A History of
Spanish Film

A History of Spanish Film

Cinema and Society 1910–2010

SALLY FAULKNER

B L O O M S B U R Y
LONDON • NEW DELHI • NEW YORK • SYDNEY

Bloomsbury Academic

An imprint of Bloomsbury Publishing Plc

175 Fifth Avenue	50 Bedford Square
New York	London
NY 10010	WC1B 3DP
USA	UK

www.bloomsbury.com

First published 2013

© Sally Faulkner, 2013

Library of Congress Cataloging-in-Publication Data

A catalogue record for this book is available from the Library of Congress

ISBN: HB: 978-0-8264-1666-7
PB: 978-0-8264-1667-4

Typeset by Fakenham Prepress Solutions, Fakenham, Norfolk NR21 8NN
Printed and bound in the United States of America

For Rowan and Cameron McDowell

Contents

Acknowledgements

Part of the research on which this book is based was funded by a grant from Spain's 'Ministerio de Asuntos Exteriores' (Becas MAE); I was able to complete the project thanks to my award of an Arts and Humanities Research Fellowship, and to sabbatical leave, granted by the University of Exeter.

I presented some of the ideas I explore in this book at the following gatherings: the 50th Anniversary Conference of the Association of Hispanists of Great Britain and Ireland, Valencia, Spain (which I attended thanks to a British Academy Overseas Conference Grant) in 2005; the European Culture Research Seminar, University of Bath, UK, in 2006; the 'Contested Memories: War and Dictatorship in Contemporary Spanish and Portuguese Culture' Conference, University College Dublin, Ireland, in 2007; the Centre for Research in Film Studies and the Centre for Interdisciplinary Film Research, University of Exeter, UK in 2008 and 2011; the 'Middlebrow Cinema' Panel, 21st International Screen Studies Conference, University of Glasgow, in 2011 (which I attended thanks to the support of the University of Exeter's Keith Whinnom Memorial Fund); the 2011 Pérez Galdós Lecture, University of Sheffield, UK; and the 'Middlebrow Cinema' Symposium University of Exeter, UK, in 2012. I would like to thank organizers and audiences for their support.

Earlier versions of my work on some of the films appeared in *Spanishness in the Spanish Novel and Cinema of the 20th–21st Century* ('*Solas* [Zambrano, 1999]): Andalousian, European, Spanish?', edited by Cristina Sánchez-Conejero, Newcastle: Cambridge Scholars Publishing, 2007); *Journal of Iberian and Latin American Research* ('Imagining Time, Embodying Time in David Trueba's *Soldados de Salamina* (2003)', 17, 1, 2011); *Revista Arbor* ('*El príncipe destronado* [Miguel Delibes 1973]/*La guerra de papá* [Antonio Mercero 1977] and Third Way Spanish Cinema', 187, 748, 2011) and *A Companion to Spanish Cinema* ('Literary Adaptations', edited by Jo Labanyi and Tatjana Pavlovic, Oxford: Wiley–Blackwell, 2012).

The following colleagues and friends have been especially generous in sharing ideas, books and films, sending me their own work, and reading my work: Mark Allinson; Chris Cagle; Núria Capdevila-Argüelles; Fernando Canet; Peter Evans; Derek Flitter; Santiago Fouz-Hernández; Rosalind Galt; Andrew

Ginger; Alexis Grohmann; Helen Hanson; Will Higbee; John Hopewell; Antonio Lázaro-Reboll; Chloe Paver; Chris Perriam; Antonia del Rey Reguillo; Alison Ribeiro de Menezes; Alejandro Melero; Maruja Rincón; Alison Sinclair; Paul Julian Smith; Núria Triana-Toribio; Katy Vernon; Belén Vidal; Tom Whittaker; Eva Woods and Sarah Wright. Many thanks are also due to my colleagues and students in Hispanic Studies, Film Studies and Modern Languages at the University of Exeter, UK. Marga Lobo, Trinidad del Río and Javier Herrera have provided tremendous support from the Filmoteca Española, Madrid, Spain. My parents, Anthony and Helen Faulkner, and parents-in-law, Brian and Kaye McDowell, have been supportive throughout. I would also like to thank my Continuum editors David Barker and Katie Gallof for their support, and, especially, for tolerating the delays brought about by two periods of maternity leave. These 'delays' are my sons, Rowan and Cameron McDowell. The sentence I have most enjoyed writing in this book is the one that dedicates it to them. Last, but only in this list, comes Nicholas McDowell, for his generosity and companionship.

List of illustrations

Textual note

A list of abbreviations and a glossary of frequently-used terms is included at the end of the text. All translations from Spanish are my own, unless otherwise indicated. I have included the Spanish original when referring to literary texts and film scripts; I have included the English translation only when referring to secondary criticism.

I have included both original title and an English translation as well as the year of release on first mention of each film; thereafter I have used the English title, occasionally abbreviated. I have taken English titles from the International Movie Data Base (www.imdb.com); when none is available I have indicated this by an asterisk in the index and on first mention of the film in the text; I have followed Bernard Bentley's Filmography for English translations (2008, 353–99), or offered my own.

All audience figures are from the 'Datos de películas clasificadas' link from the cinema section of the Spanish Ministry of Education, Culture and Sport website, www.mcu.es/cine/index; all references to prizes are taken from www.imdb.com.

Introduction:
Cinema and Society
1910–2010

This book is a history of Spanish cinema that brings the question of class mobility to the fore. The key term here is 'mobility'. Its opposite, stasis, is the explicit or implicit object of critique of much political film. From Luis Buñuel's denunciation of rural poverty in *Land Without Bread, Las Hurdes* (*Tierra sin pan* 1933), to the multi-authored critique of contemporary democracy, *There's Good Cause!** (*¡Hay motivo!* 2004) – with a series of anti-Franco films in between – Spanish political cinema has proved to be no exception here, predominantly offering a Marxist critique of apparently unassailable class privileges and exclusions.[1] It has been demonstrated that key cultural gatekeepers, both inside and outside Spain, have tended to favour this left-wing political cinema: Spanish prize-giving and subsidy-awarding bodies, along with national broadsheet press critics on the one hand;[2] international film festival programmers and foreign film distributors on the other.[3] Scholars such as Núria Triana-Toribio and Steven Marsh[4] have demonstrated that the preference for this political cinema has led to the exclusion of other tendencies in writing on Spanish film. Challenging these exclusions has led to vital work on the recovery of popular traditions. From the same starting point I take the argument in a new direction. The tendency to highlight the Spanish cinema of 'denunciation', 'critique', and 'anti-Francoism' – to reprise the words I used above – has highlighted films that impugn class stasis. Besides popular film, something else has been lost in this approach. By considering the question of class mobility throughout Spanish cinema's century of existence, *A History of Spanish Film* explores, first, the cinema's representation of upwardly and downwardly mobile groups on-screen, and places this representation, second, alongside class realignments in Spanish society off-screen. It weaves together these strands by arguing for the importance of a thus-far unexplored Spanish middlebrow cinema.

The need to address these areas is all the more urgent if we acknowledge that the single most important social change that has occurred in twentieth-century Spain, in tandem with the existence of cinema, has been class mobility, or, more specifically, a general upward movement of citizens into the middle classes – though by no means has this been uniform, or uninterrupted. The significance of this historical fact is thrown into relief through comparison. Other Western nations, like Britain and the US, became industrialized, urbanized and mesocratized in the nineteenth century.[5] In comparison, then, their cinemas have less of a tale to tell about class mobility. When the first cinematic images were shown in Spain in 1896 they were projected onto a predominantly agrarian nation, with high levels of poverty and illiteracy (one estimate puts the peasant population at 68 per cent; illiteracy at 50 per cent [Pérez Perucha 1995, 22–3]). While the 1920s saw a remarkable economic boom, the Spanish Civil War (1936–9), then the disasterous policy of autarky imposed in the 1940s by the Franco dictatorship (1939–75), led to downward social mobility far more severe than that experienced by nations recovering from the Second World War (Tortella 2000, 229–30). Following the 'hinge decade' of the 1950s, in which autarky was abandoned for capitalism through the 1959 Stabilization Plan, 1960s Spain experienced a boom. Economists have suggested that the period be described as 'Fraguismo', rather than 'Franquismo' (Francoism), owing to the importance of technocrat Minister of Information and Tourism Manuel Fraga's period in office (1962–9) (Pavlovic 2011, 1), which helpfully uncouples this period of prosperity from the person of the dictator who remained in power right up to his death from natural causes in 1975.[6] In 1987 Stanley Payne outlined how a 'new' middle class came into existence from 1950–75 (1987, 463–88), with 'the greatest sustained economic development and general improvement in living standards in all Spanish history', a level of growth only exceeded in this period by Japan (1987, 463). Alex Longhurst's 1995 sociological survey of occupation, education, income and expenditure in the second half of the century adds further detail to this acknowledged mesocratization. Statistics relating to education reveal a striking eightfold increase in secondary education and a fourfold increase in higher education from 1960–80, with women benefitting in particular; a 1993 survey found that 47 per cent of those who had gone to university had a father who had only been to primary school (Longhurst 1999, 114). Employment data is also compelling: 'the agricultural sector has gone from being the largest work provider by a very considerable margin in 1960 to being the smallest by far' (1999, 113); the service sector employed 60 per cent of the population by the 1990s (Longhurst 1995, 4). Consumerism offers further confirmation, with TV ownership at 70 per cent and washing-machine/fridge ownership at 84 per cent of households by 1974; in 1960 1 in 55 Spaniards owned a car, by 1974, 1 in 9 (de Riquer i Permanyer 1995, 265). Thus while at the start of the 1960s most sociological measures put the working class at 60 per cent of the population, by the 1990s this had decreased to below 40 per cent, even 30 per cent (Longhurst 1999, 113). Spain of the second half of the twentieth century thus experienced accelerated – if uneven – modernization and a period of widespread – if patchy – prosperity. The contours of this map of a rising middle class are thrown sharply into relief at the time of writing (summer 2012) as Spain struggles with the crisis of the Euro.[7]

One need only turn to the novels of Spain's great nineteenth-century realist writer, Benito Pérez Galdós, to give nuance to this description of a largely agrarian nation awaiting the implementation of capitalism by the 1950s technocrats. Galdós memorably portrays the new members of Madrid's bourgeoisie in his great 'Contemporary Novels' of the Spanish capital, though such class mobility was confined to a few urban centres in this period.[8] If limited in reach, this uneven, or patchy, modernization in the nineteenth century had interestingly distorting and disruptive effects on culture, which have been addressed by cultural historians of the period (Moreno Hernández 1995; Valis 2002). The term 'cursi', which describes the affected performance of a cultural sophistication one does not possess, emerged as a result of this uneven modernity, where old and new coexist in uneasy proximity.[9] *A History of Spanish Film* turns to the twentieth century (more properly, a 'long' twentieth century to 2010) for its historical focus, and to the new medium of cinema for its object of analysis, but asks similar questions about the relationship between culture and society: what is the impact of social mobility, which occurred piecemeal prior to the 1960s, but on an unprecedented national scale from that decade onwards, on the domestic cinema?

In answering this question, I aim to do more than adjust our critical focus in order to fill in the gaps of previous accounts. Moving the question of mobility from background to foreground seeks to innovate in two areas of writing on Spanish film history. First, this book brings mobility to the fore through textual analysis. In order to achieve this, I have organized the book into seven chapters that proceed chronologically and each offers six close readings of exemplary films. The reader will not find here, then, an encyclopaedic coverage of all Spanish films – surveys of this type already exist in both Spanish and English – but close analysis of some 42 fiction films.[10] This number of close readings allows me to explore the plural ways Spanish filmmakers, working in genres as diverse as the folkloric film, comedy and melodrama, with both contemporary and historical settings, have reflected, critiqued, celebrated and compensated for upward and downward social mobility over the long twentieth century.[11]

Chapter 1, 'Questions of Art and Questions of Class in Early Film', explores

the national cinema's first bid for upwardly mobile audiences through adaptations of literary texts (both novels and theatre), and through technological
prestige, with examples drawn from the silent and early sound eras, and
from political contexts that include Primo de Rivera's dictatorship and the
Second Republic. The Spanish Civil War was a rupture in every sense of the
word, shattering these connections I explore between cinema and society.
A History of Spanish Film does not, therefore, focus on this period,[12] and
Chapter 2 begins in the 1940s to explore the films with, by, and through
which Spaniards endured the post-war depression and economic deprivation
that lasted well into the 1950s. The 'Consolation and Condemnation' of the
chapter title refer to some of the uses audiences made of these films as
downward social mobility and frustrating stasis were endured. As upward
social mobility gathered pace from the 1960s onwards, I increase the intensity
of my focus to select six films from each of the decades of the 1960s-2000s.
While convenient, these decade breaks help disassociate the narrative of
this national cinema from the 'key dates' approach, which necessarily yokes
films to politics by stressing, for example, whether they are pre-1975 and
thus 'Francoist', or post-1975 (the democratic constitution was passed in
1978) and thus 'democratic'. This leveling effect of the decade-divisions is
particularly helpful in Chapter 4 on the 1970s, allowing me to uncover continuities between the beginning and end of the decade, rather than repeat the
truism of the transformation of Spanish film following the dictator's death.
Chapter 4 also puts forward my thesis concerning a new type of film. While
the six close readings of the preceding Chapter 3, which I call 'Charting Social
Mobility', map the presence of both the middle classes and middle-class
culture on-screen, I describe the films as either art cinema or popular cinema.
In the 1970s there is a crucial shift: the films often continue to portray the
middle class, but they also seek Spain's new middle-class audiences: they are
middle-class cinema.

   The second innovation of this book is to argue, then, that from the 1970s
onwards a whole new category of film comes into existence, which has
thus far never been fully explored. The denomination 'middle-class film'
foregrounds the audience at which such films were aimed, but I argue that
the pursuit of this new audience also transformed the films' aesthetics.
Textual analysis reveals that these films charted an original terrain that was
in-between previous 'art' and 'popular' alternatives: I argue that the best way of
analyzing this in-betweenness is with the term 'middlebrow'. The description
and analysis of this as yet unstudied and unnamed area of cinematic activity
in Spain will occupy my final four chapters, from the 1970s to the 2000s.[13]
As in the first three chapters, I proceed by close textual analysis, and like
these three, my close readings include bold revisions of films that frequently

occur in accounts of Spanish national cinema – including Luis Buñuel's 1970 *Tristana*, which is discussed here for the first time as a middlebrow film – and work that has never received scholarly attention before in any language – like Roberto Bodegas's frequently-mentioned but never analysed 1971 *Spaniards in Paris* (*Españolas en París*). Chapter 4, 'The "Third Way" and the Spanish Middlebrow Film', maps the early manifestations of the middlebrow, through producer José Luis Dibildos's 'Third Way' and the 'Madrid Comedy'; Chapter 5 connects this to the early films of the re-established democracy financed by the controversial legislation of the PSOE government, 'Miró Films'; Chapter 6 argues that the 'Third Way' also re-emerges in the social-realist 'cine social', while Chapter 7 brings the argument to the present day with a new reading of 'heritage' as middlebrow. The focus on social mobility – upward, downward and stalled – knits together all seven chapters to offer a dynamic new reading of this national cinema.

The 'middlebrow' in Spanish cinema studies

The application of 'middlebrow' to post-1970 Spanish film looks unpromising: not only is it an English term, but it originates in the even more specific context of 1920s and 1930s Britain. Scornfully applied to mass Anglophone culture from the 1920s (including mass-produced novels, Hollywood cinema and BBC television), the early uses of 'middlebrow' (first recorded in the Oxford English Dictionary in 1924) tell us less about the objects of denigration than about the denigrators, the artistic elites whose role as arbiters of taste was threatened by these mass-cultural developments (Hess 2009, 330). Cultural historians publishing from the 1990s onwards have helpfully shifted attention away from the anxieties of these elitist denigrators to re-evaluate the objects of their denigration (Rubin 1992; Radway 1993; Fowler 1995; Hess 2009; Hinds 2009). Two characteristics of middlebrow culture emerge as especially important for this study: first, its irreverent mixing, blurring or fusion of 'high' and 'low' (the scare marks indicate that these are also contested categories);[14] second, its especial ability to 'work through' or 'handle' change.[15] While there is no direct equivalent of the term 'middlebrow' in Spanish, I will argue that these two characteristics are especially pertinent to its post-1970 cinema. Spanish middlebrow films also mix and fuse at the level of form; on a thematic level, they also tend to 'work through' change.

The example of 'cursilería' discussed above reveals that modern Spain is not just interested in, but fascinated by, questions of class and questions of taste, as any reader of its nineteenth-century novels will confirm. That an equivalent of the term 'middlebrow' did not emerge in Spain in response to mass culture in the early twentieth century may be explained by vastly different context. Different literacy levels in the period are crucial, with Spain considerably lower than Britain at 60 per cent in 1931.[16] Language is another key distinction. The response of the British cultural custodians to American mass culture from the 1910s onwards has everything to do with the common tongue. The success of Hollywood films in the Spanish market was also a deep cause of concern (it became deeper still when the Franco regime introduced blanket dubbing of foreign films into Spanish in 1941, which damages the national industry to this day), but in the British context it posed nothing less than the threat of annihilation. Events preceding and succeeding the Civil War constitute a further distinction. While the economic boom of the 1920s led to limited social mobility, the fragile new middle class scarcely had time to generate a middlebrow culture before the ruptures of the 1930s (though films like José Buchs's 1925 adaptation of Galdós's *The Grandfather** [*El abuelo* see Chapter 1] indicate its beginnings). Civil War and dictatorship then meant that questions of politics, rather than questions of class, became the immediate preoccupations of Spanish culture and Spanish cultural theory.[17]

Historians concur that from the 1960s onwards Spain possessed an increasingly substantial middle class, which enjoyed a standard of living comparable to contemporary Western nations. The impact of this new class can be traced in politics, for new political parties like Alfonso Suárez's UCD were created in the 1970s to represent it (Torreiro 1995a, 360). This book traces the cultural impact of this new class on the national cinema. Owing to the particular circumstances of its early twentieth century, Spanish cultural commentators could not retrieve a previously-coined autochtonous term to describe this phenomenon, though the labels I will now briefly explore all share the twin characteristics of the 'middlebrow': formal fusion and thematic 'working through'.

Responding to the change in the market, José Luis Dibildos, who had begun his career as a scriptwriter and in 1956 established his own production company, Ágata Films, produced a series of films in the early-mid 1970s that sought to steer a middle course between the cerebral arthouse and crass commercial tendencies that dominated the market in the period. The films I analyse in Chapter 3, which range from aesthetic preoccupations of *Summer Night* (*Noche de verano* Grau 1963), with its tiny audience of 141,000, to the popular pranks of Marisol in blockbuster *Marisol's Four Weddings** (*Las cuatro bodas de Marisol* Lucia 1967), with an audience of over 2.5 million, demonstrate this polarized market. Dibildos described his efforts as 'popular cinema with critical bite' (quoted in Hopewell 1986, 82), while the film writing collective Marta Hernández proposed it was 'commercial cinema plus auteur cinema divided by two' (quoted in Torreiro 1995a, 361), but the label that stuck was 'Tercera vía' (Third Way). While Dibildos's particular formula for the fusion of accessible genres like comedy with the serious social issues faced by a rapidly changing Spain faded fast, the principle of fusion proved influential on large and small screens from then on.[18] I trace this influence first in the Madrid Comedies of the late 1970s and early 1980s, which similarly adopt an in-between formal approach to negotiate the vertiginous changes of the Transition from dictatorship to democracy. José Luis Garci, who directed the first of these Comedies, Unfinished Business (Asignatura pendiente 1977; analysed in Chapter 4), and thus established a blueprint for the formula, referred to the approach as 'auteur cinema for majorities' (Triana Toribio 2003, 114). Dibildos reappears as producer and scriptwriter for an early 1980s film that, again, brings together a formal fusion of 'high' and 'low' culture in a Transitional context of change: Mario Camus's 1982 adaptation of complex Modernist novel The Beehive (La colmena) through the familiar actors and conventional linear narrative of the mainstream. Moving away from the much-quoted interpretation of 1970s efforts as 'Third Way', Esteve Riambau coined a new term to describe the films funded by the new Socialist government's 'Miró' legislation that followed the The Beehive model. Cited with similar frequency, 'cine polivalente' (multipurpose cinema) (1995, 421; translated in Jordan and Morgan-Tamosunas 1998, 33) would be the label that stuck to 1980s Mirovian film. All of these terms tiptoe around a middlebrow that they fail to name.[19] Alberto Mira explains this failure through the Marxist inheritance of the Spanish cultural establishment examined above: 'The notion of solid entertainment on a middle point between art and trash had no place in critical discussions. Films, for critics brought up with the left-wing ideas of the 1960s and the 1970s, were either profound or worthless' (2005, 6).

My approach to the 'middlebrow' foregrounds its connection to social mobility and also forms part of the recent critical drive in cultural studies and film studies to rehabilitate the term.[20] It is instructive to compare this process to the recovery of the 'popular' in critical work of the 1990s and 2000s. Despite insistence that popular culture may be aesthetically mediocre and politically conservative, critics tend to focus on previously-overlooked examples to uncover unexpected aesthetic accomplishment and decode political critique.[21] Critics of the middlebrow culture may also stress its potential to be formally interesting and politically oppositional; in this vein I read films as varied as Tormento (Olea 1974), Mambrú Went to War (Mambrú se fue a la guerra Fernán Gómez 1986) or The Dog in the Manger (El perro del hortelano Miró 1996) as questioning of their contemporary contexts of Francoism, Socialism and patriarchy. It is crucial to point out, however, that scholars of middlebrow culture often explore formal mediocrity and political conservatism. In this vein, I analyse films like *The Grandfather* (*El abuelo* Garci 1998), *Alone* (*Solas* Zambrano 1999) and *Lope* (Waddington 2010) and stress in particular their conservative approaches to gender. Scholars of middlebrow culture thus avoid the critical obsession with the subversive, the radical and the oppositional, an approach that may ultimately speak more of the critics' own fetishization of dissent, than of the texts themselves and the ways they were consumed by audiences.[22] Through close reading, *A History of Spanish Film* pays attention to films as texts and, through a consideration of context, addresses the ways audiences may have consumed them. In Chapters 4–7 it highlights the in-betweenness of the middlebrow film, which often fuses high production values, serious – but not challenging – subject matter, high – but not obscure – cultural references, and accessible form.[23] The qualifications I typographically emphasize here are a reminder of contingency: there are different middlebrows at different moments and in different contexts, each one requiring its own particular analysis.[24] By linking up the middlebrow in the 1970s Third Way, the 1980s Mirovian Cinema, the 1990s 'cine social' and the 2000s 'heritage', my intention is thus not to flatten the field, but draw out the fascinating continuities of Spanish film from the 1970s to the present day.

Notes

1 The production context of *Land Without Bread* cautions against any straightforward application of 'Marxist', 'left-wing' or 'political': it was commissioned by the first government of the left-wing Second Republic, then banned by it when the government entered a new phase (D'Lugo 1997, 6). Buñuel, whose politics, like his films, defy easy categorization, went into exile during the Spanish Civil War, but Marxism became the key channel for expressing opposition to the dictatorship, as is evident in work produced from the 1950s onwards, though Francoist censorship meant knowledge of Marxist texts was partial (Graham and Labanyi 1995, 3–4). Marxist positions were adopted by the 32 directors of the collective film of protest against José María Aznar's right-wing Popular Party *There's Good Cause!*.

2 If some of the anti-Franco work produced during the dictatorship is today dismissed as naïve (including by its authors), post-Franco, as Jo Labanyi has shown, 'the largely Marxist inheritance of the anti-Francoist opposition' has proved highly influential. 'Its members played a major role in shaping cultural policy and habits, as well as in revitalizing the university system, [...] particularly under the Socialist government of 1982–95 when many of them held political positions' (2002a, 11). Focussing his attention on cinema under dictatorship, Steven Marsh has insisted that the films that criticized the Franco regime, or, in the words of the title of his book 'weaken[ed] the state' (2006), were not limited to those made by filmmakers associated with the

Spanish Communist Party. Núria Triana-Toribio notes that these anti-Franco directors associated with the Communist Party became the architects of film policy in the 1980s and 1990s (2003, 113). This promoted a broadly Marxist 'quality' cinema through subsidies in the 1980s (2003, 113–42), then a left-wing 'cine social' (social-realist cinema) through the Goya prizes in the 1990s (2003, 155–63) – both to the exclusion of popular film. Influential film critic of Spain's leading daily *El País* for over twenty years before his death in 2004, Ángel Fernández-Santos had been scriptwriter of the key oppositional film of the dictatorship, *The Spirit of the Beehive* (*El espíritu de la colmena* 1973); his daughter still writes for the film section (Smith 2003, 147).

3 Triana-Toribio traces the connections between the type of films distributed outside Spain and the slanted version of the national cinema that arises. Marsha Kinder's *Blood Cinema* (1993), whose 'shrewd analysis' Triana-Toribio stresses, is an example of a study that ignores popular film (2003, 9–10).

4 I choose Triana-Toribio and Marsh as the authors of book-length analyses with contrasting emphases on popular culture in the Franco (Marsh 2006) and democratic periods (Triana-Toribio 2003), but would stress that these studies build on the pioneering work of film scholars such as Peter Evans (1995; 2000; 2004) Jo Labanyi (1995; 1997; 2000; 2007b); Paul Julian Smith (1994 and 2000) and Katy Vernon (1999).

5 I take the term 'mesocratization', a movement to the middle class, from Longhurst 1999.

6 Even though Fraga was a Francoist minister, this neologism helps disassociate the economic boom from the dictatorship. In 1995, Helen Graham condemned the 'conservative orthodoxy' by which 'developmental dictatorship, rising from the ashes of the 1940s, authored the [economic] "miracle" and through it the democratic transition itself. By this sleight of hand, political democracy and cultural plurality become the legacy of a benevolent dictator' (1995, 244). Paul Preston reports that to this day Franco receives a good press, owing in part to this 'carefully constructed idea that he masterminded Spain's economic "miracle" in the 1960s' (2012, xii).

7 In this context Gabriel Tortella observations in 2000 are prophetic and reassuring: Spain's 'economic evolution is now advanced enough to sustain that center that was lacking in the nineteenth century – a socio-cultural middle class – that will probably serve well as keel, ballast, and rudder for whatever stormy passages may lie ahead in the oceans of the twenty-first century' (2000, 458).

8 The facts that this small middle class was 'still largely marginalized' and 'increasingly internally fragmented', 'permit[ted] the old regime to continue holding sway over what was still a predominantly rural country' (Graham and Labanyi 1995, 9).

9 This lengthy description of the adjective confirms Noël Valis's insightful summary that, 'cursi' 'is hard to define since all the English synonyms typically given in dictionaries to explain it – "in bad taste, vulgar," "showy, flashy," or "pseudo-refined, affected" – merely point to its symptoms, not its underlying condition, cause, or context' (2002, 3).

10 In Spanish, see Román Gubern et al.'s 1995 *Historia del cine español* (expanded and updated in 2009), in English, Bernard Bentley's 2008 *A Companion to Spanish Cinema*, which includes children's films, animation and documentary. Dictionaries include D'Lugo 1997 and Mira 2010. *A History of Spanish Film* does not focus on cinema of Spain's autonomous communities: as Triana-Toribio points out, Catalan and Basque cinemas, for instance, deserve separate coverage, rather than being 'shoe-horned' into books concerned with Spanish examples (2003,12).

11 This book therefore hopes to explore, if only through cinema rather than culture as a whole, Labanyi's observation that 'given the huge social changes that have taken place in twentieth-century Spain, there is important work to be done on the ways in which upwardly and downwardly mobile groups have charted their social realignment through their modes of cultural consumption,' which include 'the forgotten issue of the "middlebrow"' (2002a, 2).

12 For an analysis of Spanish cinema during the Civil War, see Gubern 1986.

13 Paul Julian Smith 'Pubic Service, Literarity, and the Middle-brow' in a chapter on the Classic Serial in Spanish TV (2006, 27–57).

14 I am drawing on Pierre Bourdieu, author of the now classic study of the co-dependency of class and taste (1999), in stressing the formal 'fusion' of the middlebrow. In Bourdieu's hostile approach, however, 'middle-brow culture' offers not 'fusion' but 'confusion', as in 'accessible versions of avant-garde experiments or accessible works which pass for avant-garde experiments, film "adaptations" of classic drama and literature, "popular arrangements" of classical music or "orchestral versions" [...] [these combine] two normally exclusive characteristics, immediate accessibility and the outward signs of cultural legitimacy' (1999, 323).

15 Lawrence Napper, whose study of the denigrated 'quota quickies' of the British inter-war period vitally reassesses the term in British film studies, chooses 'handle' (2009, 9). I take 'work through' from TV historian John Ellis (2002, 2).

16 Álvarez Junco 1995, 50. Literacy improvement was a central objective of the Second Republic through programmes like the 'Misiones Pedagógicas' (Pedagogical Missions) (Cobb 1995).

17 See Graham and Labanyi's invaluable survey of the attempt to establish cultural theory in twentieth-century Spain (1995).

18 Beyond the scope of this book lies the question of the middlebrow in Spanish TV, on which see Smith 2006, 27–57, though throughout this text I indicate where overlaps between film and TV work occur.

19 In Spanish sociology, 'middlebrow' culture may be rendered as 'pretenciosa' (pretentious) 'burguesa' (bourgeois), 'mediocre' (mediocre) and 'el gusto pretencioso de la pequeña burguesía' (the pretentious taste of the petite bourgeoisie) (Busquet 2008, 96–104). 'Cultura pretenciosa' is the translation offered for the 'culture moyenne' of Bourdieu's *Distinction* (1999) which was translated as 'middlebrow' in the 1984 English version (1999, 323).

Colloquially, diminutives of 'cultura' like 'culturilla' and 'culturetas' may be used. These equivalents unsatisfactorily stress either class ('bourgeois', the derogatory equivalent of 'middle class') or scorn ('pretentious', 'mediocre', or the diminutive), failing to capture the ways 'middlebrow' may refer to both class and aesthetics.

20 In addition to the studies published in the 1990s and 2000s mentioned above, note the activities of the 'Middlebrow Network', established in 2008 (www.middlebrow-network.com). The proceedings of a symposium I hosted on 'Middlebrow Cinema' at the University of Exeter, UK, in July 2012 are in preparation.

21 The recovery of the popular has characterized cinema studies of the 1990s and 2000. In European cinema the key text is Dyer and Vincendeau 1992b; in Spanish cinema, Triana-Toribio 2003 and Lázaro Reboll and Willis 2004b. Richard Dyer and Ginnette Vincendeau stress that the popular is not always subversive (1992a, 5), but rarely do studies of popular culture linger on conservatism (though there are important exceptions, like Leonard 2004). My own published work on popular film under Franco, for instance, stressed unexpected formal accomplishment and political critique (in connection, for example, to *The Big Family* [*La gran familia*] [2006a 27–48]); in Chapter 2 of this book I emphasize the plural uses of popular cinema by audiences under dictatorship.

22 Paul Julian Smith has argued that cultural theory, like the work of Bourdieu, may 'side-step' this 'exhausted debate' of consent and dissent, or 'hegemony and resistance' (2003, 6).

23 In this blurring of high cultural references and accessible form there are some points of continuity between the 'middlebrow' and the contested aesthetic descriptor 'pretty'. Rosalind Galt hints at these continuities in her study of the subject, with references to the 'discomfort with a style of heightened aesthetics that is too decorative, too sensorially pleasurable to be high art, and yet too composed and "arty" to be efficient entertainment' (2011, 12).

24 Deborah Shaw makes this point in 'The Emergence of Mexican Middlebrow Filmmaking: From the National to the Transnational', unpublished paper presented at the 'Middlebrow Cinema' symposium, University of Exeter, July 2012. Beyond the scope of this book, which locates particular films in their historical context, lies the movement of films between categories over time. Lázaro Reboll and Willis offer the example of *Welcome Mr Marshall!* (*Bienvenido Míster Marshall* Berlanga 1952), as a text that shifts 'from "popular" to "middlebrow" dependent upon the taste formations of those watching' (2004a, 6).

1

Questions of Class and Questions of Art in Early Cinema

Only 10 per cent of pre-Civil War Spanish films are extant,[1] and considerable, though diminishing, challenges of availability hamper efforts to engage with them.[2] Alluding to problems of preservation, David George, Susan Larson and Leigh Mercer name the study of early Spanish film 'a shadowy game of hide and seek with images whose traces grow dimmer with each passing day' (2007, 73) – but stress that the game is as important as it is difficult. If High Modernism was occasionally sceptical of cinema as a mass cultural form,[3] while the Avant-Garde, on the other hand, was frequently stimulated by its formal novelty,[4] scholars of early cinema stress that the influence of the new medium of film – much like the new form of transport of the train – stretched far beyond artistic elites to contribute to nothing less than the whole-scale reconceptualization of time and space in the modern era.[5] Film could at once replicate real time in its succession of 24 frames a second, could manipulate 'contingent, unpredictable, and unknowable instants' (an especial source of stimulation for early audiences [Woods 2012, 32]), and, as the technology advanced to allow montage, control time through editing (speed it up, slow it down, even still its inexorable flow).[6] Film, at the same time, was spatially promiscuous, able to represent both the reassuringly familiar (like *La Puerta del Sol* [Promio 1896], Madrid's central square) and the excitingly exotic (like *The Life of Mexican Gauchos* [*La vida de los gauchos en México* 1898]) (Woods 2012, 35). The camera could also break down the barrier between the public and private with shocking directness, making private spaces public, the invisible, visible. What Larson summarizes as a 'new experience of space' (2007, 112) extended to the material viewing context too, for the movie theatre constituted a 'significant new social space' (George, Larson and Mercer 2007, 74).

For Spanish film history, the insights provided by the study of its early cinema offer both salutary correctives to and productive connections with later periods. Even if the Franco regime's control of cinema was uneven (as I explore in Chapter 2), common knowledge of its repressive deployment of censorship and dubbing has led to a truism that associates Spanish cinema prior to the 1970s Transition with the political state. Eva Woods dissolves this association:

> Despite the Franco regime's grip on the cinema after the war, the Spanish national industry began not because of the state, but [...] in the realms of the popular and eventually private capital interests, even though these sectors would succumb to nationalist control after the war. (2005a, 49)

Another myth challenged by the study of Spanish film pre-Franco is that of national audiences' rejection of their own cinema. During the Second Republic (1931–6) and prior to Francoism's 1941 imposition of dubbing of foreign films (the crippling effect of which on the national cinema can still be felt today), audiences were particularly loyal to the domestic product (Fanés 1989, 148), which enjoyed nothing less than a golden age.[7]

Transnationality is an important point of connection between early cinema and later periods. Many of the pioneers were especially cosmopolitan. Segundo de Chomón, for example, worked for both Pathé in Paris and Itala Film of Turin, founded the first Spanish film production company, Macaya y Carro, and claimed other firsts, like the tracking shot and colouring techniques. Mercer shows that de Chomón developed an experimental film language that looks forward to European Surrealism (2007, 80). Moving from the experimental to the mainstream, another example is politician, writer and filmmaker Vicente Blasco Ibáñez, whose Blood and Sand (Sangre y arena) I analyse below, who was the most widely-read Spanish writer outside Spain in the 1920s (Sánchez Salas 2007, 79). Ibáñez and his work crossed both borders and media: to date, his name features as director, scriptwriter or author of the original novel of 29 films and TV series, made in Spain, France and the US from 1913–2008. The incipient star culture of the 1910s and 1920s also confirms internationalization, with Zaragoza-born Raquel Meller (Francisca Romana Margués López) working in multiple countries and media (Woods 2012, 74–100). Spain also hosted international creative personnel, including French and Italians directors seeking a neutral country in the First World War (Herrera 2005, 327). Julio Pérez Perucha negatively interprets this internationalism by summarizing it as 'emigrées and colonizers' (1995, 73–80); I inflect it positively as a process of transnational enriching of film cultures. Early Spanish film itself also frequently travelled beyond its borders. Bernard

Bentley stresses the international success of Catalan serial films in the 1900s and 1910s (2008, 22), while Woods notes of the 1920s that 'transport-ability and translatability (lack of sound), enabled [Spanish cinema's] massive dissemination throughout the West, demonstrating Spain's arrival to the world market' (2005b, 297). CIFESA, a leading production company of the Second Republic, also successfully exported Spanish films to foreign markets in the mid-1930s.

Turning to historical context, when the Lumière brothers' cinematograph was first screened in Spain in 1896,[8] its flickering images were projected onto a country that still clung on to the last vestiges of empire (the loss of Cuba and the Philippines to the US, known as the 'Disaster', was just around the corner in 1898), had an illiteracy rate of 50 per cent,[9] endured a corrupt political system of constitutional monarchy with rigged elections ensuring that two main parties took it in turns to be in power (the 'turno pacífico'), was predominantly rural at 68 per cent (Pérez Perucha 1995, 22) (though industrial labour unrest lay around the corner in 1900s Catalonia), and endured both entrenched class positions and a repressive Catholic Church. Luis Buñuel's autobiography has been cited elsewhere for its pithy summary of this situation, but it bears repetition. Referring to the Aragonese village of Calanda where he was born in 1900, he makes a remark that has widespread application to a country that was still predominantly rural: 'the Middle Ages lasted until World War I' (1994, 8).

Weakened by the Disaster, by labour unrest in industrial Barcelona, and by the continuing struggle to retain control and influence in Morocco,[10] Spain was neutral in the First World War. It abandoned the 'turno' system in 1917, but endured its first military dictatorship of the twentieth century between 1923 and 1930 under General Miguel Primo de Rivera, who fell, in part, owing to the worldwide repercussions of the 1929 Wall Street Crash. Military government continued under General Belanguer, but electoral gains in 1931 by Republicans led to the declaration of the Second Republic (the short-lived First Republic only lasted from 1873–4) and King Alfonso XIII left Spain. In a context of economic problems and industrial strife, politics became increas-ingly polarized over the 1930s, and on 17–18 July 1936 rebel Republican army General Francisco Franco led an uprising against the democratically-elected government; there followed a Civil War that ended with Franco's declaration of victory on 1 April 1939.

Against this historical backdrop film developed in fits and starts. Pérez Perucha, whose work has been widely quoted by subsequent historians, writes dismissively that, in the period 1896–1905 'fiction film in Spain totalled all of 2 comic scenes and 4 "trick" films' (1995, 29; translated in Jordan and Allinson 2005, 5), and that prior to 1910, Spanish cinema went through a period of 'prolonged pioneerism' (1995, 28; quoted in Gubern 1996, 12).[11] Early film scholars have more recently questioned the tendency to date the birth of narrative film at 1910, querying the use of terms like 'primitive' cinema, and probing the shift from what Noël Burch named the 'Primitive Mode of Representation' to the 'Institutional Mode of Representation' in the 1910s (see Kember and Popple 2004, 34, who note that Burch himself later revised these terms). In this spirit, Mercer's study of Segundo de Chomón's pre-1910 work (2007) highlights the importance of visual spectacle before narrative became the dominant fictional form. In this book I nonetheless return to 1910 as a starting point as I focus on the intertwined questions of art and questions of class in the narrative feature film. I select six films from the 1910s-1930s (a selection of a selection, of course, with only 10 per cent availability) to explore, for example, the ways the off-screen pursuit of middle-class audiences for the new medium was conducted through an on-screen appeal to artistic respectability in the form of literary and historical references.

While the first films screened in Spain were viewed in the Spanish capital, cinema initially failed to lure Madrid audiences away from established diversions like popular theatre, and Barcelona, with its small but established bourgeoisie and its proximity to France, became the context for the shift from fairground spectacle to seventh art. This shift is illustrated by the launch of the Barcelona-based journal *Arte y Cinematografía* (Art and Filmmaking), which ran from 1910–36. (Riciotto Canudo published *The Birth of the Seventh Art* in 1911.) Pérez Perucha gloomily dismisses Barcelona-based production of the 1910s as an effort based on 'enthusiasm and volunteering rather than means and possibilities' (1995, 47), hampered by severe industrial instability (most production companies only lasted four years, making an average of 4/5 titles [1995, 48; Bentley 2008, 18]); a Catholic church that dismissed cinema as 'a spectacle likely to dilute morals and provoke insanity, idiocy and blindness' (1995, 50; translated in Triana-Toribio 2003, 16);[12] exacerbating factors like the lack of celluloid in the First World War (1995, 53); and a conservative Catalan bourgeoisie uninterested in the new medium (Jordan and Allinson 2003, 173). This chapter nonetheless focuses on the attempt – rather than the overall failure – to recruit the middle classes to the cinema through artistic respectability. This attempt was already evident in the 1900s, in the theatre references of *Lethal Love** (*Amor que mata* Frutuós Gelabert 1908) for example (Pavlovic et al. 2009, 5), and by the 1910s even the largely indifferent state was briefly persuaded of film's artistic worth and invested in American Charles J. Drossner expensive historical biopic *The Life of Christopher Columbus** (*La vida de Cristóbal Colón* 1916), which was treated with enthusiasm by contemporary commentators, indifference by contemporary audiences and disdain by subsequent critics (Pérez Perucha 1995, 79–80). From this period I analyse Vicente Blasco Ibáñez's bid for respectability through the adaptation of his own novel *Sangre y arena* (*Blood and Sand* 1916), which even hostile critics acknowledge was successful (Pérez Perucha 1995, 8).

Film production shifted from Barcelona to Madrid in the 1920s, partly due to the difficulties outlined above, partly to the centralizing policies of new dictator Primo de Rivera, and partly to a new receptiveness to film among the capital's audiences (especially when it adapted popular theatrical forms like the zarzuela and sainete). The shift coincided with the economic boom that saw a staggering increase of 40 per cent in industrial activity over the decade (Barton 2004, 207),[13] with a concomitant programme of public investment and a doubling of Madrid's population over three decades to a million by 1930. If Spain as a whole possessed 1,497 cinema theatres by 1925, some 10 per cent of the European total (Pérez Perucha 1995, 88), Madrid in particular possessed only 26 in 1907 (Mercer 2007, 83), but the figure almost tripled by 1936.[14] Bentley distinguishes between the tendency for the 'Catalan pioneers' pre-1910 to be photographers and the four prominent Madrid-based directors (José Buchs, Benito Perojo, Fernando Delgado and Florián Rey) to be former actors (2008, 28), which may point to a shift of interest from visual spectacle to narrative and characterization. This is apparently confirmed by another shift over the 1920s from popular operatic adaptations (zarzuela and sainete) to novel adaptations, which Daniel Sánchez Salas dates at 1925 with Manuel Noriega and Alejandro Pérez Lugín's *College Boarding House* (*La casa de la Troya* 1925) (2007, 408; Sánchez Vidal 1991, 29), though zarzuela and sainete adaptations increased their appeal in the 1930s and 1940s. From this period I analyse the de Baños brothers' adaptation (1922) of José Zorrilla's famous 1884 play *Don Juan Tenorio*; then turn to the novel, with José Buchs's version (1925) of Benito Pérez Galdós' *The Grandfather** (*El abuelo*, first published as a novel in 1897, then as a play in 1904), and finally to Francisco Elías's *The Mystery of the Puerta del Sol** (*El misterio de la Puerta del Sol* 1929), an original comedy (not an adaptation) that was Spain's first sound film. All three attest to cinema's pursuit of new upwardly-mobile audiences in the 1920s, through both intermedial and international references.

The coming of sound was disastrous for this developing Spanish cinema. The first talkie, *The Jazz Singer* (1927), was screened silently in Madrid in 1929 as the technical equipment for exhibition did not exist (Gubern 1977, 14). Its installation was patchy, appearing in Barcelona in 1929 (Gubern 1977, 15), though the incompatibility of various systems meant that the only cities able to exhibit *Puerta del Sol* were Burgos and Zamora (Colorado 1997, 80). With insufficient exhibition equipment, the emigration of film personnel abroad to make Spanish-language versions of Hollywood film (for example for Paramount at Joinville in France [Gubern 1977, 10n. 1]), and the ever-increasing dominance of Hollywood cinema (aided by the slow-down in production among those nations who fought in the First World War), only one Spanish film was made in 1931.[15] However, as audiences grew accustomed to sound and personnel returned with technical knowledge acquired abroad, Spanish cinema under the Second Republic enjoyed a golden age that perhaps glitters all the more brightly today given our knowledge that the Civil War lay ahead. From this period I analyse *The Cursed Village* (*La aldea maldita* Rey 1930), which I interpret as a watershed piece not only for its acknowledged position as one of the best – but also one of the last – Spanish silent films. The film also misogynistically aligns upward social mobility with female moral decline, which is evident in earlier features like Buchs's *The Grandfather* and *Pilar Guerra* (1926), and looks forward to the treatment of social mobility to be discussed in later chapters of this book. A study of economic deprivation, *The Cursed Village*'s portrait of rural exodus in Castile also encapsulates the way the whole world was plunged into crisis following the Wall Street Crash, with political polarization and the outbreak of Civil and World Wars at the end of the 1930s its devastating corollaries. With such events in mind, it is impossible not to view the optimistic films of the Second Republic as poignantly backlit by the imminent crisis. I analyse *The Fair of the Dove* (*La verbena de la paloma* 1935) as a conciliatory vision that manages to combine entrenched class division with reconciliation between the classes through its breezy narrative of cross-class love affairs and communal festivities (a similar approach has been adopted to Rey's *Dark and Bright* (*Morena clara*) of the following year).[16] It was enjoyed over 1935–6 by a huge national audience loyal to domestic films precisely in the moment before such cross-class alliance and communality were catastrophically to shatter with the outbreak of the Civil War.

Blood and Sand (*Sangre y arena* André and Ibáñez 1916)

Eminent philosopher Miguel de Unamuno was unfortunately to declare in 1923 that 'Literature has no role to play in the cinema' (quoted and translated in Morris 1980, 30); popular author, journalist and distinguished Republican politician Vicente Blasco Ibáñez stands at the other end of the spectrum. Ibáñez does not just use cinema as a narrative subject in his work (like Ramón Gómez de la Serna's *Cinelandia* [1923] [Parsons 2003, 90–2]), or just incorporate film techniques like visual blurring in his literary approach (as in *Cinelandia*, again, or in Ramón del Valle-Inclán's in *Luces de Bohemia*

[Parsons 2003, 87–90]). Ibáñez is instead early Spanish cinema's icon of inter-mediality, writing filmic novels and making literary films, penning film scripts and adapting his own work to the screen, an indisputably talented pioneer filmmaker (George 2007, 91) – even if his literary oeuvre is treated more sceptically (George 2007, 94–5; Murphy 2010) – who revelled in the kind of promiscuous artistic impurity to which Unamuno solemnly objected.[17]

The success of the first versions of his work, José María Codina's *The Orchard Idiot** (*El tonto de la huerta* 1914, based on *La barraca* [1898]) and Alberto Marro's *In the Orange Grove** (*Entre naranjos* 1915, on which the author collaborated), encouraged Ibáñez to direct, with Max André, his own novel *Blood and Sand* (1908).[18] Financed by his successful publishing house, he founded Prometeo Films during a stay in Paris in 1915 and planned three further films – though only one, *The Old Woman of the Cinema** (*La vieille du cinema* André 1917), was made before the company collapsed (George 2007, 97; Ruiz 2004, 183–4). Shot on location in Madrid and Seville, with interiors in Barcelona and post-production in Paris (George 2007, 97), the film's enormous commercial success in both France and Spain (where it showed for several months) (Ruiz 2004, 185), led Ibáñez to declare that, along with Giovanni Pastrone's 1914 *Cabiria*, his *Blood and Sand* 'opens up a new literary period that elevates the artistic level of cinema' (quoted in Ruiz 2004, 185).

This 'elevation' may be traced in the film's literarity, both extra-textual and textual. The publicity poster (reproduced in Ruiz 2004, 184) mentions the original novel twice, and makes further reference to 'adaptation', Ibáñez's 'quill' and Spanish 'letters'. The text itself not only uses common visual tricks of early cinema like the iris-in (where the shot fades in and out to a circle) and contrasts between close-ups and wide-angle long shots (George 2007, 2007, 101–3), but also deploys editing in a way that recalls literary technique. In 1942 Sergei Eisenstein demonstrated that montage was a key shared feature of narrative film and the novel by comparing pre-cinematic 'montage' in Dickens's novels with cinematic montage in D. W. Griffith's films (1999). While strictly comparable parallel action through cross-cutting is absent from *Blood and Sand*, in the early sequence that narrates the bullfighter Juan Gallardo's rise to fame, Ibáñez and André cut from a sequence in the family kitchen that features Juan's mother, to a sequence of the crowd's applause for the bullfighter, then another cut back to the kitchen, where the mother is now accompanied by relatives who share coffee and anís. No provocative levelling of private and public spaces seems implied by the editing here (as in the more formally challenging *The Sixth Sense** [*El sexto sentido* Sobrevila 1929] for example); it suggests that domestic financial need motivates Juan's efforts in the public arena, which successfully lead to his family's prosperity. The juxtaposition of shots also points to one of the lessons imparted by the film: that public celebrity threatens private life, for Juan will end up being controlled by the crowd who created him (George 2007). In the novel, Ibáñez begins with the bullfighter's success in Chapter 1 (1967, 119–41), then shifts back to the village and the hardship of his fatherless upbringing in Chapter 2 (1967, 141–58), before returning to the present in Chapter 3 (1967, 158–78). While the film adaptation favours chronology, it both replicates the novel's switches of focus in Chapters 1–3, and is far more succinct.

An experienced politician and a popular author, Ibáñez as a director shrewdly articulates this literary appeal and didactic message in the vernacular idioms of melodrama and folklore, two dominant tendencies of the popular theatre from which early cinema drew its audiences and on which early films were thematically reliant. He thus aims to attract new audiences without alienating traditional ones. From melodrama, Ibáñez and André take *Blood and Sand*'s sub-plot, whereby Juan's increasing celebrity and narcissistic obsession with the fans that have created him are conveyed through the familiar trope of marriage and adultery. His wife Carmen, with village origins and familiar Christian name, is contrasted with aristocratic Doña Sol (sun), whose surname speaks of the bright lights of fickle fame and fortune. In the end, Icarus-Juan will fly too close to the 'sun' and die in the ring before a crowd disdainful of his extra-marital affair. From Spanish folklore, often disdainfully labelled the *españolada* for its promotion to domestic audiences of the stereotypes commonly held by foreigners about Spain, Ibáñez takes the bullfight. *Bête noire* of the Generation of 1898, to which Ibáñez partially belongs, the novelist and director has it both ways: he features the spectacle of bullfighting, while also using the hated national sport to launch a 'scathing critique of stardom and of the role mass audiences play in the creation of popular heroes' and to call for education as a means to free the individual (George 2007, 92–3). While Ibáñez and André knowingly criticize the clichéd rags-to-riches plot of the bullfighting *españolada*, Ibáñez unselfconsciously adopts the hackneyed fidelity/adultery opposition of melodrama in order to drive home his political message concerning individual responsibility.

Ibáñez as commercially-successful businessman thus conceived of the 'elevation' of cinema via literature as a means of increasing audiences for film by attracting the middle-class demographic through the prestige pull of liter-ature, as the Hollywood-based Vitagraph Company had done via authors like Shakespeare, Dickens and Tennyson in the late 1900s and early 1910s (Pearson and Uricchio 2004, 157), and Alberto Marro with brothers Ricardo and Ramón de Baños had done in Barcelona-based Hispano Films from 1911–16 (Bentley 2008, 15–17).[19] However, Ibáñez as Republican politician also interprets 'elevation' as the ability of film, like the novel, to convey his political views on individual responsibility and education. David George pinpoints a contradiction in this desire to attract as wide an audience as possible off-screen, while simultaneously critiquing mass audiences through the representation of the crowd and its treatment of the bullfighter on-screen (2007, 105). George shows that at first Ibáñez-director replicates Ibáñez-novelist's portrayal of the crowd as a 'beast' that both creates and devours its 'prey', the bullfighter-star. After establishing identification between the audience gathered before the film, and the crowd gathered to watch Juan (by allowing individuals of the crowd to look directly at the camera, for instance [2007, 101]), Ibáñez and André condemn both audience and crowd as 'feminized' and 'degenerate' via close-ups of a female fan and a drunkard fan (2007, 102–4). The contradiction is resolved by Juan's death. This is a turning point in the film, after which the off-screen audience is encouraged to disassociate itself from an on-screen crowd that is now only allowed to occupy the top third or half of the frame and is shown to be shackled by the ropes that separate it from the bullring (2007, 104). Crucial too is the fact that the film, unlike the novel, stresses the working-class nature of the crowd (George 2007, 105) through dress. Thus for all Ibáñez's democratic approach, *Blood and Sand* in fact ultimately divides the people by flattering only a distinct, middle-class audience.

Don Juan Tenorio (de Baños 1922)

The literary adaptation *Blood and Sand*, which features the popular spectacle of bullfighting but is taken from a novel that condemns the national sport, ultimately undermines its crossover appeal by condemning the on-screen working-class crowd. Conversely, Ricardo de Baños, who had previously adapted *Don Juan Tenorio* in both 1908 and 1910 (with Albert Marro),[20] offers in 1922 a film I analyse as crossover in three ways. It combines the literary pedigree of Zorrilla with the pleasures of popular theatre, fuses the theatrical and the cinematic in its formal approach and merges the national legend with Hollywood film techniques.

Palmira González López, writing on the 1910 version, stresses the huge cross-class popularity of Zorrilla's play, which is performed at All Souls (owing to its ghosts) in Spain to this day. This made it the ideal vehicle for Hispano films to explore 'a new type of cinema without running the risk of losing alienating the audience' (1997, 30). She nonetheless concludes that in 1910 de Baños does not stray far from 'popular spectacle models' and rejects interpreting *Don Juan Tenorio* as a Spanish equivalent of a French Film d'art (1997, 29–30). It seems reasonable to speculate that audiences' reception of *Don Juan Tenorio* changed between this second version, produced by Hispano

Films in 1910, and the third, produced by Royal Films in 1922. Cinema was notoriously unsuccessful with the established Catalan middle class of the 1900s and 1910s, whereas Royal Films in 1922 could appeal to those who were beginning to benefit from the economic boom that particularly enriched the Spanish capital. Released in Barcelona on All Souls in 1922, its Catalan reception was lukewarm, but released on the same day in Madrid in 1924, it was a runaway success (Ruiz 2004, 227–8). Thus, on the one hand, in the 1922 version de Baños does not skimp on the elements of the film drawn from the popular theatre (Eva Woods reminds us that in 1923, 50 per cent of Spanish films were still zarzuela adaptations [2005a, 48]), like a richly artificial mise en scène of both settings and costumes and an exaggerated performance style. On the other, de Baños fuses these with the more refined pleasures of Zorrilla's literary original. The imagetrack is perhaps excessively interrupted with intertitles, which every few seconds display favourite lines of the play (Wright 2007, 88) with its archaic use of the 'vos' form, for the literate and literary members of the audience to enjoy.[21]

Sarah Wright alternatively locates the film's crossover nature in its formal intermediality, for *Don Juan Tenorio* is 'happy to display its theatrical roots while simultaneously revelling in the new cinematic techniques at its disposal' (2007, 88). Rejecting the pejorative sense attached to 'theatricality', she details the visual pleasures of the film's elaborate costumes (especially those of the male characters) and sets (while de Baños employs a new cast of actors from 1908–10 to 1922, he retains many of the earlier films' tableaux) (2007, 88). Wright notes that director Ricardo de Baños, in collaboration with

FIGURE 1.1 *Don Juan seduces Dona Iñés.* Don Juan Tenorio *(de Baños 1922)*

his brother Ramón as cinematographer, takes full advantage of cinema's unique relationship with time to enhance the literary original. The pace of editing, for example, speeds time up in order efficaciously to convey Zorrilla's sense that the seducer lives on borrowed time (Ginger 2000, quoted in Wright 2007, 89), past time is evoked through flashback, and the film begins with Don Juan and Don Luis's amorous adventures in flashback before returning to the present – a beginning that might have been disorientating, were it not the case that the original play would have been well-known to much of the audience. The de Baños's *Don Juan Tenorio* even portrays invented times and spaces, by offering what Bruce Kawin was later to name a 'mindscreen' (1978), or a highly subjective 'mind's eye' view of an event. Thus we see Don Juan rescue Doña Inés from a fire at the convent which is a fabrication: Doña Inés in fact fainted and Don Juan kidnapped her. Cinematography is exploited too, with a camera that adopts different angles, opens up depth of field, and deploys close-up to underscore Don Juan's seduction of Doña Inés, thus distancing the film from the static camera of despised filmed theatre. Wright brilliantly reads the de Baños brothers' use of cinematic tricks, or what early film historian André Gaudreault termed 'trickality', to demonstrate the fusion of the theatrical and the cinematic. These tricks are deployed to portray the return of Doña Inés and Don Gonzalo's ghosts at the end of the film through double exposure, which allows the vengeful father to seep through the walls of Don Juan's residence, and the seduced nun to both appear and disappear in the blink of an eye. These techniques reveal 'the showy, spectacular and theatrical possibilities of the cinematic medium' (2007, 91).

Andrew Ginger interprets the crossover nature of the film differently again, as 'an exhilarating imitation of post-Griffith technique' in a Spanish context. In a refreshing departure from the tired thesis of a derivative Spanish cinema, Ginger interprets the deployment of Hollywood techniques, especially those connected to the energetic portrayal of time through editing, and the dynamic opening up of space through cinematography, as 'an enabling force'. Transnational fusion rather than derivative copy, *Don Juan Tenorio* offers a 'seamless synthesis between American filmmaking innovations and a national legend around which national cultural identity was constructed' (2007, 71).

If today I term the film a 'crossover' in its appeal to audiences, 'intermedial' in its fusion of the theatrical and the cinematic and 'transnational' in its grafting of American film techniques onto a Spanish legend, for its 1920s audience it was an enormously enjoyable combination of recognisability and novelty. Pleasurably familiar to all, given the play's popularity, would have been the plot of Don Juan's multiple seductions; reassuringly recognizable too would have been the film's deployment of theatrical mise en scène, including costume, setting, and the exaggerated gesturality of the actors' performances of the swooning and sleighing for which the legend is famous. A more exclusive confirmation of cultural capital would have been provided for those literate members of the audience able to read and recognize the Zorrilla quotations in the intertitles. Film form also satisfyingly fuses the familiar and unfamiliar. Audiences may have recognized cross-cuts, flash-backs, mindscreens, cinematography and trickality from the Hollywood films that were imported to Spain in ever increasing numbers over this period, but they would have enjoyed them here for the first time in connection with their own national legend. It is especially impressive that there is fusion, rather than contradiction, in the ways *Don Juan Tenorio* looks back to the popular theatrical roots of the national cinema, yet looks forward to its increasing pursuit of a socially upwardly-mobile audience.

The Grandfather* (El abuelo Buchs 1925)

A similar pursuit of this new socially upwardly-mobile audience may explain José Buchs's apparently odd decision to film the 1897 novel version of Benito Pérez Galdós's of *El abuelo*, rather than the author's 1904 theatre version.[22] This decision is peculiar first because prolific director Buchs is known principally for the enormous success of his film versions of popular theatre, especially the 1921 zarzuela *The Fair of the Dove* (*La verbena de la paloma*), which he quickly followed with *The Moorish Queen** (*La Reina Mora*) and *Carcelera, Prison Songs** (*Carceleras*) in 1922 (all three were produced by the Madrid-based Atlántida S.A.C.E). Second, the theatre version of Galdós's *El abuelo* was also very popular with audiences: it played constantly in Madrid until 1930 (especially with prestige companies) and numerous editions of the text were published (Sánchez Salas 2007, 170–2). Even if novel and theatre versions of Galdós's text are similar (the novel should be more accurately termed as a 'dialogue novel'), the choice of the novel version, along with the adaptation of another novel the following year, *Pilar Guerra* by Guillermo Díaz Caneja (1921) (both of these were produced by Film Linares), may nonetheless be taken as Buchs's bid for prestige (Sánchez Salas 2007, 398). However, this uneven film is marked by a contradiction, for while it may seek a new aspirant middle-class audience off-screen, it condemns precisely such aspirant characters on-screen.

Like Buchs, Florián Rey and Benito Perojo also turned to literary adaptation in 1925. Rey filmed a version of the anonymous 1554 classic *Lazarillo de Tormes*, while Perojo's engagement with the nation's literary hero,

Cervantes's *Don Quijote* (Part I 1605; Part II 1615) was to be titled *El Quijote*, but the project ran into difficulties (Sánchez Salas 2007, 302). Galdós was not as safely distanced in time as these other authors (he died in 1920), and his liberal, anticlerical associations meant that he was treated with suspicion by the conservative establishment. Buchs finds a successful fit between Galdós's tear-jerking plot and silent-film melodrama, with its especial attention – pre-sound – to mise en scène: in addition to costume and setting, he used colour tints. However, the veteran director of popular zarzuelas over-emphasizes the film's bid for respectability through literary adaptation, perhaps to over-compensate for the novelist's suspicious politics, or perhaps even to see good Film Linares's substantial investment in the project, for they had paid 50,000 pesetas to the Galdós estate for the novel rights (Sánchez Vidal 1991, 26). The first image of the film crystallizes this over-compensation: a respectful medium shot and 7–second take of a statue of the novelist. The film that follows partly falls into the trap of being another ossified public monument to the writer.

The problem with making a bid for respectability through a novel adaptation in silent cinema is how to incorporate the written word. One solution, as we have seen in *Don Juan Tenorio*, is an over-reliance on intertitles to ensure inclusion of all the best lines. Buchs also misjudges the intertitles. In his enthusiasm to include detail from the novel he tends to over-explain. For example, the information gleaned piecemeal by the reader concerning the character Venancio is summarized in one intertitle that precedes our first view of the character (Sánchez Salas 2007, 387–8). Here the eagerness to include novelistic detail diminishes the viewing experience, for we have little left to discover about this character when we see him on screen. Similarly, in his enthusiasm to underscore the use of premium locations in the adaptation, Buchs over-explains via intertitle: when we see a character arrive at a church we are told, as if we were tourists, where the setting is in reality (Sánchez Salas 2007, 398). Possibly mishandled through a desire to over-emphasize Galdós's literary credentials, or stress impressive locations, Buchs's use of intertitles thus occasionally undermines, rather than underscores, his bid for artistic respectability.

Galdós's tale of the penniless nobleman, Count Albrit, who returns to Spain after losing his fortune to find that his son is dead and that his daughter-in-law's adultery means one of his granddaughters is illegitimate, is perfect material for film melodrama, and Buchs takes advantage of new techniques of subjective cinematography, flashback and mindscreen efficaciously to portray Albrit's desperation to discover whether Dolly or Nelly is his blood relation. We share his point of view as he looks on the Spanish coast from a liner on returning from Peru (the coastal settings were shot in Cantabria) and even share his failing vision when he first meets his granddaughters, for Buchs blurs the focus of the point of view shots through which he gazes at the two girls, cinematically conveying the novel's reference to his frustration 'Oh! I can't see you clearly, I can't distinguish between you, you seem to me to be the same girl' (Pérez Galdós 1999, 92). A flashback conveys his imagined recreation of the scene in which his son Rafael discovers his wife Lucrecia's adultery (this event did take place), and a mindscreen represents a dream in which he imagines killing the illegitimate offspring (this event does not). But for all this formal modernity, Buchs casts Modesto Rivas as Albrit, and the actor's old-fashioned appearance with long white beard and black overall, together with his outdated performance style of exaggerated gesturality (without the justification of a theatrical source, as in *Don Juan Tenorio*), lessen our identification with him. (Sánchez Salas notes that this acting style was already being rejected as uncinematic abroad by the mid-1920s [2007, 354].)

Buchs is more successful in his portrayal of secondary characters, with whom identification is unnecessary. An excellent example is the comic treatment of the society parvenu Senén, a buffoonish character who was formerly a dependent of the Albrit estate, but is now Lucrecia's secretary. Taking from Galdós the scene where he climbs a tree to rescue the girls'

FIGURE 1.2 *Albrit is Thrown into doubt by his granddaughters, Nelly and Dolly.* The Grandfather *(El abuelo Buchs 1925)*

schoolbook, Buchs allows comic actor Emilio Santiago to indulge in caricature and climb the tree in a way that reminds us of his social climbing. Fond of the metaphor, Buchs introduces a new scene in which Senén is chased by a dog and is forced to climb again, this time up the side of the Albrit mansion. The director misses, unfortunately perhaps, Galdós's punishment of Senén's social ascendance through ignominious descent, for when, towards the end of the novel, the hapless secretary takes a short-cut by climbing up a heap of stones, he slips and falls into a pile of manure (1999, 244).

Overawed by the Galdós original, occasionally mishandling intertitles, and uneven in characterization, Buchs's *The Grandfather*, while successful on its release, ultimately failed commercially (Ruiz 2004, 299–300). Bidding for a socially-mobile new audience, its condemnation of social mobility through clichéd female characterization seems especially misjudged. If Galdós's original appeals to the stereotypes of virgin and whore, to the disappointment of readers familiar with his nuanced exploration of gender in the earlier 'Contemporary Novels' (see Chapter 6 for further details), Buchs reinforces the cliché through casting, performance style and costume. Lucrecia, first, is the socially-climbing adulteress of foreign birth (Ireland is mentioned in the novel, North America in the film). Played by Ana María Ruiz de Leyva, the actress's clothes, hair and make-up link her to the two current femme fatale stereotypes of the vamp and diva (Sánchez Salas 2007, 353–4), while her exaggerated performance style connotes inauthenticity. Dolly, second, is the domestic angel. Played by a clearly post-pubescent Josefina Ochoa o Juberías (under pseudonym Doris Wilton), the actress's own adulthood and sexuality are repressed through a simpering girlish performance style enhanced by an infantlizing wardrobe of girlish dresses with enormous bows to hide womanly curves, and hair childishly plaited and tied with ribbons. If Buchs, following Galdós, updates the obsession with honour through Albrit's statement at the end of the film that 'Between honour and love, I choose love, the eternal truth', Buchs, exaggerating Galdós, compensates for this change by stressing especially retrograde roles for women.

The Mystery of the Puerta del Sol (El misterio de la Puerta del Sol Elías 1929)*

Made at the end of the decade of extraordinary economic growth that was especially beneficial to Madrid, with population increase, employment and investment in infrastructure, Francisco Elías's *Puerta del Sol* might be read as the cultural expression of this newly confident Spain, a country to which the director returned to make his first film after gaining technical training in Paris and New York (D'Lugo 1997, 149). It celebrates the Spanish capital (its title refers to its central square, on which Elías frequently sets his camera), showcases the country's new cinema stars like Juan de Orduña and, just as its narrative stages an apparent fusion between Hollywood and Spain, so Elías plays his trump card: his Spanish film is the first to use, even if only partially, American Phonofilm sound. In the event, the wide audience of which Elías and production company Hispano de Forest Fonofilms dreamed proved as ephemeral as the protagonists' desire to become Hollywood stars, for on its release the film could not be screened in Madrid owing to technical incompatibility, and was only seen in two provincial cities.

What problems in exhibition denied most audiences the opportunity to see was how *Puerta del Sol*, in the very different genre of comic farse, nonetheless reprises some of the thematic preoccupations of José Buchs's melodramas *The Grandfather* and *Pilar Guerra*. Rather than singling out a middle-class demographic through a bid for respectability, *Puerta del Sol* sought as wide an audience as possible through the tried and tested routes of using comedy and casting stars – not to mention pioneering sound. Nonetheless the plot, once again, is fascinated by social mobility, for Elías's pair of protagonists, the farcically named Pompeyo Pimpollo (Orduña) and Rodolfo Bambolino (Antonio Barbero), dream of socially climbing above their jobs as newspaper printers by conquering the world of the seventh art. As Andrew Ginger has shown, questions of gender are crucial to the ways these questions of class and questions of art are played out (2007, 71–4). In *The Grandfather*, which centres on the patriarch Albrit's conception of honour, social mobility is repre-sented as polluting adultery through the vamp/diva Lucrecia; to compensate for this, the angel-of-the-hearth Dolly literally and figuratively soothes Albrit's wounded pride so that the film may reach its sentimental conclusion of the primacy of love. In *Puerta del Sol*, which similarly centres on male characters Pompeyo and Rodolfo, female characters also adopt conservative roles to represent male aspiration, frustration and resolution.

For all its love of apparently random farce and slapstick, the film is struc-tured around a strict Aristotelean triptych. The central dream sequence divides the film into three, and each part may be read through gender concerns. The 'thesis' outlines the protagonists' aspirations of social – and geographical – mobility by means of Hollywood film. As Ginger points out, this part of the film suggests 'apparent continuity between Madrid and America' through the frequent juxtaposition within the frame of each character with the posters of Hollywood characters that are pinned to the wall of their bedroom, and the numerous high-angle documentary-style shots of the busy traffic of Madrid's Puerta del Sol, which stress the city's shared modernity with America (2007,

71–2). (Later in the film we are treated to some of the first exhilarating aerial shots of the capital.) The protagonists' Hollywoodesque names also points to synthesis (Rodolfo Bambolino recalls Rudolfo Valentino), though, ominously, Rodolfo cannot put on his suit collar for the screen test (a problem that resurfaces in his dream in the form of the garrotte) (Ginger 2007, 72). The narrative articulates the newspaper printers' aspirations through male heterosexuality: their socio-economic desire for ascendance is articulated through their lustful desire for the It-girl film stars they meet at the Madrid-based American film studio.

Roberto's dream, which occupies the lengthy 50–minute central section of the 74–minute film, suggests 'antithesis'. He dreams that the friends invent the murder 'mystery' of the film's title in order to feature in the newspapers they are so bored of just printing. The investigating judge calls it 'una ridícula farsa cinematográfica' (a ridiculous cinematic farse), but the mystery also refers to a widely-reported actual homicide that occurred months before the shoot and also featured Madrid's Atocha station and the discovery of the murdered man's remains (Fernández Colorado 1997, 82). (Of course the Madrid and wider national audiences who read about this event in the

FIGURE 1.3 *Pompeyo is Juxtaposed with Hollywood and Catholic Iconography.*
The Mystery of the Puerta del Sol *(El misterio de la Puerta del Sol Elías 1929)*

newspapers were lamentably never to appreciate the reference as the film never reached them.) Ginger notes that the dream suggests that Spanish aspirations of American triumph end in death, for Pompeyo is murdered for his pursuit of Lía by American director Carawa in a peak of jealousy, and Rodolfo is to be wrongly executed for the crime by garrotte (2007, 73). A lengthy cross-cutting sequence opposes an ultra-modern America with a pre-modern Spain: while the American Carawa and Lía journey back to Madrid by aeroplane and car, Rodolfo is led to the gruesome medieval instrument of execution. A possible conclusion emerges: Pompeyo is murdered for his pursuit of an American It-girl Lía and Rodolfo faces execution for his pursuit of Hollywood fame. At the very time when Spanish intellectuals were rejecting the falsified image of Spain in the Spanish-language Hollywood films made, for example, by Paramount at Joinville, Elías thus apparently condemns the 'delusions' of his aspirant characters (Ginger 2007, 72–3).

Ginger shows that what I term the film's Aristotelean 'synthesis' complicates such a rejection, for when Rodolfo awakes, he and Pompeyo are successful in their pursuit of the very girls that led to their downfall in the dream. Their wooing is portrayed, furthermore, through the classic Hollywood happy ending, which is even topped off by an on-screen kiss. 'The point', Ginger suggests, is 'that a fusion between the mediatic aspirations of Madrid and Hollywood is possible, but only if it occurs on the terms of the 1920s *madrileño* male'. Since the It-girls are shown to be 'just like Spanish females', this is no less than a 'reaffirmation of Hispanic masculinity and its power over the Spanish female' (2007, 73–4).

The Cursed Village (*La aldea maldita* Rey 1930)

The introduction of sound disrupts attempts to connect extant texts with contemporary audiences. As we have seen, the partial sound film *Puerta del Sol*, packed with local references and current affairs, only had a tiny provincial release owing to lack of technological infrastructure. Just one year later, Florián Rey's *The Cursed Village* (1930), which has been celebrated by subsequent critics as a silent masterpiece, was in fact only released in 1930 in a now lost sonorized version, after only a restricted release in its original form in March (Sánchez Vidal 1997, 84). What scholars have termed the 'shadowy game of hide and seek' (George, Larson and Mercer 2007, 73) of early Spanish film still, therefore, seems difficult to play as late as 1930. If the previously-discussed films entwine questions of class and art by bidding for cultural respectability to attract a middle-class audience through literature

(*Blood and Sand*, *Don Juan Tenorio*, *The Grandfather*), and Francisco Elías's effort to attract a wide audience through technical prowess foundered in reception, Rey's today much-celebrated mastery of the silent film form was in 1930 sabotaged for the majority of audiences who could only experience a sonorized version (even though Rey added sound to the film himself). Working with a text that differs from the one known at the time, my thesis concerning social mobility and gender in the film can thus only be tentatively connected to context, for contemporary audiences would have experienced a very different sound version.

Puerta del Sol is an urban farce and Elías's first film, which he made after working as an editor in Paris then as a producer New York. He returned to his home country to pioneer sound in Spain, but went back to Paris when *Puerta del Sol* failed. *The Cursed Village*, meanwhile, is a rural tragedy whose director was a former actor and had directed numerous and varied Spanish films by 1930, including zarzuela adaptations. While Elías's *Puerta del Sol* revels in Hollywood techniques and narrative conventions, Florián Rey's *The Cursed Village* has been alternatively connected to Russian expressionism[23] for its use of close-up and shadow, avoids altogether a dynamic camera, and occasionally breaks narrative conventions by having characters apparently 'walk through' the camera (approaching it to the point of extreme close-up in one shot, moving away from it after extreme close-up in the next).[24] Nonetheless both films are fascinated by social mobility, which they explore through gender, and *The Cursed Village* dramatically and influentially emphasizes *Puerta del Sol*'s 'reaffirmation of Hispanic masculinity and its power over the Spanish female' (Ginger 2007, 74).

The Cursed Village proceeds with the force of a biblical parable, and its cultural precedents stretch back to Eve's fall in *Genesis*, taking in conservative texts like Fernán Caballero's *La gaviota* (1849),[25] and the Generation of 1898's idealization of the countryside on the way. In Rey's film, in which social mobility means the avoidance of starvation, there are apparently no shades of grey: honour must remain intact; disobedience must be punished; the Castilian village is the repository of virtue and the city (here Segovia) is a den of iniquity. Each of these truths, finally, must be acted out on the body of a woman.

The male characters of the film are initially associated with statis, which is positively coded to stand for timeless values and satisfyingly matches Rey's aesthetic choice of filming a series of carefully-crafted tableaux, avoiding altogether the then current vogue of the dynamic camera (as Rey explained in a 1942 interview, quoted in Sánchez Vidal 2005, 15), which was associated with Hollywood. To match the narrative in which farmer Juan, the husband and father, along with former farmer Martín, the blind father and grandfather, remain in the village, which has been 'cursed' by years of failed crops, characterization stresses these male characters' unyielding adherence to patriarchal honour, and the filming style favours static and eloquent tableaux. The film opens, for example, with the image of the grandfather leaning against a giant cross, with the rural landscape and village in the background. We also behold the image of the grandfather leaning on his walking stick, warming himself by the fire of the peasant cottage kitchen. As the narrative continues, Rey nonetheless questions the positive inflection of this stasis. If Juan remains in the village he does so as he has been imprisoned for his violent attack on a wealthy neighbour, Tío Lucas. If the grandfather remains in the village, our last image of him there does not connote positive immutability, but the ravages wrought by the passage of time: he takes refuge in the ruins of a castle, threatening to jump from it with the baby if his daughter-in-law Acacia tries to take the child away with her.

Acacia, conversely, connotes mobility and change, for which she is lengthily punished. Prior to her decision to leave the village, Rey misogynistically condemns female friendship, consumerism and literacy, all of which are treated as foreboding premonitions of her subsequent abandonment of her family. First, Rey shows Acacia leave her infant son in the cottage to step into the village street and chat to her female friends, including Magda, about the new shawl and necklace Magda has had sent from Segovia. Rey's framing shows that as the women gather in the medium ground, they ignore both the beggar in the foreground and the baby in the cottage in the background (who is revealed to be crying in the next shot). Next, Acacia is shown to be reading on the night of the storm that lays waste to the village's crop, casting her eyes down to the page rather than up to the heavens that open to devastate the village's livelihood (Sánchez Salas 2007, 355). It will be female friends from the village, and Magda in particular, who will encourage Acacia to leave it: the biblical precedent of her friend's name (Magdalena in full) gives forewarning of the moral outcome that will follow Acacia's decision. She is persuaded partly through her friend's account of city life, which is illustrated by Rey with a cut to cityscapes that suggest a mindscreen, as Magda conjures up an image of the busy streets she describes.

Acacia leaves the village in the rural exodus that takes on biblical proportions through the intertitle 'the tragedy of Exodus' (Kinder 1993, 44); critics have also noted that one of the departing peasants is captured by the camera with his arms open in a manner that recalls the crucifiction (Sánchez Vidal 1997, 85). We may deduce that Acacia's crucifiction begins when hunger drives her to prostitution, but Rey only depicts her torture three years later, when Juan, having been released from prison, discovers her at work with Magda in a city brothel (the film does not linger on Juan's prosperity in the

FIGURE 1.4 *Acacia (in profiles) and Friends.* The Cursed Village *(La aldea maldita* Rey 1930)

city, nor on his motivations for visiting the house of ill repute). While Rey had previously conveyed city life through the contemporary cinematic technique of Magda's mindscreen, Juan discovers Acacia by pulling back a curtain, an action that evokes the more venerable artistic precedents of the theatre, where curtains are used for often erotic discovery, and devotional painting, in which curtains symbolize Christian revelation (Wright 2007, 117). Acacia's *vía crucis* (Sánchez Vidal 1997, 85) will be to live with her family so the grandfather may die believing his honour remains intact, but Juan allows his wife no contact with her beloved child, forbidding her even to look at him, a prohibition made especially poignant when the child falls down a flight of stairs to unknown injury, yet she may not attend to him. Martín passes away and Acacia leaves to experience further torment as she wanders through the countryside: one scene shows her stumbling alone in the snow; another shows her approach a group of children and indicates that she may have lost her mind; a third evokes the biblical stoning of the adulteress, but in Rey's film this punishment is meted out by a group of children, no less; a final scene locates her in the abandoned village cottage, rocking the now empty cot. At this sight, Juan forgives her, and she recovers her wits with one kiss from the son.

Agustín Sánchez Vidal suggests shades of grey may be discerned in Rey's condemnation of womankind that indicate his disassociation from 'patriarchal morality' (1997, 85). The grandfather's blindness, so evocative in the visual medium of silent film, criticizes adherence to the honour code as unthinking. Nuance is also offered by the representation of the new generation, for the child breaks the association between male characters and stasis when he is shown playing with a toy aeroplane. Finally, Sánchez Vidal argues, Rey stresses Juan's forgiveness of his wife at the end of the film. Interpretation is, of course, another matter, and contemporary viewers like the reviewer for *La Gaceta Literaria* cite the portrayal of honour, the religious iconography and the 'exemplary punishment' of the wife to conclude that *The Cursed Village* is 'a purely Spanish film' (quoted by Sánchez Vidal 2005, 20). Marvin D'Lugo argues that the film's conservative values would become 'official Francoist cultural ideology within a decade' (1997, 30) (Rey made another sonorized version in 1942). In the next chapters of this book, we will see that directors gladly reprise its misogynistic association of the city and female adultery (for instance, in the auteurist *Furrows* [*Surcos*], analysed in Chapter 2), or the commercial *La ciudad no es para mí* (*City Life is not for Me*, analysed in Chapter 3). Rey's own attenuation of this association, along with the extraordinary formal accomplishment of the film, perhaps deserve a better inheritance.

The Fair of the Dove (*La verbena de la paloma* Perojo 1935)

Benito Perojo's *The Fair* is one of the high points of a period that is itself recognized as a high point of Spanish cinema by the epithet 'Golden Age'. An adaptation of the 1894 zarzuela by Ricardo de la Vega (libretto) and Tomás Bretón (music), it is preceded by an unacknowledged silent version, *Of the Forty** (*De los cuarenta* Roesset 1915), and José Buchs's acknowledged one in 1921. With none of the anxieties that often characterize responses to film adaptations of novels (like soul-searching about the purity of artistic media), contemporary and subsequent commentators alike enthusiastically embrace Perojo's brilliant transposition of the text from page and musical score to the cinema screen – now fully equipped with sound. In a 1936 interview, Raquel Rodrigo, for example, who plays Susana in the film, wondered if 'From now on *The Fair* may not be staged theatrically as audiences will find Perojo's film more enjoyable, pretty and accurate' (quoted in Gubern 1994, 277), while later scholars note the felicitous fit between the original zarzuela and the concurrently ascendant American musical film (Fanes 1989, 78; Gubern 1998, 56, who also stresses the influence of René Clair; Mira 2005). An 'Americanized zarzuela' (Fanés 1989, 78), or 'Saxonized comedy' (Gubern 1994, 289), this thoroughly transnational super-production (it cost 940,000 pesetas) also enjoyed thoroughly transnational reception, with success in the new markets in which CIFESA established branches in 1935 (Woods 2004, 49), including America, France and Germany.

Juxtaposing solemn rural silent tragedy *The Cursed Village* and riotous urban musical comedy *The Fair* as this chapter does, it is difficult to resist the critical commonplace of opposing Rey and Perojo, one traditional and conservative, the other liberal and cosmopolitan (Gubern 1994, 267). In fact, both made successful zarzuela adaptations (eg Rey's *The Mischief-Maker** [*La revoltosa* 1924]; Perojo's *The Fair*), both worked in shrewd collaboration with female stars (eg Rey with Imperio Argentina, whom he married in 1935; Perojo with Estrellita de Castro), both were leading directors of enormously popular films for CIFESA in the 1930s (Rey made *Rustic Chivalry/Aragonese Virtue* [*Nobleza baturra* 1935] and *Dark and Bright* [1936]; Perojo, besides *The Fair*, *Our Natasha** [*Nuestra Natacha* 1936]), both made folkloric films for Hispano-Film Produktion in Nazi Germany during the Civil War (Rey directed, for example, *Carmen* [*Carmen, la de Triana* 1938] and Perojo, *Spanish Sighs** [*Suspiros de España* 1938]) and both enjoyed continued success under the Franco dictatorship (Rey, through direction, like *La Dolores* [1940]; Perojo, through production, like the re-remake of *The Fair* [Saénz de Heredia 1962]).

Nonetheless, comparing *The Cursed Village* and *The Fair* uncovers the extraordinary diversity of 1930s Spanish cinema. Take film form. Rey masters the hauntingly poetic static and silent tableaux, and occasionally breaks classic editing conventions at moments of heightened poignancy, as when Acacia appears to 'walk through' the camera when starvation forces her to abandon her family. Perojo, meanwhile, favours fluid dynamism in cinematography and editing that brilliantly conveys the film's celebration of festivity and romance (the title and setting refer to the Madrid festival of the Virgin of the Paloma [Dove]; the action refers to the challenge to, then reconfirmation of, Susana and Julián's courtship). Matching tilts, for example, convey the couple's affections in a public context, as the camera tracks up the building in which Susana lives from Julián's perspective, then down it to Julián in the street from Susana's. Graphic matches link the couple's world, in which the wheel of printer Julián's printing press becomes the wheel of seamstress Susana's sewing machine while both characters are at work. The circular motif, with its associations of profitable employment and marital courtship, recurs at the fair through the horizontal rotation of the merry-go-round and the vertical rotation of the ferris wheel – these two efficaciously combined within one shot in homage to Eisenstein's theory of conflicting forms (Gubern 1998, 55). Elsewhere editing choices like ellipses and swipes, and cinematographic decisions to use an energetically mobile camera, link up both the narrative and the community. The irony of *The Fair* is that this dazzling cinematic modernity is deployed to portray an idealized pre-modern past of the August 1893 of the zarzuela: somewhere in the way the film smoothes this contradiction away lies Perojo's genius.

Turning to social mobility, we shift from Rey's dismal diatribe against city Segovia and fallen woman Acacia, to Perojo's animated celebration of Madrid festivity with feisty, flirtatious sisters Susana (Rodrigo) and Casta (Charito Leonis) – though both films in fact end with a reaffirmation of marriage, through Juan's forgiveness of his wife in *The Cursed Village* and Julián and Susana's reconciliation in *The Fair*. However, for all *The Cursed Village*'s formal stasis and punishment of female activity, it does portray Juan's transformation from ruined rural farmer to prosperous city foreman (an ascendance stressed by the intertitle that refers to his 'posición desahogada' [comfortable position]). Meanwhile, despite the frenetic activities of the characters at the fair, matched by Perojo's dynamic cinematography and editing, *The Fair* circles around a stasis and fails to engage with the 'struggles and woes of the popular classes, anxious for social mobility and success in a hard, hierarchical and unchanging social order' (Jordan and Allinson 2005, 10). Herein lies the reason why contemporary and subsequent Republican intellectuals

FIGURE 1.5 *The Merry-go-round, the Ferris Wheel and the Ebullient Crowd.* The Fair of the Dove *(La verbena de la paloma Perojo 1935)*

condemned zarzuelas, for they fail to address the class struggle (Triana-Toribio 2003, 33). Conversely, if *The Fair* ultimately offers a wish fulfilment in which its characters accept class status quo, this vision offered consoling reassurance to audiences living through a period when that status quo was breaking apart (I develop this thesis of 'consolation' in relation to 1940s and 1950s film in Chapter 2). Second, we may today appreciate that the film's bid for the coalescence of the community was especially urgent as we must now inevitably locate *The Fair* on the eve of Civil War.

Cross-class mobility is treated as both absurd and hilarious in Perojo's treatment of the relationship between cheeky working-class sisters Susana and Chato and the affluent apothecary, deliberately named Don Hilarión, a lecherous stereotype effortlessly embodied by key comic actor of the period Miguel Ligero. If stereotypical characterization dismisses the possibility for Susana to cross classes through marriage as ridiculous (in other CIFESA comedies of the period it is conversely shown to be possible, as in *Dark and Bright* [1936]), every other filmic resource is deployed to rejoice in a community based on the status quo. Unlike Ibáñez's negative reflection on the crowd in *Blood and Sand*, in *The Fair*, choral scenes are used positively throughout to stress the collective and the immutable. Such is the purpose of the particular scenes of the wedding breakfast and the aristocratic ball, and the general scenes of the street crowds. At the wedding breakfast of the film's opening, Julián is treated as an equal, despite being the groom's employee at the printing press (as well as noting that this is optimistic, Felix Fanés also observes how unrealistic it is that Julián should be able change from his worker's overall to a morning suit [1989, 78 and 111n. 49]). The ball is the film's only sequence to be shot in technicolour, and, in contrast to the cavalier approach to realism in the rest of the film, Perojo here uses well-known aristocrats as extras (Gubern 1994, 271). But the point is not to condemn upper-class difference, it is rather to stress similarity, for the soundtrack reveals that the aristocrats at the ball, like the workers in the street, enjoy the same music. The film's musical numbers are thus crucial: they display the popular theatrical roots of the picture, showcase Perojo's talent as a filmmaker in the ways he makes the songs entirely cinematic (Mira 2005, 37), and link up every character and location as participants in the festival. With its pre-capitalist setting, *The Fair* thus sings and laughs away class conflict, to the enormous enjoyment of audiences, who flocked to a film that was screened continuously for almost seven months. It premiered in Madrid two days before what is of course the winter's equivalent of the communal summer fair, Christmas Day, and played right up to the outbreak of war.

Given the myth of domestic rejection of the national cinema, it is tempting to create a rosy counter-myth, through films like *The Fair*, of the hugely popular Spanish film of the Second Republic. It should be stated, however, that the political censorship we might more commonly associate with dictatorship was also exercised in democracy. The treatment of Luis Buñuel is a good example. His association with the Republic has been stressed by his participation in the Madrid cineclubs, which screened mainly foreign films and fostered intellectual discussion of the medium, and his employment at the production company Filmófono, CIFESA's rival in the period. (A number of the Filmófono films have been recently re-released on DVD by Divisa, with Buñuel's name as 'supervisor' given equal billing to those of the directors.) In addition, as is well known, Buñuel left Spain when the Republic fell to become the country's most famous exile. It is logical, then, that the Republican government should commission the first film he shot on Spanish soil (he had made his first two films, *Un Chien andalou* [1929] and *L'Age d'or* [1930], in Paris in collaboration with Salvador Dalí). However, *Land Without Bread* (1933) was such a shocking denunciation of rural deprivation through pseudo-documentary that the Republican government immediately banned it. Such would be the fate of the second film Buñuel shot in Spain, *Viridiana* (1961), but this time the dictatorship banned it. With the aim of avoiding easy oppositions like Republic versus dictatorship, I move on, in Chapter 2, to one of the most contentious periods of the history of the national cinema: Spanish film under Franco.

Notes

1 Gubern 1995, 11. This statistic has since been nuanced: a 1998 estimate judged that only 5 per cent of 1920s were extant (Del Rey Reguillo 1998, 14); in 2007 20 per cent of literary adaptations of the period were judged to be available (Sánchez Salas 2007, p); in 2008 14 per cent of 1931–9 films were judged extant (Bentley 2008, 75). Spain's national film archive (Filmoteca Española) was only established as late as 1953. Prior to this, celluloid simply deteriorated or was recycled for other uses; a highly flammable material, fires also contributed to losses (Ruiz 2004, 8).

2 As the Acknowledgements of almost every book on Spanish cinema attest, Spain's film archives and affiliated libraries are essential for research, all the more so for earlier periods. The distribution of films on DVD, like the recent releases by Divisa, and their occasional availability on-line, are also extremely helpful for studying early film. I have used the following sources for films discussed in this chapter: Filmoteca Española; the pay-per-view www.filmotech.es; and Divisa DVDs.

3 In the Spanish context this scepticism was voiced most famously be Miguel

de Unamuno, who declared in 1923 that the 'baleful' cinema 'will only ruin the minds of those writers who set themselves to pen pantomimes' (translated in Morris 1980, 30).

4   See George, Larson and Mercer 2007, 75–6 for a summary of film's influence on the Avant-Garde in Spain and, for more detail, Morris 1980.

5   As has been frequently pointed out, it is no accident that the Lumière brothers' first pictures in the 1890s united film and train. Stephen Kern argued in 1983 that 'sweeping changes in technology and culture created distinctive new modes of thinking about and experiencing time and space' (summarized in Larson 2005, 264). Andrew Ginger (2007, 69) discusses the cinema's 'wider reconfiguration of space and time' in Spanish film of the 1920s.

6   See Eva Woods' reflections on the particular importance of the time-based medium of film in early twentieth-century Spain in conveying the nation's desire to '"catch up" to European time' (2012, 31).

7   Apart from the 1930s Golden Age, the audience figures cited throughout this book show that domestic audiences have flocked to Spanish films throughout the cinema's existence. What lies behind many criticisms of the domestic cinema in Spain is a Marxist-inflected hostility to popular culture, especially popular culture under Franco, which was deemed to be pro-regime (see Faulkner 2006, 7–8).

8   Robert-William Paul's animatograph was first used in Madrid 11 May 1896; the Lumière brothers' cinematograph, on 13 May (Herrera 2005, 326).

9   Spain's 'first Education Minister was not appointed until 1900, and compulsory education to the age of 12 only became law in 1908' (Bentley 2008, 3). To overcome illiteracy, 'explicadores' or 'voceadores' (explainers, speakers) explained silent films to audiences unable to read intertitles. In the United States (US) the term used was 'lecturer' (Elsaesser 1990, 165).

10   'Under the Franco-Moroccan treaty of 1912 Spain was allocated a "zone" in northern Morocco as a Protectorate, but her hold was constantly threatened by the inhospitable terrain and the resistance of local tribes' (Ross 2000, 58).

11   1910 is the year most commonly associated with change. It is cited, for example by Christian Metz, who describes the period 1910–15 as the 'beginning of the cinema as we know it' (1999, 70).

12   Bentley compares reactions to early cinema with those to seventeenth-century theatre: 'both were criticized for enticing immorality and corrupting the minds of weaker individuals' (2008, 46).

13   Nonetheless, the inevitable comparison with Northern Europe reveals that 'In 1930, Spain's industrial output per person was still only 30 per cent that of Britain, 32 per cent that of France and 39 per cent that of Germany' (Barton 2004, 179).

14   Deborah Parsons cites 21 film theatres in 1920 and over 60 by 1936 (2003, 86).

15   The dominance of US films in Spain continued in the 1920s and 1930s,

constituting 33 per cent of imports in 1922–30, but 67 per cent in 1931–9 (Ginger 2007, 70).

16 My thanks to Eva Woods for reminding me of this similarity.

17 Katharine Murphy (2010) has identified this intermediality in her study of ekphrasis in Ibáñez's novel *La maja desnuda* (1906), but does not include film in her analysis. Pío Baroja is a contemporary writer who was also involved in the cinema through adaptations of his work, collaborations with scriptwriters and articles on the subject (Bentley 2008, 35).

18 Adapted in Hollywood as *Blood and Sand* in 1922 (by Niblo), 1941 (Mamoulian) and 1989 (Elorrieta).

19 Bentley uses the Catalan spelling of the brothers' Christian names; I have used the Castilian form, which is more commonly used by historians. Javier Herrera also names Films Barcelona and Film de Arte Español as equivalents of the French Société de Film d'Art (2005, 327).

20 According to Luis Enrique Ruiz, between the 1910 and the 1922 adaptations de Baños made a pornographic version, a commissioned film only viewed in restricted circles (2004, 227).

21 In 1900 illiteracy was judged to be 50 per cent; by 1931, it was still as high as 40 per cent (Álvarez Junco 1995, 50).

22 Evidence of this pursuit may be deduced from specialist film magazines of the period, like *El cine*, *La Pantalla* and *Popular Film*. Daniel Sánchez Salas's analysis of these reveal an 'evolution in the social and artistic consideration of film' over the 1920s (2007, 413).

23 Julio Pérez Perucha puts to bed the argument that the film was influenced by Russian Olga Prebajenskaia's *The Village of Sin* (1992, 40) as it was not shown in Madrid until after Rey's was finished (1992, 42).

24 'This underlines the violence of characters' reactions, or visualizes the rupture in social conventions posed by the character involved' (Sánchez Vidal 1997, 85). The technique is used at the end of *Spaniards in Paris* (Bodegas 1971) to convey the protagonist's triumph (see Chapter 4).

25 I am grateful to Alison Sinclair for this reference. See Sinclair 2004 on the status of the rural in Spain in the slightly later period of the early 1930s of Buñuel's *Land Without Bread* (1933) and the reports of the Republic's 'Pedagogical Missions'.

2

Social Mobility and Cinema of the 1940s and 1950s: Consolation and Condemnation

An analysis of post-war Spanish cinema that places politics centre stage is persuasive. Such an approach bears witness to the devastation endured by the nation after an appalling three-year fratricidal Civil War (1936–9), then the long years of economic hardship and political reprisals, which were both the result of the repressive policies of a dictatorship forged in the context of 1930s European fascism.[1] A nation weakened by war, it is estimated that 200,000 perished from starvation or illness from 1939–44. The disastrous policy of autarky (economic isolationism), put in place while the Falangists dominated government in the early 1940s,[2] made an ideological virtue of necessity, for fascist Spain was internationally isolated until the deal with the United States in 1953 that gave the world's number one power Spanish military bases of strategic necessity in the Cold War in exchange for economic aid. Spain then entered the United Nations in 1955. Alongside economic hardship in the 1940s came political repression. The regime executed 20,000 Republicans in 1939 alone; almost a million Spaniards ended up in punishing Spanish concentration camps and labour battalions; there were a further half a million Republican refugees (many of whom perished in French and German concentration camps). Although the Civil War supposedly ended when Nationalist leader Francisco Franco declared victory on 1 April 1939, according to various measures it therefore extended to at least 1951. Fifteen years after the start of the conflict, this was the year that rationing ended and the year that the Spanish Communist Party ended military action by withdrawing its guerrilla cadre from Spain.

A history of film cannot ignore such contexts, but neither can it be a pseudo-history, with events and ideologies merely illustrated by films, or with the role of film limited to providing camouflage or distraction. For all their important attention to repressive context, the initial interpretation of Spanish film of early Francoism, which held sway until well into the 1990s, tends to use films in this way (eg Caparrós Lera 1983, especially 27–34; or Galán 2000, 133 [first published 1997]). *Race* (*Raza* Saénz de Heredia 1941) is the classic example used, irresistible to scholars as the script was penned by the dictator himself.[3] Thus while Franco's government enacted policies to protect what Bernard Bentley summarizes as 'Franco's three "F"s: Fatherland, Family and Faith' (2008, 87), the film *Race* illustrates those same three by exalting the apparently nationalist, patriarchal and Catholic motivations of the dictator in this loosely autobiographical pic (one obvious difference is that the hero's sons in the film contrast with the Caudillo's own lack of a male heir [Gómez 2002, 580]). Further examples of single films and whole genres have been used to bolster the narrative of cinema at the service of the state, which intervened to ensure the projection of its vision by active means like subsidies, official prizes and the award of import licences, and reactive mechanisms like censorship and blanket dubbing from 1941.[4] In the first part of the 1940s, when the Falangists dominated the cabinet, fascist war films like *Race* glorified the Nationalists' bravery during the Civil War and exalted their victory (*The Siege of the Alcázar** [*Sin novedad en el alcázar* 1940], actually shot by Italian Augusto Genina, is another example of this trend, detailing the endurance and valour of besieged Nationalist Spaniards in Toledo's military headquarters). However, these war films constituted a small proportion of production in the period (which was dominated by comedies and folkloric films) (Hernández and Revuelta 1976, quoted in Montiel Mues 2002, 237); they were abandoned altogether by 1942 (Labanyi 2000, 172).

Franco's 1945 cabinet reshuffle demoted Falangists further in response to the defeat of Axis powers in the Second World War, replacing them with politicians connected to the Church. What Stanley Payne named the 'realignment' of the regime (1987, 343) saw a corresponding cultural shift from war films to historical or period films that paid homage to Francoism by connecting the 'Caudillo' and his dictatorship with earlier periods of history. The supposedly Nationalist and religious fervour behind the Catholic monarchs' unification of Spain and sponsorship of the conquest of the Americas in the fifteenth and sixteenth centuries was a favourite period (*Dawn of America** [*Alba de América* 1951] offering a key example), while the defence of the 'Patria' (fatherland) against the French during the 1800s was also attractive (*Agustina de Aragón*, which details the defence of Zaragoza, is a good illustration here). The cycle of period pictures that adapted conservative authors such as Pedro

Antonio de Alarcón (I analyse *The Nail* [*El clavo*] below) or Armando Palacio Valdés also apparently offered a vision of the past that mirrored the Francoist present. The Catholic emphasis of post-1945 Francoism is even more explicit in the missionary films and priest-protagonist films (*Reckless* [*Balarrasa* Nieves Conde 1950] represents a transition movie from military to missionary tendencies),[5] and films exalting the family with a child protagonist (the big hit for this trend came in 1955 with *The Miracle of Marcelino* [*Marcelino, pan y vino* Vajda]). The other major Spanish genre of the period, the folkloric film or 'españolada', was dismissed as mere escapism by pre- (and many post-) 1990s film historians, alongside other supposedly diverting spectacles encouraged by the dictatorship like bull-fighting and football.

The persuasive early narrative of films of the 1940s and 1950s ends with a move from darkness to light, or political awakening. For example, José María Caparrós Lera's narrative of the period, which includes interviews with 40 film professionals (every one, incidentally, a male), stresses left-wing art cinema as pivotal by naming the New Spanish Cinema of the early 1960s as the 'climax' of Spanish cinema (1983, 41). This narrative of progress features key milestones along the way: the opening of the state film school in Madrid in 1947 ('The Institute of Cinematic Investigation and Experience', renamed 'Official Film School' in 1962), the increased availability of foreign film, and the often-repeated intervention of the hero of anti-Franco Marxist culture in Spain, Juan Antonio Bardem, a member of the clandestine Spanish Communist Party. At a conference in 1955 (The Salamanca Conversations) he dismissed Spanish cinema as 'politically ineffectual, socially false, intellectually poverty-stricken, aesthetically void and industrially stunted' (Marsh 2006, 1) and called for a Marxist cinema to 'bear witness to its human moment' (Santos Fontenla 1966, 192). The films that followed, like *That Happy Couple** (*Esa pareja feliz* Bardem and Berlanga 1951), were all originally interpreted as embodying this political zeal. The left-wing narrative of a move from darkness into light remained surprisingly tenacious in Spain thanks to the protacted period in which Marxism channelled dissent under the dictatorship, and the fact that the anti-Franco intelligentsia held key cultural posts in Spain post-Franco (Labanyi 2002a, 11; Castro de Paz 2002, 13). While examples of the tenacity of post-Franco dismissal of 'Francoist' cinema might still be found in scholarly articles and the specialist film press in Spain today (as I detail in Chapter 7, it still resurfaces in response to the 2000s heritage cinema), revisionist accounts of the received narrative of cinema of the period are robust.

From the 1990s, scholars productively deployed cultural theory, especially psychoanalysis, gender studies and, more recently, cultural studies,[6] to offer alternative accounts. Off-message commentators like John Hopewell had already pointed out in 1986 that 1940s Spanish cinema was not '"Francoist"' if the term is to suggest a large, homogeneous corpus of para-governmental production', and quotes maverick director Berlanga's recollection that 'I never saw any of that fierce direct control ('dirigismo') or horrendous repression that critics and historians claim characterize cinema in the 40s' (1986, 34). Through close analysis of specific texts, critics have uncovered so many cracks in the supposedly unyielding triptych of 'father, faith, family' that the edifice of uniformity crumbles (Castro de Paz and Cerdán summarize this shift in 2011, 33–42). Homosexuality has been stressed in the war film's portrayal of male comradeship (eg ¡Harka! [1940], Hopewell 1986, 35; Fanés 1989, 91–2; Evans 1995, 219); while feminist subtexts have been uncovered in the melodramatic historical epics and period films with forceful female protagonists (eg Agustina de Aragón [1950], Labanyi 2000); and an intriguingly critical 'family in crisis' in melodramas like Ábel Sánchez (1947) (Labanyi 1995). The supposedly escapist folkloric films, meanwhile, have been thoughtfully revised to account for their frequent 'disruption of official dichotomies and the fabrication of consent' (Woods 2004, 201, summarizing Labanyi 2001 and 2002b, Marsh 1999 and Vernon 1999). Eva Woods's analysis of Whirlwind (Torbellino Marquina 1941), whose title points to disruption, is a good example of this; questions of race have also been explored in both the folkloric film and the missionary film (Labanyi 1997; Woods 2012). The assumption that 1940s film directors adapted conservative authors in a necessarily conservative way has also been questioned (Castro de Paz 2002, 17), a point I will stress in my analysis of the surprising counter-reading that Rafael Gil offers of Alarcón in his adaptation of The Nail (1944).

Moving away from theory and textual analysis, critics have addressed production contexts further to dismantle the common place of a monolithic 1940s Francoist cinema. Labanyi draws on scholarship of fascism to suggest, first, that propaganda (Race notwithstanding) may have been avoided as it was understood that it directly generated resistance; second, while Franco's interest in cinema is demonstrated by his scripting of Race, Spain never had a Cinecittá, like Mussolini's Italy, indeed film production remained in the hands of private individuals whose motivation was commercial rather than political; third, the inherently collective nature of filmmaking points to a plurality of perspective that auteurist studies tend to forget (2007b, 23–4). While an auteurist director such as Saura or producer like Querejeta might assemble uniform creative 'teams' for their political cinema of the 1960s and 1970s, plurality characterizes studio-bound Spanish production of the 1940s, where creative personnel included Jewish refugees from Nazi Germany (they came to Spain prior to anti-Semitic Franco's coup), those previously employed in the Republican cinema of the 1930s, as well as those sympathetic to the regime. Indeed, it is particularly mistaken to divorce Republican cinema of the 1930s from cinema under Franco in the 1940s (a divorce I unfortunately suggest by my own chapter break), for despite the inestimable interruption of the Civil War, and the fully never forgotten (or forgiven) exile of Buñuel and others,[7] the continuities were many. Left-wing Filmófono may have lost Buñuel, who worked for the production company in the 1930s, and the 16 projects announced for 1936–7, including Brontë, Valle-Inclán and Baroja adaptations, may have folded (Hopewell 1986, 24), but it continued to produce films till 1951 (Bentley 2008, 62). CIFESA (Compañía Industrial Film Española S.A.), which was originally set up in Valencia by the Trénor family in 1932 – though quickly taken over by the Casanova family – continued to make films in both Republican and dictatorship periods up to 1956. Not only does this signal conservative cultural tendencies under the Republic (against which some of its directors like Benito Perojo might have pushed [Pavlovic 2009, 24]), but also stresses cultural continuities between the periods of Republic and dictatorship.[8] In matters of production, the achievements of the 1930s Golden Age were carried over in the 1940s: the high production values of its studio sets; its star system of quality actors; its highly-trained and skilled directors and creative personnel. Its distribution channels of multiple cinemas in rural as well as urban locales enabled Spain to have the highest rate of film attendance in Europe in the period (Santaolalla 2005b, 51). Thus the paradox may be explained: an especially impoverished post-war nation was able to enjoy an especially high-quality native post-war cinema. Finally, the 1940s film corpus has itself been skewed by the repeated focus on *Race*, in fact the only film Franco penned, and on the historical epic, of which there were only four.[9] Steven Marsh concludes that only 20 of the more than 500 films made in Spain between 1939 and 1951 conform to the 'nation-building propaganda [...] caricature' (2006, 1–2).

Turning to reception, scholars have convincingly argued for the existence of a diverse post-war audience with varied emotional and ideological invest-ments in cinema of the period. They have highlighted the roles of actors like Aurora Bautista, whose vigorous performances as historical heroines at once embody a jingoistic view of Spanish history for Nationalist audiences, but whose on-screen suffering and defiance also 'unexpectedly mediate[...] the experience of ordinary women living under dictatorship' (Evans 1995, 220), or folkloric films that offered audiences that included 'the victims of Francoist repression a cathartic release from their own relations of dependency, while allowing members of the establishment the illusion of "loving" (literally "patronizing") the lower classes' (Labanyi 1997, 226).[10] If academic criticism was slow to study what I summarize as the 'consolation' and 'condemnation' offered by post-war cinema, this role had long been acknowledged in the cultural arena. Literary reflections on the post-war period written in the late

1960s onwards display 'the contestatory potential' of popular Hollywood cinema and popular Spanish cinema and songs (Labanyi 2007a, 3–4). Basilio Martín Patino's extraordinary documentary memorial *Songs for after a War* (*Canciones para después de una guerra* of 1971 (only released 1976) bears witness to what I call the 'consoling' and 'condemning' roles that may have been played by popular song in the period (it refers to cinema too) (see Graham 1995 for an academic study inspired by this film). In it Patino includes the poignant line in voiceover: 'eran canciones para sobrevivir' (they were songs for survival).

Ann Davies questions the 'worthiness' that sometimes surrounds the study of audience reception and popular cinema, stressing that audience views are no more 'factual', or unmediated, than those of film scholars,[11] and that: 'It becomes all too easy to assume that because popular cinema carries with it the potential to subvert and resist dominant ideologies, this is what it inevitably does' (2011, 10). Consequently, I emphasize that my choice of films is selective; and that my interpretative approach is open. Avoiding the extremes of submission to dominant ideologies and subversion of those ideologies, I propose 'consolation' as a term that enables us to analyse how audiences might 'work through' their own experiences through the films they watched (I take the expression from TV studies [Ellis 2002, 2]). Rather than political ideology, I stress the widespread economic deprivation highlighted by historians like Richards (1998) and Tortella (2000) to ask how audiences negotiated this downward social mobility through the texts they consumed. Thus while in the earlier and remaining chapters of this book I chart the related question of the impact of upward social mobility on culture, and argue for the existence of middlebrow films consumed by increasingly upwardly-mobile middle-class audiences, I chart here the related question of the impact of downward social mobility on culture.

I have subtitled this chapter 'consolation and condemnation' rather than 'from consolation to condemnation' to stress that the uses audiences make of films may be multiple. The first three films selected, *The Nail* (1944), *She, He and His Millions** (*Ella, él y sus millones* 1944) and *From Woman to Woman* (*De mujer a mujer* 1950) (all produced by CIFESA), might be more readily associated with the thesis of consolation, which is explained by the context of the political defeat suffered by half of society but also the economic hardship endured by almost all. However, I will attend to those aspects of these CIFESA comedies and melodramas that might be interpreted as condemnatory of the current climate too. My next set of films *Furrows* (*Surcos* Nieves Conde 1951), *That Happy Couple* (Bardem and Berlanga 1951) and *Main Street* (*Calle Mayor* Bardem 1956), meanwhile, have been frequently analysed as a cinema of political dissent that condemns Francoism. If

1940s Spanish cinema responded to the needs of audiences experiencing downward social mobility for the first time in living memory, I will argue for a 1950s cinema that is especially attuned to frustrated upward social mobility and frustrating stasis (frustrations that are also acutely observed in the first two films I analyse in Chapter 3, *Plácido* [Berlanga 1961] and *Life Goes On** [*El mundo sigue* Fernán Gómez 1964]). For even though economists labelled the 1950s the 'hinge decade' (Pavlovic 2011, 1), when autarky was abandoned and the so-called 'technocrat' ministers (brought in by the cabinet re-shuffle of 1957) opened up Spanish markets, the upward social mobility that followed this about-turn in policy was not seen till the 1960s. *Surcos* combines a political condemnation of economic stasis with a paternalist condemnation of the distracting consolation of popular culture; more nuanced are *That Happy Couple* and *Main Street*, which merge political critique with a surprisingly sensitive response to audiences' use of cinema as consolation.

The Nail (*El clavo* Gil 1944)

Scholarly work on Spanish cinema has always stressed its international influences, a tendency given increased momentum by the recent 'transnational' turn in current Film Studies, which has given a name to these multiple border-crossings (see, for instance, Evans, Perriam, Santaolalla 2007; López 2010). While the influence of Italian Neorealism on dissident Spanish cinema of the 1950s onwards (following the 1951 Film Week) has long been stressed (Kinder 1993, 18), scholars have more recently added German Expressionism (via cinematographers escaping Nazism in the 1930s, see Llinàs 1989, 15–16), and, above all, Hollywood: film noir and melodrama (Marsha Kinder provocatively proposed a dissident Spanish cinema that was a 'transcultural reinscription' of these last two [1993, 17]), the youth movie (Delgado 1999, 43) and comedy (Evans 1995, 222; Marsh 2006, 10). In this section I will examine CIFESA's deployment of the 'prestige' picture of the contemporary Hollywood studio system, an influence that has received less attention.

The dominant Spanish production company of the 1930s and 1940s, CIFESA's preeminence (it made some 41 films between 1931 and 1950) would only be rivalled towards the end of the decade by Cesáreo González's Suevia Films, Ignacio Iquino's Emisora Films and Aureliano Campa (Pavolvić 2009, 63). It has been noted that this Spanish company imitated the American studio system, such as Paramount, by creating a 'house style' through its motto 'the torch of hits' (Mira 2010, 81), its use of a roster of gifted directors and creative personnel, star system and studios (though it did not possess its own, renting CEA studios in Madrid [Jordan and Allinson 2005, 8]). While CIFESA's big-budget films are thus comparable to Hollywood's high-A film output, a number may be more specifically termed 'prestige'. Not a genre, 'prestige' is a term that describes these films by fusing questions of production and reception (and in this sense overlaps in an interesting way with the 'middlebrow', discussed in Chapters 4–7).[12] Its cross-generic formal characteristics include recourse to high-culture, especially 'literary sources', along with '"serious" themes and lavish production values' (Cagle 2007, 292).[13] Period melodramas The Nail and From Woman to Woman fit this description, while the contemporary comedy She, He and His Millions* partially fits with its high production values. Equally important to defining 'prestige' is reception: 'Product prestige can be thought of as the extent to which the films of a studio are perceived to be of "quality" by contemporary molders of public opinion about film – commentators and critics in the trade and the general press' (Allen 1995, 130). While the three examples of Spanish prestige films I explore in this chapter variously display the formal charac-teristics of the tendency, when considering the equivalent of Hollywood's 'contemporary molders of public opinion about film' in Franco's Spain we cannot avoid political context. Not only did Spain's 'Commentators and critics' write in a censored press, but the state, while falling short of propa-ganda (Labanyi 2007b, 22), nonetheless intervened to promote a cinema that complemented its ideology of 'Faith, Fatherland and Family' through subsidies and the control of import licences: the greater the official approval of the film, the greater the subsidy and the greater the number of licences to distribute foreign films (up to 15).[14] The term 'prestige' can thus only be applied to Spanish film with qualifications.

Awarded one of the state's first interés nacional (National Interest) certif-icate (a prize given to films that supposedly embodied Nationalist values), Rafael Gil's The Nail consequently received the top subsidy of 50 per cent of its immense production costs of nearly three million pesetas, and won its producer 15 import licences, the maximum possible (Fanés 1989, 115). Its formal characteristics suggest the prestige picture, with its high culture intertext (an adaptation of Pedro Antonio de Alarcón's novel), 'serious' theme of a miscarriage of justice, and costly production values that made it the most expensive Spanish film to date. These costs included billing acting stars (Amparito Rivelles as Blanca/Gabriela and Rafael Durán as Javier) alongside 23 further actors and 1000 extras,[15] constructing expensive sets (no fewer than ten were especially created to replicate the 1850s setting of Alarcón's original novel [1853]), using a specially composed music score (to stress extremes of emotion) and buying precious and pricey Kodak-Dupont stock (to enhance emotional contrast through claroscuro). The case for prestige in reception is harder to make, since the assignation of cultural value by the censored press or the Francoist authorities is inextricably linked with pro-regime ideology. However, if we make state intervention in filmmaking the dominant factor, only a curiously tautological interpretation of films can ever follow: a movie supports the values of the state that supported it. Questioning this reflective model of the relationship between film and state, Federico Bonaddio suggests 'These [funding] circumstances arouse the suspicion that the ideological stance adopted by many historical dramas may itself have been nothing more than a sham' (2004, 31). In what follows I work with the grain of such revisionist accounts of Spanish cinema of the 1940s by placing textual analysis, not funding circumstances, first, to consider The Nail's display of the key characteristics of the prestige picture. Stressing funding circumstances has also led some critics to dismiss films of the period 'simply as a means of earning very profitable import licences' for their producers (Jordan and Allinson 2005, 16). Yet The Nail was immensely successful at the box office (Bentley 2008, 96). Thus I consider, second, the potential attraction of the film to audiences according to the ideas of consolation and condemnation.

The film's sumptuous production values immediately point to the thesis of consolation. Popular stars Rivelles and Durán enjoy star treatment in cinematography, mise en scène and music. The actors' polished performances draw on the gesturality and excess that characterizes melodrama of the period. Prestige aesthetics are all about consistency, thus such extravagant performances are enhanced by cinematographer Alfredo Fraile's admiring medium and close-ups, flattering key lighting, and the soaring strings of Juan Quintero's musical score that stress emotions. Take the climactic moment towards the end of the film in the court room. Judge Javier learns what the audience has guessed long before: that the mysterious Blanca whom he pursues as a lover (her false name meaning 'white' and 'blank' underlines how little he knows of her origins), is in fact Gabriela, the murderess whom he pursues as a judge. A resplendent Rivelles enters the densely populated and decorated courtroom (the set decorator was Enrique Alarcón) wearing a black gown with a black lace veil over her face (José Montfort and Humberto Cornejo y Raula were responsible for wardrobe). By dressing and accessorizing his actress in monochrome, Gil implies that this public and legal encounter between Blanca/Gabriela and Javier before the eyes of God (represented by the bible and the large crucifix next to the judge and the small crucifix around the neck of the accused) is a kind of tragic marriage: the virginal white of bridal tradition becomes the murderous black of Rivelles's attire. When Rivelles lifts the veil to reveal her identity, the mise en scène complements her radiance through key-lighting, the camera captures the moment in close-up, and the agitated strings of the musical score swell to a crescendo. There follows a flashy zoom in on judge Javier, in shock at this revelation of identity. The movement centres on the pained expression on Durán's face, ending in a close-up that matches the one used for Rivelles. The zoom conveys the judge's horror, but the matching close-up indicates the couple's shared destiny of loss and suffering.

To argue that the high production values of the prestige picture consoled impoverished 1940s audiences is hardly controversial. Alongside this courtroom scene, viewers could behold other elaborate interiors like the hotel, with its ornate winding staircase,[16] or the judicial office, with its towering piles of papers, or specially constructed exteriors, like the street scenes in Teruel, where the couple court, or in Madrid, where the pair are reunited. The film's wardrobe, created by Monfort and Cornejo y Raula, is another major source of visual pleasure. Rivelles's dress in the courtroom scene is in fact striking for its simplicity: in the rest of the film audiences might enjoy the extravagant adornments of the actress's twelve other outfits, or Durán's similarly resplendent attire (all lovingly displayed on the film's publicity posters assembled in the booklet accompanying the 2009 Divisa DVD release).

While acknowledging the consoling pleasures of the film's production values, an analysis of plot and characterization yields further rewards. The model for Gil's *The Nail* was José Luis Saénz de Heredia's *The Scandal* (*El escándalo*) of the previous year, another literary adaptation which used conservative Alarcón to get a racy plot about female adultery and a love affair with a priest past the censors (Labanyi 1995, 7–8).[17] Audiences seeking such sauciness would not be disappointed with *The Nail*: despite 'Fatherland, Faith and Family', the censors allowed a sympathetic portrayal of pre-marital sex. This is not a matter of explicit details, unthinkable in this period, but the nonetheless enjoyable implications of Gil's showy cinematography. The couple retires to the hotel after a night-time walk, and a tilting long shot from outside the building reveals Javier's presence in Blanca/Gabriela's room, and absence from his own. Vital too is the key change Gil makes to the ending of the literary original, which Juan Miguel Company argues is crucial to the director's 'rigorous counter-reading' of the literary original (1997b, 180). Alarcón sends Blanca/Gabriela to the gallows, which fuses a legal condemnation of her act of murder with a moral condemnation of her sexual activities outside marriage. But Gil, after devoting the final section of the film to a sympathetic portrayal of Blanca/Gabriela's justification of her actions through an impassioned speech to the court and through a lengthy flashback, changes Alarcón's original to allow Javier to win a pardon at the eleventh hour, reducing the death sentence to life imprisonment. Gil also avoids the cliché of eternal female abnegation and suffering, for Javier will share the sentence by accompanying his lover. She will be within the prison walls, he will be without, but, in his words 'voy tras ti para compartir tu dolor' (I will follow you to share your pain).

Daring, for the period, in its sympathetic treatment of sexuality, we might also read the portrayal of gender in *The Nail* as another example of a tentative feminism and a postmodernism ahead of its time that recent critics have uncovered in some CIFESA historical dramas. The plot of *The Nail* stresses performance, role play and mistaken identities throughout. At the start of the film Javier and Blanca/Gabriela are wrongly taken to be a married couple at the country baptism; they even dress up as a peasant man and wife when they are caught in the rain and take refuge with a rural family who lend them their clothes. Significantly the scenes that most directly convey Francoist values of blessed family life in the country are the corniest in the film, and the ones in which Javier and Blanca/Gabriela play roles and pretend. Gil also profitably takes advantage of the apparently incidental, though symbolically suggestive, setting of the carnival when the couple spend a night in the hotel. Gallant galán Javier rescues distressed damsel Blanca/Gabriela on two occasions during the evening of carnival festivities by pretending to be her husband. The gallant rescue of the damsel is a clichéd scenario, but the carnival context interestingly suggests 'spouse' might be a role performed like any other in the festivities. *The Nail* thus confirms what José Luis Castro de Paz has called 'the decidedly self-conscious, reflexive and meta-cinematic tendencies' of many post-war Spanish films, which, far from being trapped in contemporary Francoism, look back to Spain's playful Cervantine heritage (2002, 113n. 1) and forward to 1990s postmodern theory. Like Benito Perojo's 1942 *Goyescas*, *The Nail* also 'anticipates Judith Butler's postmodern perception (1990) that identity is the effect resulting from a repeated performance' (Labanyi 2004, 43).

We might argue that this questioning of identity is particularly significant in relation to female characters. Rivelles's substantial screen presence and especially expressive face (her frown and the arching of her right eyebrow are conduits for the emotional intensity of the melodrama) make her an attractive figure of identification for female audiences. Historical and audience studies of the period remind us that the women of post-war Spain, while deprived of the political rights they had won under the Republic, were simultaneously tasked with supporting families in dire economic circumstances, with absent male family members lost in the war, imprisoned, exiled or executed (Graham 1995; Labanyi 2007a, 5–6). When they attended the cinema – which they did in great number as audiences were predominantly female – they were most in need of consolation (Labanyi 2007a, 5). Thus we might add Rivelles's robust embodiment of the afflicted Blanca/Gabriela in *The Nail* to the strong, textured performances of other stars of the 1940s like Aurora Bautista, Sarita Montiel and Concha Piquer analysed by Peter Evans (1995). In *The Mad Queen* (Orduña 1948), for instance, Evans shows that 'exposure of male injustice to women lifts the picture from epic to melodrama and the Cifesa equivalent of the Hollywood Woman's Picture [...] Bautista unexpectedly mediates through the representation of Juana La Loca the experience of ordinary women living under dictatorship' (1995, 220).

I inflect this argument by proposing that *The Nail*'s interest in injustice is not limited to the female character. In what follows, I propose that, given the historical context, the picture offers a surprisingly consoling, if not condemnatory, treatment of the questions of crime and justice. Let us not forget that 1944 was the height of the Francoist repression, with sentences handed down by the regime's judges and law courts that imprisoned and executed dissenters in astounding numbers (20,000 Republicans were shot after the war in 1939 alone). Alongside Nationalist soldiers and officers, fascist activists, Francoist ministers and colluding clergy and civil service, the regime's judges were thus hated figures for dissenting audiences. If Rivelles's performance and Gil's characterization of Blanca/Gabriela offer a satisfyingly nuanced portrayal of a doubly-fallen women (a murderess and a sexually-active unmarried woman), the treatment of Durán's embodiment of judge Javier is also thought-provoking. Gil dissects the hated figure of the aloof servant of justice by careful stages. First, Javier is presented to us as the impatient lover, whose sexual interest in Blanca/Gabriela is nonetheless matched by a desire to protect her. Next, we meet Javier the judge, whose casual discovery of skull with a nail embedded in its base gives him the intellectual distraction of solving an undetected crime. The viewer guesses early on, but Javier's discovery that beloved Blanca, the object of his emotional interest, and criminal Gabriela, the object of his intellectual interest, are one and the same person is presented as a shattering collision in the courtroom scene described above.

Thus through the plot's inexorable progress towards its tragic conclusion Gil relentlessly deconstructs the cliché of the detached arbitrator, to the undoubted satisfaction of audiences that had been victims of the cold legal machinery of Francoism. This is a question of deconstruction, not demolition, and Gil is as interested in consequences as he is in climaxes. It is not a question of condemning an intellectually-detached judge, but stressing that he is at one and the same time an emotionally-attached lover. This nuanced treatment of Javier is most notable in Gil's treatment of the question of suffering, a punishment often uniquely associated with women in classic melodrama. The use of Christian imagery in the film is significant in this regard. Strikingly, Gil avoids the iconography of the *mater dolorosa* that was so common in the Marian Spain of early Francoism (Graham 195, 184) in favour of Christ's passion on the cross. When judge Javier begins his investigations into the nail-murder he is ominously juxtaposed with crosses when he discovers the suspicious skull in the graveyard, and framed alongside crucifixes when he and his secretary make enquiries about the deceased in the gravedigger's lodgings and in two local churches. The climactic courtroom scene opens with a close-up of a crucifix placed in front of the judge's chair in such a way as to imply a match between Christ and judge. Gil's camera then zooms back to take in Javier's entrance. This does not mean that the judge is an all-powerful messiah, but that the judge is condemned to suffer, as Christ suffered. This fate is confirmed by the zoom into his face on seeing Blanca/Gabriela. The zoom out from the cross and the zoom into Javier provide cinematic confirmation of the mirrored suffering of each man. When Blanca/Gabriela appears she may wear a small crucifix around her neck in anticipation of her future of suffering in prison (or even death by the hangman's noose as in Alarcón's original), but Javier is juxtaposed in the frame with the far larger crucifix on his desk: his future suffering will be just as significant. And of course the nail, along with the thorns of his crown, is a privileged signifier of Christ's agony. The nail in the skull of the murdered man represents an unsolved crime and miscarriage of justice at the literal level of narrative. But in

FIGURE 2.1 *Suffering Judge Javier.* The Nail *(*El clavo *Gil 1944)*

no genre could objects be imbued with more significance than in melodrama. At a figurative level, the nail signifies first the lovers' torment: they will be parted owing to the unknowing actions of Javier the judge to the detriment to Javier the lover. Furthermore, the nail signifies punishment for the irreconcilability of Javier's character: detached judge and attached lover are condemned to a life of longing. This entirely symbolic role is most important, for while 'The nail' names the film and drives the narrative, extraordinarily, we never see an actual nail on screen, bearing witness to the exceptional power of the un-seen, and the off-screen in fictional film. In a society where church and court often colluded in enacting the Francoist repression, Gil's consoling prestige picture reconsiders justice and religion by exploring the conflicting character of a judge through Christian imagery of male suffering. In a polarized socio-political context of good and evil, Nationalist and 'rojo', victor and vanquished and even 'Spain' or 'anti-Spain', *The Nail* condemns Manichean oppositions and satisfyingly explores the overlaps between accuser and accused, criminal and judge and even justice and injustice.

She, He and His Millions* (Ella, él y sus millones Orduña 1944)

If CIFESA is today most readily associated with its four high budget epics or 1948–51, and, to a lesser extent, with its prestige melodramas like *The Nail*, comedies like Juan de Orduña's *She, He and His Millions* in fact form the majority of productions and are a reminder that the company was a commercial business not an ideological mouthpiece (a truth reinforced by the fact that, when CIFESA appealed to the government for financial aid in 1946, it was refused [Hopewell 1986, 36–7]). *Millions* is a particularly good example of profitability, enjoying an impressive run of a full four weeks in the winter 1944–5 – two of the dark early 'Years of Hunger'. The standard response to the popularity of a comedy about the wealthy aristocracy at a time of widespread economic deprivation is to dismiss it as escapism. While 'escapism' suggests a passive, distracted audience, I prefer 'consolation' as it suggests an audience actively making use of a film – even though the use was limited for an economically- and politically-repressed, predominantly female, audience. After considering the partial deployment of prestige aesthetics in the film through mise en scène (costumes and settings), I consider, second, the possibility of reading condemnation in the film. Both José Luis Castro de Paz (2002, 86) and Steven Marsh (2006, 9) have written evocatively of the 'wounded' Spain of the 1940s that is partially masked but partially also revealed by comedy. I will develop this argument in relation to Orduña's portrayal of two fascinating patriarchs: Rafael Durán's performance in the leading role of the aloof financier Arturo Salazar, which connects with his role as the detached judge in *The Nail* analysed above; and José Isbert's performance as Ramón, Duke of Hinojares, the aristocratic father of four adult children, which is a secondary role only according to the measure of screen time.[18]

As has been frequently noted, *Millions* is Spain's answer to the contemporary American comedy, 'a sometimes screwball-orientated, high-society world of fast dialogue, zany socialites, and expensive gowns and haircuts' (Evans 1995, 222), with Orduña's film drawing more specifically on *Bringing Up Baby* (Hawks 1938) and *His Girl Friday* (Hawks 1940) (Castro de Paz 2002, 89).[19] The disconnect between on-screen and off-screen worlds could not be more complete, as it encompasses both narrative content and formal presentation. First, for a nation enduring sharp downward mobility, *Millions* features the upward social mobility of financier Salazar (to whose name I will return), who, though born into poverty, has made his titular 'millions' through business, and now needs to buy an aristocratic title to match through a marriage of convenience. If it was consoling for audiences to watch a film about the social mobility that was a fantasy compared to their own lives, fanciful too was the portrayal of effortless geographical mobility in the Arturo and Diana's phony honeymoon. The disconnect between worlds conveyed by film form is especially evident in the deployment of mise en scène. Like Amparito Rivelles and Ana Mariscal in *The Nail* and *From Woman to Woman*, CIFESA poured resources into the three Hinojares sisters' Hollywood-inspired wardrobe (by Pedro Rodríguez), with simpering Ana María (Ana María Campoy) appearing at the start of the film in a shiny gown exactly like that worn by Katharine Hepburn at the hotel at the start of *Bringing Up Baby*. Lavishly-dressed characters must occupy richly furnished settings, so set decorator Enrique Alarcón contrasts the traditionally-styled sumptuous interiors of the Hinojares family mansion, including the ballroom sequence replete with chandeliers and shiny dance floor in which Arturo and Diana announce their marriage, and the modern opulence of the Salazars' marital home, in which a similar ball is hosted for Arturo to declare his feelings to his smart, scheming wife.

Áurea Ortiza's work on 1940s comedies suggests a gendered analysis as a way of reading condemnation in *Millions*. Female characters, she notes, differ wildly from contemporary official ideology: 'they don't seem to go to mass, but rather to cabarets and parties' (quoted in Castro de Paz 2002, 89)! I propose extending this gender critique to the male characters to argue that, as in *The Nail*, the examination of masculinity is even more richly contestatory of Francoism. The film opens with the industrialist Salazar (we do not even meet his co-protagonist, Diana, played by Josita Hernán, until a late minute 18, after a glimpse at minute 10): through the character's name and activity in the post-credit sequence I will argue that Orduña (both director and 'technical scriptwriter' according to the credits) sets him up as a Franco-figure for audiences. Next, through the development of his character arc, Orduña subjects this figure to a mischievous and potentially condemnatory process of feminization. The treatment is not original, as it follows the process of feminization that characterizes Hollywood screwball (Evans 1995, 222), but linking the feminized male so obviously to the dictator is extraordinary.

Salazar, of course, is the surname of Franco's contemporary right-wing dictator in neighbouring Portugal, António de Oliveira Salazar, for whom the Spanish dictator had great admiration (Preston 1993, 454), and Orduña's portrayal of the character as a sober financier reinforces the overlap with a dictator who was a professor of economics. When we meet the character in his office in the film's opening post-credit sequence, his financial expertise is stressed. This post-credit sequence bears closer scrutiny owing to its similarities with the opening sequence of the NO-DO (Noticiarios y documentales),repeated ad nauseam to audiences and thus easily recognizable by 1944. In the first NO-DO of 1 April 1943, after an image of the Spanish flag and a montage of establishing shots of El Pardo palace (Franco's seat of government), a medium shot reveals a supposedly industrious Franco, hard at work in his office attending to peacetime matters – despite his military uniform. His desk is piled with state papers, and behind him we see a framed portrait of Salazar.[20] Orduña in 1944 similarly offers an establishing shot (of Madrid), a long shot of the character Salazar arriving at work by car, then two medium shots that portray his entry in the office and application to the business of the day. Between the name Salazar, and the overlap between this presentation and the NO-DO portrayal of Franco, the invitation to read this character as a stand-in for the dictator is hard to ignore, though it was not noted by the censors.

As with his role as a judge in *The Nail* (released the month before *Millions* in Madrid), Durán's character is feminized over the course of the film. Whereas in Gil's film this feminization took the form of suffering – not a physical wound inflicted by the 'nail' of the film's title, but an emotional wound that the judge inflicts upon himself through excessive professional zeal – in Orduña's it takes the more conventional route of romantic love. Over the course of the honeymoon Salazar is to succumb to his new wife's charms (after much screwball mischief with friend Joaquín who accompanies the couple to generate a phony love triangle), the heroic façade of industry and application slips and Salazar is to reveal a human side, susceptible like any mortal to the temptations of romance. It may be noted, however, that he is never shown to neglect his business responsibilities as a consequence.

If the feminization through suffering of Durán's judge in *The Nail* potentially condemned the cold machinery of Francoist justice, the feminization through romance of Durán's industrialist is much less pointed in its critique. In fact, the character arc of Orduña's Durán character matches the goal of the dictatorship to justify its existence in peace, despite its snatching of power through a military rebellion. The first NO-DO exemplifies this propagandist objective: military general Franco dressed in uniform is filmed attending to peace-time governance, exchanging weaponry and the battlefield for a desk, pen and papers. Thus just as the military dictator is softened and domesticated by such a portrayal, so the industrialist Salazar character is softened and domesticated, while simultaneously never neglecting business matters.

Far more pointed is the role of *Millions*'s second patriarch, the Duke of Hinojares, played by José Isbert. While Durán's character changes over the course of the film, Isbert's embodiment of the bankrupt, infantile aristocrat remains static. Director and co-scriptwriter Orduña may thus be credited with assigning symbolic importance to Salazar; in the case of the Duke, however, the actor Isbert is the creative source of the character's significance. Having settled into the fast dialogue, quick pace, sumptuous settings and stereotypical characterization of the comedy, the viewer meets the duke at 12 minutes into the film. Dressed in sombre black suit and sporting a moustache, he is engaged in the apparently sober business of dictating a speech about Favila and the Bear (which relate to the founding myth of Christian Spain [Llinás 1998, 107]) to a secretary (played by the actor's daughter María). Orduña need only set the camera recording, frame the character in medium shot and opt for unobtrusive long takes as Isbert practises the speech, which is rendered hilariously meaningless by the irrelevant subject matter, constant interruptions, comic misunderstandings by the secretary and even a golf ball smashing the window and striking the Duke on the head (a slapstick detail found in such fare as *Bringing Up Baby*). Isbert's performance is paramount, for he undoes the discourse of academic rhetoric through the non-discursive means of excessive gesture and exaggerated delivery. The performance brings to mind Steven Marsh's summary of the deployment of popular culture in Berlanga's work, a director with whom Isbert would work in mischievous tandem in the 1950s and 1960s (in *Welcome Mr Marshall* [*Bienvenido míster Marshall*] and *The Executioner** [*El verdugo*]): 'subversive precisely because of its ability to weave its operations within existing power structures' (2006, 101). Contemporary audiences, whose access to current affairs in 1944 was limited to the censored press, radio and the NO-DOs (established the year before in 1943), would have been wearily familiar with the empty rhetoric of politician's empty speeches, and would surely have enjoyed the potential to read Isbert's performance as condemnation. Isbert's physique is also a source of mischief – he is significantly shorter than his wife (who refers to him with the diminutive 'Ramoncito') and all his children and children-in-law. Rotund and diminutive, it is not too much of a stretch to see Isbert's pontificating Duke, presiding over the bankruptcy of his family that his children will resolve, as a proxy for the dictator, delivering moralizing speeches as the country suffered under a system of autarky that the next generation of technocrat politicians would resolve.

Just as comic repetition is one of the strategies that undo the speech-making, so the repetition of the phrase 'you're a great father' to the Duke by two of his children contributes to this suggestive undoing of his role as a patriarch. In a further speech, the duke gathers his family to reveal the bankruptcy of the estate. The scene begins with a sombre Isbert standing before his seated relatives, the gravity of his news complemented by the way Juan Quintero's soundtrack drops the jaunty motif for serious strings. No sooner has he begun, however, than he is gloriously usurped by his off-spring, in particular his daughters, who spring to their feet, seat their

FIGURE 2.2 *Hinojares's Pompous Speech.* She, He and His Millions *(Ella, él y sus millones Orduña 1944)*

father and propose solutions to the family's finances – this being screwball comedy based on a play entitled 'Fairy tale', these include searching for a prince charming (who arrives in the form of Salazar) or a North-American fairy godmother (who does not). At this point the film takes off in pursuit of that fairy tale, and Isbert is seen little more, though he does engage in activities that further confirm his infantilization: crawling on all fours while playing with a train set and falling off a ladder to bump his head (again) at the Salazars' ball.

Isbert's performance in this CIFESA comedy condemns, through the primarily non-discursive comic means of gesture and exaggeration, at least two key aspects of 1940s Francoism: its pompous political speeches and its enshrining of patriarchy. Isbert's performance in this long-forgotten comedy is so successful that it offers a model for the much-celebrated *Welcome Mr Marshall* (1952), in which Isbert embodies another useless patriarch, the village mayor, in Berlanga's searing comic satire of the Franco regime's opportunistic and unsuccessful efforts to win American economic aid. Isbert's mayor in Berlanga's film reprises Isbert's duke in Orduña's. Both patriarchs invite mischievous comparison with the ultimate patriarch of the dictatorship, Franco, as both characters engage in hilariously hopeless speech-making – the multiply-interrupted Academy speech and the truncated family speech of *Millions* are a blueprint for the much-admired, interrupted and truncated balcony speech of *Welcome Mr Marshall*. The childish behaviour of duke and mayor point to another parallel, with the train set of the 1944 film becoming the cowboy outfit in 1952, in the first case the duke plays on all four like a child, in the second, which forms part of the mayor's dream, Isbert is dressed as a cowboy starring in a Western, with oversized hat, boots and sheriff badge to match.

Offering audiences significant pleasures through its prestige aesthetics, *Millions* is also a good example of what Steven Marsh has termed 'Comedy and the weakening of the state' (2006) in connection with other directors like Edgar Neville, Miguel Mihura, Fernando Fernán Gómez and Berlanga. José Luis Castro de Paz similarly values the connection of Orduña's film – via Isbert – to Spain's high-cultural theatre of the grotesque, the esperpento (2002, 89). Marsh has questioned, however, such a repeated appeal in Spanish film historiography to the specifically Spanish, high-cultural tradition of the esperpento, arguing instead for an approach that attends to plurality, in the sense of both national and international influences, and both popular and dominant cultural influences (2006, 72, 100–1). Along these lines I summarize Isbert's extraordinary performance as the patriarch in *Millions* as an amalgam of the esperpento of high theatre with the clowns of vaudeville, the 'gracioso' (funny man) of seventeenth-century Spanish theatre (Bentley 2008, 94n. 25) and the goof of American screwball comedy, as a multi-pronged critique of masculinity, the family, and middle age in general, and a risky spoof of the dictator himself in particular, which thereby punctures at least two principles of the regime's cherished 'Faith, Family, Fatherland'.

From Woman to Woman (De mujer a mujer Lucia 1950)

If, as recent scholarship has argued (Labanyi 2000), Spanish cinema from 1944–51 increasingly valorized the feminine, the extraordinary portrayal of the suffering – and thus feminized – male judge of Rafael Gil's 1944 *The Nail* might be regarded as an early manifestation of the process, and Luis Lucia's evocatively titled *From Woman to Woman* of 1950 its culmination. Like *The Nail*, *From Woman to Woman* deploys prestige aesthetics to consoling effect. Like *The Nail*, melodrama also proves to be a crucible for potential contestation in *From Woman to Woman*. At the height of the vindictive repression enacted by the law courts Gil offers us a male judge who breaks his own heart as a consequence of his professional zeal. Lucia explores the female experience more typically explored in the Hollywood genre (dubbed into Spanish and immensely popular in this period). Thematically, *From Woman to Woman* apparently offers a consoling account of a married upper-bourgeois woman, Isabel (played by Amparito Rivelles), who loses her child and her sanity, but regains both by the end of the film. An alternative, contestatory reading emerges on considering the role of Emilia (Ana Mariscal, who won a CEC [Círculo de Escritores Cinematográficos] award for the performance), the woman who nurses her to health, acts as her marital proxy during her illness, and commits suicide at the end of the film to offer Isabel her child, 'from woman to woman'.[21]

From Woman to Woman displays all of Chris Cagle's prestige hallmarks (2007, 292). It is an adaptation of a 'literary source', the play *Alma triunfante* (Triumphant Soul) of 1902, when the film is also set, by Jacinto Benavente, a playwright who was newly popular in the 1940s after recanting his Republican sympathies (Perriam et al. 2000, 79). Its 'serious' themes include mourning and recovery, as well solidarity and betrayal, though such seriousness might be diluted for those suspicious of an exaggerated melodramatic treatment. The film's 'lavish production values' correspond to a 1950 CIFESA at the height of its success (the *Dawn of America* flop of 1951, and decline thereafter, still lay ahead): A-list actors Eduardo Fajardo (who plays ineffectual husband Luis), Mariscal and Rivelles have their performances enhanced by the work of some of the company's technical stars, including Alfredo Fraile, the cinematographer whose 'detailed and contrasted photography' dominated 1940s and 1950s black-and-white film (Mira 2010, 136), composer Juan Quintero and editor Juan Serra (these three also worked on *The Nail*; Quintero and Serra on *Millions*), plus Russian refugee set decorator Pierre Shild. Through mise en scène this team creates an opulent turn-of-century bourgeois home for Isabel and Luis, with Baroque interiors that are brightly lit. Such aesthetics might suggest escapism, but a similar look is given to Luis and Emilia's apartment, which suggests an unexpected equivalence between the homes of respectable wife Isabel and adulterous lover Emilia. While wardrobe also initially suggests the consolations of escapism, with Rivelles's Hollywoodesque gowns and frills a major source of visual pleasure (Labanyi 2007b, 40), the deployment of dress deserves further attention. Labanyi identifies a surprising refusal to dress Isabel as the modest angel of the hearth prized by early Francoism. Nowhere might such modesty be more appropriate than in the scene where she mourns the death of her daughter, but here Rivelles wears a disruptively sexy low-cut gown (2007b, 40). Meanwhile in the scene of her confrontation with rival Emilia her showy outfit makes Rivelles appear the lover, and the soberly dressed Mariscal the wife (2007b, 40–1). Thus the dressing of both the interiors and of the two female stars implies an interesting overlap between legitimate marriage and illegitimate adultery, which may have offered audiences a consoling alternative to – if not a condemnatory rejection of – the prescriptive gender roles advocated by Manichean 1940s ideology.

If set decoration and wardrobe apparently work in tandem, so editing and music are deployed together too in order to suggest a sympathetic response to Isabel's madness. Important here is the parallel portrayal of the child Maribel's accident and the scene of disturbance in the ward on Isabel's first night in the asylum. In the first scene, the number of cuts increases and the angle of shot varies as Luis pushes Maribel higher and higher on the swing till she falls off. In tandem, the music score reaches a crescendo – with increased volume of music strangely replacing any scream from the child when she falls. Likewise, during the disturbance unleashed on the asylum ward by Isabel's discovery that her stand-in daughter-doll is missing, editor Serra increases the number of cuts in response to the varied camera angles, while composer Quintero intensifies the volume and pace of the score. The matching formal treatment of the loss of the daughter and madness on the wards sympathetically shows that the first event is a straightforward cause of the second.

Turning to plot, if we consider this sympathetic treatment of Isabel in isolation, a reading of the film according to the thesis of consolation is possible. *From Woman to Woman* opens with a scene of apparent domestic bliss, in which a montage of various shots of clocks approaching 8 o'clock in the morning ends with Isabel and Luis waking up in bed, preparing together for the day, waking up their daughter Maribel, then Luis's abandonment of the day's work to buy a swing and a bunch of flowers to celebrate his wife and daughter's saint day, followed by celebrations with parents, child, grandparents and priest: a blissful upper-bourgeois world that falls apart when Maribel falls to her death. In fact melodramatic techniques are used by Lucia and his team mawkishly to undermine this vision of domestic heaven with premonitions of the future hell. The clocks are all framed from canted, low-angle positions that evoke the perspective of the child – whose life time is nearly over when the film opens. In the first shot in the child's bedroom the camera focuses on a lifeless doll, before panning to the right to frame the living child asleep in bed, thus offering a cinematic premonition of her death. Again, the doll that Isabel buys for her daughter, which looks uncannily like the child, is used to give forewarning of her death: at the present-giving party Luis will hold the mannequin in his arms while the girl is outside, which both looks forward to Maribel's death and foretells Isabel's belief that the doll is her daughter during her period of madness. The opening clocks are not incidental to the full development of the narrative too, for Labanyi has shown that Isabel's madness and sanity turn around her interpretation of time. In her deluded belief that her

FIGURE 2.3 *Isabel, Luis and the Daughter-replacement Doll.* From Woman to Woman *(De mujer a mujer Lucia 1950)*

daughter still lives she clings to the past; her recovery entails her acceptance that the past has passed. According to the thesis of consolation, this film might be said to offer suffering audiences (female ones in particular) a means to work through loss (especially that of sons, husbands, fathers and brothers in both the war and the post-war vengeance) and look to the future.

This consoling interpretation entirely overlooks, however, the fascinating role of Mariscal's Emilia. Labanyi notes that while *From Woman to Woman* dramatizes Isabel's loss of the past in which her daughter died, which might be positively interpreted as 'bringing closure to her process of mourning', it also dramatizes the loss of her past friendship with Emilia, and thus the film alternatively stages 'a melancholic identification with a past which women resisted letting go of' (2007b, 42). Through the characterization of Emilia, Lucia offers the possibility of reading the film as an act of condemnation, rather than consolation. This extraordinary character is shot through with contradiction. For a start, she is played by Mariscal, who simultaneously embodies the utmost ideal of Francoist femininity – the dictator himself chose the actress to play the idealized female role Marisol in *Race* – and multiple and richly deviant versions of femininity in her theatrical and film roles up to 1950, which include rehearsing for a role with Federico García Lorca in his *Así que pasen cinco años* (Five Years from Now) before the war, and even playing the male role of the seducer in José Zorrilla's *Don Juan Tenorio* in 1945 (Triana-Toribio 2000b, 186). The contradictions of Mariscal's star persona are replicated in Lucia's character of Emilia. She simultaneously embodies virtue and vice, the first through the conservative feminine roles of angelic nurse (we first see her wearing a white nurse's uniform with a halo-like coif [Triana-Toribio 2000b, 193]) and angelic wife to Luis in Isabel's absence (that same coif has also been interpreted as recalling a bridal veil [Labanyi 2007b, 40]) and the second through the disruptive feminine roles of adulteress, as Luis's lover during Isabel's illness, and betrayer, as she takes her patient and friend's husband. Her fate in the film is fittingly contradictory too. She makes the ultimate sacrifice of her own life by committing suicide in order to give Isabel, the legitimate wife, her illegitimate daughter: the self-sacrificing mother is the ultimate National-Catholic female role; but her suicide is simultaneously the ultimate anti-National-Catholic act (Labanyi 2007b, 41).

The characterization of Emilia in *From Woman to Woman* offers a portrait of femininity that audiences might have found satisfyingly disruptive in the socio-political context of Francoism in 1950. The film ends by coming full circle, with a similar picture of clichéd domestic bliss with husband, wife and daughter in their brightly-lit, richly-decorated home. But while the 'happy family' at the start of the film was undercut by premonition through cinematography and mise en scène of the future catastrophe of the daughter's death, the 'happy family' at the end is undercut by the ghostly presence of Emilia's sacrifice in the past evoked by Mariscal's voice in voiceover. Núria Triana-Toribio has written persuasively of the strength and tone of Mariscal's non-accented Spanish, which, she argues, is the star's defining feature, making her stand out from a cinematic context of 'silent beauties' (2000b, 191). Mariscal has been 'disavowed' by a democratic nation keen to renounce Francoism and its culture, both of which, as we have seen, are ultimately represented by the film *Raza* in which Mariscal starred (Triana-Toribio 2000b). Just as the character Emilia returns to haunt the bourgeois happy family of the end of the film *From Woman to Woman*, so the actor returns to haunt Spanish cinema historiography. That deep, authoritative female voice means that, unusually, soundtrack dominates the clichéd imagetrack here: it speaks of a conflicting, contradictory femininity which may be erased by the conventional plot but will not go away completely. Dissident forms of femininity may have been officially erased in Franco's Spain too, but a contestatory reading of *From Woman to Woman* suggests their continued, disruptive presence, if only through ghostly returns on screen and in audiences' imaginations off screen.

Furrows (*Surcos* Nieves Conde 1951)

It has become a commonplace to describe 1951 as a hinge year in Spanish cinema. The sacking of a government minister always attracts interest, especially if that minister is a servant of the dictatorship. In 1952 that was the fate of Director-General of Cinema José María García Escudero, after awarding in 1951 the 'National Interest' prize to José Antonio Nieves Conde's *Furrows* (1951) over Juan de Orduña's ponderous Columbus biopic, *Dawn of America*, which was CIFESA's patriotic response to the unsympathetic Gainsborough treatment of Francoism's national treasure in *Christopher Columbus* (MacDonald 1949). This often-mentioned opposition of a CIFESA historical film to the first Spanish Neorealist film[22] has been unhelpful, for it has tended to distort our appreciation of both CIFESA in the 1940s (of which *Dawn of America* is taken to be a culmination) and the new political currents in the 1950s. The first three sections of this chapter have challenged the notion of CIFESA as mouthpiece of the regime by stressing the consoling uses audiences may have made of the prestige picture, and uncovering possibly contestatory readings. If *Dawn of America* corresponds to the propagandist CIFESA caricature, this film is preceded by a hinterland of CIFESA's often richly suggestive cinematic creativity.

While *Furrows* offers an extreme alternative to 1940s cinema, in the two following case studies on *That Happy Couple* (1951) and *Main Street* (1956), I will stress greater overlap between 1940s and 1950s Spanish cinema in the treatment of consolation and condemnation. *Furrows* relentlessly condemns economic deprivation and the modern city – though as Katy Vernon points out, it is 'a crisis in paternal authority' that ultimately brings ruin (1999, 257). Director and scriptwriters Eugenio Montes, Natividad Zaro and González Torrente Ballester (also a novelist) were all Falangists, one of the groups that originally constituted Francoism in 1939, but one that was wounded by the regime's demotion of Falangism over the course of the 1940s. Imanol Zumalde Arregi notes further that director and scriptwriters were drawn from a sector of Falangism that was particularly critical of the regime's social policies (1997b, 296). Francoism, in *Furrows*, is thus criticized from within. First, by exposing dire economic deprivation (with its corollaries of the black market, overcrowded housing, crime and prostitution) the film condemns the failure of Francoist autarky.[23] Second, by portraying a vice-ridden city, *Furrows* critiques Francoism's more recent shift away from eulogizing the noble peasant to accepting urban life as necessary to economic reform. At the same time, *Furrows* misogynistically condemns female audiences seeking consolation in popular culture – including Hollywood cinema and Spanish cabaret – as, at best, escapist distraction, and, at worst, moral corruption.

FIGURE 2.4 *On their Arrival in Madrid, the Pérez Family is Overwhelmed.* Furrows *(Surcos* Nieves Conde 1951)

Thus the impoverished peasant family Pérez, consisting of father, mother, daughter and two sons, move to Madrid in the hope of prosperity. The fate of the three children is exemplary. Elder son Pepe falls in with gangster Chamberlain. His horrific death, injured on an illegal job then thrown, still alive, onto a railway line by his boss, exemplifies urban vice: his burial precipitates the family's return home. Second son Manolo looks set for a similar fate until he is redeemed by the virginal, blonde Rosario (whose characterization betrays the racial fascist sympathies of the Falangist director and creative team). Anxieties about women and corruption are clearer still in the treatment of daughter Tonia. If the male characters' desire for prosperity is represented in economic terms through the struggle of father and sons to find work, this female character's desire for prosperity may only be represented in moral terms. Echoing the misogyny of Florián Rey's treatment of Acacia in *The Cursed Village* (1930, discussed in Chapter 1), Nieves Conde presents Tonia's attempt to climb socially by becoming a cabaret singer as the equivalent of prostitution in her father's eyes; next she succeeds in climbing socially by actually prostituting herself with Chamberlain. Just as the popular spectacle of the dancehall is condemned in the first attempt, the popular spectacle of cinema is implicated in the second, for when father finds daughter installed in lodgings as Chamberlain's mistress, she is juxtaposed in the frame with a glamour photograph of Hollywood's Rita Hayworth (Kinder 1993, 51). Chamberlain's previous moll confirms this link between female moral decline and 'unsuitable' films through a conversation about cinema-going: when the gangster proposes taking her to see a Neorealist film about 'social problems', she wonders why anyone 'would want to see so much misery, when millionaires' lives are so beautiful!' (translated in Vernon 1999, 257).

Much critical work has examined the affiliation of *Furrows* to Neorealist 'social problems' cinema. It is perhaps too tidy to note the increasing availability of Neorealist films through cinema clubs and film weeks in Spain (these took place in Madrid in 1951 and 1953), then link it to the birth of a Neorealist Spanish cinema. Nieves Conde denies having seen any of the films (Vernon 1999, 256), though critics have noted the extensive influence of documentary techniques in general, and the inspiration of key scenes of Roberto Rossellini's *Paisá* (1946) and *Europa 51* (1951) in particular (Zumalde Arregui 1997b, 296). More nuanced is Marsha Kinder's analysis (following Hopewell 1986, 56) of *Furrows* as a 'Falangist Neorealist' hybrid of Hollywood melodrama and Neorealism (1993, 40–53), in which the leftist politics of the Italian movement are paradoxically redeployed, in the Spanish context, for the Falangist end of criticizing urban life.

In the following readings of *That Happy Couple* and *Main Street*, I focus on the second part of the moll's comment, in which Nieves Condes self-reflexively condemns the power of cinema to distract and corrupt by showing that fallen women like the moll and Tonia enjoy escapist films about millionaires (like Hollywood and the CIFESA prestige pictures examined in this chapter). While similarly self-reflexive, Juan Antonio Bardem and Luis García Berlanga, in *That Happy Couple* (co-directed), and *Main Street* (Bardem), combine their condemnation of political and economic stasis with a far more sympathetic analysis of audiences' use of cinema as consolation.

That Happy Couple (Esa pareja feliz* Bardem and Berlanga 1951)

Separated by release dates of just one year, a comparison of *From Woman to Woman* (1950) and *Furrows* (1951) in isolation illustrates the schism in Spanish cinema described by Jo Labanyi thus: 'The year 1951 marked the end of [the] focus on the family and the feminine, as the development of an oppositional cinema led to a new stress on the political, with plot lines consequently focused on the male' (2000, 164–5). First, we move from 'massively-popular [1940s] woman-centred cinema' to 'male-dominated 1950s oppositional cinema [that] never reached beyond an intellectual elite' (2000, 165). However unreliable audience figures might be for early periods of Spanish film (accounting for box office receipts only began in 1965 [Castro de Paz and Cerdán 2011, 206]), current estimates show that the audience for *From Woman to Woman* was indeed at least five times that of *Furrows*. Second, the use of diverse creative teams in the CIFESA studio system meant that some contributions could be richly discordant, like that of Mariscal in *From Woman to Woman*. With *Furrows*, on the other hand, we shift to an auteurist model of production, with production company Atenea Films created expressly for the film, and Nieves Conde able to surround himself by a like-minded team – hence the shared, sectarian Falangist vision of director and scriptwriters. Third, while a stress 'on the family and on the feminine' remains from *From Woman to Woman* to *Furrows*, we swing from a sympathetic treatment of female suffering and illness, in which the patriarch is a background figure whose ability to father daughters can be passed 'from woman to woman' (*From Woman to Woman*), to a misogynist vision where the patriarch is pivotal (*Furrows*). It is through the father's body that Nieves Conde explores hard physical labour, as in the much-celebrated, Neorealist-inspired factory scene where Manolo faints, and it is through the father's morals that the wayward behaviour of his wife and daughter is condemned.

A reading of Spanish film history that foregrounds Italian Neorealism stresses continuity between the new directors like Luis García Berlanga and Juan Antonio Bardem trained at the state film school from 1947 onwards, and films like *Furrows*, for the students were the principal attendees of the Film Weeks and the School even owned copies of some films (like *Bicycle Thieves* [Sánchez Noriega 1998, 2]). Post-2000 Spanish film historiography has increasingly questioned the role of Neorealism, however. Steven Marsh, for example, challenges its association with Berlanga to argue instead for the director's subversive fusion of multiple, mainly comedic, sources (2006, 98). More recently, José Luis Castro de Paz and Josetxo Cerdán question Neorealism's role in Spanish oppositional cinema of the 1950s altogether (2011, 43–81), even downplaying its relevance to the work of illegal communist party member and Cesare Zavattini-enthusiast Bardem (2011, 63–80).[24] In this and the final section of this chapter I similarly demote the role of Neorealism to reconsider condemnation and consolation in *That Happy Couple* and *Main Street*. Like *Furrows*, both films self-reflexively consider the consoling potential of popular culture and cinema, but unlike *Furrows*'s misogynistic dismissal of its corrupting influence, Berlanga and Bardem offer a sympathetic treatment.

Influential readings of the film published in the late 1990s suggest two very different interpretations, one focussed on condemnation, the other on consolation. Production contexts may be called on to support the first, auteurist, interpretation. The directors set up their own production company Altamira in order to centralize creative control (as opposed to the studio system), and the industry was so affronted by the film that it received a low Second Class rating and no company dared to distribute it until Berlanga's 1952 *Welcome Mr Marshall* (co-scripted this time with Bardem) proved a commercial success. Marvin D'Lugo, first, stresses this auteurist and political *That Happy Couple*, which condemns both the dictatorship itself (one skit of a maritime opera actually includes a rotund and ridiculous Franco/Carrero Blanco figure) and, more pointedly, condemns Spaniards' distraction from the reality of dictatorship by incipient consumerism and hollow popular culture: 'clearly the critique of the sad illusions of struggling Spaniards in the face of a world that only provides the surface appearance of well-being' (1997, 53). In the same year, Román Gubern similarly stressed the film's political condemnation of mid-century Spain, especially precarious labour conditions, overcrowded living conditions, and the false illusions offered by popular culture to call for a Regenerationist call to action (1997, 304).[25] Gubern also brilliantly analyses the coming together of the very different visions of directors Bardem and Berlanga in the film, noting, for instance, that Berlanga admired Frank Capra while Bardem wrote against his cinema, and that the film 'hybridizes' Spanish sainete and Italian Neorealism (1997, 304–5). This inadvertently reveals that the co-directorship of this prized example of auteurist cinema in fact recalls some of the fruitful creative conflicts that characterized collective studio-system filmmaking, and this despite the fact that the foremost example of this system in Spain, CIFESA, is the first object of satire in the film.

In 1999 Katy Vernon offered an alternative interpretation of *That Happy Couple* that unpicks the assumption that it condemns audiences who take consolation in popular culture:

> [It] would seem to offer protagonists and audience a clear lesson on the need for resignation to reality and the fruitlessness of taking refuge in temporary illusion. Yet the film as a whole works to undercut that message [and] endorses no easy opposition between cinema and real life. (1999, 258)

That *That Happy Couple* satirically condemns the blocked attempts at social mobility of Madrid's working classes is beyond doubt, and this aspect of the film has been multiply explored (e.g. Stone 2002, 42–4]). More could be said on the surprising comic continuum between CIFESA in the 1940s and dissident cinema in the 1950s, such as the similarities between the deflation of pompous authority through the treatment of the Duke in *Millions* and the admiral in the spoof nautical opera in *That Happy Couple*. However, following Vernon, I focus here on the less-studied question of consolation.

The much-enjoyed and much-analysed opening spoof of CIFESA's historical epic *The Mad Queen* in *That Happy Couple* is a giant red herring. In it Lola Gaos takes on what is surely one of the best bit parts in Spanish film history to parody the histrionic performance style of Aurora Bautista as Joan the Mad. After much exaggerated gesture and repetition to the point of absurdity – not to mention phony set decorations, over-the-top costumes and hair-dos – Gaos hysterically flings herself from the parapets. But the runners (including co-protagonist Juan, played by Fernando Fernán Gómez) fail to catch her and she breaks a spot light, and thus brings the whole shoot crashing down, not only herself. For most critics (Hopewell 1986, 43; D'Lugo 1997, 53; Gubern 1997, 305; Stone 2002, 42), Bardem and Berlanga thus send CIFESA cinema crashing down too, in this, the precise year of the company's *Dawn of America** debacle (this film would itself be an object of satire in *Welcome Mr Marshall*). Vernon, conversely, shows that 'Despite this debunking, demystifying opening' the films as a whole shows that 'no one is immune to the lures of cinematic illusion' (1999, 257). *That Happy Couple* does not simply reject audience's use of cinema as consolation, as the opening *The Mad Queen* send-up suggests. Indeed, in later years when Berlanga himself taught at the film school, his students would recall that he returned time and again to

Orduña's epic in class, commenting 'Orduña's incredible, he believes it all so much that his emotion infects you' (Alberich 2002, 26).

Thus in the very next sequence of *That Happy Couple* we find Juan's wife Carmen (Elvira Quintillá) who is emotionally affected by watching a similar prestige picture, here a Hollywood romance at the appropriately named 'Atlantic' cinema. During the viewing Carmen ignores her husband's geekish insistence on explaining the mechanisms of a travelling shot or rear projection and stresses that the film allows her to dream. Actor-direction was the responsibility of Bardem in this team-shoot, and his sympathetic characterization of Carmen anticipates the similar treatment of Betsy Blair's Isabel in *Main Street*, two characters that embody the use of cinema as consolation.

Consolation in *That Happy Couple* is not just a question of sympathetically, and self-reflexively, evoking audience's uses of cinema within the film. As Vernon points out, *That Happy Couple* also adopts many characteristics of popular cinema within the film itself. These are not the prestige aesthetics of the CIFESA epic – however affected by these Berlanga would be later – but the tropes of romantic comedy. Gubern suggests that the scenes where Juan and Carmen reflect on their past as a couple through flashbacks and

FIGURE 2.5 *Carmen (left) Ignores Juan (centre) in the Cinema.* That Happy Couple *(Esa pareja feliz* Bardem and Berlanga 1951)

voiceover gives away the origins of the script in drama (1997, 304). For José Luis Castro de Paz and Josetxo Cerdán, meanwhile, the film's flashbacks – the only ones that Berlanga used throughout his career (2011, 61) – indicate the influence of the esperpento, for the couple's panopticon perspective on Madrid when they are stranded at the top of a fairground big wheel and when they reminisce from the rooftop of their apartment block, is a distorting perspective. While Castro de Paz and Cerdán's work importantly uncovers the links between *That Happy Couple* and the often-overlooked 1940s Spanish cinema via the esperpento (2011, 6–63), Vernon's interpretation of the flash-backs more convincingly attends to their deployment of film genre and technique. The film's two flashbacks accompanied by voiceover refer to Juan and Carmen's meeting, then wedding, which are the traditional ingredients of Hollywood romance, with the second flashback even finishing with a 'movie-kiss, the self-referential nature of which is emphasized by the camera receding through the window frame' (1999, 258). They are therefore similar to the much-admired and much-studied dream sequences of Berlanga's *Welcome Mr Marshall* of the following year (e.g. Vernon 1997, 38–42). Both films portray the importance of cinema in the characters' lives as a source of entertainment, but the flashbacks and dreams show that cinema is not just a point of reference but actually structures characters' articulation of identity – the romantic comedy provides the generic devices deployed in *That Happy Couple*, the Hollywood Western and thriller, the Spanish historical epic, German expressionism and Soviet social realism are all deployed in *Welcome Mr Marshall*. The consoling role played by cinema in both films is not limited to passive escapism: audiences actively use film to articulate their own, economically and politically disadvantaged, desires and identities.[26]

In *That Happy Couple* it is crucial that Bardem and Berlanga stress the cinematic nature of the flashbacks that console the couple in their current difficulties, for this differentiates cinema from the other areas of popular culture explored. The film's broadsides against Spain's incipient consumer culture, for instance, are barbed, like its criticism of the adverts and slogans for 'Florit' soap. The soap company runs the competition for a pair of its customers to become the titular 'Happy Couple', but in delightful light comic mode, Juan and Carmen will of course only win when in the midst of an unhappy marital row. Further slogans receive more ribbing, with the Florit representative's speech on 'clean body, clean mind' totally ignored by Juan, who is at the time engaged in an argument over his murky dealings with his dodgy business partner.[27] In contrast, and despite the influential opening spoof of *The Mad Queen*, elsewhere in *That Happy Couple*, the treatment of popular cinema is sympathetic. Tonia and the moll in *Furrows* both enjoy Hollywood cinema and both are morally condemned for it. Both intertextually and textually *That Happy Couple* acknowledges cinema's role of consolation. Likeable character Carmen represents the use of cinema to dream. The relationship between sympathetic couple Juan and Carmen is also portrayed through Hollywoodesque flashbacks that acknowledge the importance of cinema in structuring the couple's life narrative. Scholars have long argued over how to divide up the creative contributions of Bardem and Berlanga to their co-directed first feature (Castro de Paz and Cerdán 2011, 60). The next section's discussion of the ways another sympathetically-characterized female character uses cinema as a source of consolation suggests that Bardem's guidance lies behind both *That Happy Couple*'s Carmen and *Main Street*'s Isabel.

Main Street (*Calle Mayor* Bardem 1956)

It is fascinating to note that Bardem's original conception of *That Happy Couple*'s Carmen would have had her recovering from the death of a child; in the event, Berlanga overruled him on the grounds of the film's comic spirit (Stone 2002, 43). Five years on, directing alone, and working in the very different genre of melodrama, Bardem was freer to pursue his interest in female suffering. In *Main Street* we find a fascinating reprisal of the grieving young working-class mother he had planned for the Madrid-based *That Happy Couple* of 1951. On first glance, Isabel seems very different. Played by American actress Betsy Blair (whom Bardem had met and impressed at Cannes in 1955), rather than the home-grown and homely Elvira Quintillá, she is provincial (the film was shot in Cuenca, Palencia and Logroño [Roberts 1999, 20]), upper-middle class (the film details unearned income from renting land), middle-aged at 35 (by the standards of the day) and unmarried. But both Carmen and Isabel long for a better life, both long for a child, and, crucially for my argument, both make consoling use of popular cinema as a conduit for these longings.

Today considered to be Bardem's best work, critical reception of *Main Street* varies according to the intertextual reference stressed. Thus scholars keen to show the kinship between Bardem's work in Spain and left-wing auteurist cinema outside Spain – which meant Italian Neorealism in this period – have noted the similarities (acknowledged by the director) between *Main Street* and *The Young Calves* (*I vitelloni* Fellini 1948) (for a summary of this approach, an extreme version of which led to the unwarranted accusation of plagiarism, see José Luis Castro de Paz and Josetxo Cerdán [2011, 63–4]). Stephen Roberts acknowledges the film's neorealist use of real locations (alongside studio interiors), problems and characters, but emphasizes that

Main Street is plot-driven, tightly-narrated and narrowly focuses on just two characters: rather than correspond to André Bazin's definition of the Neorealism as a 'direct experience of reality itself', it suggests, rather, 'the nineteenth-century novel or Hollywood melodrama' (1999, 21–2).[28] For Roberts, the film condemns Hollywood as, in Bardem's words, 'false cinema' (31), and instead harnesses multiple Spanish literary sources to present an indictment of Franco's Spain through a 'New Spanish Realism'. These inter-texts include Leopoldo Alas's 1884–5 condemnation of provincial repression of women in the novel *La Regenta* (1999, 28–9) and the 1916 sainete play by Arniches on which the film is based (previously adapted by Neville in 1936) (1999, 25–8). To these further Spanish literary sources have been added, including 1898 Regenerationism through the character of the intellectual Don Tomás (who was originally to be called Don Miguel in homage to Unamuno, though the censors insisted on the change) (Amann 2010, 20), and José Zorrilla's 1844 *Don Juan Tenorio*, through the tale of seduction and prosopopeia of the character Juan (Amann 2010). Mark Allinson, meanwhile has stressed the film's transnational debt to Hollywood melodrama (2005, 84–6). My approach aims to synthesize these by introducing a new one: Miguel Mur Oti's 1951 *Black Sky* (*Cielo negro*). Preceding *Main Street* by five years, this film also adapts Hollywood melodrama to a Spanish context and in the process condemns Francoism. Sympathetically portraying an illusionistic and downtrodden unmarried female protagonist, *Black Sky* also invites us to reconsider popular culture as consolation.

Today scarcely-known, *Black Sky* provides much inspiration at the levels of both narrative and technique for the internationally-famous *Main Street* (Mur Oti's film was produced by Intercontinental Films, which, despite its name, was Spanish, Bardem's a co-production between Spain (Guión/Suevia) and France (Plau Arte/Iberia) with Manuel Goyanes at the helm, who would later market Marisol [see Chapter 3]). In Bardem's film a group of bored, dim, provincial and middle-class men (their professional jobs differentiate them from the youthful outsiders of *The Young Calves*, and thus make the satire of increasingly middle-class Spain all the sharper [Roberts 1999, 23]) play a cruel trick on the sensitive and intelligent Isabel, by forcing dull banker Juan (played by José Suárez, significantly the only Spanish actor among the leads) to propose and court her, only to reveal the truth of the cruel trick at the public 'Circle' dance: the courtship is a sham. The source for these narrative details is apparently Arniches, but *Black Sky* also turns around a cruel trick of sham courtship. In Mur Oti's film, the bored, urban, lower-middle-class and bitchy women of the clothes shop where the protagonist works pay the penniless poet Ángel (Fernando Rey) to assume the identity of Fortún (Luis Prendes), who is the love interest of the sensitive and intelligent Emilia (Susana Canales). Mercenary

Ángel writes sentimental love letters in the style of the novels we learn Emilia devours (an activity that has led to her deteriorating eyesight). In them the poet even proposes marriage, before suffering a crisis of conscience when he learns that Emilia's mother is dying. Both Bardem's provincial men and Mur Oti's urban women justify their actions because Isabel and Emilia are supposedly 'cursis'.[29] If Bardem critiques masculinity through these useless provincial men and Mur Oti critiques female solidarity through the barbed betrayal of Emilia by other women, male characters are also flawed in *Black Sky*. While in *From Woman to Woman* the husband was benignly irrelevant in comparison to the two women's extraordinary friendship, both *Black Sky* and *Main Street* register a desperate disjuncture between particularly strong female characters, whose only possibility for fulfilment is marriage, and particularly weak potential husbands: non-committal Fortún and the phony, if conscience-stricken, Ángel, in *Black Sky*, and spineless Juan and his pals in *Main Street*. Both Mur Oti and Bardem represent this desperate disjunture in the portrayal of romantic dates. At the fairground date of *Black Sky* Fortún is brooding, silent and often cast into shadows in contrast to animate, garrulous Emilia, often shot with full lighting. Similarly, Isabel is dynamic and talkative with Juan, who is silent and sulky. After one date Bardem crosscuts between Isabel in her brightly-lit bedroom

FIGURE 2.6 *Bright Emila and Broody Fortún.* Black Sky *(Cielo negro Mur Oti 1951)*

savouring her courtship, and Juan in his gloomy bedroom, fretting over his deceit. Juan also bears comparison with *Black Sky*'s poet Ángel, for both suffer a crisis of conscience, though Ángel, unlike Juan, reveals the truth to Emilia in person, while feeble Juan relies on a third party.

Just as Bardem positively characterizes Hollywood-fan Carmen of *That Happy Couple*, both Mur Oti's Emilia and Bardem's Isabel are shown to be avid consumers of popular culture, but both are given full and nuanced characterization – a process that is especially noticeable in contrast to both films' treatment of useless men. (In the case of Emilia, Mur Oti even refuses to condemn his heroine for her robbery of a dress from the shop where she works.) The unspecified romantic novels that Emilia reads in *Black Sky* do more than offer her consoling escapism. She uses them strategically to influence her own language – at one point at the fair with Fortún she refers to raindrops as 'her tears' – and employs them to give meaning to her own identity as Fortún's potential fiancée. Once the cruel trick is revealed, Emilia then has the strength of character to act out an engagement for the benefit of her dying mother: she thus fully understands the importance of consolation, even when she if fully conscious that it is deception. Bardem through Isabel offers a more self-reflexive treatment, for she is a Hollywood film fan. Like Emilia, these films influence her language, for she copies their declarations of love in conversation with Juan, then rehearses for future romantic scenarios by pronouncing his name in different ways, like the on-screen wives and fiancées she admires. Hollywood melodrama offers Isabel the same model of identity that romantic fiction does Emilia, the sadly restrictive role of wife. But crucially, like Emilia, Isabel is conscious of the deception offered by such films. Her acknowledgement that cinematic romance is a 'pretty lie' is pitifully relevant to her own sham romance with trickster Juan.

A key difference between Mur Oti and Bardem's films is, then, self-referentiality. *Black Sky* rejects the easy interpretation that Emilia has been literally and figuratively blinded by reading romantic fiction to portray sympathetically a courageous victim of economic, political and gender repression in 1951 Spain (we learn that Emilia's father died 15 years previous, a clear allusion to the death of a Republican at the end of the Civil War). This deployment of film melodrama (and more specifically film noir when a femme-fatale-like Emilia visits Ángel) is not self-reflexive. Bardem, in contrast, adopts and adapts precisely the Hollywood forms enjoyed by his protagonist in her favourite films. For a start, he casts the Hollywood actress Blair to play his heroine, from who he coaxes an award-winning performance as the female victim that is central to the genre (Special Mention at Venice, 1956). Particularly successful too is the melodramatic deployment of cinematography and sound. Elizabeth Amann (2010, 20–4) and Castro de Paz and Cerdán

(2011, 75–6) have offered perceptive close readings of cinematography in the cathedral scene which, with its interlacing of desire, the gaze and a religious setting also recalls the attraction of Fermín de Pas to the judge's wife in *La Regenta*. Juan and Isabel look at one another in the cathedral, and Bardem apparently employs subjective cinematography and shot-reverse shot as the standard visual grammar of film romance. But Bardem wonderfully wrong-foots the viewer by ending the sequence with a tracking shot apparently from Juan's perspective, only to reveal the presence of the phony lover in the depth of field, thus cinematographically conveying that the romance is a farce. Music is used with similar playful sensitivity. When fake fiancés Juan and Isabel are together Bardem uses extra-diegetic music, but when Juan is with the prostitute who loves him in the brothel (her name Tonia repeats that of the fallen daughter of Nieves Condes's *Furrows*) Bardem opts for diegetic music played on a radio. It is therefore consistent that at the climatic dance sequence, in which Isabel is told that her romance is a charade, Bardem begins the scene with the extra-diegetic music that connotes falsehood but ends it with the diegetic sound of truth. That this sound is made up of the discordant notes of the piano tuner succinctly, and musically, conveys Isabel's acquaintance with harsh reality.

FIGURE 2.7 *Hopeful Isabel and Hopeless Juan.* Main Street (Calle Mayor *Bardem 1956)*

Both *Black Sky* and *Main Street* portray courtships that are false, both of which end with their defeated tragic heroines trudging through the rain – to an unlikely religious rebirth in Mur Oti's piece and a more likely living death as a spinster in Bardem's. Both films explore the consoling role of popular culture through their female characters, and both films stress its strategic and self-conscious uses by the characters. *Main Street* adds a self-referential dimension by deploying and questioning the very melodramatic tropes that its heroine admires. Bardem may have declared that 'false' cinema 'sends the individual to sleep' (Roberts 1999, 31), but his character Isabel is especially wakeful, deducing for herself that such cinema is a lie. By questioning melodramatic techniques through his use of cinematography and music Bardem actually does this demystifying work for his own audience, revealing, unwittingly perhaps, that the 'false' cinema necessitates an equally, if not more, 'awake' viewer than that required by his own film.

Thus from *That Happy Couple* Bardem travels to the provinces to offer a female-focussed and character-led melodrama in 1956 that stresses cinema as consolation – even as *Main Street* is itself heralded as cinema as condemnation. As we will see in the following chapter, the other co-director of *That Happy Couple* likewise turns his attention to the provinces in 1961. However, in the choral comedy *Plácido*, Berlanga offers a raucous critique of the frustrated attempt at social mobility, a question which I will show is fundamental to Spanish cinema of the next decades.

Notes

1 In a provocative new interpretation, Paul Preston has stressed these 1930s connections by naming the horrific violence of Spain's war and post-war vengeance 'the Spanish holocaust' (2012, xi). While the motivation for the holocaust was racial, Francoism borrowed and adapted Nazi anti-semitism to condemn, pursue and attempt to exterminate a 'Jewish-Bolshevik-Masonic' conspiracy (2012, xi).

2 Francoism was an enforced amalgam of Falangists, Traditionalists (these two made up the FET y de las JONS), Catholics, monarchists, the military and Opus Dei (ultra-conservative Catholic) technocrats.

3 He used a pseudonym, Jaime de Andrade, and the public apparently did not know this was Franco until 1964, when he requested incorporation in the General Society for Authors and Editors (SGAE) (L. Navarrete 2009, 169–70). The film was re-edited and re-dubbed in 1950 to remove the now uncomfortable criticisms of foreigners and democracy for a country seeking aid from the Marshall Plan. It was re-named *The Spirit of a Race* (*El espíritu de una raza*) (L. Navarrete 2009, 175).

4 Recent studies have stressed that censorship was subjective and arbitrary, plagued by guess work as rules were not published till 1962. The case of *The Faith* (*La fe* Gil 1947) well illustrates the muddle: approved by the censors, it was banned by several bishops (Labanyi 1995, 20n. 2).

5 Carlos Heredero prefers the descriptor 'Confessional cinema' to 'Religious cinema' (2000, 140).

6 See Labanyi's summary of the ways the British Birmingham Centre for Contemporary Cultural Studies (Raymond Williams and Richard Hoggart) responded in the 1950s to the 'orthodox Marxist suspicion of mass culture' of the German Frankfurt School (Adorno and Horkheimer) by 'turn[ing] instead to heterodox Marxist cultural theorist Gramsci, whose view of culture as an interactive process whereby audiences can co-opt the cultural products they consume for their own purposes allowed a more complex reading of popular or mass culture' (2002b, 11).

7 Hopewell names the loss of Republican creative personnel such as José María Beltrán and Luis Alcoriza to exile; Juan Piqueras was shot (1986, 24).

8 The cultural continuity constituted by the folkloric film has long been acknowledged: Vernon 1999, 251.

9 *The Mad Queen* (*Locura de amor* 1948); *Agustina de Aragón* (1950); *The Lioness of Castile** (*La leona de Castilla* 1951) and *Dawn of America* (*Alba de América* 1951) (Labanyi 2007b, 25). Núria Triana-Toribio has shown that these were really 'fully-fledged melodramas disguised under a historical cloak' (2000b, 188).

10 Logically, this work has led to studies of actual audiences through interviews, see Labanyi 2007a.

11 Claire Monk's recent study of contemporary British heritage film audiences confirms precisely this point: 'far from showing audiences [...] to be free to respond to these films and use them creatively as they wish [my study] has illustrated in detail how their responses and positions are unavoidably mediated and shaped by the existing discourses' (2011, 180).

12 Owing to the lack of a middle-class audience in 1940s Spain I do not term these prestige films 'middlebrow'. North America in the period is a different matter, as Chris Cagle argues (2007, 305).

13 Cagle has differentiated between 'two modes of prestige film': 'where the *film industry* defined the prestige picture of the 1930s, the *film consumers* defined the new type of prestige film [of the 1950s] (2007, 293). I have used his argument concerning the first 'mode' for my analysis of Spanish 1940s films.

14 Fewer qualifications are required when describing CIFESA's 1930s output as prestige, as Marvin D'Lugo does (1997, 106).

15 As declared in the CIFESA guide reproduced in the Divisa DVD booklet 2009, 23.

16 Fanés points out that viewers enjoyed this especially splendid setting, in 'absolute contradiction' to the poverty of 1944 Spain (1989, 216).

17 Gil courted controversy with a further Alarcón adaptation in 1947, *The Faith*, 'in which a hysterical Amparo Rivelles tried to seduce a stolid Guillermo Marín as the local priest [...] despite its approval by the censors, it was banned by several bishops' (Labanyi 1995, 20n. 2).

18 In his unsympathetic account of Orduña's œuvre, Francisco Llinás concedes that secondary characters are particularly well deployed (1998, 106).

19 Francisco Llinás explores the overlaps between Orduña's work and that of Ernst Lubitsch (1998, 106–7).

20 This first newsreel was frequently repeated through the years in which the NO-DO was shown in Spanish film theatres (1943–81, though they ceased to be obligatory from 1975). See Tranche and Sánchez-Biosca 2002.

21 Labanyi has noted that the gift of the longed-for child from a husband's fertile mistress to his barren wife evokes Galdós's treatment in *Fortunata y Jacinta* (1886–7), but while Galdós is interested in a symbolically fruitful working class and fruitless bourgeoisie, Lucia suggests Isabel and Emilia belong to the same class through dress (2007b, 39).

22 It is not the first post-war film to focus on the working classes: CIFESA's *Two Stories for Two** (*Dos cuentos para dos* Lucia 1947) explored this terrain (Pérez Perucha quoted in Company 1997a, 219). Bernard Bentley also notices that there are plural precedents in 1940s Spanish cinema for *Furrows*'s documentary tone, even though these are most frequently attributed to Italian Neorealism (2008, 118n. 3).

23 Novelist Cela, who covered similar questions in *La colmena* published in Buenos Aires in the same year, asked Nieves Conde to adapt this novel after seeing *Furrows* (Zumalde Arregi 1997b, 296). He never did, but Mario Camus would do so in 1982 (see Chapter 5).

24 Zavattini was the Italian scriptwriter most readily associated with Neorealism, penning key works like *Bicycle Thieves* (De Sica 1948).

25 'Regenerationism' refers to Spanish intellectuals' response to existential crisis in national identity consequent of Spain's decline and final loss of empire in 1898. It advocates a top-down call to action and political awakening, and is often associated with post-1951 dissident cinema. Carlos Heredero has also written extensively on Spanish dissident cinema as Regenerationist (e.g. 1993; 2000).

26 Eva Woods writes of the dream sequences in *Welcome Mr Marshall* that the 'citizens-spectators do not consume unconditionally the American movies fed to them', in the mayor's dream, for instance, 'The fantasy [provides] a mise-en-scène for the expression of Don Pablo's desire. Unconsciously, he utilizes the fetish form for his own purposes, even though his dream remains a dream' (2008, 23). In *That Happy Couple* the use of romantic comedy is collective (both Juan and Carmen's) conscious, but similarly the tropes are strategically deployed to affirm their own identity.

27 See Marsh 2006, 126, who investigates Berlanga's witty and wicked deflation of slogans in *Welcome Mr Marshall* and *Plácido* and *The Executioner*. On *Plácido*, also see Chapter 3 of this study.

28 Post-Bazin, critics acknowledge that the movement was a fusion of melodrama and neorealist technique (Schnoover 2009). My thanks to Fiona Handyside for this reference.

29 See the discussion and translations of this term, which connects to a nineteenth-century context of uneven modernity, in my Introduction.

3

Charting Upward Social Mobility: 1960s Films about the Middle Classes and the Middlebrow

Spanish cinema of the 1950s is populated with metaphors for frustrated social stasis, from the circular big wheel on which the protagonist-couple get stranded in *That Happy Couple** (*Esa pareja feliz* Bardem and Berlanga 1951), to the name of the dance hall in which Isabel's dreams are crushed in *Main Street* (*Calle Mayor* Bardem 1955): 'Circle'. Alongside these, the train functions as the key symbol of escape. The socially-aspirant rural family of *Furrows* (*Surcos* Nieves Conde 1951) arrives in Madrid on one; when they leave the capital at the end of the film in defeat, we may assume that they do so on another. At the end of *Main Street*, Isabel, who spends time at the train station as she is fascinated by its representation of escape, refuses to board a train, choosing circularity and entrapment instead.

As Spain developed as a capitalist, consumerist society throughout the 1960s, the defining characteristic of both the country and its cinema became mobility. Tatjana Pavlović stresses this thesis in her book on the period, brilliantly entitled *The Mobile Nation: España cambia de piel* (Spain sheds [literally, changes] its skin) (2011).[1] Noting the seismic social changes of geographical relocation from country to city and class mobility, tourism, and an often upward movement into the middle classes in the period 1954–64, Pavlovic also shows that another mode of transport replaced the train as the privileged signifier of the process: the automobile (2011, 5–6, 183–95), which is literally a means of mobility, and figuratively a consumerist symbol of social mobility.[2] The films analysed in this chapter confirm Pavlovic's thesis beyond the period and texts she examines. I begin with Luis García Berlanga's *Plácido*

(1961), whose title character seeks social ascendance through ownership of a 'motocarro' (motorized cart, transformed into a carnivalesque float when necessary). Following this I examine Fernando Fernán Gómez's 1963 *Life Goes On* (El mundo sigue)*, which opens and ends with a close-up of a car's steering wheel and dashboard. At the start of the film we may read this as a reference to the desired social ascendance of the characters. By the end of the film we know that Elo's lifeless body is lying above on the car roof. The status of the car as a symbol of social ascendance is so real to Elo that she cannot bear her sister's ownership of it, so she commits suicide by throwing herself on top of it from her parents' top-floor apartment. I place *Plácido* and *Life Goes On* side by side as the directors shared an outsider status in relation to both contemporary popular cinema, known as the Viejo Cine Español (Old Spanish Cinema) (VCE), and the Nuevo Cine Español (New Spanish Cinema) (NCE), the government-sponsored art cinema associated with both Carlos Saura and the film school where he taught ('The Institute of Cinematic Investigation and Experience', which Berlanga and Bardem attended [see Chapter 2] was renamed the 'Official Film School' in 1962). Breaking strict chronology, I then turn back to 1962 to examine a pair of NCE films side by side. First Jorge Grau's *Summer Night* (*Noche de verano* 1962), where, as in *Life Goes On*, Grau opens with Paco Rabal's Roberto driving a car to establish from the outset the film's focus on his membership of a leisured middle class. In a second NCE film, Jaime Camino's *The Happy Sixties* (*Los felices sesenta* 1963), leisured Spaniards again use a car to holiday on the coast. This vehicle is intertwined with the narrative as Mónica's husband's enthusiasm for the car is the direct opposite of his wife's boredom in marriage: she even uses the car to drive away from the holiday resort to commit adultery with Víctor. I end the chapter with two examples from the VCE, Pedro Lazaga's *City Life is not for Me* (*La ciudad no es para mi* 1965) and a borderline film that presents child-star Marisol as an adult, Luis Lucia's *Marisol's Four Weddings** (*Las cuatro bodas de Marisol* 1967). In these two examples, the focus on the car has dissolved into a more general interest in the consumerist objects that represent class.

In Spanish film's last decade before it began to lose audiences to television, I chronicle a centrifugal cinema of films that sit clearly on one side or other of the art and popular cinema divide. This may be owing to the selection of only six films, of course, but the commonly-used labels of the period, 'Viejo Cine Español' and 'Nuevo Cine Español' also point to a cinema of polarized extremes. I include Berlanga and Fernán Gómez's work to trouble this over-used binary, but would argue that *Plácido* and *Life Goes On* are also examples of art cinema. My argument in this chapter is that all tendencies, popular cinema, state-sponsored art cinema, or 'outrider' art cinema,[3] for all their differences in intellectual content and formal accessibility, were preoccupied with the same concern to chart social ascendance in 1960s Spain. Berlanga and Fernán Gómez's tragic characters Plácido and Elo embody the desperate, and ultimately futile, struggle to achieve it. Grau and Camino, conversely, both focus on a new middle class that already exists. Just as Florián Rey aligned social mobility with female morality in *The Cursed Village* (*La aldea maldita* 1930, see Chapter 1), so both directors also use female characters and questions of adultery and purity as a means to explore change in the 1960s. The popular cinema betrays a similar obsession with female purity through the activities of Luchy after marriage, in *City Life*, and Marisol before it, in *Four Weddings*. It will not be until the next decade that the focus switches from films about the middle classes and their middlebrow cultural choices to middlebrow films aimed at those middle classes. Thus in the 1960s, a middlebrow cinema itself had yet to emerge, but the middlebrow was a central concern.

Plácido (Berlanga 1961)

One year into this key decade of social mobility, *Plácido* (produced by Alfredo Matas for Jet Films) is a portrait of questions of class in a provincial setting. Its subjects, both social mobility and stasis, and its methods, both the moving and the still image, *Plácido* proceeds by collapsing opposites – with brilliant comic and satiric effect. What is revealed, with wicked irony, is that this movie about social mobility turns out to be a photographic still of class stasis.

Berlanga sets up mobility as central to both plot and characterization, but in both cases this proves to be a foil. The plot concerns a Christmas Eve charitable campaign, 'Siente un pobre a su mesa' (Take a Poor Person Home to Dinner [Evans 2000, 215]), based, Berlanga claims, on an actual campaign that took place in Valencia in the late 1950s.[4] Unfolding over one day in an unnamed provincial city (the film was shot in Manresa, Valencia), the campaign is apparently all about dissolving boundaries: rich and poor alike dine together. In a parallel levelling gesture, the campaign committee invites a posse of improbably dim minor film stars to be auctioned off and also join the participants for their meal. Thus rich and poor, home-owning and destitute, humbly-anonymous and glamorously-famous are to gather together like so many shepherds and wise men of the famous Christian story.

Social mobility is also apparently fundamental to the characterization of the film's eponymous antihero, whose motorized cart is decorated with a huge Christmas star that acts as a constant visual reinforcement of the importance of the Nativity. Working in the brilliant mode of black film comedy that flourished in mid-century Spain in the hands of directors like Berlanga and Ferreri in collaboration with scriptwriter Rafael Azcona (Evans 2000, 212–13), characterization here is all about cipher not psyche. Thus the personage of Plácido Alonso, played by Castro Senra 'Cassen', is a structuring device and a symbol of social mobility in the film. His name is a double pun: an ironic reminder that the economic pressure to pay the first instalment for his cart makes him anything but 'placid', and an indication that his financial responsibility governs his entire person: 'plazo' is Spanish for 'instalment'.[5] Furthermore, we first meet a character that we assume is the titular 'Plácido' as the puppet figure of the credit sequence, who Berlanga treats as a cartoon character and infantilizes by a giant hand that feeds and waters him. The rest of the film apparently restores him the agency he is denied in the credit sequence. Unlike his war-wounded brother, he is physically mobile, and his excursions on the motorized cart link up the diverse spaces of the film's action – the public spaces of the train station, casino, public toilets, bank/ notary office and barracks, and the private ones that include the Alonso, Galán and Helguera family homes. Class mobility is seemingly the social counterpart to these geographical displacements. Just as his cart moves about the city, his ownership of it – though it is paid for by instalments – enables him to earn a wage and strive for the 1960s dream of upward social mobility. Earning a wage is no insignificant detail in this film, as Berlanga exposes an economy otherwise governed by favours, freebies and nepotism. The whole campaign revolves around ingratiating oneself with the great and the good: the townsfolk only bid at the auction to look generous in front of their bosses; the starlets are out for a free jolly to the provinces with a meal thrown in; and the city's poor (with justification) are out for free food and booze. Plácido's brother's errand delivering Christmas baskets attracts no salary – he ends up with a miserable tip of a few pesetas for his efforts. This 'Christmas basket' tradition is itself a synecdoche for an economy of favours and contacts (Cañique and Grau 1993, 35). Plácido's 'seriousness' in his efforts at self-betterment ('soy una persona seria' [I'm an upright citizen] he insists at the bank) is thrown into relief by the inveigling nepotism on which Gabino Quintanilla relies. Played by a young José Luis López Vázquez on hilarious comic form, Quintanilla only gets on through family contacts – future son-in-law of the well-to-do Galán family, he prefaces every greeting with a reminder that he is 'el hijo de Quintanilla, él de las serrerías' [Quintanilla's son, the sawmill owner]. This refrain gets funnier with each repetition, especially when, like an old married couple, Plácido completes Quintanilla's sentence for him: on the telephone to the notary, Quintanilla begins 'el hijo de...'; 'el de las serrerías' adds the impatient driver.

Berlanga has much mischief with the pseudo-charitable event and grasping inhabitants of this provincial city on Christmas Eve, mischief best summed up as the collapsing of opposites. Thus, as has been frequently discussed, disinterested charity is exposed as self-interested hypocrisy throughout *Plácido*. In particular, critics have teased out the ways garrulousness reveals a lack of communication (Zumalde Arregi 1997a, 502), physical proximity becomes a cover for existential solitude (Cañique and Grau 1993, 12; 37), and discursive expertise, whether medical or legal, is nothing but a fig leaf for sham quackery (Marsh 2006, 129–32). How Berlanga achieves these ends has again been much admired. The long take, and attendant opening out of mise en scène to reveal conflict and contradiction have been analysed in detail (Cañique and Grau 1993; Zumalde Arregi 1997a, 503; Marsh 2006, 128–9). Berlanga develops a poetics of the scrutinizing stare over the absent-minded glance, and the 'staring' rather than 'glancing' viewer is rewarded with amusing discoveries. At the station, for example, the stare rather than the gaze reveals that Señora Galán, while smiling and waving at the starlets, is simultaneously calling them 'pelanduscas' (hussies) under her breath; or, at the auction, that the plump wife of one employee is cursing her husband under her breath while smiling at the his boss and the town worthies. Steven Marsh observes that 'The comicity of this film lies not so much in the exposure of Catholic hypocrisy as in the dismemberment of social hierarchy by means of adjacence and closeness' (2006, 126), with a shrewd account of the film's portrayal of the Bakhtinian body (126–7) and sensitive study of Berlanga and scriptwriters' uses of language as a populist tool, like the slogans (126), stock phrases (134–5) and jargon (medical and legal) (130–4).

This section aims to complement this work by exploring the effects of applying the collapsing of opposites to the question of social mobility. This exploration places the film's satire within the wider context considered by this book of the rise of the middle classes, and also reveals Berlanga's self-reflexive use of the film medium. First, social mobility is an obvious foil in plot and characterization. Mobility is all about agency; charity, in this deluded Catholic version, is all about lack of agency. The city's poor are marshalled intro groups, pushed about, and bundled from one venue to another. This process of dehumanization reaches an extreme with the treatment of Pascual. Like a grotesque puppet show, Señora Galán nods the head of the listless, moribund 'pobre' to make him concede to the absurd last-minute marriage that will assure he dies in wedlock, rather than in sin.[6] When Pascual passes away soon after, his corpse is subject to similar treatment, heaved out of the Helguera apartment by the long-suffering Plácido, shunted across the city in the cart, then dumped in the hovel along with the mourning Concheta

– a vision of a newly-wed bride on her wedding night surely dark enough to match Buñuel's version in *Viridiana* of the same year.

Berlanga's satire of the condescending campaign thus enables him to demonstrate the impossibility of social mobility and expose the hypocrisy of Catholic charity. Rather than dismantling boundaries and levelling hierarchies, they are everywhere reinforced. Plácido's efforts in this context are always futile. Apparently mobile, both physically and socially, Plácido, ends where he starts, in the town's public toilets where his wife works and next to which the family lives: he thus spends the entire film running to stand still.

Close examination of cinematography also reveals that opposites collapse. While the long take allows the audience to witness frenetic activity within the frame, this is always countered by the stillness of the camera. That the characters will fail to achieve anything despite their busy efforts is thus written into the very portrayal of those efforts: the static camera. The totally futile efforts of the Helguera family to attend to the dying Pascual are a case in point. Critics have pointed to the collapse of other opposites within the frame, like the division between public and private spaces encapsulated in Plácido's family home. In my reading, however, the collapsing of opposites is also self-reflexive with regards film form, for it is the stillness of the camera itself that works to undermine the frenzied activities of the characters within the frame.

I also take the photographic camera that hangs round Quintanilla's neck throughout the film to be a self-reflexive gesture. At first I took it to be a sham reference to modernity – along with the presence of the minor film stars, the advertisements for the cooking pots, and the various gadgets flourished by the pompous and hopeless Álvaro, including the thermometer (which Álvaro is incapable of using) and the inhaler (which fails to alleviate Quintanilla's cold). But the camera goes beyond these references as it is especially signif- icant in connection with social mobility and cinema. It is no accident that the only significant photograph Quintanilla takes throughout the film is of Plácido and his family (though he does snap Señora Galán in the background at the auction too): despite all their efforts at social mobility they are captured in a static snapshot. At the same time, the camera is a highly self-reflexive prop for cinema: the photograph is the cinema's immediate aesthetic progenitor and, prior to digital filming, movies contradictorily consisted of 24 still frames a second.

The presence of the photographic camera is thus a brilliant touch that allows Berlanga to combine social satire with self-reflexivity. Every attempt at mobility in the film is therefore stalled. Social divisions are shored up by the charitable campaign rather than crossed. The promise of social mobility contained in the fact of the geographic mobility of Plácido's motorized cart

FIGURE 3.1 *Quintanilla and his Immobilizing Camera.* Plácido *(Berlanga 1961)*

is not met. The frenetic activity of the long take is undermined by the static camera. And the photographic camera swinging round Quintanilla's neck self-consciously refers to stasis: social mobility is impossible for Plácido and that impossibility is written into the very textuality of his filmic portrayal: the still frame.

Life Goes On (*El mundo sigue* Fernán Gómez 1963)

If the motorized cart of *Plácido* literally represents physical mobility (which is achieved) but figuratively portrays social mobility (which is never achieved) the motor car is likewise multiply symbolic in *Life Goes On*. In Berlanga's comedy, the motorized cart works as an effective comic prop: literally laden with religious symbols and references to the sham charitable campaign; and figuratively layered with the ironic meanings of hypocrisy and stasis. Two years later Fernando Fernán Gómez adopts melodrama, via the Spanish realist novel by Juan Antonio de Zunzunegui of 1960 on which the film is based, which itself also draws on the sainete. If the car is a prop in Berlanga's comedy, it becomes an especially significant aspect of a mise en scène in Fernán Gómez's melodrama. It encapsulates the wide narrative concerns of class mobility and consumerism and the particular plot detail of sororal conflict, for Elo would prefer to jump from the balcony of the parental home to her death on the roof of her sister's new car than tolerate Luisita's bragging about this symbolic confirmation of her social success. *Plácido* and *Life Goes On* are thus twin pieces, played first in comedy, next in melodrama; both ironically refer to serenity and resignation in their titles only to scrutinize, conversely, the whirlwind changes unleashed by the attempt to achieve social mobility in the period.

Life Goes On, alongside *Strange Journey* (*El extraño viaje*) of the previous year, are often taken as a high point of Fernando Fernán Gómez's 30–credit directing career (as an actor, the number of titles soars to 212). Produced by Juan Estelrich for Ada Films, wranglings with the authorities over its portrayal of a sordid working-class Madrid meant that *Life Goes On* failed to have a showing in the capital, premiering only at provincial theatres in Barcelona in 1965 (Tranche 1997, 432). *Strange Journey* suffered a similar fate, premiering only in minor theatres some 5 years after it was made (Téllez 1997, 587), though it has enjoyed a better after-life, re-released in a recent collection of DVDs (newspaper *El País*'s 'El País de Cine' collection, 2003), subject of thoughtful critical reappraisal (Marsh 2006, 167–88) and even hailed as his favourite Spanish film by Pedro Almodóvar (Galán 2003). *Life Goes On* continues to languish in obscurity with regards both commercial availability and critical attention. Nonetheless, Fernán Gómez's piece easily bears comparison with Berlanga's contemporary work and is among the finest indictment of Francoism of the early *desarrollo* years that we have. Nothing escapes Fernán Gómez's devastating critique, neither the older generation, represented by the rankly hypocritical parents, nor the younger, explored through the three adult children of the family, whose occupations include clerical administrator Rodolfo (played by José Morales), shop assistant-turned-high-class prostitute Luisita (Gemma Cuervo) and the heroine, downtrodden housewife and mother Elo (Lina Canalejas), whose suicide concludes the film and seals the utter condemnation of the society portrayed. If the only ethical value, religious or otherwise, to remain intact in the film is Elo's sense of maternal duty towards her four children, this is spectacularly abandoned by the end through this suicide.

The intertitle with which the film opens, from the sixteenth-century theologian Fray Luis de Granada's 1556 *Guía de pecadores* (*Sinners' Guide*), could thus be just another stanza of the carol sung off-screen at the end of *Plácido*. 'Y no existe caridad, ni la habrá nunca, ni nunca la ha habido' (And charity doesn't exist, nor will it ever, nor has it ever) we hear in the 1961 film; and in the 1963 picture we read: 'Verás maltratados los inocentes, perdonados los culpados, menospreciados los buenos' (You will see the innocent mistreated, the guilty, pardoned, the good, scorned).[7] Turning, as in *Plácido*, around the struggle for social ascendance, the driver of Berlanga's film and the desperate housewife of Fernán Gómez's are siblings trapped by immobility, while generically we shift from comedy to melodrama, geographically from the provinces to the capital, and temporally from a sunrise-sunset cycle to the misfortunes of a poverty-stricken family over at least a year, plus flashbacks to earlier periods. The generic shift is key to the adjustment of focus: *Plácido* stages the efforts of the hapless male family bread-winner in a number of public spaces (though his wife also brings in a wage and there are interesting incursions into domestic spaces); *Life Goes On*, the trials of the increasingly-desperate housewife in predominantly domestic spaces.

Just as mid-century Spanish film comedy has been applauded for its ability to 'weaken' the state (Marsh 2006), melodrama, in Fernán Gómez's hands, emerges as equally debilitating. From the post-credit sequence, the genre's key characteristics, including an attention to space, especially domestic settings, narrativized mise en scène, family relationships and a female focus, are effectively deployed in this 1960s Spanish inflection of the classic genre. Via an exploration of social mobility and consumerist society, the film charts the collapse of the family – especially the patriarchal version beloved of the state – and in the process brings various buildings of the Francoist edifice tumbling down with it, like religion, peaceful coexistence and the success of *desarrollismo*.

On a second viewing of the film, the image and sound to which the credits roll, a still frame of the dashboard and steering wheel of a luxury car, with the jaunty contemporary melody of Daniel White's score, are darkly ironic. For above these shiny symbols of consumerism and modernity, especially the steering wheel with its connotations of both social mobility and individual agency in choosing the direction of travel, lies the lifeless body of the car owner's sister. By the end of the film we also learn that the catchy tune, repeated non-diegetically throughout the piece in an acoustic reminder of this striking opening, is in fact playing diegetically on the car radio (Tranche 1997, 533).

After a fade to black, the diegetic sound of traffic anticipates the next fade to a number of high-angle shots of busy streets, more specifically those of Madrid and the borough Maravillas. This name (meaning wonderment, marvelousness) no doubt attracted the director as a knowingly incongruous setting for the tale. The irony is underscored by a flashback played twice, first from Elo's perspective, then from Andrés's, in which our protagonist is crowned beauty queen 'Miss Maravillas' – a wonderfully hybrid title that encapsulates the 1960s contradiction of pro-Americanism and traditional Catholicism.[8] After the intertitle quotation, a high-angle crane shot picks out the figure of an old lady among the busy citydwellers as she slowly makes her away across a square, shopping bag in hand. Pedro Almodóvar repeats this establishing shot in another of the capital's squares in *What Have I Done to Deserve This?! (¿Qué he hecho yo para merecer esto!!)* of 1984, an updated portrait of another long-suffering working-class housewife, which picks up many of the concerns of Fernán Gómez's piece, especially poverty, prostitution, marital breakdown and a female point-of-view.

Next, subjective cinematography announces the film's concern with a female perspective: a point-of-view shot from the old lady's position tilts up the building where the family reside on the top floor, conveying her weariness at the thought of the climb. A conversation with Andrés before she enters the building introduces her name, Luisa, and the daughter, Elo, who quickly replaces her as the focus of narrative interest. As she climbs the stairs we are reminded of the parallel importance of mise en scène on stage as on screen: as in Antonio Buero Vallejo's *Historia de una escalera* (*Story of a Stairway*, first performed 1949) the stairs are narrativized and anthropomorphized. For Luisa, like Buero's elderly characters, the stairs represent age: 'muchos escalones' (too many steps) comments a boy she meets in the stairwell who helps her with her bags, 'muchos años' (too many years) she replies.

In the rest of the film the connotations of the stairwell and its ascent are substantially developed. The stairs-corresponding-to-years conversation links this space to ageing, and in two of the three flashbacks in the film, the stairs are used to connote the transition from girlhood to adulthood of both sisters Luisita and Elo. However, through clever parallel montage in the first flashback, Fernán Gómez collapses both senses of 'getting on', as ageing and socially climbing. For, at this point in the film, Luisita's occupation as a high-class prostitute is in full swing, with clothes, make-up and accessories to match. Having left home to pursue this method of ensnaring a rich husband, the flashback precedes the reunion between mother and daughter engineered by Andrés, an insidious presence throughout the film whose vague profession as theatre critic, journalist, gossip and busybody allow him to blur boundaries and cross from public spaces (the street, the newspaper office, the beauty pageant ceremony) and private spaces (the family home) at will. After matching point-of-view zooms from mother and child's perspective, Fernán Gómez cross-cuts between Luisita as a child running up the stairs, Luisita as an adult doing the same, and various flashbacks-within-a-flashback images of her childhood – first communion, a first kiss, bathing and dress-making. But for all the innocence of the childhood memories Luisita's present occupation aligns her physical ascent of the stairs with her unscrupulous yet successful social climbing.

It is cruelly appropriate that in the second flashback of the film to use the stairwell, a girlish Elo is framed gaily skipping down the stairs to her ruin. At this point of the film Elo is pregnant with her fourth child, is penniless and has been abandoned by the useless, cowardly, adulterous, violent and gambling husband Faustino played by Fernán Gómez himself. Caring for little but the football pools, the hapless husband wins, but the takings prove paltry as there are so many other winners, and he turns his back on an Elo who needs money to feed and clothe the children to blow the cash drinking and gambling. Having failed to follow her sister's example and prostitute herself earlier in the film either with her husband's boss, through the escort agency, or on the street, Elo once again cannot bear Andrés's advances. The flashback corresponds to Andrés's memory of taking Elo's hand in the stairwell; then as now Elo refuses him to continue her literal and figurative descent, which culminates so spectacularly in the suicidal fall.

Steven Marsh has shown that Fernán Gómez's *modus operandi* in *Strange Journey* is to take a revered Spanish institution, harness every aspect of film language at his disposal – with particular attention to the non-discursive means of food, music and dress – and relentlessly deconstruct it. In *Strange Journey* his target is the village, eulogized in conservative ideology as a repository of timeless traditions and values: '*The Strange Journey* constitutes a sort of queering of that national construct. The village is riddled with dysfunction, all frontiers are perforated and hierarchical relations are up-ended' (Marsh 2006, 187). In *Life Goes On* he addresses a national treasure that is even more ubiquitous: the family. The film relentlessly charts its total collapse: his especial targets, the leading male figures of father, husband and brother, and, in the film's most original contribution to this endlessly explored subject, sisterly love.

From today's perspective, director Fernán Gómez's portrayal of masculinity, even in a genre known for its histrionic exaggeration, may seem excessive. Through father, husband and brother – and a number of secondary male characters like Andrés, and Luisita's lovers – the film demolishes the patriarchal values held dear by the regime. A state civil servant, whose military-style uniform signals Francoism's illegitimate military origins, Elo's father is a buffoon: when cash-strapped Elo visits the parental home at the start of the film, Agapito absently wonders through the apartment holding a geranium for the terrace garden. When Elo reports Luisita's dishonour to the family, Agapito's response is to cry '¡La mato!' (I'll kill her!) and hit the wayward Luisita to the ground, only to accept her back into the family bosom when she buys him off with a gold ring. 'Al dinero', he pompously declares in a staggering statement, 'no hay que mirarle su origen, sino su cantidad y su poder adquisitivo' (You shouldn't worry about where money comes from, but rather how much you've got and what it'll buy you). The characterization of a husband named 'Faustino' contains no surprises. Lacking morals, with depressing predictability he ends up turning to domestic violence and crime as his gambling debts mount. With high-angle shots and rapid editing deployed to heighten tension, in a desperate scene he beats and half-throttles his long-suffering wife as his infant daughter looks on from the cot (little is made in the film of the effects of parental behaviour on these children, though the seeds are sewn in such scenes that will grow into the sustained interest in the child's perspective on conflict in Spanish art cinema from the 1970s onwards). In an interesting generic excursion into the crime thriller, Fernán Gómez then portrays Faustino's robbery, arrest, imprisonment and insanity with extreme close ups and long takes, for instance his rubbing of his neck before the open cash till, as if his body can anticipate the punishment for the crime by garrotte or hanging that his mind denies. Saintly brother Rodolfo is likewise useless, and his ineffectual praying and recitations from the *Guía de pecadores* of the intertitle might be amusing were he not juxtaposed in the frame with his sisters fighting tooth and nail. Fernán Gómez's portrayal of religion as entirely irrelevant, in the vein of Buñuel's *Viridiana* two years previously, is reinforced by the script. 'No se trata de oraciones, se trata de ...' (It's not a question of praying, but of...) insists his irritated father rubbing his fingers together to signal cash when Rodolfo assures he has prayed for a remedy to his sister's hardship. Again, as his ageing parents try to prize apart the fighting sisters in a later scene, his mother yells in exasperation 'haz algo, Rodolfo, ¡que no es hora de rezar!' (do something, Rodolfo, this is no time for prayers!). Such obvious rejection of religion is given an extra edge that brings it up to date and links it to the regime when Luisita points out that Rodolfo isn't a priest but a 'clerical administrator': thus the critique of Rodolfo under-lines the ineffectuality of both religion and the bureaucratic state.

By choosing a sororal, rather than fraternal conflict, Fernán Gómez both investigates a new aspect of the subject of the family, and refers to the new Spain of the *desarrollo* years. Fraternal conflict, with its biblical and classical resonances across the centuries of Cain and Abel and Romulus and Remus, is the key metaphor to map the Civil War onto the family, and thus provide a narrative means by which the confrontation might be explored (its flaw is that it privileges a male-centred understanding of history, and sidelines the myriad experiences that don't correspond to the bellicose image of battling brothers).[9] *Life Goes On* portrays a world far from the political conflicts of the 1930s. Here social mobility and consumerism are portrayed as ubiquitous concerns – even beyond the family Fernán Gómez's camera records competitions and adverts in almost every street scene. Through the warring sisters the director exposes and damns a society where *desarrollismo* seems to have widened the gap between rich and poor and the only characters to achieve social mobility are gamblers or prostitutes. Thus Luisita succeeds in marrying a wealthy man who can buy her the all-significant luxury car, and has her greed and ambition spectacularly rewarded, for she is entirely without scruples, even feigning a pregnancy to extract money for an abortion from a boyfriend she actually loves.[10] Elo, on the other hand, ends up a tragic victim of her pride: housewife and mother, faithful even when abandoned by her husband, she turns to family charity and a cleaning job in the absence of the welfare state, and leaps to her death because she cannot bear the exaggerated evidence of the consumerist triumph of her sister's life choices over hers.

Despite her associations with the lowly, like the basement flat in which she lives with Faustino – her position within it frequently reinforced by high-angle shots – or her descent of the stairs in Andrés's dream, Elo occupies the high moral ground in *Life Goes On*. An unequivocal condemnation of selfishness and greed, Fernán Gómez pulls the piece back from pamphleteering propaganda through textured characterization. The only worthy character in the film, we share Elo's perspective through subjective cinematography, narrative

FIGURE 3.2 *Elo at the Bottom of a Multivalent Staircase.* Life Goes On *(El mundo sigue Fernán Gómez 1963)*

focus and the fact that the first flashback of the film is hers, in which she remembers the 'Miss Maravillas' pageant. However, she is not without her flaws, not least excessive pride and explosive temper. Fernán Gómez also gives significant narrative space to the morally-bankrupt characters of Luisita, Faustino and Andrés, to whom we also have privileged access through flashback and voiceover. Thus in two scenes, as Luisita removes her makeup she apparently bares her soul to us through voiceover; likewise, voiceover conveys Faustino's anxieties as his gambling win evaporates; Andrés's desires are also revealed to us through flashback. Such generous use of the devices that supposedly give us privileged access to character has, however, an unexpected effect, for, in each case, we in fact never learn anything new. Elo's flashback does provide us with information on the lost dreams of her youth (and indicates that she will only ever be able to look to the past rather than move on), but Luisita and Faustino's thoughts merely confirm the problems of which we are already aware through narrative and we already know of Andrés's attraction to Elo from an earlier conversation between the journalist and the mother. This is, then, a perverse use of the film techniques associated with the revelation of the richness and individuality of character. In Fernán Gómez's nihilistic vision, the techniques that should reveal depth only reinforce the surface; where they should reveal character, they only reinforce caricature.

In this particularly dark condemnation of *desarrollista* Spain, Canaleja's performance as Elo is extraordinary. Drawing on contemporary examples of outstandingly strong female leads, like Sophia Loren's Oscar-winning Cesira in *Two Women* (De Sica 1960), Canaleja's embattled but battling housewife and mother looks forward to the work of the most famous and successful enthusiast of melodrama of Spanish cinema, Almodóvar. His female-focussed Madrid melodramas like *What Have I Done?!*, *Women on the Verge of a Nervous Breakdown* (*Mujeres al borde de un ataque de nervios* 1988) and *Volver* (2006), which star Carmen Maura and Penélope Cruz respectively, bear witness to the influence of Canalejas's performance. *What Have I Done?!* in particular refers to *Life Goes On* both at the start and end of the film. At the start, Gloria is introduced in the same way as Luisa; at the end, Gloria considers, then rejects, following the example of Elo and jumping from the balcony of her Madrid flat. As Elo's horribly still corpse lies on top of the ultimate symbol of mobility at the end of the film, Fernán Gómez insists in 1963 (and Almodóvar later reminds us in 1984) that social ascent was an impossible dream for many.

Summer Night (Noche de verano Grau 1962)

Much has been made, in accounts of 1960s Spanish cinema, of the differences between the dissident work of veterans like Berlanga and Fernán Gómez, and the contemporary films of the NCE. While the 'outriders' (Bentley 2008, 176–81) struggled in opposition to the state both to make and then to distribute their films, the new directors were to enjoy protection from that same state through subsidy and access to film festival and art-house cinema circuits (Faulkner 2006, 16–18). Such an opposition needs some revision as in reality 'new' and 'outrider' auteurist directors alike suffered problems, particularly with censorship (the NCE's Miguel Picazo, for example, saw his *Aunt Tula* [*La tía Tula* 1964] substantially cut by the censors). A further opposition is held to exist between the old masters and their inspiration in native Spanish cultural forms, especially the esperpento and the sainete, and the NCE youngsters, who were supposedly in thrall to foreign models. Marsh in particular has dismantled the first cliché: while directors like Berlanga and Fernán Gómez indeed drew on autochtonous dramatic trends, they likewise dialogued with international sources such as American screwball comedy (*Plácido*) and melodrama (*Life Goes On*). As for the NCE, while Italian Neorealism, and in particular Cesare Zavattini's affirmation that to 'describe social problems is to denounce them' (Whittaker 2011, 12), is a constant concern in many films, the literary adaptations produced by the movement nonetheless reveal a national focus: Unamuno in Picazo's *Aunt Tula*, Baroja in Angelino Fons's *The Search* (*La busca* 1967) and Galdós in his *Fortunata y Jacinta* (1970).

When considered from the perspective of social mobility, the differences between the 'outriders' and the NCE are also less marked. Following Berlanga and Fernán Gómez, NCE directors tended to portray those excluded from the economic benefits of *desarrollismo*, like the struggling mechanic of the eloquently-named *Getting on in the World** (*Llegar a más* Fernández Santos 1963), or the starving actors of the also interestingly-titled *Frauds** (*Los farsantes* Camus 1963). Alternative examples showed how the privileges of the older orders remained intact despite supposed progress – thus Picazo and Basilio Martín Patino explore stifling tradition in provincial Castilian cities Guadalajara (*Aunt Tula*) and Salamanca (*Nine Letters to Bertha* [*Nueve cartas a Berta* 1965]).

The take on social mobility in *Summer Night* and *The Happy Sixties*, however, differs markedly from *Plácido* and *Life Goes On*. With only a few years between them, the worlds these films portray could not be further apart: the approach to mobility is one key difference; their aesthetic form a second. For in *Plácido* and *Life Goes On*, despite all the frenzied movement of motorized carts around the city, or warring sisters up and down stairs, the key metaphors are blockage and stasis: social mobility is a mirage for Plácido and Elo, its corollary, consumerism, a fantasy. Conversely, *Summer Night* and *The Happy Sixties*, the subjects of this and the following sections, focus not on the struggle for social mobility and consumerist aspirations, but on the facts of membership of the middle classes and enjoyment of its corollaries, leisure time and material acquisition. Grau's film explores the leisure activities of a group of wealthy friends over the titular 'summer night' of the festival of Saint Joan in Barcelona; in Camino's, we track the experiences of a pampered middle-class housewife from Barcelona on summer holiday in Cadaqués.

Summer Night and *The Happy Sixties* are thus on the fringes, in many senses, of the NCE. First, both are very early examples – Grau's being the first to receive subsidies through the *interés especial* mechanism – and second, both are set in Catalonia, whereas the movement as a whole is associated with the city of Madrid and the landscapes and provincial cities of Castile. Marginal too are the aesthetic influences of both films. The first issue of *Nuestro Cine*, the mouthpiece of the NCE in journal form, may have paraded a still of Antonioni's *L'avventura* on its cover, but in fact the NCE favoured the earlier social-realist vein of Italian Neorealism.[11] However, both Grau, who studied in the state film school in Rome (*Centro Sperimentale di Cinematografía*) in the 1950s,[12] and Camino, favoured later Italian directors, precisely like Antonioni. Off-centre too, in comparison to the rest of the movement, is the chronicle of a new middle class. *Summer Night* and *The Happy Sixties* in fact reflect what the historical record shows was central over the decade – the beginnings of a massive move of Spaniards into the middle classes – whose presence would be increasingly evident on Spanish screens as the century wore on.

The first feature-length credit for Grau, who would go on to specialize in popular horror in the 1970s, no doubt partly in response to this film's lukewarm commercial success,[13] *Summer Night* is a curious hybrid which captures well the contradictions of Francoist *desarrollismo*. On the one hand, it flaunts its cinematic modernity. A co-production, half its cast is Italian, including Marisa Solinas as the angelic student Alicia, Umberto Orsini as social-climber Miguel and Rosalba Neri as floozy Rosa. On the Spanish side, Rabal is key: his role as upper-bourgeois playboy Bernardo reprises his role as Jorge in Buñuel's *Viridiana* (1961) and echoes his Riccardo of Antonioni's *L'Eclisse*, made concurrently with *Summer Night* in 1962. Intertextual connections through casting thus refer to contemporary Italian work, as does the homage to *Chronicle of a Love* (Antonioni 1950) in the extended sequence between Miguel and Alicia as their relationship comes to an end. Its overall theme of the potential meaningless of middle-class characters' lives betrays a more disperse narrative debt to *L'avventura*. Yet ultimately this modernity is put to the service of tradition, for the film's moralizing conclusion reinforces Catholic dogma, in particular that concerning the behaviour of female characters as self-sacrificing virgins before marriage and faithful mothers after. For all the new film language, then, we get the same old story: an eloquent illustration of the contradictions of the 1960s Spain, where modern liberal economics cohabited with a dictatorship forged in the 1930s.

Hybridity and contradiction are evident in *Summer Night*, even at the level of production and financing: the lionized champion of dissident cinema from the 1960s onwards, Elías Querejeta, was a producer; Opus Dei's Madrid-based PROCUSA, and Rome-based Domiziana Internazionale David Film, the two production companies. However small Querejeta's creative contribution,[14] the combination of conflicting progressive and reactionary elements in production seep into the film. *Summer Night* proceeds on conflicting tracks. It hints at once at an unleashing of desire with the 'summer night' of its title, the urban, festive setting of Barcelona on the eve of Sant Joan, its modern cinematic aesthetics and youthful characters, all of which are encapsulated in the pre-credit sequence of a documentary montage of drunken street parties on the imagetrack and heterogeneous melodies and languages on the soundtrack (Castilian, Catalan and English can be made out).[15] Yet at the same time, it reinforces Catholic ideals of the Virgin, Madonna, and faithful wife, especially in its moralizing conclusion.

These conflicting parallel tracks are narrativized by the dual focus on two social groups, both groups defined, rather predictably, by a male character and his desire for two opposing women. The timescale explored is more unusual, pairing two Sant Joan festivals that are one year apart. In the first, we have Rabal's Bernardo, whose membership of the upper-middle class is signalled from the outset by the large car he drives round Barcelona in the film's post-credit sequence. Married to the aloof Carmen, he tries to seduce Inés in the various settings visited by the group of friends during the festivities. In the first year they attend an auction then drink at posh cocktail bars – both venues showcases for the new 1960s wealthy – they move on to Bodega Bohemia and even take a fairground roller coaster ride. In the second, Bernardo hosts the party at his country residence, and ends up fruitlessly confessing his love to Inés in an interestingly-shot scene where the cinematography conveys his friend's wife's inaccessibility, for while she is framed in a frontal close-up staring at the ceiling, he is shot from the side, head muffled in a pillow and adulterous desire thwarted.

In the second group we have failed salesman Miguel, who has to borrow money (which he never repays) from the saintly Alicia for the first Sant Joan, which they spend at dance hall Salón Venus Deporte. Miguel cannot resist,

FIGURE 3.3 *Motoring Bernardo.* Summer Night *(*Noche de verano *Grau 1962)*

however, a Rosa in full bloom (with occupation as florist and flowery dress to match), with Neri's limited acting skills compensated for by her physical similarity to the voluptuous embodiment of current beauty ideals, Sophia Loren. In the intervening year Miguel gains lucrative employment as a dubious salesman and marries her (the wallpaper of the bedroom of their marital home is decorated, of course, with roses). The second Sant Joan commences as the now nouveau-riche Miguel drives his new car – the inevitable proof of his membership of the middle classes – meets Alicia again, then tries, and fails, to seduce her. One flaw of the film – Grau's feature-length début as director – is that these two narrative strands proceed practically in isolation. They are only woven together at the start of the film when Bernardo is attracted to Rosa, who storms out of the bar on their date in disgust when his desire for Inés becomes clear.

The film therefore requires an active spectator to compare the two narrative strands, for through juxtaposition rather than direct interweaving, their meaning emerges. Through comparison, the festive diversions take second place and a primary focus comes into view: marriage. Similarly, the secondary female characters of Inés and Alicia, the married Bernardo and Miguel's 'other women', take on prominence. Both Bernardo and Miguel seem to have married unwisely, but their blame is reduced in both cases by the stereotypical characterization of their wives as faulty: frigid Carmen (played by Italian Lidia Alfonsi) and harlot Rosa. Narrative interest and nuance thus cluster around Inés and Alicia, who emerge as Grau's focus of interest and heroines of the piece. Alicia, first, in a reprise of Bardem's Matilde in *Death of a Cyclist* (*Muerte de un ciclista* Bardem 1955), is a hard-working, virginal student, capable of redeeming the hero through sound advice and impeccable behaviour. Tradition and modernity are combined in the character through her membership of a film club (Miguel interrupts her during a screening of *Journey to Italy* [Rossellini] and she participates in a discussion of *L'avventura*) and her flawless behaviour: when she first rejects the married Miguel's advances, Grau juxtaposes her with a carving of an angel. Inés, too, is likened to the idealized 'angels of the hearth' of nineteenth-century bourgeois ideology when Bernardo buys her a pair of angelic wings to wear during the dressing-up that forms part of the Sant Joan festivities. She never wears them and eventually discards them, not in a rejection of this stereotypical female role, but rather because they are a gift from an unsuitable admirer. The casting of mediocre María Cuadra as Inés compromises, however, the importance Grau assigns to her role. Her wooden performance is unconvincing, yet upon her rests the moral message of the film regarding marriage. For while she appears mildly to flirt with the lovelorn Bernardo, she in fact emerges as the beloved angel of bourgeois patriarchy. For example, after returning home from the first Sant Joan party, she goes into angelic overdrive floating around the house in a spotless white dressing gown, providing warmth to her infant daughter by tucking her in as she sleeps and nutrition to her husband by fetching a drink of – of course – milk. At the second celebration she naturally rebuts Bernardo's advances and rushes home to her husband. That her husband Alberto is the only character shown at work – he is a Barcelona businessman from whose office windows we see the cathedral – betrays again the Opus Dei spirit of the film: the hardworking entrepreneur is rewarded with the only angelic wife of the film.

The conservative Catholic press in both Spain and Italy overlooked Cuadra's lousy performance and loudly praised the film. Distributed with the title *Il peccato* (*Sin*) in Italy in reference to the sin of adultery almost committed by both Bernardo and Miguel, the Vatican's *Osservatore Romano* – only one year after condemning *Viridiana* for blasphemy – lavished praise on the film's defence of marriage ("Review of *Noche de verano*" 1963). When Spain's *Ya* reported the critical success of the film at the Mar de Plata Film Festival where it débuted it is interesting that its journalist dwells on, and thus intertwines, both Catholic tradition and cinematic modernity, for *Summer Night* won both the Mar de Plata's Oficina Católica Internacional del Cine prize (the embodiment of tradition) and its Special Mention for the director (a recognition of its modernity). This art film thus mobilizes an active spectator to appreciate its portrait of middle-class Barcelona in the 1960s. It deploys modern cinematic references and aesthetics – learnt by Grau in at film school in Rome – and employs them – ironically – to entrench conservative tradition.

The Happy Sixties (*Los felices sesenta* Camino 1963)

If Italophile Grau pays homage to Antonioni through casting Rabal, focussing on the leisured middle class and using occasionally interesting formal techniques, Jaime Camino betrays an even greater debt, with *The Happy Sixties* almost a remake of *L'avventura* – with a nod too to *Journey to Italy* – on Spanish soil. Like *Summer Night*, Camino's film has a woeful exhibition history, made in 1963 and shown in Cannes the same year (Riambau 1997, 636), it wasn't distributed in Spain till 1969, and no audience figures are currently available. However, it is of interest, first, for the evidence it provides of the transnational influences on Spanish cinema as early as 1963: such influences would be richly evident by the end of the decade in Catalonia's Barcelona School.[16] Second, its study of the bourgeoisie offers an early manifestation of a film that sympathetically explores middle-class characters. As this book aims to show, this looks forward to the middlebrow films of the 1970s and beyond.

Camino is at odds with the NCE for many of the same reasons as Grau: *The Happy Sixties* is an early film; the setting is Catalan; and Camino did not attend the Madrid film school that forged the movement, but was rather self-taught with his own production company (Tibidabo Films) (Bentley 2008, 191). A first feature like *Summer Night*, *The Happy Sixties* is mixed, combining occasionally interesting formal innovation with an often excessive reverence for contemporary Italian art cinema, which might ungenerously be dismissed as imitation. The favoured *modus operandi* is to explore obvious oppositions between concepts, but such a device is best deployed sparingly, and, if at the start of the film these clashes are suggestive, by the end they are simply overdone. What emerges only in retrospect is the prescience of Camino's occasionally thoughtful portrayal of Spain's new middle classes, at a time when, in both art cinema and popular cinema alike, the nouveaux riches were simply the objects of satire or the butt of jokes.

But while the passage of time brings the significance of the treatment of class to the fore, today, the treatment of gender in *The Happy Sixties* seems pedestrian. Before approaching the film we need to remind ourselves why the tired opposition of the virtuous wife-versus-the adulteress was so attractive to Camino in 1963. Laying aside the attractions of casting Yelena Samarina as the protagonist Mónica – Camino has her bat her eyelashes in close up and wear extra-short shorts in long shots for much of the film – a female protagonist was an ideal trope to explore the contradictions of 1960s Spain. Embodiment of tradition through her exalted role for both the Catholic church and Francoist ideology, by the 1960s, she also represented tentative change. *The Happy Sixties* refers to the current increases in female employment through Mónica's pre-credit conversation with Pablo, which reveals her middle-class husband's disapproval of her work as a nurse; *Summer Night* portrays the current boom in female university education through the student Alicia; and VCE films, to be studied in the next section show current female consumerism.

Returning to *The Happy Sixties*, the first obvious opposition of the film is provided by the credit sequence, which teams a montage of documentary images of tourism in Cadaqués with the striking soundtrack of Raimón's 'Tot sol' (All Alone).[17] With every new image, the contrast between the melancholic loneliness described in the singer's poetic verse, and the enforced community of the prosaic tourists, becomes more marked: aerial shots frame a packed beach of sun-bathers; medium shots portray groups of light-skinned North-European campers and hitch-hikers; close-ups document heaps of tacky plastic bullfighters and flamenco dancers, which lie in piles in a visual echo of the earlier aerial shots of the crowds of sprawling sun-worshipers. These documentary images also gesture towards class. The first image is an aerial shot of queue of family cars entering the once-sleepy fishing-village, while on the other side of the road there travels a workers' truck. As opposed to the truck-drivers, the occupants of the cars are wealthy enough to own them and leisured enough to use them for tourist travel. The documentary images end with a swipe from a bikini-wearing sunbather to a group of local workers wearing overalls sharing bread in the heat. As Raimón's 'sol' is repeated on the soundtrack. The clash between the mournful evocation of solitude through music, and the colourful portrayal of busy coastal tourism through image, seems to be explained by the meanings of 'sol' in Catalan – 'alone' – and in Castilian Spanish (the language of the pre-credit sequence and the majority of the rest of the film) – 'sun'. Thus Spain, internationally isolated in early Francoism, now finds the advent of sun-seeking tourism an experience of profound conflict.

However, as the song is repeated on the soundtrack, this thematic focus is narrowed: we hear the lyrics for a second time as we watch Samarina's Mónica wander through a number of iconic Cadaqués locations including the cobbled streets and the market. Thus the 'loneliness' must be that of the protagonist and an alternative 'obvious opposition' emerges: that between the happiness alluded to by the tourist-slogan-style title of the film, and the unhappiness of its bored, bourgeois protagonist. The film therefore presents the possibility that Raimón's poignant lyrics might be used to explore the protagonist's existential crisis: the singer-songwriter was renowned both for musical beauty and political commitment.[18] Closer examination of the subsequent use of music in the film unfortunately reveals, however, another narrowing of thematic focus. We hear 'Tot sol' again in a potentially interesting dovetailing of extra-diegetic and diegetic sound: Víctor, Mónica's old friend who has returned from the States to holiday on the Costa Brava, whistles Raimón's melody as the couple take a nocturnal walk together. But when Víctor becomes Mónica's lover, we must retrospectively interpret the scene. The whistling seems to indicate little more than that Víctor proposes adultery as a solution to her solitude.

The second Raimón song to be included on the soundtrack, 'Per ser cantada en la meva nit' (To Be Sung On My Night), occurs mid-way through the film, after the couple has sneaked off on a boat trip to a remote area of the coast to consummate their affair. The semantic richness of a verse like 'Enllà d'una profunda/nit sense veus, em nego' (Beyond a deep,/voiceless night, I drown) again seems to be reduced to predictable premonition: adultery will not solve Mónica's loneliness. The third, 'Perduts' ('Lost' – the original Catalan indicates the plural), comes at the end of the film, after Mónica has sought out Víctor, but realizes he will never ask her to leave her family. 'Caminem perduts, sols,/ caminem, com un home sol' (We walk along lost, alone,/we walk along, as a man alone) may express her disappointment at the failure of her affair, but a soundbridge sabotages any poignancy here, for, in a surely disasterous move, Camino has the song link the lonely image of the rejected Mónica in her car, to an image of the buffoonish Catalan estate agent (on whom more later), who has likewise been rejected by the English tourists to whom he spends most of the film trying to sell land. Raimón's fourth piece, 'La pedra' (The Stone), is likewise unwisely used at the end of the film. Mónica has returned to the certainty of her role as wife and mother, thus Raimón's musings on the open-ended possibilities – 'Tires la pedra, on anirà?' (You throw the stone, where will it go?) – seem entirely inappropriate.

A second area of obvious opposition concerns characterization, which is reinforced by casting. Rather predictably, Mónica is torn between husband and lover (her third admirer, lovelorn waiter Pep, is ignored). Her husband Pablo (played by Spaniard Germán Cobos) is a walking cliché of a newly-enriched Spain: an business-man of unspecified trade, his conversation to friends concerns how fast he can drive his car from Barcelona to Cadaqués, and to Mónica, whether she might dress up more to go out, and attend to domestic duties like instructing the domestic staff or neatening the children's hair. Víctor is afforded far more screen time. He plays the key role of the outsider other, which Tom Whittaker (2011, 29–37) has shown to be so important in Antxón Eceiza's film of another coastal village coping with the advent of tourism, the Málaga fishing village of *Next Autumn* (*El próximo otoño* 1962). While Eceiza's Monique is a French student who takes the shy fisherman Juan as a summer boyfriend only to abandon him and return to France at the onset of autumn, Camino's Víctor, though Spanish, is likewise associated with foreign countries and education. Played by Frenchman Jacques Doniol-Valcroze – surely cast more for his off-screen fame as a founding editor of *Cahiers du cinema*, than his on-screen acting abilities – Víctor is a highly-trained surgeon who lives in America and speaks English. As Mónica's love interest, his specialism is, of course, heart surgery.

If predictable at the level of plot, Mónica's amorous dilemma takes on greater meaning at the symbolic levels of the national and the cinematic. *The Happy Sixties* draws on Eceiza's *Next Autumn* (long forgotten, but recently reassessed by Whittaker) and looks forward to Basilio Martín Patino's *Nine Letters* (1965) (long admired as manifesto-film for the NCE [Torreiro 1995b, 318]). The approach in all three is straightforward: there is a Spanish protagonist or central character – in *Next Autumn*, fisherman Juan (played by Manuel Manzaneque), in *The Happy Sixties*, Mónica (actually played by Russian actress Samarina) and in *Nine Letters*, Salamanca student Lorenzo (memorably played by Emilio Gutiérrez Caba, in a key role that established his

FIGURE 3.4 *Víctor and Monica Cannot Resist the Draw of Nature.* The Happy Sixties *(Los felices sesenta* Camino 1963)

on-screen persona); the character has his or her traditional values challenged through an amorous encounter with a foreign 'other' – in *Next Autumn*, a French student on summer holidays, Monique, in *The Happy Sixties*, Spanish émigré played by French actor, Víctor, in *Nine Letters*, the titular Berta, an English student and daughter of Spanish émigrés. Traditional values may be challenged in each encounter, but in these tentative times, those values pertain mainly to heterosexual relationships, and, in each of the three cases, the director has the protagonist either reject, or be abandoned by the 'other': Monique returns to France alone; Víctor returns to the States alone; and Lorenzo stops writing to Berta and is set to marry his dull Spanish girlfriend. The point, therefore, is to subject tradition to critique, rather than reject it outright, thus Juan must continue to support his family through fishing (his father dies before the film's opening, and his grandfather dies at the film's close). Mónica, for her part, resumes her traditional family role. Like the family car in which she sits to convey her acceptance of her allotted place, she will also be an object that signifies her husband's wealth and standing. Patino's is the most trenchant treatment of the return to tradition: in a brilliant final sequence, Lorenzo's decision to marry is damningly compared to petrification, a coda that draws together the lingering shots of Salamanca's venerable stone monuments throughout the rest of the film.

The casting of Víctor is key for a metacinematic interpretation of Mónica's love triangle, for Doniol-Valcroze represents contemporary currents of art cinema outside Spain. Thus, just as this foreign actor on set in Cadaqués represented the art cinema beyond Spain to which Camino was attracted, likewise Víctor, as the 'foreign' outsider on holiday, represents an alternative to conformity to which Mónica is attracted. *The Happy Sixties* uses Mónica's adultery as a device to dramatize a Spanish cinema at a crossroads. Víctor/Doniol-Valcroze represents one direction, but, in a surprisingly twist, Mónica's middle-class husband does not represent an alternative direction – this book's contention that a Spanish middlebrow cinema did not yet exist is pertinent here, as at this point there is no 'middle' cinematic tradition with which Camino can align this middle-class husband. With mixed results, Camino introduces, instead, comic relief as a counterpoint to the cinematic traditions of the foreign New Waves. Casting is again significant here, as the secondary role as the hapless estate agent is deftly played by Catalan theatre regular Joan Capri, whose gestural performance, Catalan-accented Castilian and recourse to stereotype all shift the film register decisively into popular comedy.

In three key sections, Camino portrays the three stages of Mónica and Víctor's relationship by boldly adopting modern cinematic techniques in vogue beyond Spain's borders. In each case, the sequences relating to the couple are juxtaposed with brief comic scenes describing Capri's estate agent's attempt to sell buildings and land to his 'other', a stereotypical English tourist – complete with short shorts and photographic camera hanging around his neck – and his wife. We might explain these curious juxtapositions as Camino's metacinematic dramatization of two cinematic choices against one another – the two alternatives the director sees for contemporary Spanish cinema. On the one hand, European art cinema, with its universal themes of love, solitude and solace, on the other, local crude comedy, with its localized response to the recent tourist boom and property speculation. Thus in the first section, Monica, Víctor and friends take a boat trip to an excluded beach for a picnic. A section clearly indebted to *L'avventura*, the modern formal techniques used here include the long take, for example in a shot that frames Mónica and Víctor in isolation against an empty seascape, which anticipates their attempt to reject civilization by consummating their adulterous affair in another empty stretch of coast. However, any philosophical musings about the role of landscape on the part of the audience are interrupted by the following sequence, where Capri's character amusingly attempts to sell a similarly untouched plot of land to the tourists, who look on in confusion as he plans out a holiday villa for them, complete with two large rooms, one for their flamenco-dancer souvenirs, another for a bull's head!

In the second section, Mónica and Víctor meet at a terrace café then visit a ruined monument together. As the couple rather self-indulgently mull over their unhappiness and reject the meaningless role-playing of their respective lives, Camino rejects too the classic shot-counter shot with which to record conversation in favour of a striking 3–minute-long take and predominantly static camera. Panning from left to right, this approach means one character is only ever in the frame at a time, gazing at an interlocutor off-screen, which successfully underscores the solitude of which they complain. The take ends with a pan to the left out to sea, indicating the draw of nature. Such thoughts are again interrupted by Capri, who this time shows the tourists round a tumbling-down ruined tower. 'Va a subir?' (Will it go up?) enquires the male tourist with regards its investment potential; 'Más bien tiende a bajar' (It's more likely to come down) quips Capri, as a point-of-view reveals a crumbling wall. Such comicity means it's difficult for the audience to take seriously Mónica and Víctor's visit to another ruined monument, where *Journey to Italy* (1954) is the key intertext. As in Roberto Rossellini's film, spaces are imbued with narrative meaning, but whereas the ruins of Pompeii reflect Rossellini's lead couple's crumbling marriage, in Camino's, the ruined monument must stand for Mónica and Víctor's desire to escape the trappings of civilization that they find decrepit.

Camino is again formally innovative in the scene where the couple, unable to resist what the director presents as the draw of nature, consummate their affair. Close-ups of foaming crests and crashing waves, followed by images of still water, are perhaps a rather adolescent – and male-focussed – metaphor for sex, but they make clear to the viewer that the coastal environment stands for the couple's relationship. Fascinating, then, is the juxtaposition of extreme close-ups of pitted coastal rock faces and shimmering surfaces of the water with extreme long shots of the couple at rest in an abandoned riverbed, which thus links their behaviour to the elemental forces of nature that carved out the seascape. The striking opposition of extreme close-up and extreme long shot would be taken up and extended by Carlos Saura two years later in *The Hunt* (*La caza*), to brilliant cinematic and political effect (Faulkner 2006, 164–9). But the inexperience of Camino is thrown into relief by this comparison, for while Saura's mastery of cinematic form (in collaboration with cinematographer Luis Cuadrado) has assured his place as one of Spain's leading filmmakers, the potential interest of Camino's innovations in his portrayal of the landscape remain unresolved. The striking shots of the natural environment are followed by one of a terraced hillside, a perfect illustration of the encroachment of civilization. But in this way the thematic focus narrows, and Mónica and Víctor will return to the roles and role-playing assigned to them by the civilization they have tried to reject. While this section is not juxtaposed with a Capri sequence, by the end of the film, the hapless estate agent returns. As we have seen, the final soundbridge of Raimón's 'La pedra' links the failure of Mónica with her 'foreign' Víctor to the failure of Capri to sell land or property to his English tourists, which leaves Camino open to the criticism that the whole film collapses into Capri-esque farce (Font 2003, 186).

City Life is not for Me (*La ciudad no es para mí* Lazaga 1966)

With mixed results, then, the NCE chronicled the advent of Spain's new middle class in the 1960s. As well as an enduring interest in the struggle to 'Llegar a más' (Get on), films like *The Happy Sixties* turned to the formal innovations of foreign art cinema to fashion a 'new' film language to portray those established within the middle class. As we have seen, this treatment often turned around the characterization of a woman as the embodiment of a conflict of tradition with modernity. More specifically, the new questions of women in relation to leisure time and university education were explored.

The box-office and producer-led VCE was a precise reversal, relying on the trusted generic formula of the popular comedy to mitigate financial risk. The 'sub-genres' of the VCE that focussed on a single actor were an extreme form of this conservatism: films that trotted out the same old stories in relation to the same old star were the safest bet.[19] Following the examples of the child-star films of the 1950s and early 1960s, like those of Joselito and Marisol, a key sub-genre in the mid-1960s was the 'paleto' (country bumpkin) films starring Paco Martínez Soria; by the late-1960s and early 1970s, the sub-genre of Iberian sex comedies starring Alfredo Landa emerged, which spawned the neologism 'Landismo' films.[20] For all these formal differences, the thematic concerns of the VCE sometimes coincided with the NCE, and this is especially the case regarding the portrayal of the new middle classes. Concerns about female virtue exercise directors and scriptwriters of both the VCE and the NCE, but what is new in the popular comedy is the comic treatment of middle-class consumerism.

City Life is not for Me defined an era, as its comic portrayal of immigration from country to city was a runaway commercial success. Its critical afterlife is typical of the popular comedy under the dictatorship. The top-grossing film of the 1960s (and still one of most commercially-profitable Spanish blockbusters ever), it was first ignored by critics who focussed their attention on auteur cinema, and next dismissed as pro-Franco (Richardson 2002, 71–2). Since the new millennium, however, critics have questioned this truism and looked more closely at the film's contradictions, which include its treatment of capitalism (Richardson 2002, 71–86) and focus on female adultery (Faulkner 2006, 66–9). What interests me here is the film's chronicle of socially-mobile Spain, and in particular the attention it pays to middle-class consumerism. Mise en scène will thus be an especial focus of my study of this early document of the middlebrow in Spanish film.

It is to be expected that mise en scène should be central to a film apparently about an opposition between country and city, but actually about consumerism. This area of film form includes the portrayal of macro-space, for instance the geographical settings represented through city-, sea- or landscape shots; micro-space, for instance domestic dwellings, which are often shot in studios; plus those aspects shared with the theatre referred to in 'scène': costume, make-up and props. While today much of *City Life* seems painfully formulaic, mise en scène retains its interest as one of the more thoughtfully deployed areas of its film language.[21] Even taking into account the production constraints of working in popular comedy, and the fact that this film actually established the formula, the plot of a bumbling-yet-wily old peasant straightening out the moral behaviour of his younger urban relations is nonetheless especially contrived, as are the typecast performances, which include Martínez Soria as the 'paleto', Doris Coll as the would-be adulteress and Gracita Morales as the dim, pregnant housemaid. In contrast, the deployment of mise en scène makes possible the double interpretation of the film as apparently about rural tradition yet actually about capitalist modernity.

Urban life, modern working practices and the circulation of money are all referred to in *City Life*, but capitalist modernity is largely explored through the consumption practices of the middle-class characters. One of the first Spanish films to place middlebrow consumerism centre stage, it is helpful to consider Bourdieu's insights before examining in detail three areas of especial interest in this film: decorative art, dress and food. Bourdieu's term 'distinction', while developed in a sociological study of contemporary cultural practices in France,[22] is nonetheless useful to explore the coded consumerist behaviour of this Spanish comedy. Bourdieu reminds us that the socially-mobile seek confirmation of their membership of a new class through distinctive cultural choices. Middlebrow culture – the distinctive choice of new members of the middle class – is characterized in particular by imitation and in-betweenness (see my Introduction, note 14).

To shift from Bourdieu to Lazaga is to shift from sober academic discourse to obvious film comedy, but some of the observations regarding social mobility coincide. 'Tío Agustín', as the Martínez Soria character is fondly named, lives in Calacierva, an Aragonese village from which his son, Gusty, and daughter-in-law, Luchy, emigrated to find fortune and socially climb in Madrid – like millions of Spaniards in the boom years. Gusty is a doctor, but, as always, it is the female character that embodies these financial and social shifts, for Luchy was a poor village dressmaker, but is now a leisured bourgeois housewife. Gusty's name is explained as it differentiates his full name – Agustín – from that of his father, though given the role played by taste in the film there is possibly a pun on 'Gusty' and 'gusto' ('taste' in Spanish). Luchy's name is of greater interest. A foreignified version of the Castilian Luciana (the name her father-in-law uses), her new name conveys her new membership of the middle class through its middlebrow imitation of the foreign.

Punning names aside, *City Life* tends to explore middlebrow culture through non-discursive means.[23] Decorative art exemplifies the way *City Life* poses as a predictable treatment of country versus city, but the film is in fact an analysis of the new middle class and their middlebrow consumption. Again, we begin with a simplistic opposition between country and city: the Madrid family's prize possession, a Picasso (*Still Life With Guitar* [1922]); and Tío Agustín's, a portrait of his late wife. The clash between the two couldn't be more obvious: the 'foreign' modern art (Picasso painted it in exile) vies for place on the wall of the Madrid flat with the realist portrait of the comely matriarch. But the Picasso does not in fact refer to the city, but class. Its significance is not what it represents in pictorial terms (a Cubist treatment of a guitar), but what it represents in social terms: affluence. It is all about the 'decorative' and not at all about 'art', and therefore a good example of Bourdieu's class dissection of the apparently innocent tastes of consumers. Through its mode of consumption as an emblem of Gusti's family's new middle-class status, Picasso becomes an example of middlebrow culture. Similarly, the portrait of wife Antonia is not about the country, but about the traditional roles of wife and mother. The final scene in the Madrid flat begins and ends with a zoom out and in of the portrait: rather than a triumph of country over city, this encodes, rather, Luchy's transformation from would-be adulteress into a new version of her mother-in-law. By the end of the film, the itinerant portrait returns to the wall of Tío Agustín's Calacierva home, from which we can deduce that the Picasso is back on the wall of the Madrid flat. The middlebrow consumer choices that the film apparently critiques thus remain intact.

The treatment of dress and food reinforce the role played by consumer choices. Background information on her former profession as a dressmaker gives some justification for the reduction of Luchy to a mannequin on which Lazaga simply hangs socially-coded garments. First appearing in keep-fit leggings, vest and sweat band, Luchy's first outfit connotes the leisure time that characterizes the middle-class housewife, as it did in the case of Mónica's t-shirt and shorts in *The Happy Sixties*. As with Mónica, clothes also play the narrative role of representing adultery – thus the adulteress of *The Happy Sixties* wears a green t-shirt on the first boat trip with Víctor, then a green dress when she leaves Cadaqués to find him. If Camino's use of colour is subtle, it is not hard for the viewer to decode dress in *City Life*: the greater the adornment, the greater the risk of infidelity. Thus on an adulterous date with Ricardo (sabotaged by Tío Agustín), Luchy wears fur coat, fancy hat and sexy cocktail dress. In this scene, Lazaga further likens Luchy to an iconic 'maja' by juxtaposing her in the frame with a painting of one such Madrid beauty. Immortalized in Goya's eighteenth-century portraits, the point here is not high art intertext, but rather that 'majas' were often prostitutes. Rather obviously, then, the film therefore condemns luxury as lust, punning on the shared root of 'lujo' (luxury) and 'lujuria' (lust) in Spanish – it is not incidental that Tío Agustín remarks '¡Qué lujo!' (How luxurious!) when he first sees the Madrid flat, at a point when Luchy is wearing another snazzy frock. Not surprisingly, when Tío Agustín enforces Luchy's return to the marital hearth she exchanges her finery for a dowdy, knitted cardigan.

According to this logic, the order that Agustín restores to the family should be represented by such attire at the end of the film, when the meddling father-in-law returns to the village and the whole family joins him for a party. But, of course, *City Life* is only posing as a pro-ruralist film: its conservative message actually concerns the conflation of Catholic tradition (especially

FIGURE 3.5 *Village Priest, Agustín, Luchy in Pearls amd Gusty.* City Life is not for Me *(*La ciudad no es para mí *Lazaga 1966)*

regarding Luchy's role as a faithful wife and dutiful mother) and capitalist modernity. Thus Gusty and his family return to the village at the end of the film not to stay, but as rural tourists, whose family unity and smart clothes (Luchy herself is accessorized in pearls) connote the successful conflation of traditional social mores with their new membership of the middle class. Noting that the 'mid-1960s spectator [of *City Life*] most likely had much direct experience with the migratory wave that moved 3.8 million Spaniards to the cities between 1951 and 1970' (2002, 75), Nathan Richardson argues that the viewer too is implicated in this consumerist festival. Both the Madrid-based family and the audience become tourist consumers of the village:

> *La ciudad no es para mí* interpellated Spanish citizens as modernization-friendly consumers who could appreciate the market value of the rural. While feigning criticism of the consumer driven metropolis and superficially celebrating a premodern rural lifestyle, Lazaga's film, in fact slew the spectre of the flesh-and-blood *paleto* and the anticonsumerist ontology that he represented, positing in his stead the figure of the new consuming Spaniard. (2002, 86)

This portrait of consumerism is also clear in the treatment of food. Once again apparent and actual meanings are layered upon each other through mise en scène. Thus food is an immediately obvious symbol of the divide between rural and urban life that the film apparently illustrates, but in fact demolishes. On his arrival in the city, the hick carries crusty bread, rustic charcuterie and cheese, a *porrón* (wine skin) and a pair of chickens to be slaughtered for the freshest stew and broth. Meanwhile the Madrid family maid complains that the family rarely eat together, and when they do, favour tinned and frozen food. The uproarious sequence of the tea party for Luchy's new friends the marquesses (a brief performance by María Luisa Ponte and Margot Cottens on top comic form) moves the role played by gastronomy along another stage, for the afternoon tea with dainty pastries represents social ascendance rather than country and city. But rather than deepen the divide between a lump of village chorizo gleefully hacked off with a penknife by Tío Agustín and the dainty cheesecake half-eaten by a dieting marquess, *City Life* closes it. By the end of the film, the Madrid family return to the village as tourists, and varied gastronomic options are conflated as so many consumer choices. Richardson, again, highlights the 'veritable tourist pitch of rural products' at the end of the film (2002, 84). Thus Luchy may choose American-style cheesecake in Madrid or local cheese in Calacierva: both consumer choices represent her membership of the middle class.

Marisol's Four Weddings (Las cuatro bodas de Marisol* Lucia 1967)

No account of the rise of the middle class and middlebrow culture in 1960s Spain would be complete without Marisol. Her biographer writes that she was, 'Alongside the bullfighter El Cordobés and Spain's premier football club, Real Madrid, the cultural measure of the times' (quoted and translated by Evans 2004, 133). Marisol embodied, like Paco Martínez Soria, the enormously-popular, commercial, conservative film comedy of late Francoism. Both *City Life*, and *Marisol's Four Weddings* are especially successful examples of the ability of the VCE, in its generically preferred mode of comedy, to adapt old formulae to new conditions. In the case of the 'paleto' sub-genre, this involved, as we have seen, using the age-old conceit of country versus city, and moulding it to explore the new middle class and their new middlebrow consumption – all the while retaining traditional patriarchal values. In the Marisol films, conservative comedy is aligned with the folkloric musical, perhaps the most durable of all Spanish genres (see the analysis of *The Fair of the Dove* [*La verbena de la paloma*] in Chapter 1). The result was an incredibly successful formula whereby Marisol plays a bubbly blonde, whose narrative function is to smooth out social differences and tensions, and musical one is to perform a series of songs, ranging from flamenco to pop. This may also seem harmless enough, but in political terms, Marisol's films, like Soria's, also perform the insidious double manoeuvre of rejoicing in modernity while reinforcing tradition. Thus in *Four Weddings*, social mobility and an openness to foreign attitudes dance hand-in-hand, in Lucia's busy, brightly-coloured frame,[24] with the old Francoist chestnuts of patriarchy and nationalism. It is, in Núria Triana-Toribio's felicitous allusion to contemporary consumerism and marketing, a 'new "packaging" of old values' (2003, 87). It is not, writes Tatjana Pavlovic in her defence of the academic study of popular film, to be 'disregarded as representative of the Francoist cultural and ideological agenda. Far from being some sort of pedagogical tool of indoctrination,' she reminds us, 'films reveal tensions between tradition/modernity and immobility/movement' (2011, 116).

While mise en scène was central to the analysis of the tensions of *City Life*, it is inevitable that exploring the tensions of a Marisol film should involve a star study. This is especially the case with regards the relatively late *Four Weddings* of 1967. Born in 1948, Marisol started out as a child star, like Joselito and Pablito Calvo before her in the Spanish context and Shirley Temple in Hollywood. Manufactured and marketed by the producer Manuel J. Goyanes,[25] she was launched with the instantly successful *A Ray of Light** (*Un rayo de luz*) of 1960 (directed by Luis Lucia). After twelve films and a TV series made over an intensive decade in which Marisol matured from a still infantile 12 to a young adult, the actress rebelled, reclaimed her birth name Pepa Flores, began making more socially-committed films with directors like Juan Antonio Bardem and Mario Camus, and divorced Goyanes's son Carlos, with whom she had been persuaded into a marriage of convenience in 1969.

Four Weddings, Marisol's ninth feature, is characterized by problematic maturity. It is perhaps surprising to learn that this was Marisol's most successful film ever according to the measure of audience figures,[26] for by then the formula had become somewhat stale. By 1967, Marisol was such a household name that she simply played a fictional version of her 'self', as announced in the title. This fictional signifier 'Marisol' refers to a supposedly actual 'Marisol' who is in fact no less fabricated, as the history of her 'creation' by Goyanes through 'cultivation, sophistication and modernization' (Pavlovic 2011, 127) reveals. The whole enterprise of *Four Weddings* is thus self-reflexive, but, without the self-consciousness of art cinema, there is no critical purpose. Unmoored from a referent, *Four Weddings* spins off into a whirling spiral of clichés, becoming, as Pavlovic writes in relation to the entire Marisol construct: 'an antecedent of postmodern simulacra and pure outwardness' (2011, 127).

The star's maturity also brings about a shift in focus, which in broad strokes might be described as a move from sexuality to social mobility. On the early films, Peter Evans is right to remind us, however, that 'To overplay the sexual frisson [...] would undeniably be to detract from their many other engrossing features, to underestimate their appeal to innocence, their flickering of rebellion as well as their endorsement of tradition' (2004, 133). Nonetheless, of the seven 'recurrent themes' that Pavlovic helpfully lists in relation to the cycle, it is the 'presence of the erotic and sexual elements displaced on the child' (2011, 126) that seems to provide the key to their fascination. For both contemporary chroniclers Francisco Umbral and Manuel Vicent, and later critics Evans and Pavlovic, Marisol's Lolita effect is unsettling, and interestingly skews the festive treatment of tradition and modernity in the otherwise utopian plots (Evans 2004, 133–40; Pavlovic 2011, 128–9). Ironically, when the explicit concerns of the plot shift to heterosexual adult romance, as announced in the title of the 1967 film, the fascination fades. When the adult performer refers back to herself as a child, there is no such disturbing power. The references even run the risk of clichés of schoolgirl soft porn, as in one flashback sequence of *Four Weddings* where adult Marisol dresses up in uniform at an English boarding school.

What emerges as central in the late *Four Weddings* is another theme characteristic of the cycle, identified by Pavlovic as 'class mobility' (2011, 126). The star's biography is particularly relevant to this aspect, as it was well-known that Flores, in becoming Marisol, socially-climbed from the humble neighbourhood of Capuchinos in Málaga to stardom, when her parents allowed her to go to Madrid with Goyanes in exchange for 40,000 pesetas (Evans 2004, 130). This biographical detail of Marisol's own movement into the middle class made her repeated performance of the rags-to-riches formula newly resonant to 1960s audiences despite its hackneyed familiarity. In fact, in many of her films she represented aristocratic circles (*A Ray of Light* [*Un rayo de luz* Lucia 1960]; *Lottery** [*Tómbola* Lucia 1962]) and in others, impoverished ones (*Marisol Goes to Río** [*Marisol rumbo a Río* Palacios, 1963]), but it was the middle-class label that stuck.[27] *Find That Girl* (*Búsqueme a esa chica* Palacios 1964) – fittingly, her most commercially-successful film – is perhaps responsible for this cementing together of fiction and reality, for in it Marisol plays a working-class girl who is discovered and enriched by an American producer and thus moves into the middle class. Considering all her Goyanes films, however, both Triana-Toribio and Pavlovic nuance this 'middle-class' label. For Triana-Torbio, 'she hovers between classes [...] in transition from one to another, retaining values and tastes associated with the one as she progresses into the other' (2003, 90); Pavlovic suggests a model of 'porous boundaries and continual movements between different social strata. The erroneous impression that Marisol exemplifies solely middle-class settings comes from her ability to swiftly move from one milieu to another' (2011, 127).

Four Weddings combines both the 'natural' affiliation of Marisol and the middle class that matches the actress's off-screen trajectory, and the 'transition' and 'movement' between strata that characterize her performances on-screen. An unsympathetic reading of the film's contrived and convoluted plot, in which Marisol puts the devotion of her American fiancé to the test by introducing, via flashbacks, three former boyfriends, is that it is no more than a lazy repetition of the formula that also cashes in on the off-screen media speculation about the actress's love life and marriage possibilities. Alternatively, although chronologically unacceptable, the film's light-hearted treatment of the on-screen Marisol's difficulties with the excessively intrusive press could be read as prescient of the off-screen actress's later denunciation of Goyanes and the media for her stolen childhood and adolescence.[28] Furthermore, at the same time as the on-screen Marisol fictionally struggles to ascertain whether the film director's devotion is genuine, or just a media-orientated contrivance, off-screen, Goyanes was plotting the marriage of convenience of the star to his son. 'Una española no se divorcia' (A Spanish woman doesn't get divorced) pronounces the on-screen Marisol in an early scene of the film. It is a pronouncment that stages, through the very person of the actress, the collision of bombastic Francoist ideology with the painful reality: while in the 1960s the regime still insisted on racist religious 'difference', by the 1970s Pepa Flores would endure failed marriage and divorce.

FIGURE 3.6 *'A Spanish Woman Doesn't Get Divorced.' Marisol and Frank Moore.* Marisol's Four Weddings *(*Las cuatro bodas de Marisol *Lucia 1967)*

Read through the lens of social mobility, *Four Weddings*'s four potential 'weddings' offer four scenarios for exploring, confirming and, ultimately, bolstering the new Spanish middle class. The absurd plot of Marisol's four fiancés engineers encounters with aristocratic Europe, through *ye-yé* pop-singer and son of the Scottish laird Marvin; working-class rural Spain, through penniless orphan and aspiring bullfighter Rafael; religion and missionary work through French atheist and médecin-sans-frontières Pierre; and American modernity, through film director Frank Moore, whom Marisol eventually marries. These four scenarios are all set in the narrative frame of Marisol's 'real' life as a wealthy, middle-class film actress. She works and lives with her mother (the merry widow who is the source of many of the best wise cracks of the film), and the luxury of their dress and home furnishings display the distinctive choices that Bourdieu reminds us characterize those keen to confirm new membership of the middle class.

The first three fiancés are met in flashback. First, we find Marisol in a stereotypical Britain, whose locations include a boarding school, complete with phlegmatic teachers, suits of armour, and a headmistress still obsessed with the Empire, at which Marisol performs pop number 'Johnny'[29] in English. At an underground disco bar our feisty songstress then sings popular song 'La tarara' in Spanish, but gives the traditional piece a modern twist by performing it alongside her new *ye-yé* boyfriend and his British band 'The Green Dragons'. She then visits with him the stately home of his father, a rotund, kilt-wearing Scot, and ends up at the court of the Queen of England. The point of all this extravagant cliché is conflation: just as the Franco regime sold Spain as a tourist destination that was 'different' while trying to join the European Community as a European country that was the 'same', so Marisol may speak and sing in English, but is still 'Spanish' enough to demand Elizabeth II return Gibraltar to Spain! Here, then, is mobile Marisol in class transition: able to speak English like her contemporaries seeking class mobility through education, she is at home with the aristocracy but has retained the cheeky humour of the picaresque.

In the second flashback, Spain is subject to the same clichéd treatment as Britain, which was perhaps surprisingly tolerated by national audiences. On her Uncle's bull-rearing ranch, our heroine is aligned through family ties with the landowning wealthy, but her love interest is a member of the rural poor, who dreams of escape through bullfighting. This being popular comedy rather than the NCE, the emphasis is all on what Pavlović describes as 'lack of social conflict' and 'fantasy and pleasure' (2011, 126), so Marisol and Rafael fall in love, the impoverished labourers are treated to a ham roll in the boss's parlour, the novice bullfighter gets his break, and the absurdity of all these unlikely alliances and outcomes is danced away through Marisol's performance of 'Belén, Belén', where all may unite in admiration of the blonde flamenco-dancer.

Perhaps it is the absence of a song and dance number that lays bare the absurdity of the third flashback and fiancé, an outrageously self-indulgent foray into the Franco cinematic sub-genre of the missionary film ('cine con curas'). The sequence is of interest for exemplifying the demoted role of religion by 1967 in Spain, also noted by Pavlovic (2011, 126–8), for Lucia solves the problem of exploring Marisol's love interests while exalting the country's mission as the 'reserva espiritual de Europa' (spiritual reserve of Europe) thus: Marisol visits the jungle and incites the passion of the atheist French doctor while dressed as a nun, but, in fact, she is on the set of a missionary film where she stars as Marisol. Again, the referent 'Marisol' is lost in this vortex of ridiculous imitation.

By the film's resolution, Marisol has become a kind of go-between, scurrying between the Spanish and the foreign, the popular and the aristocratic, the secular and the religious. For Triana-Toribio, this suggests 'hovering' and 'transition' between classes (2003, 90); for Pavlovic 'porousness' and 'movement' (2011, 127). I would suggest, alternatively, that this late film points to a schizophrenia at the heart of middle-class identity in the 1960s, whereby seeming opposites are forever reconciled in the person of Marisol. Fittingly, then, the ending of the film is an act of conflation. After a traditional rustic date with Moore trout-fishing, Spanish Marisol marries the American director, then flies off into the sunset with him in a glamourously-modern privately-chartered aeroplane. 'The hybrid essence of Marisol', writes Evans, is an 'affirmation of traditional Spanishness as well as of American-style modernity' (2004, 137). By the 1970s the 'hybridity' of the persona would unravel into a series of untenable contradictions, both on-screen and off, but the 1960s closes with middle-class Marisol, the emblem, in popular film, of Spain's rushed modernity.

Notes

1 The subtitle is taken from Waldo de Mier's two books of the same name, published 1954 and 1964 (Pavlovic 2011, 6).

2 See García Ochoa 2012 on the significance of the car in Carlos Saura's 1967 *Peppermint frappé*, in which it becomes particularly aligned with questions of masculinity. My thanks to Peter Evans for this reference.

3 Bernard Bentley's description of Berlanga, Fenán Gómez and Juan Antonio Bardem in this period (2008, 176).

4 See the interview with Berlanga on the 'Extras' of the DVD *Plácido* distributed by newspaper *El País* 'Un País de Cine' in 2003.

5 I owe this insight to Dominic Keown.

6 Peter Evans notes Pascual's name ironically recalls the Paschal lamb (2000, 218, 220).

7 This epigraph precedes Part One of the novel (J. A. Zunzunegui 1960, 11–12). The epigraph for Part Two is from Quevedo (1960, 149); for Part Three, Sartre (1960, 315).

8 This improves on the novel's 'La guapa del Dos De Mayo' (The Beauty of Dos de Mayo Square) (1960, 19).

9 Thomas Deveny drew out the significance of this narrative in Spanish cinema in *Cain on Screen* (1993), a work that has been criticized for reductionism (e.g. S. Zunzunegui 1999).

10 Zunzunegui's novel implies that back-street abortion was easily available (1960, 80–1).

11 *L'avventura* was screened at the Madrid Filmoteca in 1963, but not given general distribution on Spanish screens until 1969 (Monterde 2003, 106). This lack of availability surely explains why the NCE directors turned to earlier models.

12 A film school set up by the Fascist government in the 1935, it is nonetheless associated with nurturing dissident talent. The Spanish equivalent in Madrid functioned similarly. Grau won a grant from the Spanish government to study at the Centro, which he shared with Antonio Pérez Olea, composer for *Summer Night* (accompanying notes to *Il Peccato: noche de verano* CD, released by Quartet Records 2011, 2).

13 It only attracted 141,000 spectators.

14 Tom Whittaker is no doubt right to observe that the contribution of the young producer 'does not appear to be creative in any way' (2011, 152).

15 Castilian is spoken by the middle-class groups; Catalan is only heard in snippets and only spoken by workers.

16 Domènec Font notes that both the topography (Cadaqués and the Costa Brava) looks forward to the Barcelona School, and that some of the School's future members were collaborators: Carles Durám; Annie Settimo and Joaquim Jordá (2003, 186).

17 I transcribe titles and words directly from the film.

18 Raimón was key to the 'Nova Cançó' (New Song), the musical movement that opposed Francoism through the Catalan language.

19 Jay Beck and Vicente Rodríguez Ortega note that early studies of genre in Spanish film use 'sub-genre' as a term 'to classify Spanish genre filmmaking as sub-par to American and European genres, rather than as an internal division within a larger genre's structure' (2008, 5).

20 This sub-genre is parodied in *Spaniards in Paris* (*Españolas en París* Bodegas 1971): see Chapter 4.

21 The technical crew included an art department of three (Luciano Arroyo, Tomás Fernández, Jesús Mateos), set decorator (Antonio Simont), costume design (Humberto Cornejo and Matías Montero Nanette), and makeup (Paloma Fernández and María Elena García)

22 Bourdieu's analysis of class and taste is based on a survey of French social mores carried out in a period contemporary with this film, 1963 (1999, 503); *Distinction* was first published in 1979.

23 Some fun is also had with Tío Agustín's Aragonese vocabulary and accent, as opposed to the more neutral Castilian of his young family because, as Celia Martín notes, in 1960s Spain 'speaking with a regional accent was considered *provinciano* and *retrasado* and also working class' (Martin 2003, 154–5).

24 Shot using Eastmancolor.

25 For full details of her biography, see Evans 2004, 129–33.

26 It attracted 2,506,832 spectators. *Find That Girl* (*Búsqueme a esa chica*) was more commercially successful, taking the equivalent of 291, 111.58 euros.

27 'Marisol was so successful as a fabricated middle-class role model for Spanish children that she was employed to advertise the most popular doll at the time, *Mariquita Pérez*' (Martin 2003, 155).

28 Evans notes that the earlier *Carola by Day, Carola by Night** (*Carola de día, Carola de noche*) also offered a 'self-conscious image of the star' (2004, 140).

29 Musical numbers are composed by Fernando Arbex and Adolfo Waitzman, except 'Belén Belén' by Peret, who performs alongside Marisol and 'La tarara', a popular song in an arrangement here by Aldonso Sainz.

4

The 'Third Way' and the Spanish Middlebrow Film in the 1970s

Whether one consults political accounts or national cinema histories, it is hard to get away from the polarized narrative of 1970s Spain as a decade of extremes. Take the gateway dates of 1970 and 1980. In politics, we shift from repressive dictatorship – Franco's old age did not stop him signing death sentences months before his own passing (Preston 1993, 775–6) – to constitutional monarchy and parliamentary democracy. In culture, the shift is no less pronounced. If we take the case of censorship, 1970 saw a return to a hard-line approach after the failure of the tentative 'opening up' of the 1960s. By 1980, censorship had been abolished and replaced by a system of rating (1977) and the Spanish market was flooded with previously banned material. Within these rarified contexts of censorship and freedom, polarized tendencies in cinema have often been emphasized. First, auteur film, which, by the 1970s, was highly politicized and aesthetically challenging, included what is still considered the masterpiece of the tradition, Víctor Erice's *The Spirit of the Beehive* (*El espíritu de la colmena* 1973). By 1980 the auteurist tendency also included Pedro Almodóvar's feature début, *Pepi, Luci, Bom and Other Girls on the Heap* (*Pepi, Luci, Bom y otras chicas del montón*), which was similarly experimental in aesthetics, but defiantly turned away from an overt treatment of politics. On the other hand, popular cinema continued in the vein of the VCE examined in the previous chapter, with *Landismo* films – named after the actor Alfredo Landa – a noteworthy high and low. *Thou Shalt not Covet Thy Fifth Floor Neighbour* (*No desearás al vecino del quinto* Fernández 1970), for example, was the most commercially successful Spanish film of the whole of the dictatorship era (Jordan 2005, 83), but the sleazy predictability of the subgenre in which Landa plays a repressed male has made these films a national embarrassment (though they have been recently reassessed Triana Toribio 2003, 100–4; Jordan 2003).

Neat, binary accounts rarely sustain closer scrutiny, and just as historians have revised Whiggish accounts of Spain's transition to democracy, noting that the 'desencanto' (disenchantment) began with democracy and that the transition may still not yet be complete (Vilarós 1998a; Molinero 2008), so cultural commentators too have introduced nuance and shades of grey. Censorship is a good example of this revision. The *Landismo* films themselves reveal that commercial cinema anticipated the abolition of censorship by broaching previously taboo subjects, especially regarding sexuality, as early as 1970 – though the treatment is both clichéd and timid. In this vein Esteve Riambau goes as far as affirming that the end of censorship in fact meant 'No news for genre cinema' (2000, 182). If art cinema took advantage of increased freedom, most notably in the treatment of sex and violence, film historians have emphasized that other topics, like questioning the army, monarchy and police, remained taboo (Trenzado Romero 1999, 89–91). This explains why Pilar Miró faced a military court and possible jail sentence for criticizing the Guardia Civil – albeit in a pre-Franco setting – in the post-Censorship *The Cuenca Crime* (*El crimen de Cuenca* 1979).[1]

In a similarly revisionist spirit, this chapter places the death of one man in 1975 and the alteration of one piece of legislation in 1977 in the background, while bringing to the fore continuities with events in previous and subsequent decades. In particular, the social mobility unleashed in Spain in the 1960s is of greater importance to the films under discussion than the death of Franco (but not Francoism) and the (supposed) abolition of censorship. Across multiple tendencies and genres, the 1960s films discussed responded to social mobility by chronicling the struggle to achieve it, as well as portraying the attitudes and activities of the new middle classes, including middlebrow consumption. Since pinpointing something as elusive as the rise of a new class is fraught with difficulty, I propose a more modest 'shift' that seems to occur more or less in parallel with the change of decade. This 'shift' describes the difference between 1960s cinema, when, as we have seen, auteurist and popular films alike take middle-class characters and middlebrow consumption as their subject matter, and 1970s cinema, when the middle classes become the audiences who consumed films that were themselves middlebrow.[2]

In arguing for the emergence of a new audience for Spanish cinema, and for the development of a new kind of film for their consumption, I am retracing the steps of a number of key film professionals in the period. Every history of Spanish cinema mentions the 'Tercera Vía' (Third Way) tendency of Spanish cinema of the early 1970s, but few argue for its influence beyond that period. A detailed but narrow definition of the Third Way is provided by

Casimiro Torreiro, for whom the label describes the dozen or so features[3] that resulted from the collaboration of a group of politically progressive, and in some cases left-wing, professionals, including producer José Luis Dibildos, owner of Ágata Films (who also usually contributed to the script), scriptwriter and future director José Luis Garci, directors Roberto Bodegas and Antonio Drove (both of whom had attended the state film school), actors like Ana Belén, plus the contribution of notable artists like José Agustín Goytisolo and Paco Ibáñez (1995a, 359). Torreiro notes that the Third Way

> tried to distance itself from the more coarse commercial cinema and more voluntarily auteurist and metaphorical cinema. Dibildos's aim [...] was no other than to supply products to an urban middle class that was neglected by commercial cinema [...], was by then enjoying a European standard of living, and which, very shortly afterwards, would form the electoral base of Suárez's UCD. (1995a, 360)

The Third Way was a victim of bad timing, for the early 1970s were the twilight years of the regime, quickly forgotten in a Spain looking to the vertiginous possibilities of the present as the country shifted from dictatorship to democracy after the momentous death of 1975. Torreiro, writing in a key history of Spanish cinema,[4] describes the films as 'rapidly eclipsed' (1995a, 361), an interpretation that has proved influential thereafter. Some critics have connected the Third Way to later films of the decade, but by re-considering it as a middlebrow trend, this, and the remaining chapters of this book aim to show that, in the various of forms of the Mirovian film, the *cine social* and heritage cinema, its influence resonates throughout the period stretching from 1970 to today.

The 'middlebrow' label allows us both to describe the ways these films were in-between, and connect them to similar trends in post-1970s Spanish cinema. The role of Dibildos as producer connects in interesting ways with both the auteurist and commercial strands from which he differentiated his product. Like legendary dissident producer Elías Querejeta, Dibildos was creatively involved with the film through scriptwriting and achieved aesthetic quality and continuity through a dedicated 'team', not entirely distinct from Querejeta's famous 'family' of collaborators. If, for Querejeta, politics came first in this period, Dibildos was, like commercial producers, responsive to the market. And if this process of seeking out a niche audience and ensuring a quality product may sound a rather obvious production strategy today, we must remember that, in Spanish cinema of this period, such responsiveness to the audience was uniquely associated with popular film.

Moving to the texts of the films themselves, the in-betweenness of the middlebrow is confirmed. On the one hand, publicity material for Third-Way films suggests an immediate, unfortunate connection with contemporary sleazy cinema. *Spaniards in Paris* (*Españolas en París* Bodegas 1971) and *The New Spaniards* (*Los nuevos españoles* Bodegas 1974), for example, feature clichéd images of scantily-clad women on their promotional material. This is no more than crass marketing, for both films have little interest in this area,[5] and instead gently question contemporary concerns like Spanish émigré workers, unwanted pregnancy and abortion (*Spaniards in Paris*), and contemporary capitalism (*The New Spaniards*), relatively serious subjects treated in the relatively unchallenging, light-hearted manners of melodrama in the first film, and comedy in the second. *Spaniards in Paris*, moreover, features the high-culture reference of a song written by Goytisolo sung by Ibáñez. The Third-Way mix may therefore be summarized as offering serious (but not challenging) subjects; some high-culture references; quality actors and production values; and an accessible form, which, in these early 1970s Dibildos examples, has been identified by Riambau as a generic adherence to classic North-American comedy (2000, 184). This in-betweenness has also been described by Marta Hernández as 'commercial cinema plus auteur cinema divided by two' (quoted in Torreiro 1995a, 361). This book proposes that the 'middlebrow' is a better way of describing this fusion of opposites and the present, and remaining, chapters contend that this middlebrow model of Third-Way cinema transcends the uninspiring context of the dying days of Francoism, and serves as a model for textual analysis for Spanish cinema to this day.

This process of extending the influence of the Third Way has begun with some critics writing after Torreiro in 1995. Riambau, for instance, connects it with the 1970s work of Manuel Summers – like Bodegas and Drove, an ex-film school student – the production company Kalender Films, 1970s literary adaptations of classic novels, and the directorial career of Garci, especially in *Unfinished Business* (*Asignatura pendiente* 1977) (2000, 185–6). Dibildos's former scriptwriter Garci became, for Riambau, the 'mouthpiece for a reformulation of the Third Way after the disappearance of the dictator' (2000, 186). In the final chapters of this book I will argue for further reformulations. In the present chapter, I partly follow Riambau in selecting six representative middlebrow texts, but I am guided by the potential for textual analysis according to the middlebrow model, rather than narrow definitions of the Third Way.

Proceeding in a broadly chronological fashion I begin not with Dibildos, but in fact with two literary adaptations that exemplify the four strands of middlebrow fabric identified: serious subjects; high-culture references; high production values and accessibility. This critical approach leads to a provocative interpretation of a film commonly considered to sit happily in the auteurist tradition: Luis Buñuel's 1970 adaptation of Galdós's *Tristana*. A movie that usually rubs shoulders with other works in the pantheon of work of Spain's greatest auteur, I place it here with another great Galdós adaptation, this one quickly and regrettably forgotten, Pedro Olea's *Tormento* (1974). These two sections of the chapter will set out precisely how the literary adaptation exemplifies the middlebrow. Next I turn to two examples that have been commonly subsumed into the Third-Way label, the forgotten Third-Way début film *Spaniards in Paris* (Bodegas 1971) and the remarkable *My Dearest Señorita* (*Mi querida señorita* Armiñán, 1972), the subject of sustained interest thanks to its interlinking of gender and society (Hueso 1997, 691). Following Riambau, I consider finally *Unfinished Business* and *Daddy's War* (*La guerra de papá* Mercero 1977), two films that look forward to the Mirovian cinema that will be the subject of Chapter 6.

Tristana (Buñuel 1970)

A Buñuel film can be relied upon to provoke strong reactions in its audiences – whether official offices of the state, fellow film professionals, journalists and specialist critics, or the wider public. Both of the features Buñuel made in Spain, *Viridiana* of 1961 and *Tristana* of 1970, were welcomed, enjoyed and rejected in equal measure. Anti-Franco Spanish film professionals, like Carlos Saura, who met Buñuel in Cannes in 1959, and those involved with the dissident companies UNINCI and Films 59 that produced the film, enthusiastically welcomed Buñuel and looked forward to *Viridiana* being a milestone of the oppositional national cinema. The film was much enjoyed for its irreverence by audiences at Cannes where it was first screened and where it won the Golden Palm,[6] then vigorously rejected by the Franco regime after the Vatican's *Osservatore Romano* published an article objecting to that same irreverence. The rejection meant the film was retrospectively assigned Mexican nationality and banned in Spain for 16 years. With delicious timing it was first screened on 6 April 1977 – both Easter Saturday and the day the Spanish Communist Party was legalized – but it was not re-assigned Spanish nationality until 1982.

Nine years later *Tristana* too was welcomed, enjoyed and rejected. The desperate politics of opportunism in force as Francoism entered its twilight are the only explanation for the astonishing *volte face* performed by the regime with regards the filmmaker. After the censors rejected the script several times over the course of the 1960s, Buñuel returned to Franco's

Spain in 1969 after his producers threatened to pull the project completely and shoot in Portugal (Company 1997c, 676). The director of *Viridiana* was welcomed back ('tolerated and even welcomed by the authorities' according to Román Gubern [1981, 235]), and shot *Tristana* in Toledo in the autumn. The picture itself was likewise welcomed by the regime through the assignment of the 'Interés Especial' (Special Interest) subvention, then the award of the official prize of best Spanish picture of 1970 at the annual SNE, with further prizes for actors Fernando Rey and Lola Gaos, and the ultimate accolade of being selected as the Spanish entry to the Oscars for the best foreign language film.[7] The censored press, gagged with regards any mention of *Viridiana*, was conversely allowed to celebrate *Tristana*,[8] and audience figures of nearly 2 million viewers in Spain (which made the equivalent of 400,000 euros) suggest a film that successfully resonated with the public. In a reversal of the reception of *Viridiana*, the rejection this time came from anti-Franco film professionals, who believed Buñuel had sold out to the regime. Current and ex-students of the film school condemned the cosiness between Buñuel and the dictatorship in a pamphlet, comic and letter published in *Dirigido por* in 1975 (Company 1997c, 676). Further criticism was levelled at the apparent conventionality of the film. Charles Eidsvick in 1981 wrote that it 'slipped by the Spanish censors, international audiences, and even by critics as a somber, almost humourless study of the decline of two people – a film that is the most classically structured, accessible, and readily comprehensible of [Buñuel's] recent works' (quoted in Kinder 1993, 315); Marsha Kinder in 1993 that 'both the form and content were widely perceived as fairly conventional and realistic' (314); and Rob Stone in 2002 that on its surface was a 'dull veneer of respectability' (57). I would suggest that these various references to 'accessibility', 'comprehensibility', 'conventionality', 'realism' and 'respectability' may be summarized as middlebrow.

The very suggestion of a middlebrow Buñuel has been a red rag to the bull of Buñuel-auteur studies. Víctor Fuentes (2000, 148) exemplifies the outrage: 'Apparently, after the experimental, non-realist *Milky Way*, Buñuel's formal restraint in *Tristana* could be interpreted as a step backwards. But let's not fool ourselves'. For Ángel Fernández-Santos *Tristana* in fact 'sets off a bomb with delayed effect' (quoted in Fuentes 2000, 148). Critics have rallied to the rescue of a film that is only apparently middlebrow, stressing that below the surface conventionality lies the Buñuel we know and love. Bernard Bentley summarizes the multiple approaches thus: 'While discreetly sharing the conventions of the horror film, *Tristana* has been read as a political allegory [...], a social criticism [...], an indictment of women's situation [...], and a psychoanalytic discourse [...]' (2008, 181).[9]

What I offer in this section is something of a contrary counter-reading.

The rescue of *Tristana* by auteurist criticism is highly persuasive, and its varied nature typical of a director who always managed to provoke an array of reactions in his audiences – sometimes opposite ones simultaneously.[10] Including *Tristana* in a history of Spanish cinema as an example of one of the four models of critique set out by Bentley is tempting, but something niggles regarding the film's middlebrow elements. If we don't acknowledge those elements, we are unable to acknowledge their influence on Spanish film of the early 1970s in the form of the literary adaptations boom. Katherine Kovács's observation in 1983 that 'It would be difficult to find direct evidence of Buñuel's influence on contemporary cinematographic trends' in Spain (quoted in Hopewell 1986, 163) only holds if one only seeks auteurist influence. I argue that the influence did exist if we consider the middlebrow tradition. If, in the final analysis, it is critically untenable to have it both ways – Buñuel as both dissident auteur, yet also as source of middlebrow influence – my contrary re-reading of the middlebrow elements of *Tristana* at least makes it possible to account for cinematic evolution in Spanish cinema of the period.

Buñuel critics are familiar with the need to treat carefully interviews and quotes by the director about his art. Nonetheless, the following declaration is interesting in this context: 'With Tristana I made a mistake. I said: "It will be a great success in Spain. The fat ladies and the old folks will come and they'll like it"' (quoted in Fuentes 2000, 151). Fuentes underlines the irony of the comment: '[Buñuel] knew very well that he would be wrong, that the ladies in their jewels and the rich old men, protected – though now with some degree of uncertainty – by the clergy and the Civil Guard in the final days of Francoism, couldn't like a film in which their funeral was conducted over an orthopaedic leg' (2000, 151). Viewing figures suggest, on the other hand, that Buñuel was double-bluffing, for the film did connect with this audience. However ironically deployed, and however resoundingly undermined by the political elements (Fuentes 2000, 148–51), Freudian elements (Labanyi 1999) and Galdosian formal disruption (Faulkner 2004, 148–62), the middlebrow, or Third-Way mix, is relevant to *Tristana*, and it is these middlebrow elements that would be repeated in the subsequent literary-adaptation boom.

From the outset, the film apparently flatters the viewer with a fusion of high-culture references and an accessible form. First, the credits roll to an establishing shot of a cityscape of Toledo that recalls venerable Renaissance artist and Toledo resident El Greco's treatment of the subject (viewers may miss, though subsequent critics have admired, the fact that the shabbier side of the city is actually shown by Buñuel compared to El Greco [Edwards 1982, 226]). Audiences who knew the director's oeuvre may connect this intertextual reference to an act of self-referentiality to the rest of Buñuel's filmography,[11] or indeed to the outrageous use of pictorial intertexts of

Viridiana (including, most infamously, Leonardo De Vinci's The Last Supper), but for an audience denied access to Buñuel's earlier films, like the Spanish audience of 1970, the pictorial intertext is a middlebrow fusion of accessibility and cultural homage. Characterization and mise en scène apparently continue along middlebrow lines. Our meeting with Don Lope demonstrates this point. Gone is the inscrutability of Paco Rabal's Nazarín in Buñuel's 1958 adaptation of the homonymous Galdós novel. Don Lope, as Robert Havard pointed out in 1982, is characterized by deploying the accessible conventions of the eighteenth-century Spanish exempla (69). Two such exempla are enough to summarize Lope's characterization as gentleman-yet-libertine of another age. First, as Don Juan, he leers at a young woman in the street; immediately after, as a Don Quijote, he doffs his hat at a bourgeois mother. The effect, again, is to flatter the viewer through the apparent accessibility of character, which involves, but is not dependent upon, at least four high-brow literary intertexts: the exemplum, Don Juan, Don Quijote, and of course, Galdós's original novel. High-brow pictorial and literary intertexts are thus deployed apparently to enable accessibility in the establishing shot and characterization, a fusion of high-cultural references and accessibility best described as middlebrow.

Middlebrow fusion also occurs in the area of mise en scène. Here, the two demonstrably, but only moderately, serious subjects of the narrative of Galdós's original and the changed historical setting are evoked through carefully-crafted mise en scène (Buñuel exchanges Galdós's 1890s for the period 1929–35, which includes the Primo de Rivera dictatorship and the Second Republic). The fusion of moderately serious subject matter with

FIGURE 4.1 *Don Lope as Don Juan and Don Quijote.* Tristana *(Buñuel 1970)*

quality production values likewise points to the middlebrow. Thus Buñuel, shooting in colour, adopts a sepia palette of brown and greys, and pays minute attention to objects (only some of which are imbued with narrative meaning, like the slippers that refer to Lope's age [a detail taken from Galdós [Pérez Galdós 1982, 67]) Both inside and outside the home, Buñuel presents a 'Hispanic mise en scène that has in large part now disappeared' (Fuentes 2000, 150), which includes the decoration of Lope's home, Lope and Tristana's dress, the recreated ambience of the café 'tertulia', food like the dish of 'migas' (bread crumbs) and the marrons glacés, and the brazier wheel under the table at home and the barquero wheel at the park – linked, for no apparent reason other than visual pleasure, by a graphic match (Labanyi 1999, 90). These are the characteristics of mise en scène associated with the (often hated) middlebrow period drama, though Fuentes alternatively explains their presence through Buñuel's biography: returning to Spain he displays 'the nostalgia of the exile' (2000, 151).

In this tentative re-reading of *Tristana* as middlebrow, Buñuel flatters his audience through the apparent transparency of his storytelling (many critics have observed the surprising sequential accessibility of *Tristana* as opposed to the disrupted and disruptive structure of *Milky Way* that immediately precedes it [e.g. Evans 1991, 91]). This is reinforced by the apparent accessibility of characterization and the apparent decipherability of highly-crafted mise en scène. Through historical setting and literary source *Tristana* might be linked to tentative critique rather than open controversy. Buñuel's shift of Galdós's setting to the period preceding the Civil War is challenging, but falls short of tackling the conflict itself. Turning to *Tristana* as a literary adaptation, Buñuel apparently offers an accessible version of the high-cultural reference of Galdós. This novelist may have been regarded with suspicion as a liberal writer in earlier decades of the dictatorship, but by 1970, the 50-year anniversary of Galdós's death, there was official rehabilitation in some quarters (see, for example, the comments of film censors in 1969 [quoted in R. Navarrete 2003, 80]). The timing of the adaptation to coincide with the anniversary allowed suspicious anti-Franco critics to link Buñuel's work to Francoist opportunism. In 1971, Francisco Aranda pointed out in an introduction to an English translation of the script that Galdós was 'a Liberal of the past century [who] was beginning to be officially praised. His work, till recently considered dangerous, was now acceptable with the "new look" the Government wanted to give their future activities' (1971, 6). However, it should be pointed out that Buñuel had tried to adapt *Tristana* in Spain throughout the 1960s (it was refused by the censors in 1962 and 1963): he had no interest in the regime's convenient commemoration of the author.

Buñuel purists may be appalled by a reading that lingers on carefully-crafted mise en scène rather than Tristana's Freudian nightmare of Lope's severed head; that acknowledges narrative accessibility, rather than the subtle and tricky wrong-footing of the viewer that Buñuel inherited from Galdós's prose. The charge of collusion with an opportunist regime is clearly unfair. Too much is lost, no doubt. However, it was the middlebrow Buñuel – not the Freudian Surrealist, or the artful narrator – that inspired producers seeking new middlebrow products for new middle-class audiences in the period. Rather than the familiar refrain of 'difference' 'exception' and 'lost opportunity' that usually accompanies mentions of Buñuel in histories of Spanish cinema (summarized in Faulkner 2013), this reading allows us to observe similarity and continuity, for *Tristana* was followed by both the literary adaptation mini-boom, and the Third Way.[12]

Tormento (Olea, 1974)

The mini-boom of classic literary adaptations triggered by *Tristana* in the early 1970s, like the Third Way that developed in parallel, was producer- rather than director-led. The potentially profitable connection between the new audience of Spain's recently-ascendant middle classes and middlebrow films was identified, and producers responded: Emiliano Piedra backed *Fortunata y Jacinta* (Galdós 1886–7; Fons 1970) and *La Regenta* (Alas 1884–5; Suárez 1974), both starring his wife Emma Penella; and José Frade backed *Tormento* (Galdós 1884; Olea 1974).[13] In these three cases, as in most of the others, the commissioned directors were the jobless graduates of Madrid's film school, for whom government subsidies had dried up.

José Enrique Monterde dismisses the cycle as another manifestation of the 'destape' (sleazy) cinema of the period, where the historical or social interest of the original novels is bypassed in favour of the scandalous subject matters like the love affair of a priest – to take *Tormento* as an example (1989, 50). Sleazy subjects do seem to obsess male producers in this period (like the publicity material for the Third Way discussed above, for which Dibildos was presumably responsible) – an aspect that today seems especially dated and embarrassing. However, the sleaze seems to obsess the critics too, who fail to see the rest of the film beyond it. *Tormento* is an especially good example of how mistaken this is, for the affair recounted in flashback between Amparo (played by Ana Belén) and the priest (Javier Escrivá) are the dullest sequences of the film, and the single soft-focus moment of passion between the two (which of course appears on the publicity material) is risibly contrived. In contrast, the screen crackles with wit whenever the undisputed protagonist,

Rosalía, appears, played by a splendid Conchita Velasco, whose sparkling performance is complemented by the stellar contribution of Paco Rabal in a secondary role as Agustín.

Far from another example of the embarrassing popular cinema of the period, *Tormento* brilliantly exemplifies the contemporary middlebrow, Third-Way trend. Buñuel, as we have seen, gestures towards the middlebrow, flattering the Spanish viewer of the 1970s, only gleefully to disrupt almost every sequence of the film through perverse tactics such as refusing to mark dream sequences as such, cutting the opening and closing frames (Aranda 1971, 10), and even playing key images backwards at the end of the picture, all of which, I have argued elsewhere, engineers a kind of figurative deafness, or disability in the spectator (2004, 153). José Frade and Pedro Olea are not interested in disruption, but take the same middlebrow matrix of a fusion of high production values, serious subject matter, high-culture references and accessible form, and take it in a particularly successful new direction. *Tormento* resonated with audiences, attracting over two million spectators, and with critics, winning best Spanish-language film award at the San Sebastián Film Festival, and three further prizes for Velasco.

With its highbrow literary intertext in Galdós and a demonstrable serious edge in its critique of the values of Restoration Spain, the key to *Tormento*'s success is its middlebrow fusion of these elements with high production values and accessibility. Although access to audience response to the film is restricted – only press reviews are available, and these were published in the censored press – those available at the Filmoteca Española show the importance of both Galdós and social critique. Galdós is key to reviewers hostile to the film because Olea changes the ending by explicitly verbalizing both Rosalía's annoyance and Agustín's extra-marital arrangement (Arroita Jauregui 1974, writing in *Arriba*; Ramos 1974, writing in *El Alcázar*). We may take this as moral conservatism, but, alternatively, it may be argued that invoking the question of fidelity between literary original and film version enables reviewers to display cultural capital by parading knowledge of the highbrow art. While the pro-regime press was outraged by the alteration of Galdós, a more progressive review uses the fidelity issue as a smokescreen to critique the current situation in Spain (López Sancho 1974, writing in the conservative but more open-minded *ABC*). Today, we can make explicit what was implicit here: Galdós's social critique serves as a 'scalpel' (the word used by the *ABC* reviewer) for Olea to dissect the dying days of Francoism. The censors fixated on the plot's potential sensationalism – a priest's love affair – holding up the script three times (Navarrete 2003, 134). They got it spectacularly wrong. The film's critique lies not in its anti-clericalism (from the 1960s on, progressive elements of the clergy had opposed the regime), but in its portrayal of the hollow values of the bourgeoisie and the disruptive presence of strong female characters. These two points of critique struck at the ideological core of late Francoism, whose economic policies, as we have seen, focussed on consolidating the middle classes, unleashing social mobility while continuing to protect patriarchy. The tentative nature of the film's critique is in line with the tentative approach to political change that would follow Franco's death the following year; it is appropriately set under the late nineteenth-century Restoration period (named after the restoration of the Bourbon monarchy in 1874), anticipating the second restoration of the Bourbon monarchy under Juan Carlos I, who viewers knew was Franco's designated successor.[14]

High production values and accessibility are vital aspects of the middlebrow, and *Tormento* exemplifies these in the areas of casting and generic affiliation. *Tormento* owes much of its success to acting talent. Experienced Velasco and Rabal rub shoulders with the aspiring *progre* (radical) Ana Belén, star, as we will see, of many Third-Way films. As Velasco's three awards for her role attest, her performance as Rosalía, the slightly dim, middle-aged, endlessly scheming petite bourgeoise bent on social ascent, known to Galdós enthusiasts from this novel or its sequel of the same year, *La de Bringas* (1884), was central. Drawing on her experience in popular comedy, Velasco perfectly judges her portrayal of this shrewish stereotype, presenting Rosalía's pomposity and hypocrisy as objects of satire rather than caricature. Olea and Velasco take full advantage of the prancing, puffing and preening indicated by Galdós throughout his text (the actress put on 11 kilos to take on the role). A good example is Velasco's performance of the passage where Galdós describes a conversation between Rosalía and Agustín. With a self-reflexive nod, Galdós's narrator writes that an 'attentive observer' would have noted Rosalía's desire to leave her relative in no doubt over her beauty: done up in carefully-chosen clothes and accessories, 'Cualquiera, que atentamente observara a Rosalía, podría haber sorprendido en ella [el deseo] de hacer patente su hermosura, realzada en aquella ocasión por el esmero del vestir y por aliños y adornos de mucha oportunidad. Cómo enseñaba sus blancos dientes, cómo contorneaba su cuello, cómo se erguía para dar a su bien fajado cuerpo esbeltez momentánea' (Any attentive observer would have discovered in Rosalía the desire to show off her beauty, emphasized on that occasion through carefully-chosen clothes and accessories. How she flashed her white teeth, how she showed off the shape of her neck, how straight she held herself to make her tightly corsetted body look momentarily slender) (Pérez Galdós 1977, 175). Olea is the ideal 'attentive observer' and Velasco's interpretation of Rosalía is so successful that the director expanded her role in the film compared to the novel (Navarrete 2003, 136).

The final sequence is especially revealing of Olea's intentions as it departs

FIGURE 4.2 *Rosalía on Display.* Tormento *(Olea, 1974)*

significantly from the novel. In Galdós's original, we learn that Amparo has become Agustín's mistress when Rosalía's husband Bringas alone sees Agustín off at the station (chapter 40); Rosalía's reaction occurs when he relays the information to her in the following chapter. The novelist can only signal Rosalía's disgust through language: questions, exclamations, and – a Galdós favourite – ellipsis, heavy here with pent-up, unarticulated emotion: '¿Y tuviste paciencia para presenciar tal escándalo?... Conque no la puede hacer su mujer porque es una... ¡y la hace su querida...!' (And you had the patience to witness such a scandal? ... So he can't make her his wife because she's a ... and he makes her his mistress!) (Pérez Galdós 1977, 194). In the film, both Rosalía and her husband turn up at the station to say goodbye. As Navarrete points out, this draws the adaptation full circle and conveys the impression of a closed world to the viewer (2003, 135), since Olea also eliminates the novel's opening conversation and begins with Agustín's arrival by train. Rosalía is particularly keen to see off a man she believes she has saved from a dishonourable marriage, and whom she hopes may be a future son-in-law, if not a second husband for herself. Velasco's gloating gaze at Agustín in the train clouds over with horror when her former maid Amparo steps forward in the carriage, a point emphasized cinematically through the zoom. '¡Puta, puta, puta!' (Bitch, bitch, bitch!) we hear her furiously mutter (though the script had promised the censors these words would be masked by the departing noise of the train).

Amparo's triumphant gaze is a mirror image of Rosalía's here. Up to this point, Belén's performance as the angelic Amparo – admittedly a less juicy role – had been insipid compared to Velasco, even though the maid's past shadowy love affair with a priest and present rosy romance drive the film narrative. Turning to diegesis, the final shot of Belén's Amparo is climactic: through it, the viewer learns that Amparo and Agustín will live in sin. But there is an extra-diegetic story here too about the two actresses' performance style. The matching shots of Velasco's and Belén's gloating gazes triggers Belén's performance to shift gear from holier-than-thou servant-girl to triumphant mistress, as if she had learned from the more experienced actress in the course of the shoot. This apprenticeship would serve her well when she embodied Galdós's most famous working-class girl, Fortunata, in Camus's 1980 TV series *Fortunata y Jacinta* – though her performance there is again slightly uneven.

A brilliant Velasco and an improving Bélen aside, another success of Olea's *Tormento* is its attention to secondary roles. The character of the wealthy relative who returns to Madrid after making his fortune abroad, Agustín Caballero, was hardly a challenge for the experienced Paco Rabal, but his own star trajectory, which included portraying the cock-sure Jorge of Buñuel's *Viridiana* (1961), repeated in his performance of playboy Roberto in *Summer Night* (*Noche de verano* Grau 1962; see Chapter 3), then earning his colours with other major auteurs of the day such as Michelangelo Antonioni (*The Eclipse* 1962), matches felicitously his on-screen role in *Tormento*. With this film, the glamorous star returns to Spanish cinema, just as the exotic Agustín returns to Madrid. Thus, as Rabal's Agustín draws Belén's Amparo into view for the triumphant final shot described above, it again seems that an older generation of veteran actors is guiding a newer generation forwards.

Melodrama proves the ideal cradle in which to nurture this acting talent. In Olea's hands it fuses the accessibility associated with popular alternatives and the critique associated with the auteurist tradition – even if the fusion may make the critical edge blunter. Olea's adaptive method is to harness the original novel's explicit melodramatic qualities to the film genre of melodrama.[15] It has frequently been stated that the nineteenth-century realist novel provided fiction film with its narrative codes. Galdós's *Tormento* demonstrates that it provided film with a model for melodrama too. Olea reads his source text through the lens of the female-focussed narratives, theatrical performance style, and narrativized mise en scène of film melodramas made in Hollywood (e.g. Douglas Sirk) and Spain (e.g. Rafael Gil, see Chapter 2). The film's mise en scène in general and costume in particular illustrate this influence. Setting underlines characterization in *Tormento*, inviting viewers to contrast the tacky pretentiousness of the Bringas apartment with the austerity of Amparo's home and the grandeur of Agustín's mansion. But the use of costume is multi-layered. In the light, perhaps, of the attention given to dress in the sequel novel, *La de Bringas*, Olea expands on Galdós's description of Rosalía's role as chief purchaser of Amparo's new clothes, following the announcement of her engagement to Agustín (Pérez Galdós 1977, 129). Costume is thus narrativized, as Amparo's shift from servant to Señora must be registered in her dress. But for Rosalía this is about control. Amparo may have won the battle for Agustín, but Rosalía will win the war of clothes: Rosalía accuses Amparo of lacking 'taste' and 'style' (those ultimate signifiers of class) (1977, 129; 1977, 134), and takes more care to dress sexily herself, in the home and out, following the engagement (1977, 135). As the example of Amparo's attire in the last scene demonstrates, Rosalía's attempt to pin her down and hem her in through clothes fails. Olea, working in a visual medium and a genre attentive to mise en scène, is able throughout the film to capitalize on this power-dressing.

Such a commercially- and critically-successful middlebrow fusion-film was not reached again in the other films of the 1970s literary adaptations cycle, though Emma Penella's bold performance as Galdós's lusty working-class heroine Fortunata in the Angelino Fons 1970 version of *Fortunata y Jacinta*, for which she won best actress prize at the Círculo de Escritores Cinematográficos (Screenwriters' Circle), comes a good second.

Spaniards in Paris[16] (*Españolas en París* Bodegas 1971)

While immigration to Spain is a frequent concern in Spanish cinema studies, with numerous articles (Nair 2004; Van Liew 2008) and a book-length study (Santaolalla 2005a), little has been written on emigration from Spain. There are obvious reasons for this. Statistically, immigration to Spain (largely from Spanish-speaking America, North Africa and Europe) in the past thirty years is a matter of millions; emigration from Spain (to Northern Europe) during the Franco period, a matter of tens of thousands. And while immigration has attracted 'a substantial number of filmmakers' (Nair 2004, 104), the lesser but nonetheless significant phenomenon of emigration is 'an aspect of reality that is conspicuously rare in Spanish cinema' (Bentley 2008, 217n. 30). The handful of features that deal with the subject in the 1970s include Pedro Lazaga's sleazy *Come to Germany, Pepe* (*Vente a alemania, Pepe* 1971), starring Alfredo Landa, and Buñuel's *That Obscure Object of Desire* (1977) (Bentley 2008, 217), the latter made when the exiled auteur was himself working in France. The first film of Dibildos's Third Way, *Spaniards in Paris*, offers a middlebrow treatment that parodies the clichés of the *Landista* film, and favours formal accessibility over the challenging experimentation of Buñuel. Aimed at Spain's new middle-class audience, its portrayal of economic migration was a reminder that social mobility in Spain was not achieved by all.

Studies of Spanish immigration cinema have focussed on the ways it addresses racism and questions constructions of national identity. In this section I will consider *Spaniards* as an example of Spanish emigration cinema that explores similar issues.[17] The dual treatment in *Spaniards* of emigration-from-Spain and immigration-to-France offers precisely the serious subject matter that, I argue, is a key characteristic of the middlebrow. After analysing this question alongside the film's tentative testing of other subjects like unwanted pregnancy and abortion, I devote the rest of this section to other characteristics of the middlebrow, especially the accessibility provided by the safe deployment of familiar melodramatic tropes, high production values guaranteed by casting, and high-cultural references, especially the use of oppositional poetry and music at the film's extraordinary conclusion.

In the four decades since the release of *Spaniards*, economic migration has soared, a reality that has fascinated world cinema, leading to numerous films about such matters as multiculturalism and racism. In the context of films like *La Haine* (Kassouvitz 1995), a landmark piece in the French context, *Spaniards*, which is also set in Paris, is relatively tame, but nonetheless deserves sympathetic attention for its prescient attention to the issue. A surprising aspect of the treatment is that the titular 'Spanish girls' face no xenophobia or racism. Ana Belén's Isabel, the innocent girl from Sigüenza who arrives in the capital to be a maid, works for a responsible couple – her boss even learns Spanish and takes classes in Spanish culture to make her feel at home. The trials encountered by Belén's character are linked to Spain: the caddish boyfriend who leaves her pregnant is Spanish; the abortionists he contracts Spanish too. France, in fact, emerges as a haven for the character. Her sympathetic, Spanish-speaking French doctor informs her that the French state does not differentiate between wed- and unwed mothers-to-be for medical care, her French boss is unconcerned, and the improbably happy ending – which breaks with the socio-realist tone of the rest of the film – is nothing short of a hymn to a nation that allows an unmarried mother to work and prosper.

Francophile Bodegas, who himself worked in Paris at the start of his direc-torial career, reserves his critique for his home country. Spain emerges as the 'invertebrada' (spineless) nation referred to in the title of Ortega y Gasset's famous work of 1921 *España invertebrada* (*Invertebrate Spain*) – a high-cultural reference sewn into the narrative as Emilia is sent this book as a gift. Such a critique of spinelessness proceeds in a manner far removed from Ortega y Gasset's philosophical observations by parodying instead the stereotypes of popular Spanish sleazy comedy. Emilia spices up her dull day-job as a maid and purges her bitter memories of abandonment by a Spanish partner who returns to his wife by posing as a high-class French prostitute and preying on a series of male Spanish tourists. Inspired by the Landa-type, these clichés of cultural, linguistic and sexual incompetence are deftly embodied by comedy-trained actors José Luis López Vázquez and José Sacristán. The only racism of the film is that of these Spanish sex tourists towards French women.

What rescues the film from being a pamphleteering condemnation of spineless Spanish masculinity is female characterization. First, Bodegas gestures towards plurality by exploring the lives of four girls, a plurality repeated by Icíar Bollaín in the 1990s, whose *Flowers of Another World* (*Flores de otro mundo* 1999) also begins with the arrival of a coach-load of female migrants and explores in detail the lives of three. The 'Spanish Women' of Bodegas's film's title are four maids to wealthy Parisian families. First, embittered and worldly-wise Emilia fleeces Spanish tourists; next timid Francisca gives up on France and returns to Spain. The measured performance of Elena María Tejero as a third maid, Dioni, conveys particularly well the experience of an ageing, weary fiancée, who stoically accepts deferred maternity by looking after the children of her French boss. After a seemingly eternal courtship and endless saving, the couple reunite after five years apart working in France and Germany respectively. Bodegas wisely resists the easy clichés of rosy romance in his portrayal of their reunion, retaining instead an unsentimental tone as the couple pack the car with hard-won household furniture and goods finally to return to Spain and marry.

The undisputed protagonist is Isabel, the fourth maid, played by Belén in her first feature as an adult. She finds a different path to fulfilment to the others, and the film traces a straightforward character arc of her transformation from the bewildered, plainly-dressed village girl who steps off the coach at the start of the film to the worldly, glamourous city woman at the end. Script and plot development ensure Isabel is the film's narrative focus – most scenes feature her and her reactions, but Bodegas ensures this focus is matched by cinematography and soundtrack. If his choices are not revolutionary, they are thoughtfully chosen and successfully deployed, thus promoting both the formal accessibility and quality that characterize the middlebrow Third Way. Thus, as well as medium shots and close-ups that focus on Belén, subjective cinematography enhances our identification. For example, low-angle point-of-view shots register her feeling of being overwhelmed by the unfamiliar city at the start of the film; in a second early scene where she meets her employer, a canted shot conveys her disorientation as she looks around the glamorous Parisian apartment.

Identification with Isabel is also underscored by the soundtrack. The lack of subtitles throughout the film means that the non-French speaker can appreciate the initially monolingual Isabel's feelings of isolation as she meets her boss. Bodegas is sensitive to sound as well as image in the sequence of Isabel's announcement of her pregnancy to Manolo. Rather than subjective cinematography, it is subjective sound that encourages us to identify with the maid's predicament. Useless Manolo's voice is drowned out by traffic on the Parisian street; Isabel's voice, conversely, is loud and clear.

In keeping with the generic mode of melodrama, Bodegas is attentive to mise en scène too, and Isabel's innocence in the French capital is conveyed through the white colour of her coat, which she exchanges for a sunny yellow mac as she settles into the new city. Belén's make-up also changes over the course of *Spaniards*. Predictably, but effectively nonetheless, she wears little make-up at the start of the film; her transformation into a confident working woman at the end signalled by heavy cosmetics.

In a film that predominantly traces one character arc, casting and performance style are critical. Belén embodies the intertextual reference to her own performance as a child star in *Zampo and Me* (*Zampo y yo* Lucia 1965) and Bodegas uses this to convey the childish naivety and vulnerability of Isabel on her arrival. As we have seen in Chapter 3, in Luis Lucia's comedy *Marisol's Four Weddings (Las cuatro bodas de Marisol)* similar references to the actress's on-screen childhood backfire as the plot propels her into the adult scenario of multiple marriage suitors. *Spaniards*, adopting melodrama rather than comedy, proceeds more cautiously and thus the child-star intertext helpfully underscores the narrative shift from innocence to knowledge. Isabel's back story is believable: from a large family she works abroad so her only brother Andrés may receive an education. Her own lack of education is confirmed not only through her monolingualism, but through her complete lack of knowledge of her own fertility, which leads, predictably, to unwanted pregnancy.

This intertwining of the on-screen plot of Isabel's maturing, and the off-screen development of the actress's own career as she moved from child- to adult-star is felicitous. Two scenes stand out for their importance to the narrative, the character arc, and the shift in Belén's performance. First, Isabel's angry rejection of both Manolo and the abortion he has organized is the film's turning point. The melodramatic hallmarks of contrast and excess are efficaciously judged in Bodegas's attention to performance as well as details of image and soundtracks. Mise en scène is immediately striking. The décor of the French kitchen is dazzling and white, the black clothes of the women sinister and dark: Isabel's scarlet jumper a striking splash of colour that looks forward to the red blood about to be spilled. Close-ups of silver medical instruments confirm the planned event as Isabel is guided to the table and lies on her back. Next, an arresting point-of-view from Isabel's perspective captures the lined faces of the women. Framed against the white ceiling, they peer and prod, mutter terrifying reassurances, their age and clothing recalling Goya's pictorial treatment of witches. *The Spell* of 1797–8 is particularly relevant, with its preying figures clad in black and basket of dead infants. Meanwhile discordant strings and jarring chords screech out on the soundtrack. Bodegas's anti-abortion stance, conveyed through colour, music, subjective cinematography and composition within the frame could not be clearer. Isabel's moment of clarity is conveyed through an unexpected cut to black, a dark moment that the audience might at first associate with death. In fact it is a violent moment of birth. First, the birth of a self-affirming Isabel, who springs into life, unceremoniously throws Manolo and the women out of the flat and wildly smashes up the instruments of their trade, with soundtrack returning to the film's theme tune and imagetrack following her movements, even as blurring and rapid editing convey their urgency. Second, this is of course a premonition of the birth of the child whose life she has just saved, her red jumper now symbolizing the blood of childbirth. But, importantly, the scene does not end there. Belén's performance shifts from an aberrant fit of rage to the self-composure she has exhibited elsewhere in the film. First, Bodegas cuts to a Paris cityscape, only explicable as Isabel's mind's eye at this point; next the telephone rings. Straightening her clothes, she answers. Apparently incidental, these details are important, for they convey her ability to survive and thus be able to raise, as a single mother, the child she has just saved. In aural terms, this competence is conveyed by her confident French as she speaks on the phone. In visual terms, Bodegas chooses this pivotal moment to break fictional convention and have his protagonist stare at the camera, the significance of which is reinforced by the interruption of the image with flashes of white light. This 9–second long take of a defiant Belén looking straight at the camera in medium shot is a celebration of her simultaneous and inseparable self-affirmation and motherhood. This scene is aesthetically inventive, but not wilfully obscure; it is thematically serious, but not overly-challenging in adopting an anti-abortion stance; and it intertextually cites high art through Goya. This is quality and accessible – middlebrow – filmmaking at its best.

The next and final sequence of the film is similar. It begins with the affirmation of identity at the level of the state by the stamping of Isabel's new passport. She returns home, stubs out a cigarette (the first she has smoked in the whole film) then lifts her baby boy into her arms to make a second visit to the passport office with her son. The exchange in Spanish with the office worker reveals her social ascendance from domestic help to shop worker, while the words she coos in French to the boy reveal her bilingualism.

Turning to mise en scène, it at first seems inconsistent to see Isabel wearing a white coat again, for the colour had previously symbolized naivety, and was replaced by the jaunty yellow mac, then the blood red jumper symbolizing death, Isabel's rebirth and Andrés's birth. As she returns to her flat the reason becomes clear. Since red is coded as new life Bodegas reserves it for the baby: the large cot that now dominates Isabel's room is scarlet, as is the child's all-in-one.

Cinematography links this confident, maternal Isabel to the city. We first see her purposefully walking through the streets alone in high-angle and eye-level long shots that indicate her harmony with her surroundings. After returning to the passport office to register baby Andrés – named after her brother – high-angle long and eye-level long shots are again employed to capture her striding through the streets, this time proudly clasping her red-clothed son. This portrayal of the city as a welcoming space for single mothers echoes the earlier scene where Isabel announces her pregnancy to Manolo: the traffic drowns out the male voice, but complements the female voice. The way Bodegas shoots the street scene again dismisses the importance of the lack of a husband or father. Bodegas frames Belén and the boy through the windows of a bridal shop, the brilliant red of the baby's outfit the only focus of the image, not the black and white of the bride and groom's attire on sale.

This celebration of single motherhood is reconfirmed by soundtrack. Just as this celebration of single motherhood is extraordinary given the date of the film, 1971, when the Franco regime, and its refusal of alternative family structures, was still in place, so the incorporation of the particularly famous political

FIGURE 4.3 *Triumphant Single Mother Isabel.* Spaniards in Paris *(Españolas en París Bodegas 1971)*

work of oppositional poet Agustín Goytisolo and oppositional musician Paco Ibáñez on the soundtrack is extraordinary too. The educated audiences that Diblidos and team sought for the Third Way would have been well aware that 'Palabras para Julia' (Words for Julia) was written by Goytisolo in memory of his mother, who was killed by a Nationalist bomb in Civil-War Barcelona, and in honour of his daughter, whom he named after her. Ibáñez, it would have been equally well-known, had been censored by the regime and was working in exile in the early 1970s. In addition to these political strands, Bodegas and Belén use the poem's references to resilience in the face of adversity, which I transcribe below, to encourage the viewer to imagine Isabel's determination as both mother and worker: she brings up the boy alone, has risen the ranks of employment, and exudes self-confidence through gait, dress, cosmetics and smoking:[18]

Tú no puedes volver atrás
porque la vida ya te empuja
como un aullido interminable,
 interminable.

You cannot go back
because life pushes you forward
like an endless, endless howl.

Te sentirás acorralada
te sentirás perdida o sola
tal vez querrás no haber nacido,
 no haber nacido.

You will feel cornered
you will feel lost or alone
you will perhaps wish you had never
 been born, never been born.

Pero tu siempre acuérdate
de lo que un día yo escribí
pensando en tí, pensando en tí,
 como ahora pienso.

But you must always remember
what I wrote one day
thinking of you, thinking of you, as I
 now think of you.

La vida es bella, ya verás
como a pesar de los pesares
tendrás amigos, tendrás amor,
 tendrás amigos.

Life is beautiful, you will see
how despite sorrows
you will have friends, you will have
 love, you will have friends.

Nunca te entregues ni te apartes,
junto al camino, nunca digas:
no puedo más y aquí me quedo,
 y aquí me quedo.

Never give in, never stray,
next to the road, never say:
I can't go on, I'll stay here, I'll stay
 here.

This conclusion of *Spaniards* offers an intermedial constellation between poet, musician, director and actress, which combines dissident culture under

Franco with a promotion of single motherhood, in a middlebrow fusion of high culture with an accessible treatment. It is both astonishingly political and unashamedly upbeat in its hymn to single motherhood. If the starting point of the film is emigration from Spain for economic necessity, it is only fair, though, to criticize Bodegas for failing to address the economic realities of the single mother. How, one wonders, does Isabel fund the childcare she must need to get a new job in a shop? Overly optimistic too is the film's insistence on the intertwining of female independence and maternity – that Isabel gains a sense of identity and purpose by rejecting abortion is plausible, that she gains promotion in work while her child is an infant is less so. This intertwining is in fact the means by which Bodegas negotiates the contradiction that lies at the heart of the film: its modern desire to celebrate Isabel's identity as an independent, successful Paris resident may only be achieved by the traditional means of a celebration of maternity. If this pro-natalism seems dated, a film like Benito Zambrano's *Alone* (*Solas* 1999), which I address in Chapter 6, proves that it continues to resonate with audiences, for *Alone* maps out the similar redemption of an urban-dwelling independent young woman through maternity.

Of the Third Way, Marvin D'Lugo pronounces that, 'Presenting issues of the day, but seldom moving beyond the surface topicality, these Dibildos-Bodegas collaborations, especially the comic works, seemed to hark back to the folkloric comedies directed by Pedro Masó and Pedro Lazaga in the previous decade' (1997, 131). The Dibildos comedies like *The New Spaniards* did fail to meet the Third way criteria, and fell into familiar cliché – perhaps working in the same genre of comedy meant the pull of the Viejo Cine Español was overwhelming. A melodrama like *Spaniards*, however, exemplifies the middlebrow trend, and may thus be considered alongside *Tormento* of 1974 (which as we have seen also features Belén) and *My Dearest Señorita*, of 1972.

My Dearest Señorita (*Mi Querida Señorita* Armiñán 1972)

For Marta Hernández, as we have seen, the middlebrow Third Way was 'commercial cinema plus auteur cinema divided by two' (quoted in Torreiro 1995a, 361). Hardly a methodology, the mathematical aphorism nonetheless usefully highlights diverse elements ('plus') and process ('divided by'). Diversity is not difficult to identify in considering the background of the creators of *My Dearest Señorita*, a commercial and critical success at the time of its release, and one of the few Spanish films of the period to retain its interest for critics today.[19] Director Jaime de Armiñán brought to the film his previous experience of directing Marisol's *Carola by Day, Carola by Night** (*Carola de día, Carola de noche* 1969) for the popular cinema, as well as a much admired record in television (Hueso 1997, 691). Co-scriptwriter and producer José Luis Borau also brought the diverse professional experiences of directing popular film (eg *Brandy* [1963]), teaching scriptwriting at the auteur-focussed film school, and producing films with his company El Imán – which also backed *Señorita*. The name of main actor José Luis López Vázquez must also be added as a creator of the film: as Armiñán has declared in a recent interview, without this actor as protagonist, *Señorita* could not have been made.[20] We have seen elsewhere in this book his contributions as one of Spain's foremost comic actors of the period: he perfectly judges his portrayal of feckless Quintanilla in *Plácido* (Berlanga 1961); his talents are wasted in embodying the witless sex tourist in *Spaniards in Paris* (Bodegas 1970). Unanimous critical admiration of his role in *Señorita* is usually prefaced by highlighting his star persona as a comic actor, usually of the popular Spanish cinema. This study will also bring to the fore his further associations with key Spanish auteur Carlos Saura in non-comic roles in *Peppermint frappé* (1967) and *The Garden of Delights* (*El jardín de las delicias* 1970).

However, noting the diversity of elements of the Third Way is list-making, not film analysis. I will devote the rest of this section to process. I replace what Hernández unsatisfactorily calls 'dividing by two' with an analysis of *Señorita* as middlebrow. The most striking feature of *Señorita* is its brilliantly original subject matter, which was surprisingly passed by the censors without revision. López Vázquez, one of the most popular Spanish actors of all time and thus very well-known to audiences as a man, plays Adela, the provincial stereotype of a modestly well-off, leisured, God-fearing spinster, which filmgoers might link to the similar roles played by Betsy Blair in *Main Street* (*Calle Mayor* Bardem 1956; see Chapter 2), or Aurora Bautista in *Aunt Tula* (*La tía Tula* Picazo 1964). Adela shaves her face daily and is sexually-attracted to her maid Isabelita, but it is a marriage proposal from local bank manager Santiago that prompts a visit to a sympathetic, non-judgmental confessor, then a similarly benign male doctor (played in cameo by Borau), who reveals that her biological sex is male. Next seen having grown a moustache, wearing a suit and arriving at Madrid's Atocha station, the confused Adela has become the bewildered Juan, who struggles to establish his male identity in both professional and personal terms in the Spanish capital. Critics have speculated on sex change operations (Hueso 1997, 689) and Hermaphroditism (Hontanilla 2006), but, as Armiñán has confirmed in interview, it is simply a mistake: Adela is a man but believes he's a woman. That Adela is a man may make the sexual politics of the film less interesting, but it makes the oppositional politics of the film explosive. Armiñán insists in the same interview that such cases of mistaken identity exist in reality, citing (unspecified) medical evidence. D'Lugo is surely right to argue that it is both the mistaken identity and the fact that such cases are unusual that lead to the political critique: 'The film's improbable premise that Juan – under the protected identity of Adela – could, in fact, grow to adulthood never seeing another person naked nor recognizing his own biological gender poses a biting criticism of the repressive environment nurtured by the conservatism of the Franco dictatorship' (1997, 71).

Such a reference to 'biting criticism' is characteristic of scholarly responses to anti-Franco auteur cinema of the period. Clearly, as with *Tristana*, a case may be made for inclusion of *Señorita* in this revered group (and this case has been made by Triana-Toribio 2003, 97). *Señorita*'s oppositional politics are unquestionable, especially in the areas of mistaken identity, useless female education, and the bewildering encounter with modernity. However, just as in *Spaniards in Paris* Bodegas undercut his modern portrayal of female independence with a conservative insistence on the inextricability of female self-affirmation and motherhood, so *Señorita*'s modern oppositional politics are undercut by conservative sexual politics. While the first part of the film, which takes place in Pontevedra, bristles with the disruptive possibilities of lesbian desire, the revelation of Adela's biological sex simply re-establishes heteronormativity. Institutions of Church and Science, both represented by sympathetic men, emerge as benign agents of 'liberation' and purveyors of 'truth'. Ana Hontanilla is right to pose the feminist question: 'what happens to those women educated during the long, post-war Francoist period who, unable to enjoy an opportune mix-up of nature – or of society – have the fortunate option of actually being biological men definitively close to them' (2006, 120)?

It would be unfair to dismiss *Señorita* for falling short of twenty-first century feminist expectations. But neither is it my intention to rescue *Señorita* as an insufficiently-admired auteurist piece in spite of its conservative heteronormativity. Instead, the Third Way, or middlebrow framework allows us to analyse *Señorita* both because of its serious engagement with its subject and because of its unadventurous undercurrent of conservatism.

Beginning with subject matter, Armiñán and Borau's script brilliantly answers the question of how to portray the provinces and capital of 1970s Spain in an original way. As I have suggested, the representation of Pontevedra is particularly effective. Casting is key to the ways Bardem and Picazo highlight provincial prejudice in *Main Street* and *Aunt Tula*: American actress Blair provides an outsider's perspective to her portrayal of jilted Cuenca spinster in the 1950s; and Bautista's bombastic previous roles in historical melodramas serve as an ironic counterpoint to her stifled Guadalajara spinster in the 1960s. But Armiñán and Borau surely trump them both with ugly López Vázquez as spinster Adela in 1970s Pontevedra. Importantly, López Vázquez exhibits the dramatic restraint honed in his roles as Julián and Antonio in Saura's *Peppermint* and *The Garden*, and plays Adela absolutely deadpan. The combination of the audience's full awareness of the actor's sex, and the actor's 'straight' performance of the role, makes for a simple twist that utterly skews the portrayal of the provincial city. For example, the charitable church-led activities of the leisured middle-class women of Pontevedra are rendered absurd by Adela's presence, especially when she athletically wellies a ball off the pitch at a charitable football match. Similarly, the film's opposition between the formal female dress of mantilla and comb, and the casual clothes of the new generation of ye-yé girls takes on a new dimension as López Vázquez wears the traditional attire. Most interestingly, Adela's homosexual desire for Isabelita disruptively queers domestic space. Otherwise evoked through a mise en scène of ultra-traditional furnishings and exceptionally sober colours – a point narrativized when the Señorita announces her desire to modernize the flat – this is the unlikely scenario for the point of view shots that reveal Adela's desire. Underpinning all of this is a critique of a society that could so neglect female education and so repress the body that Adela's mistaken identity could occur. Particularly devastating, then, is the scene of Adela's pique of lesbian jealousy when Isabelita gets a boyfriend. Mobilizing her hopelessly limited knowledge of physical corporeal reality but using too the powerful clichés of a patriarchal ideology that regulate female sexuality, Adela warns Isabelita about the dangers of associating with men before marriage.

The film's twist enables Armiñán to critique provincial Spain through the highly-original lens of lesbian desire. It also allows him to adopt a new perspective on urban experience, though the coming-of-age story of a male, heterosexual encounter with the city is as old as the hills. A viewer who only starts watching *Señorita* from the Atocha station arrival might be forgiven for taking it to be yet another story of the bewildered *paleto* (country bumpkin) in the capital, of the type Paco Martínez Soria made famous in the VCE. *Señorita* shares with art cinema the mobilization of an active spectator, for each of Juan's experiences in the capital is meaningful only if viewed through the memory of his earlier provincial life as a spinster. Thus Juan finds himself woefully ill-equipped in professional terms. The exchange between this middle-aged man and the typist about his curriculum vitae at the employment office is a powerful indictment of the hopeless inadequacy of female provincial education in the post-war: when asked what he has studied, he replies 'cultura general y dos años de piano' (general culture and two years' piano practice). If he is uneducated and insufficiently experienced in professional terms, he is overwhelmed and bewildered in personal terms, unable to cope with either the easy manners of tart-with-a-heart Celia/Patricia, nor the formal courtship with Isabelita, with whom he has an apparently chance encounter in the capital. It is the simplicity of the single plot twist that makes this wider critique so impressive, for there could be no better way of representing the disorientating clash of tradition and modernity than through the body of a particularly well-known male comic actor in the part of a man who has lived to the age of forty-three in the belief he is a woman.

A serious critique of a repressive environment that is not overly-challenging in its insistence on heteronormativity, *Señorita* also exhibits middlebrow traits in its formal accessibility, high production values and occasional reference to elite culture. These elements coalesce in the casting and performance of López Vázquez; I choose two sequences for close reading in which this performance is complemented particularly well by José Massagué's mise en scène, shot by veteran art-cinema cinematographer Luis Cuadrado. The first sequence is found in part one, the portrait of the provinces, when Adela receives a bunch of red roses from hopeful suitor Santiago. By this point of the film, flowers in mise en scène have become imbued with a narrative role that is not complex to decipher. The close relationship between Señorita and maid is established from the first post-credit sequence by the giving of a red carnation as an apparently innocent token of affection. On a second viewing, the audience understands that Adela's giving of a flower to Isabelita represents exactly the same thing as Santiago's giving of flowers to her: heterosexual romance and a desired future marriage. The profession of Isabelita's boyfriend as a florist further reinforces this association. After giving and receiving the flowers, Armiñán locates Adela in her drably-furnished apartment wearing a dull grey house dress and slippers that match the furnishings. Both vases of flowers flood the image with colour, and the simple plot twist promotes fascinating possible readings. First, Santiago's formal flowers, which are located in the drawing room, stand for traditional provincial courtship – but they are actually a gift of love between men. Second, the single carnation that Adela gives Isabelita, which is a splash of colour in a vase in the white kitchen, symbolizes Adela's homosexual desire for Isabelita – which is ultimately revealed to be heterosexual attraction. For audiences who knew López Vázquez's previous art cinema work with Saura, this skewing of potentially transparent situations would be familiar. In *Peppermint*, for example, López Vázquez's Julián appears to be a serious doctor with designs on marrying his assistant (played by Geraldine Chaplin). In reality, he is sexually-obsessed with his friend's American wife (also played by Chaplin); unable to tolerate the confusion, he murders both friend and wife.

The second sequence concerns Juan's residence in a cheap guest-house in

FIGURE 4.4 *Queering Provincial Spain. Isabelita and Adela.* My Dearest Señorita *(Mi Querida Señorita Armiñán 1972)*

Madrid. Juan is given the 'habitación de paso' (provisional or temporary room, 'de paso' also gives the sense of 'passing through') because it is on budget and all that is available. The space and its name become richly evocative of his current struggle to establish his identity. First, the space is not private, for other guests may pass through; second his residency is not permanent: he is only passing through. It is in this transitory, traversable space that Juan attempts to forge his new identity – ultimately its traversability ensures it is transitory, for the landlady's niece riffles through his private possessions, discovers the suitcase of woman's clothing and her aunt throws him out. A telling sequence concerns Juan's discovery of the sewing machine in the room. His education of 'general culture and two years' piano practice' has equipped him with the ability to sew, and he sets to work cutting up his old female clothes to make new items, described as 'de fantasía' (fantasy) by the shop-owner who buys them from Juan, thinking they are made by a sister, Adela. The scene in which he rips up the female-coded clothes of his former existence to fashion something new effectively conveys Juan's own struggle to make something modern and new from his old provincial self as a woman. Interesting too is the fact that this refashioning of an old identity into a new one should itself take place in a space coded as 'passing through'. All identity, Armiñán seems to suggest, is provisional.

Middlebrow for its high production values, its accessible formal treatment, occasional high-cultural reference and at once provocative-yet-conservative subject matter, *Señorita* is brilliantly original in its skewed portrait of a provincial spinster, and offers an interesting new take on the male story of coming-of-age in the city that ends with the loss of virginity. The interesting provisionality of Juan's bewildering struggle to establish his identity in the city is diffused by the coda, however. Juan returns to Pontevedra to pick up Adela's money, then he buys one of the new flats on Madrid's outskirts that symbolize the social mobility of the 1960s and readies himself to install Isabelita as his wife. Most critics have interpreted Isabelita's comment to Juan while the couple are in bed at the end of the film as an interesting admission of the intermingling of homosexual and heterosexual desire. '¿Qué me vas a contar, Señorita?' could be taken to mean the innocent 'What are you going to tell me, Señorita?', or to mean the knowing 'You can't tell me anything I don't all ready know, Señorita'. In summarizing this ambiguity, John Hopewell suggests an alternative, conservative and patriarchal interpretation: 'the ex-maid calls her ex-mistress "Señorita". Perhaps she knows his identity. Or perhaps she equates her ex-mistress with the bachelor because she regards him, as the man she will marry, as her new master' (1986, 99). Somewhere in-between D'Lugo's identification of the film's 'biting criticism' in political terms, and Hontanilla's identification of its failure in feminist terms, we might ultimately locate this extraordinary 1972 film.

Unfinished Business (*Asignatura pendiente* Garci 1977)

I end this chapter on the middlebrow Third Way of the 1970s with two films that demonstrate the continuities in this area across the decade. José Luis Garci is widely acknowledged to be the bridge for those continuities. Dibildos's scriptwriter, Garci, was a 'pillar' (Peláez Paz 1997, 765) of the Third Way at the start of the decade; with his first film *Unfinished Business*, he is credited with developing and politicizing the trend towards the end of it. New names were needed for new, post-Franco times, and *Unfinished Business* has been included, first, in a group of films termed the 'Cine de la Reforma' (Reform Cinema) (Heredero 1989, 23), a label that emphasizes the ideological links between the films and political reform following the dictator's death; and, second, it has been included in a group termed 'comedias madrileñas' (Madrid comedies), which emphasizes genre and location. In the final section of this chapter I consider Antonio Mercero as another example of a director of the middlebrow tendency. Like Armiñán, Mercero intertwines work for small and large screen (a process of crossover recently discussed in Paul Julian Smith's discussion of the figure in a chapter entitled 'Auteur TV' [2006, 145–74]), bringing to *Daddy's War* (*La guerra de papá* 1977) the experience of TVE's highly popular *Village Chronicles (Crónicas de un pueblo* 1971–4) and *The Phone Box* (*La cabina* 1972) – the only Spanish programme to have won a US Emmy (Smith 2006, 30). Released just a few months after *Unfinished Business*, his *Daddy's War* is a key example of Reform Cinema, is also set in Madrid, but, rather than comedy, is generically affiliated to melodrama and child-star cinema.

The sub-genre of the 'Madrid Comedies', which was prominent in the late 1970s and early 1980s, is an important manifestation of the middlebrow trend in Spanish cinema. *Unfinished Business* was the first, with *First Work* (*Ópera prima* Trueba 1980), to be analysed in Chapter 5, another notable success. Densely-scripted and closely-observed, critics have noted the adherence of the 'Madrid Comedies' to an originally theatrical sub-genre, often associated with the middlebrow, the 'Comedias de costumbres' (Comedy of Manners) (e.g. Fiddian 1999, 242), a connection that allows us to trace an affiliation between twentieth-century Spanish film to both nineteenth-century Spanish theatre,[21] and to other national cinemas where this sub-genre is prominent, like the French.[22] In both Spanish and French cases, the distinction between 'Comedy' and 'Comedy of Manners' is similar, the former associated with crude traditions both north and south of the Pyrenees. Conversely, the Comedy of Manners in both France and Spain exemplifies the middlebrow. Darren Waldron and Isabelle Vanderschelden's description of the French version alludes to the characteristic middlebrow hallmark of fusion of serious subject matter with accessible, yet thoughtful, form, which I have defended throughout this study: 'an established sub-genre that tackles questions of class, gender and sexuality through the medium of light entertainment, but which also bears the personal, authorial signature of the director' (2007, 6).

Rob Stone calls the successful development of the Third Way in Madrid Comedies like *Unfinished Business* and Fernando Colomo's *Paper Tigers** (*Tigres de papel* 1977) 'a clear instance of cinematic evolution' (2002, 120). By re-locating the films in the framework of the middlebrow, such continuities can be further underlined. Co-author of key Dibildos scripts like *Healthy Married Life* (1973) and *The New Spaniards* (1974), Garci collaborated with José María González Sinde on the script of *Unfinished Business*, which, after a surprising rejection from his former mentor Dibildos, was taken on by producer José Luis Tafur. The tentatively serious plot was typical of the middlebrow. Shot at the end of 1976 and released in April 1977, the film's narrative deals with a romantic affair that unfolds in the months leading up to and following the dictator's death. In the early Dibildos films the links between the personal and political were only implied, thus in *Spaniards in Paris* the causes of economic migration from Spain to Paris for girls like Isabel must be deduced by the audience; in the same film, Spanish sex tourism is addressed only as a symptom of Francoist repression: there is no analysis of its cause. Seven years later, Garci's approach is to make the political causes of individual behaviour explicit. Almost every key event in the personal experience of José and Elena's romance is interwoven with a political event.

With the exception of a brief quotation from Pablo Neruda,[23] *Unfinished Business* lacks the highbrow cultural intertexts we have seen elsewhere in this chapter such as reference, through adaptation, to literary classics, or reference, through citation, to canonical art, music or poetry. Instead, the film is notable for its repeated references to the particularity of the political context. Such references do not confer cultural capital in the manner described by Bourdieu, but they nonetheless point to the key middlebrow characteristic of a serious subject matter. This politicization of the personal thus lifts the rather silly narrative of a bored lawyer allaying his mid-life crisis through an extra-marital affair above the crass clichés of saccharine romance.

For example, boy meets girl, in Garci's hands, is an event that occurs in the middle of a political rally. The personal and the political are inextricably interwoven as the commotion caused on the Madrid street by the distribution of leaflets intermingles with the commotion caused by José's abandonment of his car in the middle of the street in order to attract Elena's attention. The subsequent reunion between the two in a café unfolds to the sound of a speech on the radio by Franco with subsequent cheers by the crowd. During their first illicit date José compares himself to Arías Navarro (vice-president of Franco's last government). And when the two have sex – the 'pending exam', or 'unfinished business' of the title, for they had been prevented from such intimacy during the Franco years of their adolescence – it seems inevitable that the moment should occur in a heavily politicized context. José borrows an apartment from his friend and colleague nicknamed 'Trotsky', and just in case the audience misses the name, the walls are painted red, festooned with images of communist propaganda, and, to top it all, a huge poster of Lenin hangs above the bed. Subtlety, then, is not Garci's aim. The intertwining is emphasized too through José's job as a left-wing labour lawyer. The case of his client bears a clear resemblance to Marcelino Camacho, renowned Comisiones Obreras (Workers' Commissions) militant, and his difficulty in securing his release despite the end of the dictatorship matches his disappointment with the affair with Elena. Elena is the girlfriend of José's adolescence; on their first date 20 years later his monologue is especially explicit in interlinking of the political and the personal:

Nos han robado tantas cosas. Las veces que tú y yo tuvimos que hacer el amor y no lo hicimos. Los libros que debimos leer... No sé, pero me parece que es como si nos hubiera quedado algo colgado, como aquellas asignaturas que quedaban pendientes de un curso para otro. (They've stolen so much from us. The times you and I should have made love and didn't. The books we should have read... I don't know, it seems to me as if we've got unfinished business, like those exams we needed to pass that we carried over from one school year to the next.)

The purpose of all this intertwining is explicitly to denounce the repressive impact on personal relations of the dictatorship. *Unfinished Business* seems, furthermore, to advocate a disengagement from politics to pursue personal pleasure, for José and Elena will ignore the rallies and the speeches to pursue their affair. Óscar Pereira sees this 'lack of articulation' (1998, 161) between the 'microtext' of the affair and the 'macrotext' of political events (1998, 160) as the 'defining element in the ideology of the *desencanto*, which marked the reform process undertaken by Franco's government after his death' (1998, 161). For Pereira, *Unfinished Business* emerges as a film that actively promotes (1998, 161) the disenchantment with politics that characterized Spain's transition to democracy, laying the blame at the door of the middlebrow intertwining of personal and political, whereby 'The trivial love story is [...] contaminated with the prestige of the historical, the real'; the result is that 'We have no understanding of history in depth, but instead are offered a contemporary creation, more costume drama and re-enactment than critical discourse' (Pereira quoting R. Lewison 1998, 163).

All the elements of the hostility towards the middlebrow are present here: treading a middle path it 'contaminates'; fails to plumb adequate 'depth' and even favours such suspicious aesthetic forms as the 'costume drama'. However, a sympathetic approach to the intertwining of the personal and the political in the film's serious, but relatively unchallenging, subject matter allows us to appreciate the ways it captures the spirit of the times to such an extent that it became known as 'the film of the Transition' (Peláez Paz 1997, 766). Like Pereira, I find the disengagement with politics that characterized the *desencanto* profoundly relevant to the film, but would stress, first, that José does re-engage with politics towards the end of the film. His mid-life crisis abates, his career takes off and he dispenses with the childish affair. His cynicism may reach a new low as he drunkenly urinates against 'a billboard that welcomes the union of democracy with consumerism ("35 million political parties vote for Condor socks"), but over which has been scrawled the infamous slogan "We lived better under Franco"' (Stone 2002, 122), but in Stone's pithy aphorism: 'he is doomed to live long and prosper' (2002, 122).

Second, Pereira's dismissal of the film also misses the attention paid to the portrayal of Elena. Fiorella Faltoyano conveys the ennui of a wealthy bourgeois housewife and pampered mistress through rather off-putting impassivity, which at least comes as a relief compared with the irritating chitter chatter of José Sacristán's Woody Allen-inspired portrayal of José (D'Lugo 1997, 256). It is difficult for the audience to identify with a dull character evoked through a somewhat deaden performance, but by the end of the film Elena is the only partner to articulate a sensible interpretation of the affair. While she constantly stresses her age (33) and adult life as a wife and mother of two girls, she points out that José only ever sees her as the 15–year-old of his teenage years. Stone is right to note that the sex, for José, 'is a regression tactic that identifies him as a similarly infantilised male to that of Saura's *La prima Angélica*' (2002, 122). Depressingly enough, childish José will prosper; adult Elena, however, is left behind.

Reviewing the film from a gender perspective, she is the victim of two particularly bad choices. First, in the scene of the distribution of the political rally where José spots her from his car, she is actually in the process of reading the leaflet when her childhood boyfriend calls out to her. She follows his instruction to throw it away to talk to him, her acquiescence to José, then actions of screwing it up and casting it aside, represent the choice of pursuing a pointless affair rather than potentially engaging with politics. Second, in the sequence discussed above where José is lost in the past lamenting the sex he didn't have and the books he didn't read, Elena looks to the future. Their amusing conversation at cross purposes portrays another lost opportunity for this woman. While José proposes that they sleep together, she ignores him and voices her plans to go to university and study. His response is to insist on the sex. When he finally engages with her and asks which university, she has taken her second bad decision: she abandons her plans for study to instead make the arrangements for the affair. When the romance flounders, she is cast aside, in John Hopewell's summary: José 'never asks Elena to be part of the transition with him. She – like the Hollywood woman – remains historical flotsam, left in the wake of the history-makers' (1986, 111; this point is also emphasized by Barry Jordan and Rikki Morgan-Tamosunas 1998, 68).

Middlebrow in its serious, but tentative subjective matter, *Unfinished Business* also exemplifies the middlebrow formal traits of high production values and accessibility. Garci's formula was a successful one: the script is wordy and peppered with contemporary political references; the cast includes popular actors like Sacristán and Faltoyano, even if their performances are somewhat derivative and deaden; the soundtrack nostalgically refers to 1960s hits from groups like the Duo Dinámico; and the settings portray contemporary Madrid and nearby Castile. All of this brought profits at the box

FIGURE 4.5 *Elena Chooses Romance over the Rally.* Unfinished Business
(Asignatura pendiente Garci 1977)

office (though beyond the reach of this study, it would be interesting to break down audience figures of 2,300,000 viewers by community and discover if such Madrid comedies were so successful in, say, Catalonia). A further key characteristic of the film is its significant intertextual debts. Andrés Peláez Paz insists on the autochtonous influences of the sainete and costumbrismo, citing the portrayal of secondary characters, the use of popular language laden with references to current affairs, plus allusions to radio, cinema and song (1997, 766). But the debt to Hollywood romantic comedy is even more extensive and specific, feeding into the very formal characteristics of the film as well as the multiple allusions by the character José within the diegesis. Peláez Paz himself notes *An Affair to Remember* (McCarey 1957); Stone highlights Robert Redford (2002, 122); and Marvin D'Lugo mentions *The Way We Were* (1973) and *The Graduate* (1967) (1997, 33) to defend a convincing summary of the indebted stylistic structure of the entire film as:

> Imitat[ing] patterns of visual-narrative construction of Hollywood films. An insistence on extravagant establishing shots and a rigorous emulation of Hollywood shot/reverse-shot construction of scenes suggest a blatant imitation of the 'look' of Hollywood cinema of the period. (1997, 160)

One critic's creative 'influence' might be another critic's derivative 'imitation'; rather than engage in this endless discussion,[24] I would stress that inter-textual references in *Unfinished Business* made the film both accessible to audiences, and brought with it the added pleasure of recognition. Criticized, then, for being insufficiently original in its formal construction and insufficiently profound in its political engagement, *Unfinished Business* exemplifies the risks run by the middlebrow film. Yet the film was successful with audiences and continued to resonate beyond its release to be seen as emblematic of its decade. This study has argued that this success and resonance may be accounted for because, rather than in spite of, it being a middlebrow film.

Daddy's War (*La guerra de papá* Mercero 1977)

While it failed to achieve the emblematic status of *Unfinished Business*, Antonio Mercero's *Daddy's War* (*La guerra de papá*) was nonetheless a key Transition film that was even more successful at the box office than *Unfinished Business*. With almost a million more viewers (3,524,450 as opposed to 2,306,007), it took top place for a Spanish film in 1977 – a period that just still precedes the haemorrhaging of the film audience to television that was around the corner.[25] Like *Unfinished Business*, the film exemplifies the key middlebrow traits of serious, yet reasonably unchallenging subject matter and high quality, accessible form. Again, like *Unfinished Business*, *Daddy's War* looks forward to middlebrow films of the 1980s. The Madrid comedies would continue in the hands of directors like Fernando Trueba, with whose *First Work* (1980) I begin Chapter 5; though Garci's own career would lurch from the highest international accolade for *Begin the Beguine* (*Volver a empezar* 1982) in the form of Spain's first Oscar for best foreign language film, to hostile critical dismissal of his work as outdated (Mira 2010, 142). Produced by José Frade, *Daddy's War*, on the other hand, is a family melodrama and adaptation of contemporary novelist Miguel Delibes's 1973 *The Dethroned Prince* (*El príncipe destronado*). As such, it looks forward to the Mirovian films to be discussed in Chapter 5, which also often favoured literary adaptations. A key example, Mario Camus's *The Holy Innocents* (*Los santos inocentes* 1984) also adapted a brief Delibes novel (first published in 1981), which, like *Prince*, similarly chronicled lost innocence and the impact of history in the 1960s.

I begin this section with an analysis of *Daddy's War* as a literary adaptation. Unlike the Galdós adaptations considered at the beginning of this chapter, Delibes does not have the 'classic' cachet, but nonetheless brings highbrow cultural prestige to the film as one of the key novelists of Spain's mid-century. I will argue, however, that the middlebrow textures I read in the film – its simultaneous seriousness, yet accessibility – are equally applicable to the novel. Though published in 1973, *Prince* was written in 1963, a point of relevance to both the novelist's biography and Spanish cinema. The declared inspiration for the novel is the activities of Delibes's own son Adolfo, to whom he dedicated the book, and who drew its illustrations. An undeclared influence may have also been Spanish cinema's child stars, for, as we have seen, the late 1950s and early 1960s were the heyday for such figures as Pablito Calvo, Joselito and Marisol. The novella charts eleven hours of one day in the life of Quico, the three-year-old protagonist. The fifth of six children, Quico has been recently 'dethroned' by a baby sister – hence Delibes's title. Delibes's uses of dialogue and third-person objectivist description are designed to represent this moment of childhood. While Quico is dynamic and imaginative, he is a three-year-old: his world is thus one of action and experience, rather than consideration and interpretation. Were it not for the way Delibes plays with socio-political context, the novel would be a whimsical, if amusing, record of childhood play. However, Delibes places his young protagonist in an upper-middle-class Madrid family that is still torn apart by the hostilities that remain even 25 years after the Civil War. Just as Garci intertwines the personal and the political through a sentimental romance shot through with allusions to lost opportunites and current political upheaval, Delibes also interweaves two worlds: one of childhood innocence and one of adult resentment (a third one is touched upon through reference to the oldest son's attitude to his father's politics [Delibes 1974, 153–4]). The role of the reader is, then, not just to enjoy the description of childish pranks, but also to ask what is the effect on Quico of growing up in this context of confrontation? The wider relevance of this question – posed by Delibes when he wrote the piece in the 1960s and again when he published it in the 1970s – is not difficult to deduce. This is yet another of the overdetermined families that dominated Spanish culture of the period (to name but a few others, consider *The Disenchantment* [*El desencanto* Chávarri 1976], *Ana and the Wolves* [*Ana y los lobos* Saura, 1973]): the father stands for an all-powerful and arrogant dictatorship, the mother, a defeated and resentful Republican Spain, and the infant, the future generation caught up in the conflict between these two.

For experienced and multi-award-winning TV director Mercero, the novel's middlebrow intertwining of the personal and the political, and disarmingly naive formal presentation were effortless to adapt to the screen. Delibes's dialogue translates easily into Mercero and Horacio Valcárcel's script; and detailed, objectivist description of the objects that catch Quico's attention can be conveyed by point of view shots of those same objects from the child's perspective in the film. Likewise, just as Delibes withholds any explicit commentary on the part of the narrator regarding Quico's struggle to understand the world of adult confrontation, thus leaving this act of interpretation to the reader, Mercero too resists excessive didacticism and leaves to his viewer the admittedly straightforward interpretative task of drawing out the significance of the contrast between childhood innocence and adult sophistication. One key difference, however, is that Mercero's viewer is primed to look for political interpretations, as the director changes Delibes's original title *The Dethroned Prince*, which focuses on the family, to *La guerra de papá*, which focuses on the Civil War.

Two examples illustrate the middlebrow intertwining of family life and politics on the page and on the screen. First, during the tense family lunch, Quico's mother scolds him for eating with his left, rather than his right hand, and there follows a lecture by his father on virtues and qualities of left-handed and right-handed people, which has clear political overtones of Left-wing and Right-wing (Delibes 1974, 66). Identical on page and screen – Delibes's dialogue is transposed by Mercero and Valcárcel to the script – the sequence illustrates how Quico causes and witnesses adult confrontations that he, as a child, does not understand, but that the reader or viewer, as an adult, does.

A second example of childhood innocence in confrontation with adult sophistication can be seen in the sequence where Quico and his older brother Juan play at war with their father's gun (Delibes 1974, 78–81). This sequence also illustrates the way Mercero expands on Delibes's original. Both reader and viewer are accustomed to Quico and Juan's investment of everyday household objects with a symbolism that speaks of the values and obsessions that surround them. Thus the tube of toothpaste Quico keeps in

FIGURE 4.6 *Quico Tries to Comprehend a War-torn Adult World. Vito and Quico.* Daddy's War *(La guerra de papá Mercero 1977)*

his pocket is, variously, a 'truck', a 'boat', and a 'canon', or the lamp with a winged shade, a 'guardian angel' (Delibes 1974, 12, 13, 15, 78). In the context of this playful symbolism, it comes as a shock when Juan, after rummaging around in the drawer of his father's library, finds a real gun, and with it, pretends to shoot Quico. Our protagonist assumes this to be a game of Cowboys and Indians, but it is actually, his older brother insists, the Civil War, or, as he calls it, 'la guerra de Papá' (Daddy's war) (Delibes 1974, 79). In the treatment of this scene in the novel, the narrator passes no comment: it is for the reader to intuit the horror of a three-year-old and seven-year-old acting out a Civil-War battle with a real gun. Further, Delibes's dispassionate narrator adds to the sense of danger with the chilling detail that it lacks a safety catch (Delibes 1974, 79).

This is obviously a key scene for Mercero as it gives him the title of his film version, *Daddy's War*. With respect to dialogue, Mercero and Valcárcel change the order of the boys' conversation, which otherwise remains unaltered in its passage from novel to script. In mise en scène, we see the setting (the library) and actions (the war game) that Delibes's narrator describes. However, Mercero uses other resources that are specific to film to emphasize the sinister political dimension of this childhood game, which is only implied in Delibes's original. First, as soon as the boys enter the library, Mercero uses lighting and introduces a musical score to imply foreboding and suspense. Next, on the desk where the boys find the gun, Mercero places a photo of the father as a soldier, a red and yellow Spanish flag, and a black and red Falangist flag (none of these details is present in Delibes's original) and ensures the viewer notes their presence through medium shots. Mercero thereby expands on the literary original to apportion blame more specifically: the victorious Nationalists are responsible for the perpetuation of Civil War rivalries, and the damaging impact of these on the young.

As we have seen in *Unfinished Business*, this interweaving of the personal and the political, or introduction of more explicitly political elements to the original formulation of the Third Way in the early 1970s, is a key characteristic of late Third-Way, or Reform cinema. It is a middlebrow approach, which in Mercero's hands combines the escapism of o the child-star films with tentative political critique. But *Daddy's War* is middlebrow in aesthetic as well as political terms. Whereas Garci invested in multiple and lavish sweeping establishing shots of Madrid in his romantic comedy *Unfinished Business*, Mercero largely confined the action of *Daddy's War* to the events that unfold in the family flat, an apparent limitation that in fact works particularly well for this family melodrama. With little distraction from ostentatious cinematography, then, the performance of actors was key. Competent comedy actress Veronica Forqué plays Vito (her jolly vivacity and affection towards children two qualities reprised by Pedro Almodóvar when he cast her as Cristal in *What Have I Done to Deserve This?!* [¿*Qué he hecho yo para merecer esto?!!* 1984]); Héctor Alterio showcases his sinister set piece as the insensitive Nationalist father (already seen in his role in Saura's *Raise Ravens* [*Cría cuervos* 1975], and extended in both Pilar Miró's *The Cuenca Crime* [1981], and Luis Puenzo's *Official Story* [*La historia oficial* 1985]); and finally, Teresa Gimpera portrays the downtrodden mother, whose Left-wing views and family background continue to irritate her husband, even now, twenty-five years after the Civil War. While the novel is set, specifically, on 'Tuesday, 3 December, 1963' (Delibes 1974, 7), the first post-credit intertitle of the film states 'Any day in March, 1964'. Mercero perhaps made this change in order ironically to place the parents' arguments in the year of Franco's celebrations of '25 Years of Peace'. A Catalan model, Gimpera became the face of Avant-Garde Catalan film movement known as the Barcelona School (thanks to her début in Vicente Aranda's *Fata Morgana* [1965]), she also plays the mother of the most famous precocious child of art cinema of the period, Teresa in Erice's *The Spirit of the Beehive*. Mercero draws excellent performances from these three actors, and through them gestures to both commercial and auteurist traditions in the Spanish cinema. Forqué offers the archetypal happy, ditzy maid, recalling the roles played by the likes of Gracita Morales in the 1960s VCE. Alterio is a brooding presence here in a brief performance that recalls his auteurist work with Saura and looks forward to similar collaborations with Miró and Puenzo. And Gimpera's radiant beauty – which recalls her work in Catalan art cinema – contrasts with her gloomy life, thus emphasizing the tedium of her existence.

Mercero has been particularly praised for the performance he coaxes from Lolo García as Quico: his directorial 'trump card', according to Philip Mitchell, is 'his portrayal of childhood disrupted by a precocious exposure to adult sadness' (2004, 180). While some sequences are slightly saccharine – Mercero lets cinematographer Manuel Rojas focus too long on García's thick, blond curls and big, blue eyes – the director does draw out a convincing performance in order to make the serious point of this film: the sins of the parents are visited upon the children, or, more specifically, Quico is psycho-logically affected by growing up in a house full of stories of the Civil War. At the end of the day of which the narrative consists, Quico is frightened and unable to sleep as he re-tells himself the stories about war, punishment and blood-letting that he has heard throughout the day. Here the end of the film neatly answers the question posed about Quico's bed-wetting at the start: we understand that its cause is the fears that arise from the stories.

The conceit that future generations are tortured by the actions of previous ones is central to Spanish art cinema of the period: Erice and Saura made precisely the same point through casting child actress Ana Torrent in *The Spirit of the Beehive* and *Raise Ravens*. As we would expect in the work of Spain's key art directors, Erice and Saura rely on enigmatic silences, complex plot construction and intertextual references to draw their audiences towards this interpretation. Mercero, as we would expect in the middlebrow mode, requires much less work from the spectator. While referencing the art tradition, he draws too on the long tradition of celebrating innocent childhood in the popular Spanish cinema; the result is a middlebrow film that was both commercially successful, and influential upon cinema of the following decade.[26]

Notes

1 The film narrates a miscarriage of justice that took place in Osa de la Vega, Cuenca, in 1912. The case was transferred to a Civil Court and dismissed. The film was released in 1981.

2 Francesc Llinás summarizes the change thus: 'by the time of the transition, the traditionally large popular cinema audiences for low quality sex films and comedies were being drawn to television and home video. Increasingly, the new cinema-going public saw itself as middle-class, educated and liberal' (quoted in Jordan and Morgan-Tamosunas 1998, 32).

3 Torreiro lists *Spaniards in Paris* (*Españolas en París* Bodegas 1971) as the first example (1995a, 359); *Healthy Married Life* (*Vida conyugal sana* Bodegas 1973); *The New Spaniards* (*Los nuevos españoles* Bodegas 1974); *My Wife is Very Respectable, Given the Circumstances** (*Mi mujer es muy decente dentro de los que cabe* Drove 1974) and *Women, a Man's Thing** (*La mujer es cosa de hombres* Yagüe 1975) as the foremost examples (1995a, 361).

4 Gubern et al. 1995, re-published and expanded in 2006 and 2009.

5 The wedge that Dibildos succeeded in inserting between the Third Way and the sleazy cinema began to slip as time wore on. Rob Stone notes that certain (unnamed) examples in the late 1970s betray a 'gradual surrender to the smutty softcore of the post-dictatorship destape' (Stone 2004, 167).

6 Shared with *The Long Absence* (Colpi 1961).

7 The Oscar was won by Elio Petri for *Investigation of a Citizen Above Suspicion* (1970).

8 See, for instance, the enthusiastic reception of the film in *El Alcázar* ('*Tristana*, de Luis Buñuel' 1970) and *Solidaridad Nacional* (Munsó Cabús 1971, in which the reviewer describes it as 'the film best film of the year').

9 To these we might add the further strand of approaching the film as a Galdós adaptation.

10 *Nazarín* (1958), for example, attracted both pro- and anti-Catholic responses (Faulkner 2004, 137).

11 See Faulkner 2004, 150.

12 Barry Jordan and Mark Allinson also connect *Tristana*, the literary adaptations boom and the Third Way (2005, 23).

13 Other titles include *Marianela* (Galdós 1878; Fons 1972); *Doubt* (*La duda*, based on *El abuelo*, Galdós 1897; Gil 1972); *Doña Perfecta* (Galdós 1876; Fernández Ardavín 1977); *Pepita Jiménez* (Valera 1874; Moreno Alba 1975).

14 My thanks to Jo Labanyi, who suggested the importance of the second restoration in her comments on an earlier version of this section.

15 In film studies, the term 'melodrama' no longer has the negative associations it had in literature in Galdós's day, which led him to parody the popular folletín (penny dreadful) in *Tormento*'s first chapter.

16 Literally, Spanish women in Paris.

17 A recent chapter on immigration cinema concludes by anticipating that 'What should happen in the near future is the expansion of this [...] in the hands of non-native Spanish direction that will tell yet "Other" stories that continue to question established notions of Spanish national identity' (Van Liew 2008, 274). It would be ambitious, but interesting to consider *Spaniards* a French immigration film, whereby in 1971 Bodegas provides the 'non-native' perspective on French national identity that this critic looks forward to in 2008.

18 I transcribe this text from the audio-track of the film.

19 With 1,783,000 spectators, a fistful of prizes at the CEC (Círculo de Escritores Cinematográficos), the SNE (Sindicato Nacional de Espectáculo), the Sant Jordi Awards and the Chicago International Film Festival, it was also Spain's Oscar nomination in 1973.

20 El País de Cine DVD Extras.

21 Beyond the scope of this study, the intermedial connections between the middlebrow Comedy of Manners in twentieth-century Spanish film and nineteenth-century Spanish theatre are suggestive. My thanks to Derek Flitter for suggesting this area of convergence to me.

22 See Sarah Leahy's excellent study of the genre in French cinema in relation to *The Taste of Others* (2007).

23 As Óscar Pereira points out (1998, 164), the card that José includes with the red carnations reads '"We are not the ones we once were" Robert Redford', from poem 20 of the Neruda's *Veinte poemas de amor y una canción desesperada* (*Twenty Love Poems and a Song of Despair* 1924), a suitable intertext for *Unfinished Business* as this poetry collection was both adolescent in tone (Neruda wrote it at 20) and immensely popular with readers.

24 Belén Vidal's recent (2008) and forthcoming work on cinephilia in Spanish cinema bypasses this redundant debate to offer a fresh approach.

25 In 1973, the film audience was 86 million; in 1978, 51.5; in 1979, 35.6 (Riambau 2000, 180).

26 Consideration of the influence of the film for the small screen lies beyond the scope of this book, though its salient formal features of a domestic setting, the medium shot and family narrative predict television drama such as *Tell Me How It Happened* (*Cuéntame cómo pasó* 2001–).

5

Miró Films and Middlebrow Cinema in the 1980s

Accounts of 1980s Spain may emphasize continuity or change, depending on the point being made. The rhetoric of change voiced by the champions of Spain's new democracy is difficult to resist. Franco was dead, the dictatorship over, the PSOE won a landslide victory at the elections of 1982 on a slogan that used precisely that word 'cambio' (change), and a changed, democratic Spain won the ultimate accolade of European approval in the form of joining the EEC in 1986.

A sceptical account might stress, however, that while Franco was dead, his anointed successor, Juan Carlos I, was king. The dictatorship was over, but a number of its key ministers remained in public life (Triana Toribio 2000a, 275), like Manuel Fraga. (A Francoist minster, he was president of Galicia for 15 year in democracy, and, incredibly, remained politically active as a Partido Popular Senator until as late as November 2011, passing away two months later.) Furthermore, the path that led Spain to Europe did not begin in 1982, but stretches back to the economic reform under the dictatorship in the late 1950s. And looking ahead, by the 1990s Felipe González's inspirational party of 'change' became mired in the kind of corruption that was all too familiar, including illegal party financing (the FILESA scandal) and illegal anti-terrorist groups (GAL).

A sceptical account that stresses continuity may assemble further evidence to make its case. In 1981 army officers led by Colonel Tejero stormed the parliament in an attempted coup. It may be noted, however, that the effect of this bid for continuity in military rule ironically had the opposite effect of bolstering the new, changed Spain of democracy by forcing the country to leap to its defence (though how quickly the country 'lept' has been recently questioned [Cercas 2009]). Euphoric rhetoric about political change in Spain is also punctured by the fact that with democracy was born 'desencanto' (disenchantment), and its crushingly nihilistic complaint that 'Bajo Franco vivíamos mejor' (We lived better under Franco). Some may argue, however, that this disillusionment was just as much a response to economic diffi- culties as to the political system. It is clear, then, that any attempt to order untidy socio-political realities into convenient categories like 'continuity' and 'change' may be perpetually frustrated.

In Spanish film historiography too, contrasting accounts of 'change' and 'continuity' are both tempting and frustrating. Accounts that emphasize change, rupture and innovation tend to cluster around the figure of Pedro Almodóvar, whose first feature *Pepi, Luci, Bom and Other Girls on the Heap* (*Pepi, Luci, Bom y otras chicas del montón*) was released in 1980, and who, until *Live Flesh* (*Carne trémula* 1997) stressed that the dictator was irrelevant to his work (Smith 2000, 185). Almodóvar-scholars have demolished the self- interested, nationalist co-option of the director by the establishment, pointing out that his adoption only occurred much later. Núria Triana-Toribio's work, for example, traces the transformation of Almodóvar from 'punk' outsider, which lasted well into the 1980s, to his awkward and ironic status as something of a national treasure (Triana Toribio 2000a; 2003, 132–42). Embodiment of the counter-cultural 'Movida' in the early 1980s with the low-budget *Pepi, Luci, Bom* and *Labyrinth of Passions* (*Laberinto de pasiones* 1982), only as the decade wore on did his fortunes with the political and critical Spanish establishment change. If the award of government subsidies may be taken as an indication of acceptance by the political establishment, he first received these for *Matador* in 1986, though still had difficultly securing them again for *Law of Desire* (*La ley del deseo* 1987) (Smith 2000, 10). Triana-Toribio notes, however, that he continued to receive hostile treatment by the Spanish specialized press until the international success of *Women on the Verge of a Nervous Breakdown* (*Mujeres al borde de un ataque de nervios*) in 1988 (2000a, 279). By 2000, though, his grungy début *Pepi, Luci, Bom* was given a prime time screening on Spanish TV's respected Spanish Cinema programme 'Versión Española' (Spanish Version). Broadcast in November, it was aligned with Spain's celebration of 'the twenty-fifth anniversary of Franco's death, and the triumph of a consolidated democracy' (Triana Toribio 2003, 142). If this was 'a sort of canonization' in his home country (Triana-Toribio 2003, 142), the director nonetheless continues to attract controversy (take, for instance, his infamous spat with unsympathetic *El País* journalist Carlos Boyero in 2008 [Jordan 2011, 31–3]).

Identifying 'change' in 1980s Spanish cinema is therefore a controversial business. Besides Almodóvar, the PSOE's new policy for film funding once in power was another, no less heated, locus of debate. Pilar Miró, oppositional filmmaker under the dictatorship and veteran of the notorious censorship affair provoked by her *The Cuenca Crime* (see Chapter 4, note 1), was appointed Director General of Cinema in 1982, a role that changed in name only to Director General of the Institute for Cinema and Audio-Visual Arts in 1985; she resigned in 1986, but her legislation remained in place, with only a few alterations, until the PSOE lost power in 1996. That legislation, the 'ley Miró' (Miró law), was passed in December 1983. In industrial terms its key innovation was to establish a system of *avance sur recettes* whereby a film could receive a state subsidy. The arbitrators of the Film Protection Fund who distributed these subsidies were of course able to impose their selection criteria. The argument has been rehearsed many times that their selection led to the imposition of a certain view of Spanish cinema. Accounts vary. On the one hand, there are those that describe the encouragement of a quality cinema, with high budgets, a preference for literary adaptations, and an eye for international distribution and festivals – these accounts are in the minority; an example might be Ramiro Gómez B. de Castro's descriptive survey (1989). On the other hand, there are those that condemn the legislation for its cronyism, for its imposition of a uniform, politicized view of Spanish culture and for its corollary effects of shrinking the variety of output and stifling in particular its popular, commercial trends. These accounts are in the vast majority, and a snapshot might include Tatjana Pavlovic's reference to the 'preposterous classification standards for Spanish films [...] They were frequently expensive, ponderous, often period literary adaptations, technically proficient but soulless (2004, 135, 148); Peter Besas's reference to Miró's 'lavishing a great deal of public money on her ageing, left-wing, auteurist "centurions", all of whom were keen to develop an intellectually respectable, anti-Francoist and internationally competitive film "culture"' (summarized in Jordan 2000b, 182); John Hopewell's reference to its effect of creating a cinema whose big budgets led to glossy American production values that were 'visually pleasing at any cost' (1986, 227); or Paul Julian Smith's reference to a 'Socialist government which sponsored a cinema intended to mirror its own consensus politics, a cinema specializing in adaptations of literary classics with unimpeachable anti-authoritarian credentials' (1996, 25).

Digging deeper, fascinating questions of continuity and change arise from this near blanket condemnation of Mirovian cinema. While the aim was change, whereby directors were freed from the constrictions of censorship and a lack of financing, for all the key commentators the effect was – ironically and troubling – continuity. For one thing, the decisions of the Film Protection Fund could easily be seen as a new form of censorship: certain films were favoured, others were discouraged. For another, the democratic state's policy of subsidizing films that were left-wing, well-made, with auteurist directors and the potential to win prizes at foreign film festivals troublingly repeats the dictatorship's film policy in the 1960s, where the films known collectively as NCE were subsidized, albeit through different mechanisms with different names, for exactly the same reasons (for details see Faulkner 2006, 13–20). Continuity may be stressed once again by the fact that many of the directors who received such subsidies had themselves been precisely those dissident, NCE directors, like Vicente Aranda, Mario Camus or Manuel Gutiérrez Aragón. Triana-Toribio also detects an alarming continuity between Mirovian cinema and an earlier period of the dictatorship in a Nationalist desire to construct, through cinema, a new narrative of the nation (2003, 118). 'The rhetoric (if not the explicit content) of the PSOE manifesto calling for *good* democratic films echoes the language of the *nacionales* who in the 1940s argued that celebrating the heritage of *Hispanidad* was conducive to *good* films' (Triana-Toribio 2003, 117).

One way to counter this blanket condemnation of Mirovian cinema is to stress positive change, and point out that the policy did support the work of new directors like Almodóvar. Gómez B. de Castro's statistical data on the films subsidized, the subsidy received and the amount recouped (1989, 252–3, 266–7) shows support for some directors who were not Miró's cronies in black and white, and lays out the financial fortunes of the films. Given the immeasurable contribution Almodóvar has made to the cultural prestige of democratic Spain, which is impossible to quantify in financial terms, it seems ungenerous to mention Gómez B. de Castro's statistics, even more so as they only include domestic sales to 1987. Nonetheless figures that balance the Miró subsidy against recuperation at the box office reveal that *Matador* cost the state nearly 30 million pesetas (1989, 252) and *Law of Desire* over 90 million (1989, 266).[1] Conversely, Carlos Saura's *A Love Bewitched* (*El amor brujo* 1985) and Camus's *The House of Bernarda Alba* (*La casa de Bernarda Alba* 1986) made 47 and 35 million respectively (1989, 252, 267). *El viaje a ninguna parte* (*Voyage to Nowhere*) and *Half of Heaven* (*La mitad del cielo*), on the other hand, to be discussed below, lost 8 million and 57 million (1989, 252–3).

An alternative way to answer blanket condemnation of Mirovian cinema is counter-attack, and elsewhere I have dismantled in detail the rejection of the aesthetics, ideology and commercial performance of a Mirovian film like *The Holy Innocents* (*Los santos inocentes*), to highlight its formal innovation in the area of rural cinema; its ideological questioning of new issues beyond the tired political opposition of dictatorship/democracy like nostalgia, and its commercial success (2004, 60–6). My aim in the present study is not to replace condemnation with celebration: cronyism has been rightly exposed; many films lost taxpayers' money; the corollary of stifling less favoured genres was disasterous; and many of the films abundantly deserve the title 'the Subsidised Assassination' (José Luis Guarner in his review of the appalling *Requiem for a Spanish Farmhand** (*Réquiem por un campesino español* Betriu 1984], quoted in Hopewell 1986, 240). Nonetheless, I will treat a number of Mirovian films with sympathetic attention in the defence I am mounting of Spanish middlebrow cinema from the 1970s on. 'Middlebrow' is an adjective almost always used by Anglophone critics in connection with Mirovian cinema, and almost always used negatively. For Hopewell, for instance, 'middlebrow' describes the ways Mirovian cinema breaks with Spanish traditions of gritty Social Realism and adopts a polished formal look he describes as 'American' (1986, 227). I use the term 'middlebrow' to reassess the ways these films lie in-between art and popular trends.

This chapter will stress in particular the formal characteristics of middlebrow cinema already explored in six very different films of the 1970s. Questions of the rise of a new middle class (highlighted in the chapter on the 1960s) and consequent birth of a new audience, identified first by producer José Luis Dibildos (explored in Chapter 4), will play less of a role in the 1980s. Films of this decade take the existence of this class as a given. Take the two gate-post films of 1980, for example, the previously-mentioned *Pepi, Luci, Bom* and Fernando Trueba's first film, to be discussed in detail in the first section, *First Work* (*Ópera prima*). Both narratives turn on the lives of two young women who appear to own their own Madrid apartments, initially at least have little or no financial worries, and are free to pursue leisure (Pepa's job as an advertising executive is taken more for laughs than financial need; if Violeta is learning the violin to become a paid member of an orchestra, this is never mentioned). Likewise, the middle-class audience is also taken as a given in this period. Indeed, the major question concerning the audience in the 1980s regards its desertion rather than its arrival. As in analogous national cinemas, the cinema audience haemorrhaged in favour of TV in this period, where appetites for film were met by broadcasting features originally meant for the large-screen, and by the rise in number of quality television serials, which adopted and adapted supposedly 'filmic' characteristics like star actors and high production values.[2] However, and crucially for the argument of the rest of this book, enough of a middle-class audience remained for the continuation of Spanish middlebrow cinema – right up to the present day.

A stress on the formal characteristics of the middlebrow also enables me to address other examples from the 1980s that are not the Mirovian 'usual suspects'. Mirovian cinema remains central to this chapter, and indeed this book. Even a cursory examination of existing Spanish film histories written in English reveals that the adjective 'middlebrow' almost exclusively occurs in connection with Mirovian cinema – and almost exclusively for the purposes of dismissal. However, by emphasizing continuity with 1970s Third-Way cinema, and especially its reformulation by José Luis Garci in the 1977 Madrid Comedy *Unfinished Business (Asignatura pendiente)*, I will begin with an examination of Trueba's 1980 *First Work* as a second comic manifestation of the middlebrow in Spanish cinema. Another important thread cast from the 1970s Third Way is the literary adaptation, three examples of which I examine in this chapter. I begin with one of a trilogy of musical films Saura made with Emiliano Piedra, his ballet adaptation of Federico García Lorca's *Blood Wedding (Bodas de sangre* 1981). Saura is, of course, the great dissident Spanish auteur of the dictatorship period – but I'm interested here in the fact that producer Piedra was a key proponent of the Third Way via literary adaptations in the early 1970s, with both classic adaptations *Fortunata y Jacinta* (Fons 1970) and *La Regenta* (Suárez 1974) backed by his production company Emiliano Piedra PC. Next, I consider Camus's controversial adaptation of Camilo José Cela's *The Beehive (La colmena* 1982), a film whose connection to the Third Way could hardly be clearer as it was produced and scripted by the instigator of the trend, José Luis Dibildos himself. *Diamond Square* (La plaza del diamante* 1982), Francesc Betriú's adaptation of Mercè Rodoreda's novel, was, like *The Beehive*, a result of the UCD's TV-film financing deal, though both are commonly associated with Mirovian cinema as they look forward to its key characteristics. I close this chapter with two examples of middlebrow, Mirovian cinema that are successful in creative terms. Modest in budget, subsidy and commercial success, Fernando Fernán Gómez's *Mambrú Went to War (Mambrú se fue a la guerra* 1986) made a modest profit too for the government (Gómez B. de Castro 1989, 252). Reprising the sainete tradition for a 1980s context, the film seems to have gone somewhat unnoticed – overshadowed, no doubt, by the showy *Voyage to Nowhere* Fernán Gómez released the same year. Manuel Gutiérrez Aragón's *Half of Heaven* (1986), meanwhile, had a huge budget (Hopewell 1986, 242), the largest subsidy awarded any film in 1985–6 (Hopewell 1986, 241), and, despite a large audience, still ran a loss for the government (Gómez B. de Castro 1989, 253). Working in the very different idioms of comedy and melodrama, both *Mambrú* and *Heaven* find a means to address the past and relate it to the present that is both intelligent and accessible.

First Work (Ópera prima Trueba 1980)

In many ways Fernando Trueba's Madrid Comedy *First Work (Ópera prima)* picked up where Garci's 1977 *Unfinished Business (Asignatura pendiente*, discussed in Chapter 4) left off. Garci passed the baton to Fernando Colomo, who directed *Paper Tigers* (*Tigres de papel* 1977) and *What's a Girl Like You Doing in a Place Like This?* (*Qué hace una chica como tu en un sitio como éste* 1978) in this generic vein, then produced Trueba's film (by all accounts, on a shoestring). A script-led comedy of manners, Trueba's first work exemplifies middlebrow Spanish cinema in comic mode, all of which is encapsulated in the film's title. That 'Opera prima' means 'first work' is the film's first linguistic pun; that it is a film about the protagonist's affair with his female cousin ('prima' means female cousin), who lives in the 'Opera' borough of Madrid, is its second.

And so the film goes on. The wordy script is absolutely central. Written by Trueba in collaboration with Óscar Ladoire, who plays the protagonist Matías, it made Colomo weep with laughter when he first read it in 1979.[3] Transcribed onto the pages of this book, the jokes are triply removed from their original context: the linguistic one of Spanish; the formal one of film; the geo-temporal one of Madrid in 1980. Nonetheless, the opening sally, transcribed and translated by Stone, conveys some of the flavour: when a young woman creeps up behind Matías and covers his eyes with her hands teasing 'Who am I?', he responds by asking '"Almudena? Wait, don't tell me. Milagros? Mari Puri? Mari Pili? María Luisa?" on and on until he runs out of fingers and turns to confront his beautiful young cousin' (2002, 123). An alternative might be the sequence inspired by the Parvulesco interview in *Breathless* (Godard 1959), which takes place at an airport, and in which the author's words are partially drowned out by the diegetic sound of aircraft. In *First Work*, Matías carries out another interview with an author, similarly interrupted by the diegetic sound of aircraft, at Barajas airport. As pompous and sexist as Parvulesco in Godard's version, Trueba's American author is foul-mouthed, whisky-swigging and belching to boot. Straight-faced, dead-pan, with both perfect comic timing and a nod to knowing English-speakers in the audience, Ladoire's Matías ventures, 'Señor Belch, se dice que su último viaje a Madrid es para promocionar su última novela ... *Mierda seca*' (Mr Belch, Sir, it is said that your latest trip to Madrid is to promote your latest novel ... *Dry Shit*), amusingly, if not especially originally, undoing the formality of the Spanish second person 'Usted' with the tentative insertion of the scatological title. All this amounts to a middlebrow fusion of the immediate accessibility of comedy – its cruder manifestations being ever-familiar and ever-successful in Spain – with the witty intertexts, puns, contrasts and timing of the Comedy of Manners

Despite budgetary constraints, then, *First Work* manifests some of the high production values that constitute another formal characteristic of the middlebrow. Besides the quality of the script, the film is reliant on the ability of the actors. Many of the much-loved and much-prized actors of democratic Spain cut their teeth on Madrid comedies such as this: Paulina Molina (the titular cousin, Violeta); Antonio Resines (Matías's thrill-seeking best friend, León); Kitty Manver (Matías's ex-wife Ana) and Marisa Paredes (in a brief cameo as a porn-film director) all inject intelligence and wit into secondary and potentially highly clichéd roles. Chief among the successes, though, is Ladoire, the protagonist on whose shoulders the film rests. Here is Spain's answer to Woody Allen, an actor who also draws on José Sacristán's embodiment of the Allen-type, analysed in *Unfinished Business* in Chapter 4. Fast-talking and wise-cracking, Ladoire offers a witty performance as wimpy intellectual Matías. The conflation of his physically underwhelming presence on the screen and acoustically overwhelming endless prattle encapsulates a crisis of masculinity that may now sound clichéd, but was in 1980 both subversive and new.

The analysis thus far defends *First Work* as a middlebrow film on the basis of its fusion of generic accessibility, and high production values of script and acting. I have suggested that in the previous chapter that another trait of the middlebrow film is the deployment of highbrow cultural references. This characteristic is especially clear in a literary adaptation of a canonical text (see the analysis of *Tristana* and *Tormento* in Chapter 4); or in a film that emulates an admired auteurist genre like Neorealism (see the analysis of *cine social* in Chapter 6); or in a film that didactically approaches a historical period considered important (see the analysis of heritage cinema in Chapter 7). It is already clear that the cultural references in *First Work* are diverse: I have mentioned Jean-Luc Godard, whose *Breathless* is one of the high points of European art cinema; pornographic cinema, which is an internationally recognized synonym for devalued low-brow culture;[4] and actor-director Woody Allen, whose name is synonymous with US Comedies of Manners. It is clear, then, that the Madrid Comedies are characterized by an especially wide

FIGURE 5.1 *All Talk. Matias.* First Work *(Ópera prima Trueba 1980)*

range of varied cinematic intertexts, a characteristic suggestively explored as 'cinephilia' in Belén Vidal's work on Spanish film (2008). It may be argued that this irreverent pillaging of 'high' and 'low' intertexts is characteristic of postmodernism. However, a postmodern text deploys such references in jarring juxtaposition with the effect of disorientating the spectator, an example of which in Spanish cinema might be Almodóvar's disruption of a viewer's response to a rape-revenge narrative through the distancing device of disparate references to comic book intertexts and Spain's light operatic sub-genre, the zarzuela, in *Pepi, Luci, Bom. First Work*, on the other hand, is middlebrow rather than postmodern as it fuses its plural intertexts through the person of Matías and performance of Ladoire, for all references, from Godard to porn, are harnessed to explore, often to amusing effect, his political *desencanto* and personal mid-life crisis.

Matías's endless musings about politics and personal relations as he lives out what amounts to a heterosexual male fantasy in the arms of a sexually-generous young relative with no family ties or financial constraints, may be dismissed as pointlessly facetious. 'Although they are often attacked for their facetiousness' John Hopewell writes in an early defence of the Madrid Comedies, 'it is this very quality which gives [them] much of their social point' (1986, 224–5). More specifically, Robin Fiddian aligns the 'social point' of the films to an investigation of gender. With reference to Colomo's later *This Happy Life** (*La vida alegre* 1986), he argues that the sub-genre was a crucible that allowed filmmakers 'to show the obsolescence of institution-alized masculinism and to unsettle stereotypes of gender at a fascinating moment of fluidity in the historical evolution of Spanish society' (1999, 252). With reference to female characters in particular, Stone notes that while certain manifestations of the Third Way veered very close to the *destape* cinema (he does not name them) it was meant to oppose, 'the separate evolution of the social commentary and satire of the best of the *tercera vía* resulted in the *comedias madrileñas* (the Madrid comedies), in which liberated females [...] flaunted the subjectivity of their libertine desire in front of bemused heterosexual males' (2004, 167).

All of these descriptions of apparent 'facetiousness' with a 'social point' that 'show obsolescence' and 'unsettle' through gendered 'social commentary and satire' suggest the middlebrow for their grafting of serious, but not overly-challenging, social commentary onto accessible, but well-crafted form. Once again, we see that the critique is explored in connection with female characters – forever tasked, it would seem, as the vessel to work through social change. Through Violeta, then, we meet, again, the leisured, middle-class, financially-carefree and sexually-active woman explored by Camino in *The Happy Sixties* (*Los felices sesenta* 1962), or Lazaga in *City Life is not for Me* (*La ciudad no es para mí* 1965) (Chapter 3), or, more recently, Garci in *Unfinished Business* (1977) (Chapter 4). Violeta doesn't fair well in comparison with Elena in Garci's film, however. While Fiorella Faltoyano's character Elena may at first reference the cliché of the adulterous bourgeois housewife, she is ultimately charged to represent the not-insignificant adulthood that is entirely absent from her lover José's childish activities. Molina's character Violeta, on the other hand, only initially connotes positive generational change: she pursues her own intellectual ambitions as a violinist, and her liberated attitude to sex not only unsettles fumbling Matías but even renders him temporally impotent. With the benefit of hindsight, it is difficult not to see Violeta's behaviour – if not maternally preparing food she is temptingly stripping off her clothes – as a forerunner of the cliché of heterosexual male fantasy that Trueba would go on to develop fully in *Belle Époque* (1992). Nonetheless, such po-faced complaints seem somehow to go against the youthful, experimental spirit of this fresh, witty film, which is an important reminder that the middlebrow includes film comedy, not just literary adaptations or historical film.

Blood Wedding (*Bodas de sangre* Saura 1981)

One of the consequences of the way this book brings middlebrow trends into view is the occasionally jarring juxtaposition of films. This section provides one such instance, where Trueba's jokey, Madrid Comedy début *First Work* sits alongside an austere flamenco ballet, *Blood Wedding* (*Bodas de sangre*). Carlos Saura's musical begins with a documentary prologue of the arrival of dancers to a studio, then features the hour-long dress rehearsal of Antonio Gades's dance adaptation of Federico García Lorca's rural tragedy, *Blood Wedding* (1933). Trueba's Comedy of Manners, like its French and North-American equivalents, turns on a wordy script replete with heterogeneous cultural, especially cinephilic, references. The Spanish strain of the Comedy of Manners in this period is also especially tied to place, with one of Madrid's boroughs even featuring in the film's title (Ópera). Saura's *Wedding*, meanwhile, might generically fit into the musical, but the humour that we might typically associate with this tendency is stripped away to the point of making discipline and severity one of its thematic concerns. Lorca and flamenco might be tied to Andalousia, but in Saura's hands this specificity of place is also stripped away by the rootless location of the dance studio setting (which banishes geographical markers of place) and wordless adaptation of the play (which banishes acoustic markers of place like the strong Andalousian accent). Trueba's web of cultural references, with its gleeful disrespect for hierarchies of 'high' and 'low' is here replaced by the reverent adaptation of Spain's most celebrated playwright. Ultimately, the convergence of the 20-something-year-old newcomers to film like Trueba, Colomo and Ladoire resulted in *First Work*. Seemingly at the other end of the cinematic scale, *Blood Wedding* was authored by a holy trilogy of Spain's revered left-wing intellectuals:[5] Saura, dissident auteur *par excellence* of late Francoism, with such brilliant political work as *The Delinquents* (*Los golfos* 1959), *The Hunt* (*La caza* 1966) and *Raise Ravens* (*Cría cuervos* 1976) to his name; Gades, professional dancer and well-known communist, with films like Mario Camus's remarkable recovery of Spain's *maquis* (anti-Franco resistant fighters), *The Days of the Past* (*Los días del pasado* 1977), part of his acting record; and Lorca, whose complex poetic work is forever backlit by his political martyrdom, slaughtered at the start of the Civil War by the Nationalists in 1936.[6]

Yet this study argues that these two cinematic opposites may both be analysed according to the characteristics of the middlebrow. They both address middle-class audiences, whose presence in film theatres was consolidated in the 1970s, and who, despite the formidable competition of television, could be enticed back to it for quality middlebrow films. Middlebrow *First Work* upgrades crude *destape* comedies to the cerebral, but nonetheless still accessible, Comedy of Manners, in order to explore the serious impact of vertiginous generational change through a light-touch romantic examination of gender relations. Middlebrow *Wedding*, meanwhile, likewise upgrades the musical from its association with the popular folkloric film (see Chapter 1), by connecting it instead with documentary, which has high-brow political associations, and ballet, which has high-brow cultural associations. It examines social conformity and rebellion through an accessible dance format, which, while sustaining a political reading, nonetheless avoids other challenging subjects that may have been developed in connection to Lorca's original, like homosexuality and rural deprivation.

My interpretation of the film as middlebrow apparently finds common ground with the initial hostile reception of the director's dance trilogy, of which *Wedding* forms the first part.[7] In an influential account, Esteve Riambau denounces Saura as a 'paradigmatic case' (1995, 447) of the 1980s tendency for filmmakers to 'renounce a certain personal trajectory in favour of the requirements for a multipurpose cinema made by a much reduced and exclusive market' (1995, 446). Auteurist Saura, Barry Jordan and Rikki Morgan-Tamosunas apparently concur, 'seemed to have opted for the middlebrow mainstream' (1998, 28). 'Multipurpose' and 'middlebrow' are terms of critique here; I aim to analyse the film through this lens.

Thus far *Wedding* and the dance trilogy have been defended by critics in auteurist terms. Hopewell, for instance, offers a sensitive reading of *Wedding* as the 'poetic' work of a political auteur undiminished by the challenges of adjusting his art to new democratic contexts (1986, 151–4). Robin Fiddian and Peter Evans also stress continuity in Saura's auteurism from dictatorship to democracy in their study of *Carmen* (1988) (for an auteurist defence, also see D'Lugo 1991, 192–201; Jordan and Morgan-Tamosunas 1998, 28–9; Stone 2002, 75–6; and Bentley 2008, 250). While Núria Triana-Toribio's off-beat critique of the collaboration between Saura and Gades reaches a very different conclusion to these critics, it is nonetheless also carried out in auteurist terms. For her, films like *Wedding* exemplify a problematic hostility to popular culture and a naive belief that a 'pure' flamenco may be rescued:

certain opposition filmmakers took it upon themselves to 'cleanse' the folkloric musical cinema of the music which they considered had been hijacked by the regime through the *españolada* [...] [Saura and Gades's] Marxist-informed attitudes towards popular music were partly responsible for attempts to expunge flamenco of some of its clichés and perceived 'impurities' or 'foreign elements'. (2003, 125–6)[8]

This book offers a conciliatory reading of *Wedding* that maintains the sympathetic analysis of Saura's treatment defended by most auteurist critics, and accepts the scepticism on which Triana-Toribio insists regarding attitudes to popular culture. I take the interpretation in a new direction through the middlebrow focus, however. My starting point is a brief comment made by Tom Whittaker in his excellent study of dissident producer Elías Querejeta: 'The hermetic and modernist *Sweet Hours* (*Dulces horas* 1981), the thirteenth and final Saura/Querejeta collaboration, is vastly different in tone from the dance films which [Saura] would later go on to direct' (2011, 10). Just as Whittaker shows the creative contribution of Querejeta to Saura's work, I posit the connected though more tentative thesis that producer Piedra, who backed the 1980s flamenco trilogy, was also influential. Piedra's name is rarely mentioned, cast into the shadows by the considerable presences of Lorca, Gades and Saura. There is little evidence of any creative input; certainly nothing like the influence Querejeta wielded. Nonetheless, his role in connecting Saura's work to Spain's middlebrow tradition deserves recognition.

Crucially, Piedra had been a key proponent of the middlebrow Third Way in the 1970s. His *Fortunata y Jacinta* (Fons 1970) and *La Regenta* (Suárez 1974) also show his interpretation of this middle path of filmmaking as synonymous with adapting literary classics (giants of nineteenth-century Spanish literature

Benito Pérez Galdós and Leopoldo Alas in these two cases). D'Lugo describes Piedra's role in *Wedding* as Saura's 'friend and sometime distributor of his films' (1991, 203), but this downplays the producer's role. This study contends that *Wedding*, like *Fortunata y Jacinta* and *La Regenta*, reveals Piedra's vision of a middlebrow cinema, with a didactic mission to present classics of Spanish literature to audiences, through an accessible form and high production values. The role of Alfredo Mañas, listed in the credits of *Wedding* as 'literary adapter', is important too. This writer had also worked for Piedra on the script of *Fortunata y Jacinta*, and with other credits including two further Galdós adaptations in the intervening period, the film adaptation of *Marianela* (Fons 1972) and the TV adaptation of *Misericordia* (Alonso and Mediavilla, Estudio I, 1977), he constitutes, through literary adaptation, another bridge back to the Third Way.

The adaptation of Lorca's text to musical film is middlebrow because, in creative continuum with the 1970s Third Way, it treads a middle path. Turning to thematic concerns first, the film offers a reading of the text that is at once politicized, and pared-down. The basic – and highly effective – conceit of the dance adaptation is that submission to the rules and rigours of dance match submission to the rules and rigours of society. Thus when the ballet performer Cristina Hoyos makes three mistakes in the warm-up section of the documentary prologue of the film, she is scolded by dance director Gades and must better learn her steps. In parallel, the character Hoyos embodies in the play, the bride, must learn her place within patriarchy and, when she transgresses, face punishment from the community by being forever stained by the blood the two men spill for her (a point powerfully conveyed by the twin crimson stains made on her spotless white wedding gown). Ironically, however, while Gades is the dance director, and is thus representative of order for the ballet performance, in the play he plays Leonardo, the bride's adulterous lover, and thus represents the disruption of that order within patriarchy. Auteurist critic D'Lugo is right to note that this paralleling turns around the human body, 'the battleground on which the struggle between instinct and conformity to social regulation will be played out' (1991, 200). An unruly force of disruption, the body must be trained, through dance, to follow the prescribed steps; likewise society must rein in the body's desires by the prohibition of adultery. The wedding scene is thus central:

> the dance of the wedding couples embodies the obstacles the community erects to constrain renegade desire. Leonardo's circling movement under-scores that communal interdiction. In order to achieve his union with his lover he must therefore somehow disrupt the conventions of the dance. (D'Lugo 1991, 200)

As we might expect, given the director's achievements, Saura perfectly complements the dance adaptation through filmic means. For example, he underscores the overlap between the regulation of dance and the regulation of society through the studio mirror. Just as the dancers check their bodies in the mirror for their correct execution of the steps, so society checks its members for the correct execution of its rules. For D'Lugo, again, the mirror emerges as a 'socially regulating apparatus' that implies 'the off-screen presence of a social community' (1991, 199). Indicative of a wider community too is the film's prologue – apparently only added to expand the hour duration of the ballet to a length sufficient for commercial distribution (D'Lugo 1991, 194). Hopewell picks out the fact that each dancer is assigned a specific space in the make-up and changing rooms, which looks forward to the social hierarchy observed then challenged in the play that follows. Intriguing too is his observation of on- and off-stage overlaps in the behaviour of the dancer who plays Leonardo's wife. In the changing room she arranges photos of a child (most likely her son), Christ and a saint with a boy, which reveal the centrality of the Catholic family in her value system; on stage, her character will defend the same by revealing and condemning her husband's adultery.[9] Hopewell makes the point too that at the heart of the film as a whole lies an ambivalence: 'self-control and discipline in the dancers leads to a ballet of great beauty; the self-repression of Leonardo and the bride leads to great self-torment' (1986, 153). A political reading is encouraged as we identify with the leading role of the outsider figure of Leonardo, played by committed communist Gades; simultaneously our enjoyment of the disciplined ballet is encouraged in aesthetic terms. The two cannot be reconciled: Leonardo and the groom kill one another and the film ends.

While the intellect may ponder this exploration of desire and prohibition, the eye and ear are entertained by a film that is a perfect hybrid. Popular flamenco music, Spain's best-known folkloric form that is also associated with the gypsy community, is grafted onto the high-art form of classical ballet in an instance of middlebrow fusion. A good example of this is 'La nana' (Lullaby), sung by a Marisol who herself embodies the hybridity of an acting career as a child star in popular film (see Chapter 3) and adult life as a committed communist (at this point she was also married to Gades). The performance consists of her lone female vocal, an austerity matched by the tortured ballet steps performed by Leonardo's rejected wife. In combination they convey a wounded woman in love: simultaneously proud of her baby, yet rejected by her husband.

Saura also matches this middlebrow approach. His authorial signature is particularly legible in cinematography, and critics have admired its 'poetry' (Hopewell 1986, 152). Hopewell appreciates the ways the camera's movement

FIGURE 5.2 *Marisol and Classical Ballet.* Blood Wedding *(*Bodas de sangre *Saura 1981)*

underscores the dancers' stillness, whereas their movement is, conversely, captured by the camera's stasis (1986, 152); Stone notes that through cinematography and editing Saura expresses time through 'the *compás* or rhythm of the dance' (2011, 47). Film form thus complements Gades's choreography particularly well, and should be celebrated as an outstanding example of intermedial adaptation. We are, of course, a long way here from the kind of narrative disruptions Saura deployed for pointed political critique in, say, *Raise Ravens*. But the point is that *Wedding* should be admired as an accessible, high-quality, serious, but not overly-challenging example of Spanish middlebrow cinema; we should not try to force it into a constricting auteurist interpretation of Saura's cinema.

Some directors maintain a unique vision throughout their careers, of course. But others may shift back or forth between art cinema and other, less critically-admired, trends. Approaching a film like *Wedding* as middlebrow frees us from the insistence on Saura's auteurism. Thus we have Saura, particularly in collaboration with Querejeta, as the great art film director of the late Franco era, dissecting with brilliant incision the neuroses of the Spanish middle class. And we have Saura, post-Franco, in a new collaboration with Emiliano Piedra, making middlebrow films for that middle class. Both Sauras deserve our serious and sympathetic attention.

The Beehive (*La colmena* Camus 1982)

The Beehive (*La colmena*) was commissioned and funded by Spain's first TV-film financing deal, the '1.300 million competition' put in place by the UCD in 1979. Its cultural purpose was didactic, 'a preference for series based on the great works of Spanish literature', and its industrial purpose was to foster TV-film collaboration, 'filmed material of a cultural nature to be broadcast on TVE and exhibited in other media' (Ministerial Order quoted in Gómez B. de Castro, 151). Mario Camus's *The Beehive* (a feature-length film), and Francesc Betriú's *La plaza del diamante* (a feature-length film plus four, one-hour parts for a TV series; with both original Catalan and dubbed Castilian Spanish versions of both film and series), both 1982, are often mistaken for Mirovian cinema because the UCD's model of state subsidies formed the basis of the amplified and extended Miró legislation, passed the following year.

The Beehive exemplifies each of the four middlebrow characteristics explored in this book thus far. None is more prominent than the use of a high-brow cultural reference, Cela's much-admired modernist portrait of 1940s Madrid as a fractured society of atomized lives, summarized in the 'beehive' metaphor of its title. Cela's politics are ambivalent: a Franco censor himself, his novel *The Beehive* was nonetheless originally banned in Spain and therefore published in Buenos Aires in 1951. But the nihilistic portrayal of the 1940s, a decade which was termed in the dictatorship's propaganda as Franco's 'años triunfales' (years of triumph), made the novel attractive to a UCD government, a film producer and a film director all keen to recover an alternative version of Spanish history through recourse to its literature.

Producer Dibildos's role is particularly interesting in this regard. Producer-founder of the Third Way, *The Beehive* may be seen as the culmination of Dibildos's vision to make quality, accessible, yet reasonably serious cinema with high cultural capital for Spain's middle-class audiences (it was to be his penultimate film). It is too easy just to criticize his script for the reductive changes it made to the original novel, a mistake made by a 'Fidelity Criticism' approach to adaptation. More interesting and more important is to address his script according to his aim to produce middlebrow cinema in this particularly contentious moment of transition. Thus while Mañas, Gades and Saura adapt Lorca through a process of brutal pruning that reveals an austere and universally-comprehensible opposition of conformity and rebellion (though Saura's work was always well received on the festival circuit, the dance trilogy was his first commercial hit overseas as it was easily legible to international audiences), Dibildos proceeds by retaining and enhancing elements of the original. The Madrid setting remains, and while international audiences may miss some of the local references, national audiences would have recognized many of the exteriors, including the Retiro park, numerous street scenes (often shot at night so more contemporary markers would be hidden), and even an interpolated section of archive footage of the capital's old tram network. The majority of the novel's staggering 296 characters are cut (to the consternation of Cela purists), but some 27 are retained, a not insignificant number in a feature-length film, conveying some of the sense of plural, purposeless lives. Dibildos retains much of the language of the original through dialogue, and deploys further strategies to incorporate Cela's original prose. First, the novelist himself plays a cameo role as Matías Martí, allowing Dibildos to incorporate an element from one of Cela's short stories, rather than the novel, and thus bring, quite literally, the authorial voice to the adaptation. Second, Dibildos smuggles in a reading from the novel that cleverly avoids the often unsatisfying strategy of voiceover: penniless writer Martín (played by José Sacristán) reads a section of the text (Cela 1998, 319) to his prostitute sweetheart, ironically named Purita (little pure one) (Conchita Velasco), in a tame bedroom scene. Dibildos succumbs to voiceover, however, in the final section, where a gruff male voice reads the famous lines 'esta mañana eternamente repetida...' (this morning, eternally repeated, ...)

FIGURE 5.3 *Martin reads Purita a Section of the Novel on which the Film is Based.* The Beehive *(*La colmena *Camus 1982)*

(Cela 1998, 320), while Camus's cinematography indulges in rather stylized tracking shots and fades in a fairly successful attempt to convey the drifting of time described.

In French theorist of taste Pierre Bourdieu's terms all this reverent reference would constitute a classic example of the petite bourgeoisie's attempt to acquire cultural capital through the short-cut of a film adaptation, thus bypassing the educational and class dispositions necessary for familiarity with the novel.[10] But Spain of the 1980s differs from Bourdieu's France of the 1960s chiefly because of politics. This was Spain of the transition and Dibildos's script can also be seen as a didactic text, informing a nation emerging from dictatorship of the value of its cultural traditions; though it may be pointed out, of course, that this mission is highly paternalistic. In Dibildos's hands, then, the middlebrow trend acquires a new, urgent mission. It may offer serious instruction regarding urban deprivation in the 1940s, referencing prostitution, illness, hunger, the black market and homelessness. The treatment of all of these, however, is cosy: the prostitutes look healthy and have time for love affairs; we witness no death from illness; characters talk of hunger but none look gaunt, and in any case goodies like cheese and cakes are shown to get through to the capital from relatives in the provinces; the black market is given the most human of faces through its association with beloved José Luis López Vázquez's portrayal of Leonardo Meléndez; and Martín always manages to find a bed. The post-Civil War society of political winners and losers is also portrayed through the antagonism between former-Republican Martín and his pro-Franco brother-in-law, though this is mediated by sister and wife Filo (Fiorella Faltoyano), rather like the UCD mediated political antagonisms in the transition. In this middlebrow film, the instruction is not too serious, not too challenging and not too politicized. Here then the middlebrow seems the perfect vessel for the consensus politics of the transition. Undoubtedly a film that is more about Spain of the 1980s than Spain of the 1940s, if you expect your historical cinema to portray the past like a factual textbook, you will be disappointed. If, however, you allow updating to be one of the purposes of historical cinema, the film is a success, with each decision taken by Dibildos and Camus relevant to the consensus values of the transition.

If Dibildos authored the script, Camus's contribution to this middlebrow project relates to the accessibility of the formal treatment and the deployment of high production values. Director of a successful and lavish 10-part TV adaptation of Galdós's *Fortunata y Jacinta* two years previously, with *The Beehive* Camus seems oddly out of his depth. The film's awkward, hybrid form is problematic. That there is a lack of fidelity to the novel is not the problem, it is rather film director Camus's fundamental mishandling of the question of film genre. The best adaptations allow film genres productively to interact with the source, as in the comic and melodramatic elements of Pedro Olea's *Tormento*, which playfully (not reverently) replicate and extend the comic and melodramatic elements of Galdós's original novel (see Chapter 4). With *The Beehive* we have a modernist, experimental, fragmentary novel adapted to a film genre that clumsily fuses gritty social realism with stylized melodrama, and there are no points of convergence.

Worse is Camus's use of a big budget, where another comparison is also helpful. Whereas Almodóvar came from a context of low-budget cinema too, when he was awarded subsidies and began to make higher-budget pictures he spent the money wisely. The sophisticated and expensive mise en scène of *Matador* and *Law of Desire*, for example, enhance his preferred genre of melodrama. Camus spends his budget on star actors and refined mise en scène too, but such stylization sabotages, rather than enhances, his preferred genre of social realism. Take the formal treatment of the scenes at the brothel. Fidelity to Cela's portrayal of the misery, disease, hunger and cold of these abandoned women is not the point; it is rather Camus's mishandling of the generic affiliation to social realism. This former director of the NCE, who portrayed the economic deprivation of a group of travelling actors in *Frauds** (*Los farsantes* 1963) so well, attempts to do the same in *The Beehive*. But the portrayal of misery, disease, hunger and cold are undone by the expensive soft lighting, casting of glamorous star actors (like Velasco), and the pictorial mise en scène. Particularly disconcerting is the dawn scene of the brothel's kitchen, spotless bed linen neatly hung above the stove to dry. As the visual equivalent of Homer's soft fingers of the dawn light lovingly caress the pristine white linen, the viewer would be forgiven for forgetting that this is a post-war Madrid whore-house. This does not confirm Hopewell's argument that Spanish cinema is unsuited to 'American' big budgets, but that Camus, in this particular case, let the big budget that should have ensured his success instead author his undoing. Low-budget *Frauds* is, ironically, a more successful work than high-budget *The Beehive*.

For its content, then, *The Beehive* is an important document of the transition and interesting example of historical cinema's tendency to update. For its form, however, this particular film reveals the ways the middlebrow may fail. Critics today may complain; but contemporary audiences and critics did not seem to mind: it was the highest-grossing Spanish film of 1982 in Spain, and won the Golden Bear in 1983 at Berlin.

Diamond Square (La plaza del diamante* Betriu 1982)

Diamond Square (*La plaza del diamante*) is similar to *The Beehive* in many ways. It was also funded by the UCD's 1979 '1.300 million competition' TV-film financing deal, and its director, Francesc Betriu, has a similar profile to Mario Camus, director of *The Beehive*. Both Betriu and Camus attended the film school in the 1960s and both were associated with the dissident NCE film movement. In democracy, both would turn to state-subsidized literary adaptations. Besides *Diamond Square* and *The Beehive*, Betriu would go on to make Ramón Sender's *Requiem for a Spanish Farmhand** (1985); Camus would adapt Miguel Delibes's *The Holy Innocents* (1984) and Federico García Lorca's *The House of Bernarda Alba* (1986). *Diamond Square*, like *The Beehive*, is an adaptation of a key post-war novel. Mercè Rodoreda's *La plaça del Diamant* was written in Catalan while the author was in exile from Franco's Spain in Geneva, and published in Barcelona in 1962. Such overlaps have no doubt led to the similarities in negative critical response to literary adaptations outlined at the start of this chapter. In this section I will refute, first, the triple condemnation of middlebrow cinema, historical cinema and literary adaptations in José Luis Monterde's dismissal of *Diamond Square* as 'one of the films that was most damaged by the standardization of the "look" of our historical cinema' (1989, 60). Second, I will use the shared profile of Betriu and Camus's films as a starting point for a comparison that will ultimately argue that *Diamond Square* is a very different, and far more successful, film.

Like *The Beehive*, *Diamond Square* is quintessentially middlebrow: this does not, however, imply 'standardization' (Monterde 1989, 60), for they are middlebrow in different ways, and with differing degrees of success. Both films exemplify the middlebrow as they are both adaptations, in fictional, feature-length format, of two giants of post-war Spanish literature's modernist novels of dissent: Cela's evocation of a fractured post-war Madrid through multiple characters; Rodoreda's portrayal of a similarly fractured single female life in Barcelona from the 1920s to 1952. Readers seeking fidelity between novels of approximately 300 pages and films of less than two hours will be disappointed – and that disappointment has been frequently expressed. To complain of such an inevitable reduction in length seems pointless. To note that decisions about what to keep and what to exclude amount to a process of sanitization seems more justified: gone from Camus's *The Beehive*, for example, is disturbing concluding allusion to a miscarriage of justice (Cela 1998, 325–6); gone from Betriu's *Diamond Square*, for example, is some of

Rodoreda's grotesque imagery, like the monstruous pregnancy implied by Quimet's tapeworm (1997, 84).

This is proof that a 'Fidelity Criticism' approach to adaptations simply sends us back to the originals, while failing to address the films in any adequate way. A middlebrow approach to the films, however, allows us to analyse them as films and acknowledge the roles played by the literary originals. Rodoreda is fundamental to Betriu's *Diamond Square*, providing the high cultural reference that is a key component of the middlebrow. Both textual and extra-textual elements underscore this importance. Within the text, film and novel share, of course, the same name, and the film is bookended by respectful references to the novel. At the opening, after the acknowledgement of the support of TVE (Televisión Española), and details of the production company Fígaro Films, the novelist's name and book title constitute the first credit, which is rolled against a black and white photograph of the smiling author. The end credits of the film, meanwhile, roll to a respectful static medium shot of a monument to both the author and her novel, located in Barcelona's actual Diamante square. Outside the text, the importance of Rodoreda to the adaptation was underlined by the press: her views were sought and any participation recorded (see, for example, Casals 1984).

The reading of the novel performed by the film's scriptwriters – Betriu in collaboration with Gustau Hernández and Benet Rossel – also exemplifies the middlebrow. By reducing the original – which is the inevitable effect of adapting to a time-pressured medium – and sanitizing it – which is the effect of creative decisions – they produce a serious consideration of female, working-class experience across three decades of terrible economic hardship and tumultuous political change, which nonetheless draws back from outright provocation. The content of the film is hard. Consider, for instance, the scenes where a desperate Natalia is forced to leave her son at an orphanage because she no longer has enough money to feed him; or where a famished Natalia lies in bed between her two children during an air raid as she is too weak to take them to the bomb shelter; or where a despairing Natalia's plans the murder of her starving children and her own suicide 'por que ya nadie nos quiere' (because nobody wants us anymore) – though they are saved by Antoni before she can carry out her plan.

So far, so similar to *The Beehive*, for the perspective on pre-Civil-War, Civil-War and post-Civil-War Barcelona might be termed a transition perspective: the film's didactic mission to emphasize hardship but not apportion blame matches the transition's pacifist politics of avoiding a return to Civil War at all costs by avoiding retaliation against its perpetrators and the dictatorship they set up in victory. (Often summarized as the amnesiac 'Pacto de olvido' [Pact of Oblivion] this description of the politics of the transition needs to be carefully nuanced, for the period was in fact characterized by continual, if partial, remembering.) Natalia's second husband Antoni (Joaquim Cardona) may be interpreted as something of an embodiment of this transition spirit. Wounded in the war he is rendered impotent, but rather than be consumed by frustration and revenge, he works hard as a shopkeeper in the post-war, seeking a quiet, comfortable life, and offering material and emotional support to Natalia, whom he pulls back from the brink of the infanticide and suicide she plans as she is unable to support her children as a friendless wartime Republican widow.

It is regarding the matter of film form that the differences between Camus and Betriu's works become pronounced. *Diamond Square* is something of a gift to the student of film form, for we may analyse in turn its five key elements (audio track; cinematography; mise en scène; editing; and casting) with rich rewards. Take audio track first. The use of a voiceover to read original lines from canonical texts is a quintessential middlebrow strategy. In film studies, we should bear in mind, voiceover has the stigma of being considered an insufficiently-cinematic adaptive short cut (utterly avoided, for example, by auteurist director Saura in his wordless version of *Blood Wedding*). In Spanish film studies, furthermore, voiceover has the added stigma of its association with the NO-DO, the newsreels that were commonly understood to be the regime's ideological mouthpiece. They preceded all film screenings and were thus a means of broadcasting a slanted version of current affairs that was not affected by levels of literacy. A key formal feature of these reels was the irritatingly pompous male narrator of the events – inevitably, the pompous male voiceover became associated with the partial political perspective offered. Camus's recourse to voiceover in *The Beehive*, therefore, while brief, is problematic for its use of a gruff, male voice that brings with it these associations of authority and authoritarianism.

Betriu's extensive use of Silvia Munt's voice in voiceover to convey Natalia's perspective on life avoids the mistakes committed by Camus. Fans of Rodoreda may complain that her voice is much reduced by Betriu, and that the film cannot reproduce the intense interiority of the first-person voice of the novel. Nonetheless, the fact that the voice is female, that it is timid in delivery and often apparently inconsequential in content means that it overturns the associations of the NO-DO, and offers an accessible and effective – middlebrow – version of the novel's portrayal of Natalia's subjectivity.

In *Diamond Square*, Betriu is also sensitive in his deployment of cinematography – the key filmic means by which subjectivity may be rendered. First, his unexpected strategy of avoiding subjective cinematography in the portrayal of Natalia is both simple and effective. The avoidance of point-of-view shots from Natalia's perspective conveys her lack of confidence as a character and her lack of agency according to class (working class) and gender (womanhood). The gendered interpretation is particularly clear in the opening shots where Natalia meets her future, machista and domineering husband Quimet (Lluis Homar) at a dance at the Diamante square of the novel and film's title. Not only is there no subjective cinematography, but there is not even a close-up of Natalia's face until she is dancing in Quimet's arms. In this way Betriu conveys that heterosexual romance, future marriage and maternity (all implied by Quimet's arms) are the only means by which a woman may acquire an identity (an identity implied by the first close-up of her face). The point is reinforced at Natalia and Quimet's wedding, where Betrui offers the only extreme close-ups of the film. Cinematography thus underscores again the alignment between marriage and acquisition of female identity.

Hostile critics who dismiss Betriu's rendering of Natalia's subjectivity as 'an effect of superficial realism' (Company Ramón 1989, 86) also miss the remarkable sequence of Natalia's monologue when she learns of the death of Quimet during the Civil War. Not difficult for the viewer.to understand, and not outrageously experimental, the fact that Betriu breaks fictional illusion and has Munt address the camera directly effectively conveys the magnitude of the loss for Natalia's life. In a long take of 60 seconds the camera zooms in to a medium shot of Natalia as she stands on her balcony at night and articulates her torture thus:

> Tuve que hacerme de corcho ... Con el corazón de nieve ... Por que si hubiese sido como antes, de carne, que cuando te pellizcan te duele, no hubiese podido pasar por un puente tan alto, tan estrecho, y tan largo. (I had to harden my heart ... turn myself into stone.[11] Because if I'd been like before, flesh and blood that hurts when you pinch it, I wouldn't have been able to cross such a high, such a narrow, such a long bridge.)

Munt's Natalia casts a sisterly gaze back across the decade to Ana Belén's Isabel of *Españolas en París* (*Spaniards in Paris*): both characters find strength in adversity; both directors convey this strength through an interesting but not obscure anti-illusionistic use of cinematography.

The power of the scene in *Diamond Square* is also underscored by the deployment of mise en scène, which critics have already acknowledged to be a strength of the adaptation (Hopewell 1986, 124; Balló, Espelt and Lorente 1990, 286–8). Whereas Camus's rosy-tinged dawn shots of the brothel in *The Beehive* are misjudged, Betriu uses blue filters in *Diamond Square* to great poetic effect. First, there is diegetic justification for these filters, for

FIGURE 5.4 *Natalia at the Limit.* Diamond Square *(La plaza del diamante Betriu 1982)*

in wartime Barcelona the Defensa Civil ordered that windows be painted blue and taped over to prevent glass shattering on the impact of Nationalist bombs. With blue-tinted windows taped over with diagonal crosses, Natalia's flat is transformed into an eerie and melancholic space of blue shadows. The colour becomes associated with Natalia's widowhood as she delivers her monologue on the terrace, surrounded by blue light. The effect is not dissimilar to Víctor Erice's use of amber-coloured, meshed windows in *The Spirit of the Beehive* (*El espíritu de la colmena* 1973), where the yellow light filtering into the post-war family house effectively conveyed the sense of life trapped in a beehive. Jordi Balló has also notes that the diegetically-justified use of the blue filter in the central section of the film that corresponds to the Civil War forms an effective part of a sequence of colours throughout the movie. The colour for the first section, which corresponds to Natalia's youth and innocence, is white, as in the dress she wears when she meets Quimet and her wedding dress; the Republican period is associated with the colour red, as in the scarlet coat we see the married Natalia wear in the street when out shopping with husband and son; the Civil War is conveyed through the afore-mentioned blue and through black, as in the colour of moribund and widowed Natalia's coat when she drags herself onto the streets to find food for her children; the post-war period corresponds, finally, to the colour grey, the colour of Natalia's clothes and hair in middle age (Balló, Espelt and Lorente 1990, 287).

The use of objects in mise en scène is similarly effective. Central to the characterization of Natalia in the film, as in the novel, is her association with the pigeon. Quimet names her 'Colometa' (little pigeon) when the couple meet and never calls her anything else. The feminist reading of Quimet naming his wife after a bird, then immediately trying to clip her wings by stopping her working, and ultimately installing her in a dovecot-like apartment, is straight-forward. There are further dimensions to the overlaps between ornithological and human life, for Quimet will establish a pigeon roost on the balcony in order to make money from the birds that end up invading the whole flat. Natalia may be named Colometa, and even her gentle second husband keeps a china pigeon on his mantelpiece, but it is Quimet's life that is ultimately linked to the birds: we see the last pigeon expires on the balcony, and in the next sequence Natalia receives the news that Quimet too has died in the war.

In *Diamond Square*, not only does animal life symbolize human life, but objects do too. Juan Company Ramón offered an early analysis of the role of the mechanical bear in the toy shop window in relation to Natalia. 'Colometa first sees it during the Republic, when a subjective shot establishes her as doing something active if only looking. By the 1940s the bear has come to symbolise "an artificial palpitation ... a mechanical movement comparable to the blind and instinctive action of bees in a beehive"' (Company Ramón, summarized and translated in Hopewell 1986, 124). Natalia turns to other objects to make sense of her existence. Company Ramón notes the ways she traces her finger around the engraving of scales on the apartment corridor, or scrapes her fingernail along a groove in the dining table: without any education, 'she has to cling to domestic objects, to everyday details as the only referential item which makes the surrounding world natural and partially comprehensible' (quoted in Hopewell 1986, 124). The point is made again through the shape of the star that she traces on Antoni's table after his proposal: like mariners of yesteryear, the star may provide her with the co-ordinates with which to orient her life.

This accessible yet effective handling of film form also applies to editing, and in particular the interesting use of parallel montage during Natalia's first pregnancy. Literary critics have focussed on the way that Rodoreda describes pregnancy as an experience of alienation: described with disarming simplicity in the first person thus 'era com si m'haguessin buidat de mi per omplirme d'una cosa molt estranya' (it was as if I'd been emptied out myself and filled up with something very strange) (1997, 64). Betriu takes advantage of Natalia and Quimet's trip to a fair, complete with street march of 'cabezudos' (grotesque giant figures made of papier mâché) to convey this sense. On their return home, a heavily pregnant Natalia lies on her back (in surprising comfort) next to Quimet in bed; Betriu then cross-cuts between the bedroom scene and Natalia's flashback memories of the cabezudos. Both her swollen pregnant belly and the cabezudos papier-mâché heads seem unnaturally large: through association, Betriu, following Rodoreda, overturns the ideology of woman's experience of maternity as natural, to show its distorting, alienating side.

Impressive as Betriu's multiple deployment of film form is, it all hinges on the performance of his protagonist, Silvia Munt, cast here in her break-through film (Bentley 2008, 248). The physicality of the actress is key. Exceptionally slight of frame, her voice may take on the fragile, timid tone necessary to portray the bewildered, uneducated Natalia at various points of her life. Her slightness also throws into relief the deforming effect of pregnancy on her body. Most importantly, however, is the ways, with appropriate make-up, lighting and wardrobe choices, the slender actress may be transformed into the skeletal Natalia on the brink of starvation. Munt's physique might also be described as bird-like, rendering the key metaphor, derived from the novel, of Natalia as a pigeon work on the screen. While all this fragility may effectively convey Natalia's perilous existence at the mercy of patriarchy via domineering Quimet, or at the mercy of economic injustice and political abandonment as a destitute war-widow, Munt is also able to convey strength. The previously mentioned scene where she addresses the camera directly, for example, frames a defiant actress. Again, the scene of the birth of her first child successfully privileges the visual over the audio through Munt's body. Avoiding the extravagant yelling that characterizes unconvincing filmic representations of childbirth, Betrui employs close-up, where the beads of sweat on Munt's brow convey the physical trial of labour. Natalia's single scream as her first child is born is echoed decades later as she wanders back to Diamante square late on the New Year's Eve that inaugurates 1952. In a rare point-of-view shot the now middle-aged Natalia looks up at a tear in the awning above the dance hall as another scream of self-affirmation rips from her body.

A serious, if not provocative, adaptation of a canonical novel, *Diamond Square* represents the best of the middlebrow trend. The avoidance of provocation is typical of the middlebrow across the examples studied in this book, but must also be linked to the particular historical context of the consensus politics and treatment of the past during the Spanish transition. Betriu's decisions in film form tread an admirably effective middle path between obviousness and obscurity, offering a treatment that is at once accessible and thought-provoking.

Mambrú Went to War (Mambrú se fue a la guerra Fernán Gómez 1986)

The final two films for analysis are chosen to explore some successes of Mirovian cinema in creative terms; in financial terms, while *Mambrú Went to War* (*Mambrú se fue a la guerra*) was a modest success, *Half of Heaven* was an outright failure.[12] Both funded by the 'ley Miró', both were also directed by filmmakers renowned for their edgy, highly-political and unquestionably auteurist work in late Francoism and the transition. Both films reveal a formerly veteran auteur, Fernando Fernán Gómez and Manuel Gutiérrez Aragón moving from left field to centre.

In a study of Basilio Martín Patino, a director with a·similar, dissident profile, Tatjana Pavlović argues that when he made films under the 'ley Miró', his auteurist critique remained as sharp as ever (2008, 120). As opposed to the single example of Patino, almost every other formerly dissident director moving mainstream has been accused of blunting their critique: to the examples of Saura, Camus and Betriu, examined earlier in this chapter, we might add Juan Antonio Bardem (for whom one might compare the stinging *Death of a Cyclist* [*Muerte de un ciclista* 1955] to the sentimental *Lorca, the Death of a Poet* [*Lorca, muerte de un poeta* 1986]). At the heart of both Pavolvic's admiration for Patino's immutability, and of the multiple condemnation of other directors' malleability, lies an auteurist conception of Spanish cinema. This book's focus on the middlebrow, however, allows us to address Mirovian films by formerly dissident directors without automatic disappointment. While some films deserve the scorn heaped upon them by most critics, others warrant more sympathetic reading. Through an analysis of *Mambrú* and *Heaven* that attends to the middlebrow, I propose such a reading here.

Fernando Fernán Gómez – iconic actor, writer, playwright and film director whom we have met in Chapter 3 – made two films in 1986 that, incredibly, exemplify the best and the worst of Mirovian cinema. *Voyage to Nowhere* (*El viaje a ninguna parte*) was high-budget, highly nostalgic, rather derivate and too long; in addition, it was a commercial flop in the sense that it failed to recoup its subsidy at the box office (Gómez B. de Castro 1989. 253). Nonetheless, it was fêted through multiple Goya prizes in 1987, awarded by the newly created AACC (Academia de las Artes y las Ciencias Cinematográficas de España), including best film. (As Núria Triana-Toribio points out, the vision of Spanish cinema promoted by the Goyas would be a continuation of that supported by the ley Miró, for it was set up by Miró's successor as Director-General, Fernando Méndez Leite [2003, 116]).

Let's get the easy pun out of the way first: this film encapsulated a mid-1980s Spanish cinema on the road to nowhere. Every age re-tells stories according to its own concerns, so the fact that *Voyage* retreads the ground covered, for example, by Bardem's *Thespians** (*Cómicos* 1954) and Camus's *Frauds* (1964) is not a problem in itself.[13] The problem with the existence of such successful precedents is that it invites unflattering comparison. Both Bardem and Camus adopted the perspective of a group of travelling actors to explore and critique contemporary provincial towns and cities in the 1950s and 1960s respectively. Fernán Gómez covers the same post-war periods, so by 1986, this temporal focus constituted historical recreation. On paper, the director's addition of a temporal frame, whereby former actor Carlos Galván (José Sacristán) reminisces about the period from the perspective of an old people's home in 1973, looks like an interesting approach to the question of memory, whose importance in the period cannot be overestimated. In fact, the unreliability of Galván's memory is too often just played for laughs, as when he recalls the fictional memory of dancing with Marilyn Monroe, and Fernán Gómez cuts to doctored archive footage of the blonde icon swooning at the sight of a weedy Sacristán. Another problem is that the representation of the rural Spain in which the story unfolds is also reduced to clichéd touristy tableaux, like set-piece scenes of picturesque villages, town criers in sunny village squares, and country cottages decorated with carefully-positioned wooden carts and geranium pots. With the same producer as *The Holy Innocents* (Camus 1984), Julián Mateos, *Voyage* plugs into the same nostalgia for rural space as Mario Camus's film. (Spain had only recently experienced internal migration to the cities in the 1960s.) However, in *Innocents*, Camus manages to draw out some of the contradictions of nostalgia, where picturesque cinematography interestingly counters the hardship portrayed (Faulkner 2006b). Fernán Gómez fails to tease out similar contradictions, as the framing device that features the actor Sacristán unconvincingly aged by make-up and wig is too weak – so we are just left with the nostalgia. Both middlebrow *Innocents* and *Voyage* are straightforward and serious treatments of the rural past; both are rooted in a cultural context of conflicting amnesia and remembrance; and both use temporal frames to explore the past: but where *Innocents* has some success, *Voyage* does not.

Released earlier in the same year, Fernán Gómez's *Mambrú*, with a script by Pedro Beltrán, also succeeds where *Voyage* fails. The main thrust of the film is similar: both try to play past off against present via the memory of an individual man. In *Voyage*, Fernán Gómez offers a historical recreation and melodrama, lavishing his efforts (and budget) on recreating the post-war period, and adding a flawed temporal frame. But in *Mambrú* he focuses on the development of one central conceit through tragic-comedy with greater success. The director himself plays the grandfather Emiliano, a former Republican drummer-boy who had gone into hiding for the duration of the 36-year dictatorship, and has re-emerged on Franco's death (20 November 1975): such cases were known as 'topos' (moles) (Deveny 1990).[14] It could be argued that the tragi-comic figure of Emiliano, played by Fernán Gómez with a mixture of dignity and mischief that earned him a Goya in 1987 for Best Actor, transcends the 1980s Spanish context to represent the universal experience of bewilderment and disorientation consequent of change and absence. But in the 1980s Spanish context the plot device is bitterly satirical. Through Emiliano, Fernán Gómez is able to offer a critique that looks two ways. First, Emiliano embodies the past of the Civil-War and pre-Civil War Spain known to him as a drummer-boy and chemist's assistant in his youth; second, his bewilderment on emerging from thirty-six years of voluntary imprisonment in a cellar beneath the water trough in the family yard makes reference to the months immediately following Franco's death. Take the early scene in which Florentina invites her husband to inspect the town centre through a spyglass. Emiliano puts it to his eye and we share a point-of-view spy-hole as he trains the lens on what was, before his incarceration, the centre of power in the town: the church. His wife's instruction to shift his attention to the town hall and mayor (flanked by Civil Guards) encapsulates the disturbing continuities and changes of 1980s Spain described at the beginning of this chapter. While the change is the shift away from ecclesiastical power, the continuity is that power now apparently rests in a neighbouring institution, whose importance is also underscored architecturally: the town hall. While Franco may be dead, the town hall is still led by a male figure-head, the mayor, Emilano's former political rival during the war. Named Paco, a diminutive of Francisco, this short and rotund character clearly overlaps with the similarly-shaped former dictator, Francisco Franco.

This critical view of the present is reinforced by the next central plot development. First, democracy brings change and justice: after thirty-six years, Emiliano's 'widow', Florentina, who has feigned his death to cover up his hiding, will receive the war-widow's pension she is due with arrears. But with all this democracy, change and justice come materialism, self interest and dodgy deals: Emiliano's family won't allow his 'resurrection' as it means sacrificing the cash. In the scene where the problem is first presented to him, Emiliano's eyes are obscured by the dark glasses he wears to get used to the sun, so the viewer must partly imagine Emiliano's devastated expression as his family voice the new materialistic values of 1980s Spain: they prefer to pretend he is still dead in order to enjoy spending the pension.

The film proceeds, then, by straightforward opposition between the political idealism and moral honour of Emiliano, and the materialism represented, in particular, by the next generation: first, his daughter, Emma Cohen's Encarna, whose name conveys her concern for bodily comfort (a shortened form of the religious 'Encarnación', 'incarnation' or 'making into flesh') and second, his son-in-law Hilario, played by an Agustín González reprising what seems to be the only role he ever plays as the materialist cynic. Hilario in particular conveys the family's irritation that Emiliano is alive, as he jeopardizes their worldy comfort thanks to the pension. Thomas Deveny suggests that two scenes highlight this point, both of which are succinct but straightforward. First, Fernán Gómez offers the scene where Hilario carries Emiliano home on his back after he has twisted his ankle when leaving the home where he is now unwelcome. 'Metaphorically,' writes Deveny, 'Hilario feels that he has carried Emiliano for many years'. Second, Fernán Gómez exploits the metaphor of vision developed elsewhere through the blinding effect of the present on the former mole. While the present-day sun, which represents present-day values, may obscure Emiliano's vision, Encarna and Hilario plunge the whole house into literal and metaphorical darkness through their materialist acquisition of new electrical devices: when both the new television set and new vacuum cleaner are in use 'they symbolically blow the fuses' (Deveny 1990, 393).

FIGURE 5.5 *Family Relations Post-Franco. Encarna (Left) and Hilario (Right) Regard Emiliano (Centre) as a Burden.* Mambrú Went to War *(Mambrú se fue a la guerra Fernán Gómez 1986)*

Another straightforward opposition is that between Emiliano and his grandchildren, Manolín and Juanita. When Manolín asks his grandfather if he was 'decent', he retorts 'yo era honrado' (I was honourable); in a mirror interrogation of grandson by grandfather concerning politics, Manolín retorts 'yo de política paso' (I couldn't care less about politics). In these examples, Emiliano's political and moral idealism is presented in opposition to the 'pasotismo' (couldn't-care-less-attitude) said to define Spanish youth under democracy (though today this may be contrasted with the activism of the understandably indignant youth of the anti-capitalist 'indignados' [outraged] movement). Elsewhere the inability of this generation to escape a conflictive Spanish past is represented by Emiliano's granddaughter Juanita, who is having a relationship with Rafa, right-wing mayor Paco's grandson. The pair are perplexed by their families' opposition to their relationship, but the image of the water wheel before which they sit as they plan to elope neatly encapsulates history repeating itself (Deveny 1990, 393).

This is high-quality and highly-successful middlebrow fare: thought-provoking and straightforward. The accessibility also derives from the use of comedy. Scripted by Beltrán, who had collaborated with Fernán Gómez on the script of *Strange Journey* (*El extraño viaje* 1963) and had also previously worked with Berlanga, *Mambrú* turns around a comic plot concerning hypocrisy. Like Berlanga's work, Fernán Gómez's *Mambrú* also displays a generic affiliation to the sainete comedy, characterized by the choral effect brought about by using a wide range of usually working-class characters, and offering closely-observed attention to location. Like Berlanga's *Plácido* (analysed in Chapter 3), *Mambrú* deploys comedy for dark satiric effect, with 1980s hypocrisy in a materialist context Fernán Gómez's target and 1960s hypocrisy in a Catholic context Berlanga's. What differentiates the two, and makes *Mambrú* middlebrow and *Plácido* not, is the shade of darkness. Two similar sequences illustrate the point. When Hilario carries the injured Emilano on his back the metaphor is satirical, but the comic treatment is light rather than grotesque. When Pascual passes away in Berlanga's film, the treatment of his inconvenient corpse, unceremoniously heaved onto Plácido's motorized cart and dumped in his house, is both comic and grotesque: black humour at its darkest.

Middlebrow *Mambrú* constitutes a subsidy well-spent. While its treatment of the past undeniably replicates the 'unimpeachable anti-authoritarian credentials' that Smith identifies in the type of literary texts Mirovian cinema often chose to adapt (1996, 25), its treatment of the present is refreshing. José Ramón Pérez Ornia's summary for an *El País* review as 'a bitter film about the death of pre-war ideals and hopes and about disappointment with today's left' (quoted in Deveny 1990, 394) points to its sly irreverence towards the Socialist government that subsidized it.

Half of Heaven (*La mitad del cielo* Gutiérrez Aragón 1986)

John Hopewell identifies a hiatus in the career of Manuel Gutiérrez Aragón in 1981:

> Up to *Sonámbulos* [1978 ...], he had thought that cinema 'necessarily explored its own language as poetry and painting had done'. Now he saw the danger of films becoming 'art for cinephiles' when they should be mass art. From [...] *Maravillas* [1981], Gutiérrez Aragón has usually worked within genres, used stars, and adopted the pictorial plushness favoured by the PSOE film authorities from 1982. (1999, 166)

Hopewell usefully outlines the movement to centre that I have described already in the works of Saura, Camus, Betriu and Fernán Gómez in this chapter.[15] The middlebrow framework adopted in this book allows us sympathetically to analyse such centripetal work, balancing contextual questions with close textual analysis. At the same time, it allows us to remain sensitive to what might be termed the 'auteurist residue'[16] left by a director like Gutiérrez Aragón, once at the vanguard of anti-Franco art cinema (Hopewell 1986, 164).

Hopewell's dig at PSOE cinema policy is a reminder that films like *Mambrú*, *Half of Heaven* (*La mitad del cielo*) and *The Dumbfounded King* (*El rey pasmado* Uribe 1991), discussed in Chapter 6, will always be associated with the controversial system of subsidies that financed them. This book proposes that it is now time to prise some of these films out of the smothering embrace of the 'ley Miró' and analyse them, rather than automatically condemn them, as middlebrow. In the following chapters I will suggest that another way of releasing them from the context of 1980s subsidies is to show that they were more than a contrived result of state interference in culture, as they have gone on to influence Spanish cinema in subsequent decades, as middlebrow films continue to find audiences to this day.

Prising Gutiérrez Aragón's ninth feature, *Heaven*, from the smothering embrace of the 'ley Miró' seems straightforward. One way of releasing it is to stress the film's auteuristic characteristics, as Bernard Bentley does in a sensitive study that uses a close reading of film form in the credit sequence as a spring board to analyse questions of politics and gender in the picture as a whole (1995). I will draw on Bentley's study to make the complementary case for Gutiérrez Aragón's *Heaven* as a middlebrow film. But while Bentley implicitly views the film through the lens of the brilliant auteurist work the director had already completed, I allow myself the benefit of hindsight and view it through the lens of the middlebrow work the director would go on to complete, especially the television series *El Quijote de Miguel de Cervantes* (1991).

Whereas *Mambrú* is both challenging and accessible in its comic development of the basic plot conceit of the Republican mole's clash with his contemporary surroundings, *Heaven* achieves a similarly middlebrow result by very different means. This beautifully- and carefully-observed melodrama traces the pivotal decades of the life of a young woman, Rosa, from 1959 (announced at the start of the film by intertitle) to the 1970s, a temporal period that may also be inferred from references to the shift in the political balance of power during the dictatorship from Falangists (who dominated the 1940s and 1950s) to technocrats (who dominated the 1960s and 1970s). Part biopic along the lines of the nineteenth-century *Bildungsroman*, part chronicle of the migration from country to city, part critical document of the central decades of Francoism and part feminist study of one woman's overcoming of adversity in a patriarchal context, Bentley is right to highlight the possibility of 'a number of readings' as a key to approaching the film (1995, 260). But while interpretative multiplicity may be taken as a hallmark of auteurist cinema, especially in a Spanish context where directors and audiences had learned the technique in order to elude censorship, in *Heaven*, this multiplicity may be described as middlebrow owing to the accessibility of treatment.

We are a long way here, then, from Gutiérrez Aragón's 'barely comprehensible' political cinema of the dictatorship and transition (Vilarós 1998b, 188). The four 'parts' I identify in *Heaven* clearly overlap with one another. While the film begins with a prologue that features Rosa's 'abuela' (grandmother, played by a statuesque Margarita Lozano), this hardly disorientates the viewer who may quickly identify Rosa (a brilliant Angelina Molina in an award-winning performance)[17] as the protagonist. The film then traces her character arc from hard-working daughter of a power-station worker in rural Cantabria (the credits detail 'un pueblo en la Cordillera Cantábrica' [a mountain village in Cantabria]) through plucky, resourceful and intelligent wet-nurse, then market-stall owner and finally successful restaurateur in the Spanish capital. The opposition traced between rural and urban Spains is also not complex, and is achieved through the inclusion of the rural prologue, then presence of Rosa's family, especially the *abuela*, in the city with her. Barry Jordan and Rikki Morgan-Tamosunas argue that the presence of the *abuela* points to the 'impossibility of integration' (1998, 49) between rural and urban worlds, citing the iconic shot of Lozano shod in traditional wooden clogs marching down Madrid's M30 motorway. However, the ways Rosa puts her rural knowledge of food and nutrition to use in the urban context points to perfect integration:

having born her deceased husband's daughter in the village, she is able also to breastfeed the son of the Falangist politician Don Pedro (memorably played by Fernando Fernán Gómez),[18] which gives her the opportunity to move to the city; her knowledge of food and cooking earns her the support of Don Pedro and gives her the ability to run an offal stall at the market; similarly, contacts, ability and sheer hard work earn her success as a restaurateur. In a surprising further reading, then, the film is something of an instruction manual for how to get on in a capitalist market context.

With regards the potentially challenging questions of anti-Francoism and feminism, Gutiérrez Aragón's treatment is also middlebrow. With his principal focus on Rosa's life, the director reserves his anti-Franco critique for the background, rather as Camus does in *The Beehive*. As in *The Beehive*, the regime is represented through unsettling references to a hostile institution, not provocative references to a terrifying one. Thus, just as Camus's Martín is stopped in the street and asked for his papers, then arrested for a crime he did not commit, only finally to be released, so *Heaven* stages a similar encounter with the authorities. At the market, Rosa's customer and future lover, the student Juan, refuses to be searched and Rosa gives manager Delgado a bloody nose. Both end up in the Francoist cells, but nepotism rides to the rescue of both: kindly Don Pedro secures Rosa's release, while a family contact ensures Juan's. It is food, again, that mediates other politically-significant sequences in the film, such as Ramiro's 'address to the carcasses as if they were grandees' (Bentley 1995, 262) at the slaughterhouse, and the speeches and behaviour of government ministers as they dine at Rosa's restaurant. The portrait of Francoism is unflattering, rather than damning; its execution interesting, but not obscure.

Food, once again, is central to a feminist interpretation of the film. Gutiérrez Aragón's treatment of this area is tentative, and he may be criticized for failing to address questions of rural poverty and inadequate female education – though Olvido, unlike her mother, is shown studying and attending school. It seems rather ungenerous to dismiss Rosa's 'feminist' ascendance as the combined product of the character's endless good luck and the actress's extraordinary good looks. If the viewer accepts the tentative treatment, and does not question the film's problematic division of politics as a realm of male power and food as a 'realm of female power' (Katherine Kovács, quoted in Bentley 1995, 264), the reading is both rewarding and straightforward. 'Feminist militancy' and 'breast-feeding'/'making rice-pudding'/'making potato-croquets' looks, on paper, like the impossible and slightly risibly conflation of opposites, but Gutiérrez Aragón's careful treatment, and Molina's intelligent performance, may convince the viewer. Bentley, for example, argues that:

Traditional feminine occupations are no longer shown to be subservient or demeaning but, in the case of Rosa as the narrative moves forward, they gradually become a source of power and authority that bring economic independence and allow her to reject the social and sexual proposals put to her. (1995, 266)

The cautious, middlebrow, approach is, then, to take a realm that is universally-understood, here food and nutrition, and imbue it with tentative political relevance. Gutiérrez Aragón performs the same manoeuvre with another widely-accessible area, fairytales. While re-reading fairytales from a feminist perspective is less original, the version of Cinderella offered ('Cenicientas' in Spanish) is still thoughtful. Thus Cinderella-Rosa copes with the obstacles of humble origins, an ineffectual father and ugly sisters, and through determination, ingenuity and a fairy-godmother in the sizable shape of the *abuela*, finds fortune. Her fate is not to cram a tiny foot into a dainty shoe and marry Prince Charming, but to find independent economic security and conduct sexual relations on her own terms: her restaurant is a runaway success and she attains satisfaction of sorts in a complex three-way relationship between herself, Don Pedro and Juan. Having refused both men's hands in marriage, that security and satisfaction is conveyed in the final shot of Rosa in the film. Played by a resplendent Molina in heavy make-up, black-lace dress and diamond accessories, Rosa sits in her restaurant at Juan's wedding reception, flanked on her right by Juan, the groom, and on her left by Don Pedro, her protector.

The generic affiliation of the film as a whole to melodrama is at once easily legible, and complemented by the high production values controversially financed by the 'ley Miró' subsidy. As we would expect in this genre, settings are carefully and convincingly evoked, like the rural spaces of the prologue, the market where Rosa has her stall, and the restaurant that is the setting for her success. The aspect of mise en scène that refers to costume and props is crucial too. We have seen numerous examples in this book of a middlebrow film that harnesses references to high culture, often through literary adaptation, and one could argue that in a film like *Heaven*, it is the auteurist cachet of a director with a record like Gutiérrez Aragón that fulfils this aspect. The film also includes a clear reference to one of the best-known works of Spanish renaissance art in the form of Velázquez's *Las meninas*. The reference isn't just there to flatter members of the audiences who recognize it, but it plays an important role in underscoring the importance of mise en scène in melodrama. Just as *Las meninas* is one of the most self-reflective works of world art – in both literal and figurative senses – so Gutiérrez Aragón deploys it self-reflectively to draw attention to Rosa's clothes. In an earlier dressing-up scene the *abuela*'s ghost had warned Rosa, via Olvido, that 'ponerse muchos adornos es cosa de nuevos ricos' (too much bling makes you look nouveau riche); in the *Las meninas* dressing-up scene before her lover Juan's wedding reception Rosa needs no advice. Her clothes convey, rather than exaggerate, her social ascendance; the colour black not the mourning attire of a widow, but a knowing counterpoint to the bridal white of her lover's new wife.

The *abuela*'s traditional wooden clogs are also dripping with narrative significance, symbolizing both rural space and the character's magical ability to predict the future. Rosa's daughter Olvido inherits the *abuela*'s gift, and summons her great-grandmother's ghost after she has passed away by wearing the clogs. When Rosa's daughter makes the same prediction about Juan's death as the *abuela* did about Antonio's, Rosa's first husband, who dies before Olvido is born, our protagonist is set on breaking the cycle of super-stition. This is conveyed by mise en scène, not script. At Juan's wedding, having dressed herself so carefully, Rosa then adorns Olvido with her own jewellery and puts away the *abuela*'s clogs. Symbolically accessorized in her mother's jewels rather than shod in her great-grandmother's clogs, Olvido is thus unable to summon up the *abuela* and by forgetting her (an action promised all along by her name – 'Olvido' means 'I forget'), she begins to live in the present instead.

The key to the film's success, both as a melodrama, and as a middlebrow treatment of its overlapping concerns as biopic, study of the rural-urban

FIGURE 5.6 *The Velázquez Intertext. Olvido (Left), the Boy, Rosa and Juan.* Half of Heaven *(La mitad del cielo Gutiérrez Aragón 1986)*

divide, political document and feminist fairytale, is the performances Gutiérrez Aragón draws from his actors. Principal among these is Molina's unfussy portrayal of the similarly unfussy Rosa. Fundamental too is Fernán Gómez's reaching for nuance in his portrayal of the kindly protector and Falangist politician Don Pedro, who provokes a complicated mixture of filial gratitude, class-based respect and sexual love in Rosa. Finally, Lozano,[19] even as her voice is dubbed owing to her Italian accent (Torres 1992, 203), manages to avoid cliché as she embodies the superstitions and traditions of rural Spain.

Notes

1   Triana-Toribio notes that the international success of *What Have I Done?!* meant that 'the administration did not have any other choice than to support financially his next two projects *Matador* (1985) [...] and *La ley del deseo* (1986)' (2003, 138). While Hopewell argues that big budgets sabotaged the desire for social realism in films like *The Holy Innocents* (*Los santos inocentes*), Almodóvar wisely spent budgets on wardrobe and set design (Triana-Toribio 2003, 138) enhancing his generic preference for melodrama, rather than undermining any attempt at realism. Carlos Losilla cannot resist a jibe at *Matador* for its budget, however: 'even someone like Almodóvar jumps on the bandwagon of luxury' (1989, 41).

2   A good example of this is Camus's ten–part *Fortunata y Jacinta*, first broadcast in 1980. Over the period 1973–89, the number of cinemas fell from 5,632 to 2,234; and the audience fell from 86 million in 1973 to less than 13 million by 1989. (Carlos Losilla 1989, 33).

3   Interview with director on DVD extras, El País de Cine DVD.

4   This trend was especially visibly in Spain post-censorship and pre-ley Miró, when, from 1975–82, pornographic S-rated films were allowed to flourish (Kowalsky 2004).

5   This authorial 'trilogy' is reinforced by the first credit (in blood red, of course): 'LORCA, GADES, SAURA en BODAS DE SANGRE'.

6   Jo Labanyi is surely right to suggest literary studies 'undo the tendency to back-project his tragic death [...] onto his writing' (2010, 8), but the politics of his death are relevant to this adaptation.

7   He followed it with *Carmen* (1983) and *A Love Bewitched* (1986), both also produced by Piedra. He followed these with *Sevillanas* (1992), *Flamenco* (1995) and *Tango* (2008).

8   In any earlier exposition of this argument, Triana-Toribio (1999, 233–9) contrasts Saura and Gades's rejection of the *españolada* with Almodóvar's playful recognition of the role it played in everyday life through the jokey treatment of 'La bien pagá' (The Well-Paid Woman) in *What Have I Done?!* (1984). Basilio Martín Patino's *Songs for after a War* (*Canciones para después de una guerra* 1971; released 1977) combines a critique of the

Franco regime's propagandist use of popular music with a recognition of the role it played in post-war emotional life as a tool of survival.

9 As Hopewell points out, Saura develops these off- and on-stage overlaps in *Carmen* (1986, 154).

10 Triana-Toribio notes the 'appeal' of 'concepts of taste and distinction in a country that is obviously organized in terms of class but in which the "privileges" of education and access to middle-class culture were closed to many until the 1960s, and even then restricted by the dictatorship's censorship and lack of funding. Culture became big business in the 1980s and so did cultural consumption' (2008, 266).

11 Literally 'cork' and 'snow'.

12 Gómez B. de Castro's statistics (1989), cited above, do not take into account subsequent DVD or video sales. See also Hopewell 1986, 242.

13 Bentley 2008, 262n. 10. Saura would also use the conceit of travelling actors in *¡Ay Carmela!* (1990).

14 Emiliano's musical occupation explains the film's title: 'the first line of a popular song originally sung by Napoleon's soldiers, the reference is to the Duke of Malborough, and the British troops replied with the same tune: "For he's a jolly good fellow..."' (Bentley 2008, 263). *¡Ay Carmela!* also uses the title of a popular song.

15 Of Gutiérrez Aragón's *Heaven* Carlos Losilla angrily writes 'cineastes who formerly offered highly personal work now champion showy vulgarization' (1989, 41).

16 I thank Susan Martin-Márquez for suggesting this phrase in response to a paper I gave at Screen 2011.

17 Best actress at the 'Fotogramas de Plata'; best actress at San Sebastián and nominated for a Goya.

18 Winner of best actor at the 'Fotogramas de Plata'.

19 Lozano won Best Supporting Actress at the ACE awards.

6

Middlebrow Cinema of the 1990s: From Miró to *Cine Social*

I n the 1990s, democratic Spain, member of North Atlantic Treaty Organization (from 1982) and the European Community (from 1986), saw the PSOE (Partido Socialista Obrero Español), in power since 1982, lose the elections in 1996 to José María Aznar's PP (Partido Popular). This event could be described as an unremarkable change of power in an established democracy – though it did institute a right-wing government in Spain for the first time since democracy returned. My choice of six films for close reading in this chapter is inevitably partial; however, analysis of the selection suggests a shift away from concerns with the immediate political and economic contexts that characterized many of the films analysed in this book thus far, and a shift towards an interest in the wider contextual questions of gender and memory.[1] On the first, commentators on the post-Franco period have noted that Spanish culture frequently refracts questions of socio-political change through gender – though this book in fact offers numerous instances of such refraction in early periods. Barry Jordan and Rikki Morgan-Tamosunas write at the end of the 1990s, for instance, that 'the role and status of women have been at the epicentre of the social, economic and legislative changes which have reverberated throughout contemporary Spanish society since the end of the dictatorship' (1998, 117). With my mention of 'memory', I look forward' to the Zapatero government's passing of the Law of Historical Memory in 2007, which forms part of the cultural background to the next chapter. While in Chapter 7 I examine two middlebrow films that form part of the cultural context of José Luis Rodríguez Zapatero's controversial piece of legislation, I mention it here as the focus on the Civil War and its legacy in the 2000s was far from new. In Spanish cinema, it was arguably first addressed by Carlos

Saura's watershed work of dissident cinema, *The Hunt* (*La caza* 1966); in this chapter I analyse its middlebrow treatment in Antonio Mercero' s moderately successful *A Time for Defiance* (*La hora de los valientes* 1998).

In many important critical accounts of 1990s Spanish cinema, the middlebrow is absent owing to a frequent focus on the extremes of auteurist and popular trends, and moderate attainment is overlooked owing to a recurrent emphasis on disasterous failure or triumphant success. At the start of the decade, for example, assessments of the national cinema were exceptionally dismal. A conference in 1992 chaired by Pilar Miró (creator of the subsidy system discussed in Chapter 5) concluded that 'there was no more cinema in Spain, that the industry was "humiliated"' (translated in Smith 2000, 138). By the end of the decade that same cinema was attracting high praise. Producer-director José Luis Borau, for instance, claimed in 1999 that 'Spanish cinema is going through its best period', though he qualifies the statement by limiting it to auteurist film (1999, xxi). Leaving aside the question of whether commentators on Spanish film are somewhat given to hyperbole, an alternative explanation for the transformation in assessments lies in the thesis of novelty that has been influential among many accounts of the decade.

Carlos Heredero, for instance, wrote in *20 nuevos directores del cine español* (*20 New Spanish Film Directors*) in 1999 that 'Something is on the move in Spanish cinema' (11). Novel and exciting, certainly, were many of the new directors débuting in the decade, some of which are the subject of Heredero's monograph. Compared to 62 new directors making their first films between 1984 and 1989 (Heredero 1999, 11), over 200 débuted between 1990 and 2001 (Pavlovic et al. 2009, 184). Writing from the perspective of 2012, we can now test Heredero's predictive powers in his analysis of twenty, and note that many, like Alejandro Amenábar or Icíar Bollain, went on vigorously to confirm their initial promise.

'Industrial and legislative mutations', mentioned, but not analysed, by Heredero (1999, 11), certainly also took place. Passed in 1983, the 'ley Miró' of advance subsidies for quality Spanish cinema was already being rationalized in 1988 by Jorge Semprún, then Minister of Culture, but by 1994, under another Socialist Minister, Carmen Alborch, the system was 'virtually dismantled':

With film subsidies thus largely decoupled from government committees in favour of market performance, this arguably shifted the balance of power away from directors (who had previously been the custodians of government subsidies) to producers, who would now take on the economic risks of film production. (Jordan and Morgan-Tamosunas 1998, 3)

As for the market in which 1990s film would perform, Heredero also mentions 'transformations in the sociological characteristics of its audience' (1999, 11). Núria Triana-Toribio points out, however, that the rejuvenation of the 'new cinema-going public' actually took place over the 1980s, when the percentage of the audience under the age of 25 reached 80. In the 1980s that rejuvenated Spanish audience increasingly rejected domestic cinema: while in 1981, 21 per cent of the films seen by national audiences were Spanish, by 1991 this number had dropped to 11 (Deveny 1999, 22). Triana-Toribio lays the blame for this at the door of a Mirovian cinema that failed to connect with youth audiences (2003, 140–1). Heredero's assessment of the 1990s is that the decade's new generation of directors made new films with new themes in new market conditions and thus lured this new audience back to the national cinema (1999, 34).

The 1990s was undoubtedly a decade of some change and renovation, and Heredero's focus on new directors is particularly appealing. Novelty is seductive and youth is attractive, but we should remember the lessons of the historiography of Spanish film of the 1960s, in which attention to that decade's novelty and youth, the movement of new directors trained at the state film school named the 'Nuevo Cine Español' (New Spanish Cinema), monopolized critical attention at the expense, for example, of popular trends (unimaginatively dubbed the 'Viejo Cine Español' [Old Spanish Cinema] in constrast). In this vein Triana-Toribio has offered a critique of the auteurist – and patriarchal – hierarchies that govern Heredero's work on Spanish film of the 1990s. Heredero lionizes, for instance, the work of artistically-experimental auteur Julio Medem (1999, 11), who speaks an art-film language that easily translates across borders to find audiences abroad. Triana-Toribio, meanwhile, argues for the centrality of the untranslatable popular alternatives that enjoyed unprecedented blockbuster success among Spanish audiences in the same decade, like Santiago Segura's *Torrente* series. Naming these films 'New Vulgarities', and noting their debt to earlier commercially-successful low-brow formulae like the VCE of the 1960s and *destape* (sleazy) cinema of the 1970s, Triana-Toribio shows that these films found a massive audience among the adolescent, non-politicized public whose dominance she dates back to the 1980s (2003, 141).

Analysis of Spanish cinema of the 1990s thus emerges as especially polarized. We have seen, on the one hand, an enthusiasm among professionals like Borau and critics like Heredero for auteurist directors that are highly successful in artistic terms – and have also attracted audiences, on both domestic and international distribution circuits.[2] On the other, the 'New Vulgarities', made by directors who have been colourfully referred to as the 'hijos bastardos de la postmodernidad de los ochenta' (bastard children of

1980s postmodernism) (Pavlovic et al. 2009, 184), have been astoundingly successful in commercial terms. For all their vulgarity, reactionary politics and bad taste (Pavlovic et al. 2009, 185), some of them have also been 'perceived as ingenious for [their] deliberate stupidity' (Pavlovic et al. 2009, 186). Apparent opposites, auteurist and vulgar tendencies in fact both share a rebellion against the middlebrow, Mirovian cinema of the 1980s. The thesis of novelty that has been connected to auteurist cinema is an implicit rejection of the formulaic repetition of which Mirovian films were accused. The rejection of the Mirovian cinema in the 'New Vulgarities' is explicit. As Triana-Toribio notes: 'The publicity phrase that accompanied *Torrente*'s release – "just when you thought that Spanish cinema was getting better" – indicates that the neo-vulgar comedies are self-consciously rejecting the Miró legislation model of "good films"' (2003, 151).

Alternative critical accounts have begun to add shades of grey to this black-and-white portrait of a 1990s Spanish cinema of auteurism and vulgarity. For example, in Peter Evans's summary of auteurism in the period, he acknowledges a 'a New Spanish Cinema of emerging talent' (1999, 2), but is careful also to note 'a healthy balance between work by new and established directors, whose films are all characterized by a maturity of approach in form and content' (1999, 1). Writing on Spanish cinema of the period as a whole, meanwhile, Tatjana Pavlovic et al. leave aside the tired thesis of novelty and name the following trends: 'the so-called *hijos bastardos de la postmodernidad de los ochenta* [...]; a return to engaged cinema and "social realism"; historical period films; a boom of women directors; and veteran filmmakers who have reinvented themselves in the new global socio-political and cultural context' (2009, 184). These, they write, have emerged in the transformed global audio-visual sector of the 1990s, in which new distribution and exhibition structures 'relied on festival-fueled circuits of international art cinema, television funding and increased co-productions, and were characterized by a blurring of the divide between art film and commercial cinema' (2009, 182).

A contradiction therefore emerges between the persuasive interpretation of 1990s Spanish cinema as a decade of 'auteurist' and 'vulgar' extremes that reacted against the middlebrow, and the description of an audio-visual environment that actually encouraged a 'blurring of the divide between art film and commercial cinema'. A reconsideration of the tricky question of the audience may help untangle the knot. In Chapter 4 of this book I have argued that in the early 1970s producer José Luis Dibildos identified an emerging middle-class audience for Spanish middlebrow films, and that these so-called 'Third Way' films confirmed the emergence of that audience through their reasonable commercial success. The continued success of reformulations of the Third Way in some (though by no means not all) films of the 'Reform Cinema' of the late 1970s, the 'Madrid Comedies' of the late 1970s and early 1980s and the Mirovian cinema of the 1980s and early 1990s, points to the continued existence of a public interested in such middlebrow fare. An audience study by Francesc Llinás in 1986 confirms that 'Increasingly, the new cinema-going public saw itself as middle-class, educated and liberal' (quoted in Jordan and Morgan-Tamosunas 1998, 32) – though 'saw itself', rather than 'was' is an unhelpful qualification. New and reliable audience data for the 1990s, however, indicates the continued existence of a middle-class audience for middlebrow films, a hypothesis confirmed by the modest success with domestic audiences of the films discussed in this chapter and the next. In Paul Julian Smith's careful analysis of the data (2003, 146–50), he points out the new features of the 1990s audience as increasingly wealthy, literate, urban and female (148–9). While this description connects with the middle-class audience Dibildos identified in 1970, Smith's study reminds us that such an audience did not remain unchanged. Any argument that flattens its field of study is problematic; this book's analysis of Spanish middlebrow cinema aims to point out hitherto overlooked continuities, while also acknowledging differences.

In this chapter, therefore, I will argue for a 1990s Spanish middlebrow cinema that is sensitive to the changed environment of that decade but also points back to earlier manifestations of the middlebrow trend. Rather than the much-discussed 'auteurist' and 'vulgar' extremes, I will offer close analysis of examples of both the Mirovian cinema against which they rebelled, and other trends like 'social realism', 'historical period films' and the work of 'reinvented veteran filmmakers' of which Pavlovic et al. remind us. Mirovian cinema is Spain's most famous – and hated – version of middlebrow cinema, but, drawing on the thesis I have developed regarding the Spanish middlebrow film from the 1970s onwards, I will argue that, just when Santiago Segura was enjoying the thought of Spanish cinema getting vulgar (again), in fact its middlebrow trend was continuing, modestly, to flourish. For while some professionals and commentators wrung their hands over the failure of the Socialists' subsidized middlebrow cinema, others, including no less a figure than Pedro Almodóvar, adopted and adapted the formal characteristics of the middlebrow to make films that would continue to appeal to Spanish audiences in the 1990s and beyond.

I begin with an analysis of one final Mirovian film, veteran Basque director Imanol Uribe's turn away from his auteurist signature films about contemporary political themes in the 1991 historical comedy *The Dumbfounded King* (*El rey pasmado*). Taken by key critics to be representative of all Mirovian cinema, I note many of its differences, and suggest that it looks forward to the heritage cinema that forms a key strand of Spanish middlebrow film from the mid-1990s onwards. After this section, I devote the rest of the book to exploring how Spanish middlebrow cinema reconfigured itself in the wake of the failure of the 'ley Miró'. I begin with *The Flower of My Secret* (*La flor de mi secreto* 1995), which Almodóvar specialists welcomed as a return to form after the director's 'problematic period' of *Tie Me Up! Tie Me Down!* (*¡Átame!* 1990), *High Heels* (*Tacones lejanos* 1991) and *Kika* (1993) (Pavlovic et al. 2009, 179). While some commentators have appealed to the elite discourse of high art to signal Almodóvar's change of direction as the start of a 'blue' period, as opposed to an earlier 'rose' one (Vincent Ostria, quoted in Smith 2003, 150), a shift that aligns Almodóvar with Picasso, I suggest the middlebrow as an alternative paradigm in which to locate the director's work. In *Flower* Almodóvar connects literature and film by studying the life of a writer; later in the decade two other familiar names of the modern Spanish cinema also explore literature-film connections, but they do so through a perhaps surprising return to the classic literary adaptation. Casting aside the negative associations of Mirovian cinema with adaptations of worthy literary texts, Miró herself connects with contemporary European heritage trends and offers a dynamic, witty version of Lope de Vega's 1618 classic *The Dog in the Manger* (*El perro del hortelano* 1997). A year later José Luis Garci, credited with updating the Third Way by developing Reform Cinema and the Madrid Comedy in the 1970s (see Chapter 4), releases Spanish cinema's fourth version of Galdós's *El abuelo* (*The Grandfather*, published in 1897; in Chapter 1 I analyse the first version), with a rather reverent adaptation of that title in 1998. I close the chapter with two final versions of the middlebrow. While *The Dumbfounded King*, *Flower*, *The Dog in the Manger* and *The Grandfather* turn to literary referents, Antonio Mercero (whose Delibes adaptation *Daddy's War* [*La guerra de papá*] I discuss in Chapter 4) exploits pictorial referents in his portrait of the Spanish Civil War, *Defiance* (1998). My final reading of new auteurist director Benito Zambrano's social-realist study of motherhood and domestic violence in *Alone* (*Solas* 1999) points to an interpretation of the so-called *cine social* (social-realist cinema) as a middlebrow blurring of highbrow Italian Neorealism and the lowbrow *paleto* (country bumpkin) cinema we encountered with *City Life is not For Me* (*La ciudad no es para mí*) in Chapter 3.

The Dumbfounded King (El rey pasmado Uribe 1991)

Taken by many critics to be the quintessential Mirovian film, Imanol Uribe's fifth feature and first foray into the three new areas of historical cinema, comedy, and literary adaptation, *The Dumbfounded King* (*El rey pasmado* 1991), is in many ways atypical. While period settings are familiar in Mirovian cinema, the favoured scenarios are the Spanish Civil War (as in *Requiem for a Spanish Farmhand** [*Réquiem por un campesino español* Betriu 1985]) and, more often, Francoism (as in *Half of Heaven* [*La mitad del cielo* Gutiérrez Aragón 1986, analysed in Chapter 5]). Uribe, however, following the Gonzalo Torrente Ballester novel on which the film is based, sets the piece in the so-called 'Golden Age' of Spain's seventeenth century, with a king that resembles, in action and in appearance, a young Felipe IV.[3] Many Mirovian films displayed the high-cultural references that characterize the middlebrow through references to literature via literary adaptations. Most films adapt the novels and plays of anti-authoritarian writers of the early-mid twentieth century, including Federico García Lorca (*The House of Bernarda Alba* [*La casa de Bernarda Alba* Camus 1986]) and Luis Martín Santos (*Time of Silence* [*Tiempo de silencio* Aranda 1986]). Uribe, conversely, lays aside a specific engagement with immediate twentieth-century conflict by choosing the 1989 historical novel of Torrente Ballester, whose work had already been successfully adapted to the small screen with Rafael Moreno Alba's *Joys and Shadows** (*Los gozos y las sombras* for TVE 1982) and on whose *Crónica del rey pasmado* (*Chronicle of a Dumbfounded King*) Uribe felt he could rely for a commercial success (Stone 2002, 148). *The Dumbfounded King* also differs from much Mirovian cinema in its focus on sexuality, also explored in Uribe's earlier *Mikel's Death* (*La muerte de Mikel* 1984). While a film like *The Holy Innocents* (*Los santos inocentes*), for example, studiously avoids this area in its portrayal of the 1960s peasantry,[4] *The Dumbfounded King* follows Torrente Ballester's original novel in using sexuality as a humourous trigger for the narrative of the entire film. Uribe's auteurist interests are central here, but relevant too is what Barry Jordan terms 'The Almodóvar Effect' on Spanish cinema (2000a, 72–5), which follows Marsha Kinder's observation that Almodóvar 'establish[ed] a mobile sexuality as the new cultural stereotype for a hyperliberated Socialist Spain' (1997, 3) and Paul Julian Smith's argument that after the success of *Women on the Verge of a Nervous Breakdown* (*Mujeres al borde de un ataque de nervios* 1988), Spanish films 'benefited from the frame of legibility that Almodóvar had offered foreign audiences, who now expected stylish eroticism and zany humour from Spain' (2000, 138).

Compared to *Women* of 1988, one of the most commercially successful Spanish films abroad of the time, or *Belle Époque* (Trueba) of 1992, which went on to garner the ultimate accolade of Best Foreign Picture at the 1994 Oscars, *The Dumbfounded King* did not make an enormous impact outside Spain, though it was well received at its screening at the Berlin film festival (Riambau 1995, 424) and it won a director's prize at Biarritz (D'Lugo 1997, 94). However, with its temporal focus on the seventeenth century after so much Mirovian cinema about the twentieth, its adaptation of contemporary 'magical realist' novelist Torrente Ballester (Charchalis 2005) after so much socio-realist treatment of socio-realist authors like Miguel Delibes (*The Holy Innocents*), and its post-Almodovarian focus on sexuality after so much sobriety, it enjoyed commercial and critical success in Spain, winning seven Goyas.[5]

In subsequent criticism, however, Uribe's film has been an unlucky victim of bad timing. As one of the last films funded by the Miró legislation – released the November before Miró herself condemned the national cinema as finished, and three years before the entire system was dismantled – in some critical responses it has come to stand for everything that was wrong about that subsidy system. Chief among these is Esteve Riambau's much-cited assessment of *The Dumbfounded King*, and Mirovian cinema as a whole, as 'multipurpose' (1995, 421–4; quoted, for instance, in Jordan and Morgan-Tamosunas 1998, 32–7; Triana-Toribio 2003, 119; Pavlovic et al. 2009, 154). For Riambau, 'multipurpose'[6] cinema as an amalgam of 'auteur film + genre + literary adaptation + star system + formal look' (1995, 424). The first problem with 'multipurpose' as a methodological approach is that it is a list: if applied to a film it leads to an analysis that describes a list of aspects, not the film as a whole. The listing approach also fails to highlight the key characteristic of the films, which is the fusion, blurring or overlap of these aspects. The ability to account for fusion is precisely the point of approaching such films as middlebrow. While in this book I have also 'listed' the characteristics of this trend as a matrix of high-cultural references, accessibility, high production values and a 'serious' subject matter, my emphasis throughout has been on the fusion of these four. My close readings have therefore described something new: not, for example, Riambau's 'auteur film + genre', but a 'middlebrow' film that fuses, or blurs, the contribution of a previously auteurist director with the characteristics of a popular genre. In this section I will thus offer an analysis of *The Dumbfounded King* as a blurring, middlebrow film. I will also highlight some of the risks involved in this middlebrow strategy. My critique is not intended to scapegoat the film for the failings of the Miró subsidy system, but rather to highlight some of the potential problems with blurring, especially in the film's use of highbrow pictorial references to Velázquez and Titian.

Riambau's 'listing' approach provides an interpretation of the film as a series of 'parts' with no sense of the 'sum of the parts'. Thus, in connection with the fact that *The Dumbfounded King* is an adaptation of a historical novel, Riambau attends approvingly to its features as a period film, including the contribution to historical recreation made by the extended reference to Velázquez's *Venus at Her Mirror* (1644–8) in mise en scène (this image became the publicity poster of the film); the easily recognizable characters of the king, Felipe IV (Gabino Diego), his wife Isabel de Borbón (Anne Roussel), the royal favourite Count-Duke of Olivares (Javier Gurruchaga),and the Great Inquisitor (Fernando Fernán Gómez); and the easily identifiable contextual presence of the Inquisition (we glimpse soldiers and prisoners in brief street scenes, but *autos-da-fé* are only mentioned, never seen). The problem, for Riambau, comes with the next item on his list, the affiliation of the film to popular comedy. It is a period film, he writes, 'however, the protagonist's inexperience in matters of politics and amorous conflicts makes the film as a whole *drift* towards the terrain of comedy' (1995, 423; emphasis added). This verb 'to drift' implies a lazy blurring of categories that really ought to be kept apart. Such an irritation with blurring of course characterizes the whole history of the reception of the middlebrow, as we have seen in Bourdieu's references to 'confusion' of categories (see Introduction).

This book is interested in the middlebrow blurring of categories, and offers sympathetic analysis of many, though not all, such instances. I do not interpret Uribe's fusion of period film and comedy as a 'drift' of focus. From the outset, the intertwining of formidable inquisitorial context with a comic critique seems clear. Take the opening credit sequence of the astronomical study. Mise en scène signals historical context here through director of photography Hans Burmann's warmly-lit night-time setting of a monk's attic study, complete with candles, yellowing tomes and scrolls of paper, early astronomical globe and telescope (Uribe affirms in interview that he and Burmann consciously imitated the colour palette of Velázquez's work).[7] José Nieto's original music score of adapted canticles also adds period authenticity. While sight and sound suggest an early-modern context, astronomical study also nods to the role of the church as a seat of learning in the period. We do not, however, witness the monk make a thrilling scientific discovery. On the contrary, as the camera tracks towards the monk he is revealed in medium shot to be grasping the obviously phallic telescope in a state of some agitation. Next, a point of view shot humorously reveals why. Rather than the cosmos yielding up its secrets, the monk can only see a sexually ambiguous vaginal or anal landscape. In and out of the circling clouds swim the abstract naked forms of writhing women and copulating men. The monk thus views the night sky through a thick fog of sexual obsession. After this satirical fusion of historical recreation with a comic treatment of the activities of the monk, how can the viewer expect the ensuing film to be anything but a hybrid historical comedy? Post-Riambau, recent criticism has admired it as such, with Thomas Deveny lauding its deployment of the 'libidinous gaze' (1995), Marvin D'Lugo praising both it 'lighthearted script' (co-authored by Torrente Ballester's son) and 'historical accuracy' (1997, 94), and Jordan and Morgan-Tamosunas highlighting its exploration of 'a theme central to both distant and more recent Spanish experience: the invidious and absurd effects of the imposition of a rigid authority and perverse moral code' (1998, 34).

This theme of the impact on individual's behaviour of 'rigid authority' constitutes the serious subject of the film, rather than any kind of didactic mission to instruct the viewer on the details of the seventeenth-century court. If a viewer expects commercial, feature-length film to provide him or her with the same lessons as a school textbook, they will almost always be disappointed. Uribe sets aside the history lesson and fuses his chosen theme of the conflict between individual and authority with a comic treatment. This fusion of the serious subject with accessible treatment makes the film middlebrow, and in many cases the fusion is successful. Take the early scene when the king finds his way to the queen's bed chamber barred by Juan Diego's zealous clergyman, Padre Villaescusa, brandishing a crucifix. The sequence is played for laughs, yet effectively conveys religious repression too. Another example might be the toe-curling sequence of fertility treatment, seventeenth-century style, whereby Olivares and his wife copulate in the centre of a circle of chanting nuns (with backs turned for decorum) in the back of a church, as Villaescusa moodily prays at the altar in the background! The solemn thesis of the insidious intervention of the Catholic Church on individual behaviour is told as a joke.

Further examples of middlebrow fusion relate to the combination of serious subject matter and high production values. The performances of a number of supporting actors are excellent, including Juan Diego as the twisted Villaescusa, María Barranco as willing prostitute Lucrecia, Joaquim de Almeida as sensible and authoritative embodiment of modern Catholicism Almeida, Eusebio Poncela as sexy Count of Peña Andrade, and Gurruchaga as the corpulent Olivares. These successes are only slightly let down by a wooden Gabino Diego as the gormless adolescent king, whose casting was inevitable given his remarkable physical resemblance to Felipe IV. Fernán Gómez as the Grand Inquisitor, however, gives what must be one of the most unconvincing performances of his career. 'A living compendium of bluff manliness on the Spanish screen', as Chris Perriam describes him (2003, 161), he looks uncomfortable and awkward in priestly garb. Apart from such mistakes, production values are consistently high in other areas, like the convincing use of location, with a Toledo museum, Madrid's El Escorial and a Portuguese palace standing in for the now disappeared Madrid Alcázar, and the streets and churches of Toledo a credible replication of seventeenth-century Madrid. Deveny also stresses cinematography. For example, when court theologians assemble to debate the king's behaviour, their Manichean views are conveyed in the flashiest camera-work of the whole film: 'an overhead shot taken from the cupola over the assemblage shows the beautiful black-and-white design on the marble floor of the great hall, a design which symbolizes the dialectic nature of the proceedings' (Deveny 1999, 367).

While Riambau and others take *The Dumbfounded King* to be a film that represents the end of the line by placing it in the Spanish industrial context of Miró subsidy, a different film emerges if we place it in the European context of heritage cinema. A term coined by Charles Barr in 1986 to refer to 1940s British period films like *Henry V* (Olivier 1945), heritage cinema has received much attention, especially in the British context (e.g. Higson 1993; 2003). Focussing in particular on 1990s, and taking in world cinema examples beyond the Anglophone world, Ginette Vincendeau summarizes that, with regards film form, what differentiates heritage cinema in this period is, first, an emphasis on setting and, second, a 'mannerist and postmodern' self-consciousness about narrative conventions (2001, xviii). In the context of European heritage cinema, then, *The Dumbfounded King* emerges, alongside *Cyrano de Bergerac* (Rappeneau 1990), as the beginning of the line. Uribe's film confirms, first, Vincendeau's emphasis on setting, with micro-spaces like the monk's study and the church heavily narrativized, as we have seen, and others lavishly recreated, like the court scenes. Macro-spaces too, like the street scenes, are convincingly authentic. *The Dumbfounded King* is steeped, second, in the 'mannerist and postmodern' self-consciousness indicated by Vincendeau. For example, each of the particular spaces mentioned is used ironically, the study for onanism and the church for fornication. Many of the performances exhibit knowing mannerism too, though the witty contributions of secondary actors, especially Barranco, Gurruchaga and Poncela, somewhat disconcertingly outshine those of principal actors Gabino Diego and Fernán Gómez. Nonetheless, in its early deployment of the formal characteristics of heritage cinema, *The Dumbfounded King* marks a break with the Miró formula (which is it was nonetheless taken to exemplify), and looks forward to later manifestations of Spanish heritage cinema, to be discussed in this chapter and the next.

While *The Dumbfounded King* successfully fuses the high production values of heritage cinema with a serious treatment of the repression of the individual, there are other instances in the film where fusion closes down, rather than opens up interpretation. It is this mishandling of the balance between serious subject matter and accessible treatment that is problematic

FIGURE 6.1 *Sumptuous Mise en Scène in the Recreation of the Seventeenth-century Court.* The Dumbfounded King (El rey pasmado *Uribe 1991*)

– not the middlebrow fusion itself. Take the deployment of pictorial references, mentioned by Riambau. Uribe offers a middlebrow combination of the high-culture references of Velázquez's *Venus*, his portrait of the monarch *Felipe IV in Brown and Silver* (1632) and a number of Titian nudes, with a comic, accessible treatment. Gabino Diego's juxtaposition with the latter portrait is a successful example of the middlebrow: it highlights the physical resemblance of the actor to Felipe IV, and offers informed members of the audience the pleasure of recognition. The Velázquez and Titian nudes also provide this middlebrow pleasure of recognition, but their role in the narrative is to limit, rather than enhance, interpretation. Deveny admiringly notes that pictorial references are deployed as objects of the king's 'libidinous gaze', but when renaissance art is filtered through the adolescent perspective of the boyish king, it is reduced to pornography. For example, in the film's publicity poster, Velázquez's *Venus* is doctored so we see the king's, not the Goddess's, face in the mirror.[8] Gone, then, is the question of narcissism, and the viewer's ambiguous location in the play of gazes. In their place we have a scenario in which a faceless female nude plays the role of nameless and interchangeable erotic object to an individualized, and even nameable king's heterosexual male gaze. The sexual politics of this scenario cannot be laughed away as erotic or comic, for contrasting female anonymity and interchangeability with male recognisability and specificity is problematic. *Venus* is recreated again in the opening sequence of the film that sets out the king's titular 'bewilderment' when contemplating female nudity. This time Uribe includes a reflection in a mirror, but this reveals both the king's identity in medium shot, and that of Count of Peña Andrade (extravagantly-dressed, moustache-twirling Poncela in a comic role as the fantastical erotic count-devil that he clearly relished). The body in question is Laura del Sol's (who plays society prostitute Marfisa), but with her back turned she is just anonymous, interchangeable flesh. Similarly, when the king demands entry to a secret room that contains a stash of Titian nudes, the impression is of an adolescent boy with top-shelf magazines.

The middlebrow balance between serious subjects and accessible treatment is, then, a fine one. Uribe judges it well in taking from Torrente Ballester's novel the readily comprehensible frustrations of a sexually-inexperienced adolescent to convey the nefarious effect on the individual of repressive authority. But Uribe misjudges the balance by tying a series of art references to male adolescent sexual awakening, for the effect is reductive. Sensitive to questions of sexuality elsewhere in his filmography, perhaps Uribe was constrained in *The Dumbfounded King* by respectful fidelity to his source novel, with the author's own son co-authoring – and thus monitoring – the script.[9] However, if he was inspired in part by an ambition to repeat Almodóvar's international success in exploring sexuality and desire, he fails to replicate that director's exploration of its unknowability and elusiveness. While *The Dumbfounded King* occasionally places limits on desire by reducing it to the perspective of a boy-king, Almódovar, to reprise the punning title of the first work in English on the director, presents, in contrast, 'Desire unlimited' (Smith 1994).[10] Ironically enough, as we will see in the next section, in the years when Uribe and others were imitating the 1980s Almodóvar-formula of humour and sexuality, Almodóvar himself was devising a change of direction that was both formal and thematic.

The Flower of My Secret (La flor de mi secreto Almodóvar 1995)

Accounts of Spanish film of the 1990s agree that, in the early years of the decade, it was in need of renewal. While the career of Pedro Almodóvar is often taken as an anomalous case in Spanish cinema (as we have seen in the analysis of his domestic reception over the 1980s in Chapter 5), in the early 1990s there is an unusual parallel between the two. While Almodóvar has rightly been admired for the way he burst onto the Spanish cultural scene in the late 1970s, with no formal training in film and relying on shoestring budgets provided by his then day job for Telefónica (the Spanish national telephone company), his reinvention from the mid-1990s onwards is arguably just as impressive. Whether reinvention under the weight of critical expectation, or invention in the context of anonymity, is tougher is a moot point. We should bear in mind, though, that the 1990s Spanish cinema landscape is littered with the failed attempts of previously-successful directors at reinvention. Take, for example, Francesc Betrui's effort to combine a late 1970s 'Madrid Comedy' (by casting some of its acting veterans like Antonio Resines and Kiti Manver) with the Mirovian cinema's favoured author Miguel Delibes (by adapting his *Diario de un jubilado* [*Diary of a Retired Person* 1996]) plus a re-run of the social mobility theme of a married couple entering a competition used in Juan Antonio Bardem and Luis García Berlanga's *That Happy Couple** (*Esa pareja feliz* 1952). The resulting *A Perfect Couple** (*Una pareja perfecta* 1997) was a critical failure and a commercial flop.

With the change of direction in his career begun with *Flower*, Almodóvar, in contrast, emerges as successfully sensitive to both the evolving 1990s Spanish audience and the evolving 1990s Spanish industrial context, described, as we have seen, as a 'blurring of the divide between art film and commercial cinema' (Pavlovic et al. 2009, 182). (Outside the scope of this book lies the related question of the evolving international audiences on which Almodóvar as phenomenally successful global auteur is of course also dependent, a matter on which Brad Epps and Despina Kakoudaki provide a helpful introduction [2009].) Successful at the box office and 'good business' for the film's French co-production company Ciby (Almodóvar quoted in Smith 2000, 177), *Flower* as a change of direction was not immediately greeted with delight by critics. What I will analyse as Almodóvar's 'middlebrow turn' provoked similar upset to the controversy stirred by Spain's other great international auteur, Luis Buñuel's apparent shift towards the middlebrow in *Tristana* (1970). Buñuel critics familiar with the director's earlier work queried its conventionality with some disappointment, though soon comforted themselves with the realization that 'beneath its dull veneer of respectability there lay virulent anti-clericalism and a treatise on the stagnancy of Spanish society' (Stone 2002, 75). In other words, despite the middlebrow elements, Buñuel's acerbic auteurist critique remained unchanged (for my recuperation of *Tristana* as middlebrow see Chapter 4). There are some points of comparison with the critical reception of Almodóvar's *Flower*, which Jordan and Morgan-Tamosunas describe in 1998 as 'a change in his trajectory. It totally set aside the hedonism, overblown stylisation and *auteur* as interior decorator of previous farces in favour of a rather drab naturalism and a confusingly real "reality effect"' (83). However, adopting an auteurist model that emphasizes the continuity of the directorial signature, the same authors somewhat confusingly write in the pages of the same book (though in a different chapter) that in *Flower* 'the characteristic Almodóvar strengths of style and female characterisation' remain, and the film as a whole demonstrates continuity as its themes 'recover the potential demonstrated in the sensitivity and insight of Almodóvar's earlier films' (117).[11]

Paul Julian Smith avoids both knee-jerk criticism of the director's change of direction and the comforting conclusion that the auteurist vision remains unchanged in his impressive analysis of the 'blue' trilogy, which consists of *Flower*, *Live Flesh* (*Carne trémula* 1997) and *All About My Mother* (*Todo sobre mi madre* 1999). Smith assesses the films in the light of the previously-discussed analysis of audience change in the 1990s: increasingly 'wealthy, educated and urban', 'proportionately more female', and more interested in 'literarity', in the sense of viewers also being readers of novels, newspaper cultural supplements and reviews (2003, 147–50). With competition for Spanish audiences in Spain taking the form of the twin giants of Hollywood (which in a typical year wins 85 per cent of attendances [2003, 146]) and the 'New Vulgarities' domestic blockbusters, Smith is right to note that the select demographic he identifies for films like *Flower* is 'a minority of a minority' (146), though 10 years after Smith's identification of the demographic the continued success of middlebrow films today suggests this audience continues to exist.

I take the findings of Smith's study in a complementary direction. As part of a book on Spanish middlebrow cinema, my interpretation locates *Flower* within the history of the national cinema, which is not Smith's concern. Transnational Almodóvar is of course incomprehensible without reference to the global environment in which much contemporary filmmaking takes place: the texts of his films are replete with implicit and explicit international references; their contexts of production, distribution and reception are thoroughly global. However, what I seek to do here is concentrate on the Spanish Almodóvar, for national audiences, whose middlebrow turn in *Flower* connects his work with Spanish middlebrow trends. These connections stretch back to the Third Way, the 'Madrid Comedy' and to questions of literarity explored in Mirovian cinema. The connections also look forward to films analysed in the rest of his book. In the same way that Almodóvar's 1980s work influenced the domestic cinema's turn to 'stylish eroticism and zany humour', as in *The Dumbfounded King* or *Belle Époque* (Trueba 1992) (Jordan 1999, 286 n. 1), his reinvention with *Flower* also influences a number of the middlebrow directions the domestic cinema would go on to take. The emphasis on literarity, for instance, is evident in both *The Dog in the Manger* and *The Grandfather* (to be discussed in this chapter), mother–daughter relationships in rural and urban settings re-emerge in *Alone* (also discussed here), and a middle-aged writer–protagonist enduring a mid-life crisis recurs in *Soldiers of Salamina* (*Soldados de Salamina* to be discussed in Chapter 7).

For Smith, *Flower* inaugurates a 'new kind of arthouse'; I analyse many of the same characteristics, but alternatively defend the term 'middlebrow'. While 'arthouse' helpfully positions Almodóvar in a transnational industrial context, 'middlebrow' helps us connect *Flower* to previous and subsequent aesthetic trends in Spain. *Flower* is middlebrow in its fusion of serious subject matters, accessible treatment, high production values and high-cultural references, a matrix of connections implicit in Smith's summary of the trilogy as a whole as 'Neither too challenging nor too simple, it combines in dynamic equilibrium increased measures of both aestheticization and social commentary' (2003, 153). Smith notes that this new bid for seriousness is also self-consciously sewn into the narrative of *Flower* through the details of Leo's crisis as an author ('Leo' means 'I read' in Spanish). Previously a writer of popular romantic literature termed the 'novela rosa' in Spanish (literally 'pink novel', the equivalent of Mills and Boon in England), the collapse of Leo's marriage causes her prose to darken 'no sé escribir novela rosa, me sale negra' (I don't know how to write romantic literature, it comes out serious; literally 'rather than pink, it comes out black'): '*Flower* stages the conflict between "pink" and "black": that is to say, between popular romantic fiction and novels that are serious in both senses (high in status and melancholic in tone)' (Smith 2003, 153).

In narrative terms, the conflict between 'pink' and 'black' writing remains unresolved. Leo continues to write successful 'black', or serious work. One example of this, 'Vida y dolor' (Life and Pain), is pilfered from a kitchen bin by her maid's son, converted into a film script and, in a little dig at his imitators, we learn it will be made into a film by Juan José Bigas Luna; another example becomes the plot for Almodóvar's own *Volver* of 2006. Meanwhile, Leo's sexually-ambiguous friend and possible future lover, the deliberately named Ángel, ghost-writes the romantic 'pink' novels for which she is under contractual obligation. Indeed the title of the film is an example of this ghost-writing: when Leo reveals to him that she is the author of the 'pink' novels, for which she uses the pseudonym 'Amanda Gris', Ángel offers a pretty description of the revelation as 'La flor de mi secreto'.

However, when we consider the film as a whole, *Flower* stages the fusion of 'pink' and 'black', which I argue is a key to the middlebrow. What remains 'pink' in *Flower*, or what connects it to widely-read romantic literature, is accessibility. The film may begin with a film-within-a-film of a medical training session for doctors about organ donation which is disorientating for the viewer, but the potential distancing effect of this self-conscious mise-en-abyme of the questions of representation, female disorientation and grief is quickly mitigated by the arrival of the disorientated, and soon to be grief-stricken, Leo at the seminar room. Almódovar thus avoids the deliberately obtuse, and the film's accessibility derives mainly from its deployment of the conventions of melodrama (Allinson 2001, 140–2). Almodóvar underlines in a commentary to the published script that this genre is not to be taken as the filmic equivalent of popular romantic literature (1996, 147). However, they coincide in many relevant areas. Thus *Flower* displays the readily recognisable melodramatic characteristics of a female focus (Leo), an attention to female relationships within the family and without (Leo's mother and sister for the first; Betty and Ángel for the second), a privileging of emotional life (melancholia, grief, mourning and the threat of madness partially balanced by the mother–daughter bond, sisterhood, friendship and recovery) and a characteristically close attention to sound (music is the 'melos' of 'melodrama') and mise en scène, both heavy here with narrative significance.

It could be argued that Almódovar 'blackens' this 'pink' melodrama by emphasising tragic elements, showing us just how close Leo gets to touching the abyss of suicide. But black elements are present in almost all manifestations of the genre (see the discussion of *The Nail* and *From Woman to Woman* in Chapter 3), and their relative importance is a matter of degree. Alternatively, we might contend that Almodóvar 'blackens', or makes the film more serious, through a new attention to the demonstrably serious socio-political contexts of mid-1990s Spain. These include a reference to NATO and the Bosnian conflict through the profession of Paco, Leo's cheating husband, as a Spanish army officer stationed in Brussels, and the street protests by Spanish health workers targeted at then Socialist president Felipe González's reforms (González would go on to lose the elections after 14 year in power the year after the film was made). However, these two socio-political references are red herrings, for both lead us back to the film's central theme of Leo's crisis and recovery, as her marriage falls apart and her writing changes in response. Almodóvar's script makes a bid for emotions to be given some of the recognition of military warfare when the two are equated in Leo and Paco's arguments: 'You volunteered for the Peace Mission to escape the war you've got here! And I'm the only victim in that war!' complains Leo (Almodóvar 1996, 86); Paco takes up the equation of marriage and war later in his comment to his wife that 'no war can compare to you' (Almodóvar 1996, 89). Similarly, cinematography would seem to suggest that Leo's drama equates to, or even rises above, the grievances of the crowd of striking workers. When suicidal Leo finds herself engulfed by this crowd and is rescued by her guardian 'Ángel', Almódovar ends the sequence with a tilting crane shot that lifts the image, and our attention, up and away from the workers in order – problematically perhaps – to continue the narrative focus on Leo's emotional life.

Alternatively again, we may argue that Almódovar fuses the accessible and the serious by deploying high production values, a characteristic of the middlebrow that I have emphasized throughout. Take the example of the wordy script, which fizzes with wit, comic moments, and intertextual references for the initiated, like the roll call of contemporary Anglophone women writers cited by Leo in her first interview with Ángel. This clever wordiness recalls the scripts of the Madrid Comedies of the late 1970s and early 1980s, a generic connection also made by the presence in *Flower* of some of the trend's iconic actors, like Kiti Manver as nurse Manuela and Marisa Paredes as Leo.[12] In this 1995 film, however, the emphasis has shifted, for while in *First Work* (*Ópera prima* Trueba 1980), for example, much of the dense script is devoted to the development of Woody-Allenesque humour, in *Flower*, notwithstanding moments of laugh-out-loud humour such as the response of Leo's sister Rosa (Rossy de Palma) to the Flamenco performance, the emphasis is on grief and the threat of madness, which is announced by the very first words the viewer hears – and simultaneously reads – in Leo's flat: 'defenceless and a prey to madness' (Almodóvar 1996, 6).[13]

Mise en scène and sound thus also emerge as exquisitely crafted in *Flower*. The use, for example, of mirrors, frames, fabrics and filters is, throughout the film, a joy to behold. The middlebrow balance is perfect, for this aspect requires thoughtful interpretation, but it is not overly complex. Thus, as Almodóvar himself points out (quoted in Smith 2000, 174) and critics have emphasized (for example Acevedo-Muñoz 2007, 160–1) the first kiss between Leo and Paco is perceived through multiple mirrors, which obscures a view of their lips. This succinctly and thoughtfully – though not abstrusely – conveys the fracturing of their relationship. The viewer's attention to other filters over the image is also richly rewarded, with Leo shot through a partition mesh to convey her distancing from her husband in a late-night telephone conversation with him (this contrasts with the preceding conversation with Ángel: the understanding between the two characters is portrayed by parallel montage, Almódovar respecting each interlocutor with equitable medium shots). In a visual echo of compromised visibility, when Paco returns home, Almodóvar films him through a partially-opaque shower curtain to convey the simultaneous enticing proximity yet unsurmountable distance of his body from Leo. When the marriage collapses and Leo retreats to the village Almagro with her mother to recover, her partial rebirth is again conveyed through a filter that is both appropriate to location and full of significant references to female solidarity. The bedroom where she convalesces is also partially obscure, but importantly also partially revealed through a long shot through a window hung with the lacework that is collectively and painstakingly sewn by the village women. Leo's recovery will also be painful, and achieved thanks to solidarity with other women. Her full recovery is again conveyed through a filter. Wearing a suit of a green colour that represents rebirth, she arrives at Ángel's flat at the end of the film, and Almodóvar captures the couple's reflection in a round mirror that contrasts with the broken image of Leo and Paco in the fragmented mirror. Leo then confidently brushes past the red chainmail screen at the door – a filter which, earlier in the film, might have partially obscured her.

The acoustic make-up of the film is similarly richly layered with thoughtful – but not inaccessible – significance. Original compositions by Alberto Iglesias complement developments on screen, with shrill strings, for example, aptly conveying Leo's fragility. The words of the 'boleros' (sentimental songs) included in the film, like Chavela Vargas's 'En el último trago' (In the Last Drink), which speaks of love lost, heart-break, and the temptation of alcoholism (present throughout the film) also complement the narrative. Other aspects of sound, like the life-giving gift of the mother's voice that rescues Leo from suicide, or the rhythmic, military, and cruel sound of Paco's footsteps as he departs having broken up the marriage, likewise richly reward the attentive listener.[14]

Almodóvar also appeals to his audience through recognisable high-culture references, another feature of the middlebrow that this book as described throughout. Take casting first of all. Almodóvar's choice and direction of his actors is the stuff of folklore in Spain, with cosy references to 'his family', 'his girls' and 'his boys' conveying both the actors' enthusiasm for the director, and the intensity of the engagement he requires from them. One such member of the 'family' is Paredes, whose presence in *Flower* recalls her previous appearance in Almodóvar's work (*High Heels* [*Tacones lejanos* 1991]), and her

FIGURE 6.2 *Leo and Angel in the Whole Mirror that Suggests Wholesomeness.* The Flower of My Secret (*La flor de mi secreto Almodóvar 1995*)

earlier performances in the Madrid Comedies. Smith points out too that she is renowned actor of the Spanish theatre, and that, by casting her, Almodóvar thus borrows from the prestige of the older art (2003, 134), which is a good example of the middlebrow blurring of elite culture (serious theatre) and accessible treatment (a film melodrama that follows the genre's conventions). In interview, Almodóvar has explained how he toned down the theatricality of her performance through exhaustive rehearsal ('at one point I said: "Don't move a single muscle in your face"' [quoted in Smith 2000, 176]), but a tendency to expressive excess nonetheless remains, for example in the sequence of Paco's departure. I do not interpret this as a mistake on Almodóvar's part. First, theatrical excess is entirely appropriate to the melodramatic narrative of emotional breakdown; second, the director perhaps occasionally permits some theatricality in order, precisely, to allude to the older art.[15]

Almodóvar offers his audience the pleasure of recognition, or, in Bourdieu's terms, the distinctive pleasure of confirming their cultural capital, though other elements of literarity. *Flower* offers readerly pleasures through its references to literature in the script, as we have seen, and by the presence of books in the frame, like the sweeping shots in the introduction to Leo's flat that allow the viewer to take in titles like Juan José Millás's *Ella imagina* (*She Imagines*).[16] The conversations between Leo and Ángel, especially those at the offices of the respectable Spanish daily newspaper *El País*, also allow the viewer to recognize literary references. Unlike the uneven deployment of high art in *The Dumbfounded King*, in *Flower* each writer or text mentioned enriches our understanding of the plot. *She Imagines*, for example, could be an alternative title for the entire film. Literarity is not just limited to intertextual references either, for the film also portrays the physical act of writing, like the rather obvious images of the author typing out words, but also explores the more interesting questions of what influences the creative process, whereby marital crisis causes Leo's 'pink' novels to come out 'black'.[17]

Flower, therefore, marks Almodóvar's middlebrow turn, perfectly fusing its four key elements. It deploys the readily-decipherable conventions of melodrama; offers a serious bid for emotional life to be taken as seriously as the more conventionally-worthy topics of war and strikes;[18] uses high production values, with script, sound, mise en scène and performance surely perfectly judged; and incorporates high-culture references that are both easily identifiable and rewardingly relevant to the film's narrative. This is a film to match any manifestation of Spanish middlebrow cinema. Its handling of melodrama is on a par with Olea's brilliantly critical, yet reassuringly accessible, treatment of another middle-class woman in his Third-Way *Tormento* of 1974. Its crafting of script is a match for the best moments of a Madrid Comedy like *First Work* of 1980. Given that Almodóvar's work was often seen as an attractive alternative to Mirovian cinema in the 1980s (for instance by Smith 1996, 23–34) it is perhaps ironic that it is Almódovar himself who reinvents the literarity that was so crucial to the PSOE's subsidized cinema. While the Mirovian cinema perhaps relied too heavily on connecting literature and film through literary adaptations, Almódovar's *Flower* points to new dynamic, witty, but still middlebrow version of literarity that would go on to influence Spanish films from 1995 on.

The Dog in the Manger (*El perro del hortelano* Miró 1996)

Another film director of the 1990s for whom literarity was fundamental was Pilar Miró. Frequently mentioned for her controversial establishment of state support for middlebrow films in her role as Director General of Film (1982–5), in this section of the book I examine her as a film artist in her own right. Throughout her directing career (cut short by her death from a heart attack at 57 in 1997), literature and film went hand in hand, with her filmography including five literary adaptations for cinema, alongside numerous literary adaptations for TV. In *Flower*, as we have seen, Pedro Almodóvar yokes highbrow-yet-straightforward literarity to accessible-yet-stylized melodrama; in his next project he similarly turns to literary adaptation in the classy thriller *Live Flesh* (1997). Miró's *The Dog in the Manger* (*El perro del hortelano*) links up with a number of these elements in an entirely original way. The film is an adaptation of a 1618 play by Lope de Vega, Spain's most famous Golden-Age dramatist, and dynamically combines the prestige of both the author and the classic theatre with a treatment that draws on popular romantic comedy. Relevant too is the contemporary boom in middlebrow 'heritage' cinema, of which, we recall, Uribe's *The Dumbfounded King* (1991) is an early example. *Cyrano de Bergerac* (Rappeneau 1990), an obvious model that is also scripted entirely in verse, and *Much Ado about Nothing* (Branagh 1993) are both mentioned by Miró in interview (Fernández Soto and Checa y Olmos 2010, 86), and some press critics hailed *The Dog in the Manger* as the first Spanish movie to rival these foreign successes (García-Posada 1997). Despite what many saw as the audacity of retaining almost all of Lope's original verse – only one fifth is cut (Allinson 1999, 35) – *The Dog in the Manger* attracted a domestic audience as substantial as that of *Flower* (almost one million in both cases), and a fistful of Goya awards, including Best Director and Best Actress, proving once again the success of the middlebrow in mid-1990s Spanish cinema. Central to *The Dog in the Manger* too are the feminist politics of identity, which Miró explored throughout her directorial career. On the film's release the director herself suggested it offered a reworking of Lope that is sensitive to gender critique (Torres 1997).

Writing on heritage film in 2001, Ginette Vincendeau sees the genre as 'a new type of popular cinema' (2001, xxi). Approaching Miró's *The Dog in the Manger* as popular cinema is attractive, not only because the film commanded a large audience (the first 'market' approach to popular cinema outlined by Vincendeau with co-author Richard Dyer in *Popular European Cinema* of 1992a [2]), but also for its generic deployment of romantic comedy (the second 'anthropological' approach to popular cinema offered by Vincendeau and Dyer [1992a, 2], as offering aspects aimed at a mass audience, like this ever-appealing genre). Another advantage of this approach would be to rescue dramatist Lope de Vega from the library and emphasize the huge popularity of his plays with disparate seventeenth-century audiences. However, such a reading would overlook the film's 1990s context, in which the classical theatre has a distinctive cachet, and would further ignore the question of fusion, which is central to Miró's handling of the adaptation and genre. Vincendeau seems to hint at the middlebrow when she qualifies her categorization: 'The popularity of heritage films [...] rests on their ability to straddle art/auteur and mass cinema' (xxi-iii).

As we have seen with *The Dumbfounded King*, heritage critics highlight mise en scène as crucial to the genre, a characteristic that corresponds with the emphasis on high production values that is typical of the middlebrow. Mise en scène in *The Dog in the Manger*, including the vibrant costumes worn by Emma Suárez's Diana, and the sumptuous interior and exterior settings of her palace, are a major source of visual pleasure. However, this is not a 'museum aesthetic' (Vincendeau 2001, xviii), where narrative depth is displaced by surface spectacle, because this mise en scène is carefully narrativized. We do not just marvel at the frills and bustles of Diana's dresses, which were not authentic anyway – they date from the mid-seventeenth century, whereas the play is from 1618 (Canning 2005, 84). Dress is clearly aligned with plot development, as the colours of Diana's costumes encode emotion: blue for coldness; red for passion; gold and orange at the opening and conclusion for social status (Canning 2005, 90). Settings are similarly narrativized: palatial interiors reference Diana's social standing, exteriors in the garden, a loosening of restrictions that allows her to flirt with her secretary (Canning 2005, 84). The director capitalizes too on the liminal spaces that connect these two spheres, such as the steps, and on fluid spaces such as the river (Allinson 1999, 36). If the inauthenticity in costume may have been lost on audiences, those who read the press would have been aware of the inauthentic locations. Miró explained that the film was shot in Portugal since permits were easier to obtain there (Evans 1997, 9), but this geographical displacement has the additional advantage of making it clear that the faithful portrayal of period, or 'museum aesthetic,' was not Miró's concern. The film does not therefore fully comply with Vincendeau's view of the heritage movie's attitude to setting, and avoids the superficial stress on spectacle that scholars have criticized.

If we turn to Vincendeau's second formal definition of heritage film – its self-reflexivity – an analysis of performance style in *The Dog in the Manger* allows us to appreciate how the film fuses these high production values with a progressive narrative in gender terms, which we might label 'serious', from a gender perspective. Happy cinematic couple Emma Suárez and Carmelo Gómez account for much of *The Dog in the Manger*'s appeal (they also worked in tandem in *Your Name Poisons My Dreams* [*Tu nombre envenena mis sueños* 1996]). Their success may be appreciated through their recourse to the acting conventions of foreign heritage cinema. Chris Perriam argues that Gómez's costume, long hair and beard self-consciously echo Gérard Depardieu's look in *Cyrano de Bergerac*, while the delivery of his lines is knowingly 'postmodern' (2003, 85). In the case of Suárez, the intelligence that actresses such as Emma Thompson have brought to British heritage cinema is surely a model. Elaine Canning argues that Miró's Diana is 'a more coquettish creature than her Lopean counterpart' (2005, 84), and, while we may never know for sure what an 'original' Lopean Diana may have been, her point regarding Suárez's performance stands. Breathless, wistful or lusty by turns in her delivery of Lope's lines, Suárez's Diana oozes intelligence and self-awareness. Crucial here for a gendered interpretation is Suárez's 'mannerist' performance – playfully peeping through her veil at mass, or suggestively clutching a rose as she muses 'Mil veces he advertido en la belleza,/gracia y entendimiento de Teodoro;/que a no ser desigual a mi decoro,/estimara su ingenio y gentileza' (I've noticed a thousand times in Teodoro's beauty, grace and wit that, if it were not inappropriate to my sense of decorum, I might admire their ingenuity and gallantry) (Vega 1991, 68). Seeking out the same niche audience for Spanish middlebrow cinema that Smith identifies for *Flower*, Miró ensures that her coyness merges suggestively with cunning, making Suárez's role satisfying to audiences who, post-Franco, have enjoyed increasing numbers of films (by women and otherwise) that 'articulat[e] the changing definitions of female subjectivity and the relations between the sexes' (Evans 1997, 12). *The Dog in the Manger*, then, adapts the character-istics of the heritage trend to suit its purpose. By playing down the genre's 'museum aesthetic' and playing up its self-consciousness, Miró avoids the seductions of surface and foregrounds a feminist reading of Lope's play.

Alongside this fusion of the relatively serious subject of female emancipation

FIGURE 6.3 *Emma Suárez's Playful Performance as Diana.* The Dog in the Manger *(*El perro del hortelano *Miró 1996)*

and some of the characteristic high production values of heritage cinema, another aspect of the film's success is explained by its more consistent generic affiliation with romantic comedy (Evans 1997, 10–11; Allinson 1999, 34). This blurring of canonical author with accessible genre is a key middlebrow quality. It is relevant here that Branagh's *Much Ado*, one of Miró's models, was also marketed as a romantic comedy. Thus the Portuguese palaces that provide the setting evoke romantic comedy's recourse to a lovers' 'place apart' (Evans 1997, 10), while the cinematography portrays the unfolding of romance through the point-of-view shots, facial close-ups, dissolves, and soft-focus photography that are typical of the genre (see Allinson's formal analysis of the end of Act II; 1999, 37). The opening kiss between Teodoro and Diana's love rival Marcela – a departure from the play (Canning 2005, 83) – also signals the romantic comedy genre. While Mark Allinson goes so far as to suggest that *The Dog in the Manger* does not belong to the heritage category at all (1999, 34), I would suggest that it blurs heritage movie and romantic comedy to offer an appealing treatment of a revered dramatist.

Crucial to the middlebrow mix too is the extended high-culture reference to Lope de Vega. For audiences familiar with his *The Dog in the Manger* the film offered the pleasure of recognition, or, in Bourdieu's terms, a confirmation of their distinctive choices. For audiences new to the play, the prestige of the classic theatre still rubs off on their viewing experience. Miró had herself worked extensively in the theatre in the early 1990s (Fernández Soto and Checa y Olmos 2010, 86), and her knowledge of this medium as performance art allows her to elicit Suárez and Gómez's knowing delivery of Lope's lines, and to dress, accessorize and position them within the frame in playful response to the text. At once shrewd theatre director and talented film director, *The Dog in the Manger* could not be further from filmed theatre: the formal characteristics of romantic comedy as a film genre, especially settings and cinematography, enrich performance style and mise en scène to offer a middlebrow cinematic reworking of the 1618 stage original that is at once accessible, self-reflexive and feminist. *The Dog in the Manger* was to be the first part of a trilogy of film adaptations of classic Spanish theatre (Mira 2010, 209); Miró's untimely death meant that it would be left to others to develop this successful middlebrow current of classic adaptations in the 1990s and beyond.

The Grandfather (*El abuelo* Garci 1998)

As we have seen in this chapter, despite the greater visibility of new auteurs and 'New Vulgarities', the 1990s was also time of modest potential for Spanish middlebrow cinema. *The Dumbfounded King* successfully linked Spain's rich cultural heritage to the growing contemporary boom of European heritage film; *Flower* announced Almodóvar's connection with a small but sustainable national audience that sought quality middlebrow films with a special focus on feminism and literarity; while *The Dog in the Manger* showed the potential to develop these same strands through witty literary adaptation of classical theatre. José Luis Garci's *The Grandfather* (*El abuelo*) of 1998 looked ideally placed to capitalize on this potential. Another literary adaptation with a period setting and a popular actress in a lead role, the film furthermore combined a promising trilogy of literary-cinematic names. As in Carlos Saura's 1980 *Blood Wedding* (*Bodas de sangre*) adaptation, which announces 'Lorca, Gades, Saura' in its first credit, one publicity poster for *The Grandfather* promises 'Galdòs – Fernán Gómez – Garci'.[19] *The Grandfather* is the Galdós text most frequently adapted in Spanish cinema (see Chapter 1 for my analysis of José Buchs's silent 1922 version), though the film versions vary. However, with three successful middlebrow adaptations of the novelist in the 1970s and 1980s (films *Tristana* and *Tormento*, analysed in Chapter 4, and TVE's *Fortunata y Jacinta*), there was proven potential in Spanish cinema for adapting Galdós. Second, Fernando Fernán Gómez, who it is too easy to name the 'grandfather' of Spanish cinema, brought a wealth of experience to the film through his multi-faceted knowledge of Spanish culture as actor, director and playwright. Finally, Garci had a track record of middlebrow success with his participation in José Luis Dibildos's original Third Way in the early 1970s as a scriptwriter, his updating of that trend in the Reform Cinema and Madrid Comedies of the late 1970s, and, despite a heavily sentimental turn in his 1980s work, had even managed to win the Oscar for Best Foreign Language Film in 1983 with *Begin the Beguine* (*Volver a empezar* 1982). The potential for *The Grandfather* to succeed was, therefore, immense; my thesis in this section will be, however, that the film failed to meet that potential in almost every way.

As we have seen, high-culture references are a key feature of the middlebrow, as they pleasurably confirm the distinctive cultural choices of middle-class audiences. Directors like Luis Buñuel and Pedro Olea in the early 1970s, and Mario Camus in the early 1980s, had shown that Galdós could be adapted to the Spanish screen in ways that were both generically accessible – often through fusing the novels with film melodrama – and intellectually stimulating – often through linking the novels' nineteenth-century studies of gender and social mobility to twentieth-century concerns. Compared with *Tristana*, *Tormento* and *Fortunata y Jacinta*, Galdós's *The Grandfather* is a strange choice. Perhaps Garci and fellow scriptwriter Horacio Valcárcel[20] were attracted to the ease with which they could transfer the original to a script. *The Grandfather* is one of the author's 'Dialogue Novels', which, as their name implies, read like film scripts by stripping narrative down almost completely to dialogue. The problem is that by the late 1890s (*The Grandfather* was published in 1897), Galdós's work was losing its lustre: the stimulating ambiguity of the 'Contemporary Novels' was giving way to thesis-driven didacticism. And so with *The Grandfather*. The author presents the tragic, blind Spanish King Lear in the form of Count Albrit. In step with the Generation of 1898's lament at the state of the nation, Galdós's Albrit returns from Peru, where he has lost his fortune, to a Spain characterized by the premature death of his son, the ungratefulness and materialism of his home town of Jerusa and the knowledge that one of his granddaughters, Dolly or Nelly, is illegitimate. On the shoulders of daughter-in-law Lucrecia Richmond rests the blame. Feminist literary critics have read her as a 'heartless, promiscuous society vamp' (Jagoe 1994, 163), whose adultery, and its illegitimate issue, taint the noble nation represented by impoverished nobleman Albrit.

In Garci's defence, he goes some way to mitigate the misogyny and nostalgia of Galdós's antifeminist hymn to the pure, domestic granddaughter Dolly, whose Ibsenian name belies a narrative that takes an 'anti-Ibsenian route' (Jagoe 1994, 163). The stereotype of the snooty, urban adulteress, or 'society vamp', Lucrecia, might have resonated in Buchs's 1920s, but would have hardly connected with Spanish 1990s audiences. Garci alters the character in its translation from page to screen in a number of ways. Influential *El País* critic Ángel Fernández-Santos is appalled by Garci's addition of a prologue to

the Galdós original which distracts attention from Fernán Gómez's performance as Albrit (1998). Ramón Navarrete, however, underscores its feminist
role of presenting Lucrecia in a sympathetic light (2003, 156). In the novel,
sluttish Lucrecia has a current lover, in the film's added prologue we see her
abandoned by a pusillanimous government minister, who breaks with her to
avoid the disapproval of his father-in-law, through whom he has nepotistically
secured his post. In contrast to the cowardly corruption associated with the
male character, we witness Lucrecia's admirable stoicism. Garci also adds a
later scene to the film where Lucrecia explains her conduct to Albrit, which
the audience can verify by cross-referencing her account with the information
about her failed love affair contained in the prologue. Thus director and scriptwriter offer a 'deeper and more reflexive Lucrecia than the one found in the
novel' (R. Navarrete 2003, 160). A further dimension to the feminist recasting
of Lucrecia, not mentioned by Navarrete, is Cayetana Guillén Cuervo's strong
performance, through which coolness and restraint emphasize dignity and
control, rather than aristocratic aloofness.

The despite the retrograde treatment of gender in the original novel, Garci
might have further developed the potential to link Galdós's critique of materialism, nepotism and corruption to the discredited values of Felipe González's
socialism, whose party the PSOE was thrown out of office for these reasons
two years before the film was released.[21] Garci preferred, it seems, to
lavish screen time on Fernán Gómez's performance as grandfather Albrit,
with much of the film's lengthy running time of 147 minutes devoted to his
endless monologues on honour and literature, transferred almost verbatim
from the original novel. Despite his interesting development of the character
of Lucrecia, Garci's response to the novel is otherwise one of unadventurous
fidelity.

The middlebrow, as I have argued, is all about fusion, and among Spanish
cinema's Galdós adaptations we have the excellent example of Olea's 1974
version of *Tormento*, which blurs the accessible genre of melodrama with
Galdós's novel. Navarrete argues that *The Grandfather* too is an example
of 'classic' melodrama, picking out mise en scène, narrative structure, and
the enhancement of Lucrecia's character as evidence (2004, 158). While the
treatment of Lucrecia is effective, Garci's handling of other elements leans
towards the saccharine sentimentality of which he has often been accused,
and thus misses the opportunities exploited by Olea to use these elements
to open up his reading of Galdós's novel. Choices in lighting, for example,
cast almost every scene in sepia tones – even yellowing Fernán Gómez's
saintly halo of white hair and beard in some shots. These tones may be effectively deployed in the opening scene in which Lucrecia is abandoned by her
cowardly lover, as the sepia palette conveys the staleness of his affections

for her, but elsewhere in the film they are just a lazy short hand for conveying 'pastness'.

Galdós's original novel contained great potential to critique characters through film melodrama's interest in mise en scène, which includes clothes, furnitures and accessories. Galdós is merciless with cynical, social climber Senén, who has secured a government post through Lucrecia's relationship with the minister, threatens her with blackmail when she withdraws her support, and sells Albrit an incriminating letter about his daughter-in-law in exchange for the impoverished nobleman's last possession, a ruby ring. Actor Agustín González clearly enjoys offering a performance he has been perfecting over many years as the materialist nouveau riche, but director Garci could have done more to bring out a critique of Jerusa's parvenus through the way they accessorize themselves through dress and their houses through furniture. Guillén Cuervo's Lucrecia gets the best line of the film when she tells the fawning Jerusa townsfolk that they have poor 'gusto' (taste), a criticism that devastatingly condemns both social climbing and its tacky display. For all Garci's interest in melodrama, he misses out on the opportunity to link this critique to mise en scène in the rest of the film. Instead, melodrama in Garci's hands is a genre for visual pleasure and nostalgia. Thus his choices in framing favour picturesque tableaux, with lengthy takes of country dwellings (shot in Asturias and Burgos) and coastal landscapes (shot in Asturias). For all Garci and Valcárcel's transcription of Galdós's novel in the script, the director does not make his protagonist blind, perhaps because he was unwilling to sever his links to these picture-postcard rural and coastal

FIGURE 6.4 *Bad Taste in Provincial Jerusa.* The Grandfather *(El abuelo Garci 1998)*

settings. In cinematography too, Garci chooses to link sequences through fades, again with no discernible purpose other than to offer harmonious visual pleasure. The same must be said of the musical score, which gives obvious cues for emotional moments, like Albrit's discovery that his legitimate heir is Nelly, though he prefers the domesticated Dolly. The potential significance of this rejection of the blood line for loving affection is drowned in sentimentality thanks in no small part to the soaring strings of Manuel Balboa's compositions at key moments. But the worst aspect of sound, even pointed out by the otherwise enthusiastic press, is the post-sync dubbing. In a country where it is almost impossible to watch a non-Spanish language film that has not been dubbed (specialist 'Original Version' cinemas only exist in large cities), and one where dubbing is associated with the sinister censorship of the Franco regime, which introduced the practice in 1941, it seems incredible that Garci would dub *The Grandfather*, thus echoing the artificiality of the sepia-toned interior shots and picturesque external shots on the soundtrack.

Production values in *The Grandfather* are therefore high in the sense that they are carefully crafted and expensive, but the crafting and the expense often seem misdirected. Given that the only Goya won by the film was for acting (Fernán Gómez won best actor), it seems possible to name this area as the most successful direction of resource. The Spanish press was wildly enthusiastic about Fernán Gómez's performance, with Fernández-Santos's fervent references to his climbing on the 'pinnacle' of Garci's achievement, 'raising it higher still, adding energy to its energy and genius to its genius' (1998) not untypical. Grandfathers had previously been most sighted in Spanish cinema in the shape of Paco Martínez Soria's country bumpkin stereotype in the VCE of the 1960s and 1970s, and we might perceive something of a desire to redeem the representation of old age in Spanish cinema in the adoring reception of Fernán Gómez's convincing turn as the cantankerous nobleman. Convincing too, as we have seen, are Guillén Cuervo and González, though there is little of the satisfying knowingness of Emma Suárez and Carmelo Gómez's heritage-influenced performances in *The Dog in the Manger*. What really lets the performances down, however, is the sentimental treatment of the children, often dressed in contrasting sickly pastels and with the phony voices that resulted from the post-sync dubbing.

The Grandfather, in sum, is a middlebrow fusion of high-culture Galdós with accessible melodrama, but, in far too many areas, Garci misjudges the balance. Valuing a prize-winning actor means indulgently conceding him too much screen time, while neglecting other performances, like those of the children. Appreciating melodrama means expensively emphasizing picturesque settings, while neglecting the interesting questions of social mobility and dress in mise en scène. Worst of all are Garci's shortcomings as a reader of Galdós. Not the author's greatest work, *The Grandfather* nonetheless contained a critique of corruption in 1890s Spain that suggestively match the scandals of 1990s Spain. Conversely, an *ABC* review finds Fernán Gómez to be a sensitive reader of the novelist: 'The actor seems as stuck on Galdós [...] as Garci is on the Oscar' (García Jambrina 1998). Perhaps this is Garci's ultimate failing, to choose a novel to adapt with the American Academy Awards in mind rather than Spanish audiences. When interviewed following the film's nomination for the Best Foreign Language Oscar he reveals 'I'm going [to America] going in good company, that of Benito Pérez Galdós, who is one of the most studied authors in the United States today' ('Review of *El abuelo*' 1998). Thanks in no small part to Fernán Gómez's Goya and the Oscar nomination, *The Grandfather* performed well at the Spanish box office, with over one million ticket sales. It is a miserable legacy, however, that no Spanish film director has wanted to touch a Galdós adaptation since.

A Time for Defiance (La hora de los valientes Mercero 1998)

In this chapter we have charted a number of the more and less successful attempts by directors to adapt to changing social, political and audio-visual environments. What each attempt shares is a middlebrow turn. In this section I will analyse a feature by a veteran director whose approach remains consistent. Antonio Mercero had a hit with middlebrow *Daddy's War* (*La guerra de papá*) in 1977 (analysed in Chapter 4), which was seen by over three and a half million, but his 1998 offering, *A Time for Defiance* (*La hora de los valientes*), only found an audience of 118,000. Both films are family dramas with Civil-War themes, quality actors, a domestic setting and a particular focus on children; their vastly different reception by audiences strikes a note of caution. While this book describes middlebrow films for middle-class audiences from 1970 to 2010, my thesis is not intended to flatten the field, but explore middlebrow continuities even as films and audiences change.

The drop from 1977 to 1998 for similar films by the same director is explained first by audience change. As numerous prizes attest, Mercero is a master of the small, rather than the large screen, and has recently been oxymoronically described as making 'Auteur TV' (Smith 2006, 145–74). His deployment of the televisual themes of the everyday and the televisual aesthetics of domestic drama in *Daddy's War* was enjoyed by an enormous audience. From the 1980s that audience could find such themes and aesthetics on television itself, and viewing figures for *Defiance* show that those viewers could not be lured back to the cinema for them by 1998.

In the rest of this section I will consider a further reason for *Defiance*'s failure to connect with audiences. Despite the similarities between the 1998 and 1977 films outlined above, the tricky business of a middlebrow balance between serious themes and accessible treatment was well-judged in 1977, but mishandled in 1998. At this stage, it is worth re-examining Bourdieu's description of the way middlebrow culture deploys high culture (he uses the term 'legitimate culture' to stress the ways such culture is socially-sanctioned, or legitimized). The middlebrow 'give[s] the impression of bringing legitimate culture within the reach of all, by combining two normally exclusive characteristics, immediate accessibility and the outward signs of cultural legitimacy' (1999, 323). *Defiance*'s claim to 'legitimacy' lies not just with its demonstrably serious theme of exploring the harrowing impact of the Civil War on one family, but also with its multiple high-art references to Goya. The treatment of the artist and his work could not be more 'accessible', for straightforward explanations of their significance are interweaved throughout the narrative. Scriptwriters Mercero and Horacio Valcárcel (who also penned *Daddy's War* and *The Grandfather*) take the 'plausible "urban myth"' (Mitchell 2004, 178) that one work of art was forgotten in the evacuation of the treasures of Madrid's Prado museum during the Civil War as their starting point. The not accidentally-named Manuel (after Republican president Azaña) played by Gabino Diego, works as a museum guard prior to the conflict, and the narrative of the film follows his efforts to look after a forgotten Goya self-portrait as his family life develops in the context of the war (his future wife's family and his nephew Pepito are all killed by Nationalist bombs; he marries, fights for the Republic, has a son, but is executed after Franco's victory just after returning the painting to the museum).

In *Defiance* the high-culture reference to Goya is thus narrativized in a manner that we have not seen in other films examined. In Roberto Bodegas *Spaniards in Paris* (*Españolas en París* 1971), for example, I argue that reference is made to Goya through the framing, casting, clothing and make-up of the two abortionists who evoke the witches of *The Spell* of 1797–8 (see Chapter 4). In Manuel Gutiérrez Aragón's *Half of Heaven* (*La mitad del cielo* 1986, Chapter 5), Velázquez's *Las meninas* is recreated in mise en scène through the use of the mirror and positioning of characters as Rosa dresses for Juan's wedding. These two references are not explicit, so they pleasurably endorse the cultural knowledge of initiated audiences. In narrative terms, both cases enhance the unfolding of the plot, but are not crucial to its comprehension. We might draw on Spanish cinema's most famous and infamous deployment of an intermedial reference by way of contrast. In Luis Buñuel's *Viridiana*, the audience's knowledge that the beggars recreate Leonardo Da Vinci's *Last Supper* is crucial to understand the director's vision of a degraded, Godless humanity.

In *Defiance* too, an understanding of the life and works of Goya is necessary to plot development. But 'Television auteur' Mercero takes no risks: the film offers a digest of the painter's life and his three key works *The Charge of the Mamelukes* (1814), *The Third of May* (1814) and *Self-portrait* (1815), for Manuel has learnt by heart the museum guide's introductions and is fond of repeating them. Philip Mitchell helpfully differentiates between films that 'intertextually' refer to art that lies outside the diegesis, such as *Viridiana*, and films like *Defiance*, where the art reference is 'intra-textual', and explained within the narrative. Mitchell questions the critical tendency to value the greater demands made on the viewer by 'intertextuality' as opposed to the considerably easier task of deciphering 'intra-textuality', and I follow his call to revisit the Third Way (2004, 182) and re-assess 'too fixed a polarity between an auteurist directorial tradition and a more populist one' (169), though he does not rehabilitate the term 'middlebrow'. While I argue that middlebrow efforts deserve a sympathetic approach, it is also necessary to explain why some are more, and some less, successful.

A successful middlebrow film holds Bourdieu's 'legitimacy' and 'accessibility' in a dynamic balance; in *Defiance*, however, the balance tips too far in favour of 'accessibility'. A comparison with Mercero's successful effort in *Daddy's War* is instructive. In *Daddy's War*, first, Mercero follows Miguel Delibes, the author of the source text for the film, and simultaneously adopts a child's literal and figurative points of view and contrasts these with the adult world. Thus childhood fears and games are an accessible way into the film's serious consideration of the abiding psychological effects of the Civil War, which constitutes a successful example of middlebrow blurring. Twenty years later, and working from an original script (though co-authored with the same scriptwriter), Mercero fails to perform the same balance. By giving greater emphasis to a child's point of view he simplifies events to an extent that their treatment borders on the childish. Ironically, this simplification does not take place in connection with the scenes involving Pepito, Javier González's convincing turn as a boy who loses his father in the war (a detail from Mercero's own biography), and is himself killed by a Nationalist bomb. Drawing on Mercero's own direction of Lolo García as Quico in *Daddy's War*, and Jaime Chávarri's exploration of children playing adult war games in *Bicycles are for the Summer* (*Las bicicletas son para el verano* 1984) (Mitchell 2004, 180, 185n. 18), Pepito provides an effectively inquisitive perspective on the adult worlds of both war (for example, the dreams about his father) and family (for example, his witnessing of Manolito's birth).

The simplification and infantilization in fact occur in the narrative that is not connected to a child. Ably supported by Leonor Watling's secondary part as Carmen (a role that precedes the actress's international stardom through Pedro Almodóvar and Isabel Coixet's films of the 2000s), Diego's turn as protagonist Manuel is nonetheless problematic. Chosen by Mercero for the 'childishness' of his gaze, the director persuaded comic actor Diego to take on the part of Manuel for his first dramatic role.[22] His characterization as the well-meaning anarchist and Prado guard plays up the 'childishness' to which Mercero was attracted in the actor's persona. While in *The Dumbfounded King* (1991) this childlishness effectively underscores director Imanol Uribe's critique of royalty, in *Defiance* its effect is more uneven. Diego's childishness may convey the idealism and ingenuity of the losers of the Civil War, but, perhaps audiences sought something more complex. Further, because all our information about Goya is filtered through him, we are given little more than an introductory digest, which includes the facts of his birth and the briefest narrative descriptions of his most accessible paintings. Perhaps, again, audiences didn't appreciate this heavy-handed accessibility.

In 2002 Mercero would offer another film about children that dealt with the serious topic of cancer, *The Fourth Floor* (*Planta 4ª*), which found success with an audience of over one million. Perhaps, then, the problem with *Defiance* was its treatment of history. As revisions of the Civil War and an interrogation of memory beyond nostalgia acquired greater urgency

FIGURE 6.5 *Goya Explained. Diego and* The Third of May. A Time for Defiance *(La hora de los valientes Mercero 1998)*

in all spheres of Spanish life in the new millennium, audiences would seek more challenging, though still middlebrow, revisions and interrogations, as we will see in Chapter 7's discussions of *Carol's Journey* (*El viaje de Carol* Uribe 2003), which reprises the child's perspective, and *Soldiers of Salamina* (*Soldados de Salamina* Trueba 2003), which questions memory itself.

Alone[23] (*Solas* Zambrano 1999)

First work of Benito Zambrano, trained at the Cuban film school of San Antonio de los Baños, *Alone* (*Solas*) seems a far cry from some manifestations of the middlebrow in the 1990s. The film apparently confirms the novelty and auteurism that critics like Carlos Heredero claimed characterized Spanish cinema of the 1990s. Released in the last year of the decade, *Alone* is included as a 'revelation-film' in the conclusion of Heredero's *20 New Directors* to bolster the thesis of auteurist renewal defended throughout the book (1999, 392). A commercial and critical success, the film attracted almost one million viewers and the current tally of awards currently numbers some 38 wins and 15 nominations.[24]

Alone is apparently a text-book example of the *cine social*, the collective term for social-realist cinema used by directors and critics from the 1990s on. Despite the new term, this cinema connects with Juan Antonio Bardem's call for a 'socially relevant' Spanish cinema in 1955 that is indebted to Marxist Italian Neorealism (Triana-Toribio 2003, 156). Having studied in the Cuban School founded in 1985 by the Castro government,[25] Zambrano was well placed to make a film that fitted with the ethical and aesthetic vision of the *cine social*, summarized as films that 'aim to show the effects of environmental factors on the development of character through depictions that emphasize the relationship between location and identity' (Hallam with Marshment 2000, 184) and that 'favour as subject matter present-day social problems (crime, drugs, domestic violence against women and children)' (Triana-Toribio 2003, 156–7).

Thus *Alone* privileges contemporary social problems in its plot, and the techniques of social observation loosely associated with Italian Neorealism in its form. It has the dubious honour of crossing off every item and adding more to Triana-Toribio's 'problems' list – with a plot that takes in urban poverty, unemployment, poor housing, illiteracy, lack of community, alcoholism, and unwanted pregnancy in connection with its protagonist, lonely Seville-resident María (Ana Fernández) – and broaches newer areas such as the alienation of the elderly in both rural and urban spaces and the domestic abuse suffered by María's equally lonely but village-dwelling mother, Rosa (María Galiana). *Alone* meets many of the formal conventions associated with the *cine social*'s inheritance of Italian Neorealism. First, Zambrano casts unknown actors as his leads (a fact that is all the more remarkable today, as Galiana has become a household name thanks to her post-*Alone* role in TVE's ever-popular *Cuéntame cómo pasó* [*Tell Me How It Happened* various directors 2001-present]). Authenticity, the elusive goal of social realism, was partially achieved in *Alone* by retaining local accents, including Galiana and Fernández's Andalousian accents (both are Seville-born), and Carlos Álvarez-Nóvoa's Asturian one. As the director comments in relation to accents, *Alone* 'seeks, above all, to transmit a sensation of authenticity and truth from the screen' (C.P.A. 1999); 'authenticity' is a word echoed in press reviews in praise of the film (C.P.A. 1999; E. Fernández-Santos 1999).

We should not forget that 'authenticity' is an effect brought about by the deployment of a series of techniques, and alongside casting and accents, mise en scène is also crucial in the *cine social*. As in Italian Neorealism of the 1940s onwards, Spanish social-realist cinema of the 1950s onwards, and Spanish *cine social* of the 1990s onwards, long takes are crucial to enable audiences to appreciate environment. Thus Zambrano's long takes ensure that the different settings of the film take on especial prominence and convey to the viewer the importance of environment in conditioning life. When María brings her mother home from hospital in the post-credit sequence, the camera lingers on images of urban deprivation in her neighbourhood. We behold homelessness, drug addiction and graffiti in takes of 17 and 15 seconds, and, in subsequent street sequences, our attention is also drawn to prostitution and unfinished building work in this area. As we move from public to private space there is no improvement: we cannot fail to notice that María's flat is dark, damp and run-down in takes of 15 and 30 seconds. Zambrano draws attention to class inequality through mise en scène by contrasting this interior with the neighbour's light and spacious apartment, and the shiny new buildings in which María works as a cleaner.[26] And lest we fall into the trap of admiring those luxurious interiors, Zambrano includes a scene of María at work at an art gallery when she bursts out in anger. As she cries and thrashes out in frustration, Zambrano frames her in a long shot and holds her in a long take of 11 seconds, so we cannot fail to measure her predicament against her lavish surroundings. (Though at least she and her family have access to a modern, efficient hospital, which indicates an effective welfare state – an aspect of the film Paul Julian Smith notes will particularly impress UK audiences [2001, 56]).

Read as an example of the *cine social*, *Alone* thus contradicts Aznar's smug assurance that 'España va bien' (Spain's doing well) (Saíz 1999).

Exploring familiar problems and raising new ones, Zambrano's *Alone* is also a landmark in representations of Andalousia. It is characterized by solemnity, and silence, this latter in opposition to the stereotype of garrulous 'alegría' (chirpiness) often associated, both externally and internally, with the South of Spain. A scene at María's work encapsulates this refusal of comedy. She and two fellow workers take a break from cleaning for a snack. The jocular banter of her jolly companions is interrupted and silenced when the pregnant protagonist throws up her sandwich. In other words, fun and games are banished from a film concerned with solemn social issues such as unplanned pregnancy.[27]

Alone thus narrativizes a characteristic of the *cine social* as a whole: its rejection of the often comic genres and sub-genres of the country's popular cinema. Nonetheless, I will devote the rest of this section to tracing *Alone*'s debt to precisely one such subgenre, the comic country-bumpkin cinema, often starring Paco Martínez Soria, of the 1960s–1970s. Unlikely as it may seem, *Alone* reruns key aspects of the subgenre's plot and even its portrayal of gender, as a comparison with Pedro Lazaga's *City Life is not for Me* (*La ciudad no es para mí* 1965, discussed in Chapter 3), reveals. My conclusion is that this surprising fusion of the critically-acclaimed, auteurist *cine social* with the critically-disdained, popular *paleto* cinema yields another example of 1990s Spanish cinema's middlebrow tendency.

Separated by 34 years, *City Life* and *Alone* both describe the visit of an elderly rural relative to family members in the city: Tío Agustín from his beloved Aragonese village Calacierva to his son in Madrid; Rosa from an unnamed Andalousian village to her daughter María in Seville. In both films the role of the elderly relative is to promote traditional, family values by changing the behaviour of female adults: Tío Agustín saves Luchy from adultery; Rosa saves María from abortion. In fact, neither film is really about the opposition of country and city at all; both actually explore the dangers of female sexuality, which takes the form of extra-marital sex in *City Life*, and non-procreative sex in *Alone*. As we have seen in Chapter 3's discussion of *City Life*, female sexuality acts as a screen onto which anxieties about change are projected. These changes concern upward class mobility consequent of the 1960s economic boom and its cultural corollary, middlebrow taste. *Alone*, however, exposes the negative underside of capitalist expansion, showing that not all have benefited. In the sequence at the art gallery in which María is a cleaner, *Alone* nods at the cultural consumption of the economically ascendant. However, in focussing on the cleaner, this is not a film about the new middlebrow cultural tastes. So, *City Life* explicitly addresses middlebrow culture in its plot; *Alone*, in its fusion of auteurist *cine social* and popular *paleto* cinema, is, in contrast, an example of middlebrow culture itself.

FIGURE 6.6 *Another Country Relative Arrives in the City to Regulate Female Sexuality.* Alone *(*Solas *Zambrano 1999)*

Galiana's performance as Rosa could not be further from Martínez Soria's as Tío Agustín. While the latter is all irritating chatter and slapstick comedy, Rosa wordlessly influences her daughter's behaviour; with the 'dignity' of both her performance and of the character she portrays stressed by reviewers (I take the word from the title Elsa Fernández-Santos's review for *El País*, which describes how *Alone* 'recovers the dignity of rural women' [1999]). Nonetheless, Rosa is the vehicle for the film's anti-feminist message. María might be 'alone' because she is involved in a loveless relationship with Juan, or 'alone' because she lives in a city that apparently lacks rural community (though the bar is an obvious community locale), but her mother senses a deeper solitude: her childlessness. Rosa also intuits her daughter's pregnancy, and, with remarkable subtlety, the film charts her success in saving her unborn grandchild from the abortion María at first plans, and in finding a surrogate father and grandfather for the future mother and child in the form of the avuncular neighbour. Writing from a feminist perspective, Candyce Leonard finds this treatment of gender retrograde: 'Motherhood as the single path towards self-identification or relieving loneliness is the knotty premise that threatens to erase the sexual female, the working female and the independent female' (2004, 224).

In the final sequence of the film this retrograde treatment is particularly marked, for at this point in the narrative Rosa has died, and thus events unfold without the presence of subtle Galiana's highly intelligent performance as the taciturn Rosa (recognized by a Goya award). The coda details Rosa's posthumous influence in redeeming the family and is very heavy-handed in tone. Mother, child and 'grandfather' (the kindly neighbour) visit Rosa's grave in a scene bathed in sunshine; as the three walk back to the village, an exceptionally long take of one minute and 16 seconds, and a high angle shot, draw our attention to the rural surroundings and the large cross. Meanwhile, we hear María tell her deceased mother in voiceover of her happiness in motherhood and even the new family's plans to return to the old family home in the village. Overlooking the association of that home with domestic violence, María plans an asexual existence with the 'grandfather' and thus becomes the ideal virginal mother of Christian tradition announced all along by her name. As Leonard observes, María tries sex, work and independence in the city and abandons her lonely failure in all three for motherhood in the country. But with the conclusion that María will live as a mother who is financially dependent on the 'grandfather' in the old family home in the village, Zambrano goes too far. Despite all the sunshine in the coda, we are aware of the dark associations of the family home as the odious site of Rosa's dependence and receipt of domestic abuse. Whereas *City Life* chastises its would-be adulteress Luchy, it dare not suggest the return of the family to the village as this would jeapordize the 1960s economic boom. The conclusion of *Alone* is thus even more conservative than that of its subgeneric forerunner, as Leonard convincingly argues, 'By associating procreation with innocence and failing to scrutinize the materiality that allows or denies freedom of choice, *Alone* restores the myth of motherhood' (2004, 232).

For all the stress on newness and auteurism in accounts of the *cine social*, this reading of *Alone* stresses surprising connections with alternative trends in Spanish cinema. We might provocatively name *Alone* the *City Life* of the 1990s: both feature country bumpkins in the city, and both propose an anti-feminist regulation of female sexuality. This is not to say that Zambrano's *Alone* is an example of popular cinema despite itself. It is characterized, conversely, by hybridity and fusion. *Alone* therefore reruns the accessible *paleto* plot in the highbrow register of *cine social*. This fusion makes it an example of middlebrow culture, which Bourdieu notes can be either 'accessible works of avant-garde experiments' like classic literary adaptations in film, 'or accessible works which pass for avant-garde experiments' (1999, 323), of which *Alone* is a good example.

Notes

1 Another selection of films from the 1990s, for example, may reveal closer links to political contexts, as Bernard Bentley suggests in writing that the Socialist government's 'problems and abuses of power found their way into the plots of films and may have contributed to the subsequent debacle of the PSOE' (2008, 282).

2 See, for instance, Santaolalla's summary of the commercial track record of Medem's début, *Cows* (*Vacas* 1991) (1999, 310).

3 Torrente Ballester was a former Falangist and one of the scriptwriters of *Furrows* (*Surcos*, see Chapter 2).

4 This is no doubt in order to distance the film from the previous associations of its lead actor, Alfredo Landa, star of the notorious *destape* subgenre that uses his very name, *Landismo*. Triana-Toribio notes that *Los santos inocentes* avoids dealing with comedy and modernity for similar reasons in her shrewd study (2003, 122–32).

5 Its total of 663,000 spectators is close to that of *Half of Heaven* (1986), which suggests, assuming a similar filming budget, that it may not have recouped its government subsidy. The seven Goyas did not include the top prizes of Best Film, Director, Actor.

6 The original 'polivalente' has also been translated as 'polyvalent'. Neither version captures the association of the Spanish term with the secondary school universal qualification 'Bachillerato Unificado Polivalente' (Unified Multipurpose Baccalaureate) (Triana-Toribio 2003, 173n.19).

7 DVD Extras, Círculo Digital DVD, 2002.

8 Torrente Ballester had used the original on the cover of his 1989 novel, published by Planeta.

9 In the DVD Extras (Círculo Digital 2002), the director recalls that Torrente Ballester only ceded the rights for the adaptation after gaining Uribe's reassurance that he would maintain its level of eroticism.

10 This title puns on the name of Pedro and Agustín Almodóvar's production company, El Deseo S.A.. 'S.A.' stands for 'Sociedad Anónima', which translates as 'Ltd' or 'limited' in English.

11 Núria Triana-Toribio cleverly interprets the change of direction by appealing to an auteurist filmography characterized by changes of direction (2000a 281–2).

12 Triana-Toribio highlights references to the Madrid Comedy in *What Have I Done to Deserve This?!* (*¿Qué he hecho yo para merecer esto?!!* (1999, 229).

13 The female focus, as well as the writerly interests, of the film are succinctly conveyed by Leo's correction of the adjective in this phrase, which conveys gender in Spanish: for 'indefenso' (defenceless) (male agreement) she writes 'indefensa' (female agreement).

14 The Almodóvar fan is also rewarded with intertextual references between his films, like the sound of distant high-heels in his other film starring Paredes, a sound foregrounded in the film's Spanish title *High Heels* (*Tacones lejanos*, literally, 'distant' high heels).

15 In *All About My Mother*, this theatricality is emphasized again as Paredes plays an actor in the film.

16 Millás is Almodóvar's favourite writer (Zurián 2009, 424n. 5).

17 Elsewhere in the 'blue' trilogy architectural references are also deployed in a middlebrow manner. Barcelona's La Sagrada Familia in *All About My Mother*, for example rewards audiences with the pleasure of recognition, and clearly invites them to relate the 'Holy Family' to protagonist Manuela's reconfigured family. Smith notes the director favours Gaudi's easily recognisable cathedral over the city's cutting-edge architecture (2003, 164).

18 The director would develop this bid throughout his work, summarized by Smith as 'the emotional imperative' in connection with *Talk to Her* (*Hable con ella* 2002) (2006, 14–28).

19 Featured on the video version distributed by Columbia Tristar, 1999.

20 Collaborator with director Antonio Mercero on the script of *Daddy's War* (*La guerra de papá*, see Chapter 4).

21 Ironically, like the Madrid and Jerusa of Galdós's novel, Garci was himself embroiled in a corruption scandal concerning *The Grandfather*. He was accused of purchasing votes to secure the Goya for best picture in January 1999, 'a scam somewhat reluctantly denied by Academy President Aitana Sánchez Gijón' (Jordan 2000, 190). In the event *The Grandfather* lost out to *The Girl of Your Dreams* (*La niña de tus ojos* Trueba 1998).

22 Interview with director, El País DVD 'Extras'.

23 Literally, women alone.

24 *Alone* attracted 944,573 spectators in Spain in a year when the total number of domestic viewers of Spanish films was 18.1 million. It won Goyas for best new director, best supporting actress (Galiana), best new actress (Fernández), best new actor (Álvarez-Novoa), and best original screenplay. Outside Spain, the film won prizes in France, Argentina, Mexico, Germany, Columbia, Brussels, Israel, Cuba and Japan.

25 The school's mission statement is to foster a Spanish-language 'Other cinema', which counters mainstream film, and in which 'reality and human beings stop being treated as spectacles' (www.eictv.org [accessed 9 July 2007]).

26 The celebration of the 1992 Expo in Seville saw substantial investment in new architecture.

27 Cristina Sánchez-Conejero shows that *Alone* is the antithesis of the clichéd representations of Andalousia as the home of happy-go-lucky folk interested in dancing and bullfighting, and instead portrays 'the real, not the folkloric or nationalist Andalousia' (2006, 140). She also notes that these folkloric stereotypes have been promoted by both the dictatorship and subsequent democratic autonomous governments alike.

7

From *Cine Social* to Heritage Cinema in Films of the 2000s

As the new millennium began, José María Aznar's PP remained in office in Spain, winning in 2000 a second term that was marked by the president's unpopular support for the post-9/11 war in Iraq. In 2004, political power changed hands with José Luis Rodríguez Zapatero's PSOE victorious. Apparently a case of democratic business as usual, these elections were, in fact, highly controversial. Taking place just three days after Al-Qaeda bombed commuter trains in Madrid on 11 March 2004, killing 191 people, many saw the return of the Socialists to power as the electorate's punishment of Aznar's PP, which had wrongly blamed the attacks on Basque terrorist group ETA. At the time of writing in 2012, the PP is back in government, under Aznar's hand-picked successor, Mariano Rajoy. This time there is consensus among commentators that power changed hand for more routine reasons: rather than Rajoy's PP winning the elections, Zapatero's PSOE lost them for their supposed mishandling of the economy.

On the international stage, the 2000s are thus dominated by Islamic terrorism and the controversial response of the West. In domestic legislation, the new millennium has also witnessed contentious landmarks. My selection of six films leads to an inevitably partial focus on some of these. Another author might have emphasized questions like Spain's autonomous communities, and, in particular, Basque independence and terrorism, in connection with the new wave of provocative documentaries such as *Basque Ball: Skin Against Stone* (*La pelota vasca. La piel contra la piedra* Medem 2003) and *Pursued** (*Perseguidos* Ortega Santillana 2004). Instead, the selection resumes my focus on the questions of gender and memory raised at the start of Chapter 6. Zapatero's PSOE was controversially interventionist in both areas, with legislation addressing domestic violence (2004) and legalizing same-sex marriage (2005), and the passing of the Law of Historical Memory (2007).

From the 1990s onwards, financing possibilities for Spanish films have healthily diversified to include 'subventions from the regional governments, resources from selling broadcast rights to television networks, distribution advances, home video, advanced sales of foreign distribution, official bank loans, and private financing' (Pavlovic et al. 2009, 182). Of these, Tatjana Pavlovic et al. stress investment from television and multinational multimedia conglomerates like PRISA as particularly significant (182–3); nonetheless, central government subsidies 'continue to be a major source of funding at the national level' (183). Pilar Miró's 1983 subsidy system was revised by the outgoing Socialist government in the early 1990s to link awards to market performance rather than the criteria of government committees, a process of revision consolidated by the PP when they entered office in 1996. However, in the new millennium questions have been raised about the subsidy system once again. Barry Jordan, who stresses that 'subsidies' are now 'multi-layered' and include local, regional, national and European sources, analyses the mismatch between falling audience share for Spanish films in the domestic market, and rising levels of production of subsidized films (2011, 19). Notwithstanding the golden year of 2006, when Spanish film enjoyed a historically high 20 per cent domestic audience share (Smith 2009, 13), Jordan argues that too few domestic films constitute 'appealing, mainstream cinema which both engages and entertains wider audiences' (38) – though detects a recent swing towards films that are responsive to the market, or 'in favour of the spectator' (39).

A cinema that 'engages and entertains' may be interpreted as a call for middlebrow film,[1] successful examples of which creatively fuse serious subject matters and high-cultural references with high production values and accessibility. I begin with two examples of the *cine social*, which builds on the analysis of *Solas* in the previous chapter. Dubbed variously as 'popular social realism' (which is fairly neutral) (Jordan and Allinson 2005, 163) and 'timid social realism' (which is highly critical) (Quintana 2008), this recent trend in Spanish cinema exemplifies the problematic reception of middlebrow film. While prize-giving bodies in Spain, wide audiences, and some critics welcomed the ways films like *Mondays in the Sun* (*Los lunes al sol* León de Aranoa 2002) and *Take My Eyes* (*Te doy mis ojos* Bollaín 2003) accessibly addressed social problems like unemployment and domestic violence, other critics, especially those writing from Spanish academia's ever-influential Marxist perspective, rejected the films' dramatization – in their view an obfuscation – of reality. Another middlebrow thread that crosses into the new millennium is that of the Spanish-Civil-War film, with Imanol Uribe's *Carol's Journey* (*El viaje de Carol* 2002) a successful return to the blending of childhood innocence and adult conflict explored in Chapter 6 in *A Time for*

Defiance (*La hora de los valientes* 1998), and evident in other middlebrow features of that decade like *Secrets of the Heart* (*Secretos del corazón* Armendáriz 1997) and *Butterfly's Tongue* (*La lengua de las mariposas* Cuerda 1999). While maintaining a middlebrow balance, David Trueba's *Soldiers of Salamina* (*Soldados de Salamina* 2003) takes the question of memory in a new direction, by combining its interrogation in the Javier Cercas novel on which the film is based with questions of literarity, female experience and middle age that are indebted to Almodóvar's *The Flower of My Secret* (*La flor de mi secreto* 1995; analysed in Chapter 6). Heritage cinema also returns in the 2000s with great commercial success. I analyse Agustín Díaz Yanes's *Alatriste* (2006), a blockbuster starring Viggo Mortensen that even beat Almdóvar's admired *Volver* (2006) at the box office, as a cross-over between Heritage and Western. Spanish-Brazilian co-production *Lope* (2010), directed by Brazilian Andrucha Waddington, also turns to the early-modern period to offer a fictional bio-pic of the early adulthood of its most famous dramatist, Lope de Vega, the adaptation of whose *The Dog in the Manger* (*El perro del hortelano* Miró 1997) I discuss in Chapter 6. With non-Spanish lead actors (American Mortensen in *Alatriste*; Argentinian Alberto Ammann in *Lope*) and directors (Brazilian Waddington for *Lope*), these films point to the much-discussed transnationality of contemporary Spanish cinema;[2] they also variously confirm the middlebrow potential of Spanish heritage cinema, which we may now trace back across a century of film to the silent cinema discussed in Chapter 1.

Mondays in the Sun (*Los lunes al sol* León de Aranoa 2002)

As we have seen in Chapter 6's discussion of *Alone*, Benito Zambrano's first film was ideally timed to garner admiration according to two new critical paradigms for Spanish cinema. First, it formed part of the attractive 'novelty' of 1990s, or the buzz that surrounded first-time directors making, apparently, brand new kinds of film. Second, it participated in the decade's celebrated return to social realism – given a veneer of novelty with the new 1990s description *cine social* – which, by the turn of the new millennium, was in ascendance. The work of Fernando León de Aranoa also benefits from its location within these two paradigms. Protégé of veteran left-wing producer Elías Querejeta, who backed his first three films, León de Aranoa has been a major figure of the *cine social* with features *Family* (*Familia* 1996), *Neighbourhood** (*Barrio* 1998), *Mondays* (2002), *Princesses* (*Princesas* 2005) and *Amador* (2010), though his critical and commercial success has lately fallen from the highpoint of *Mondays* – over 2 million admissions, Spanish candidate for the 2003 Best Foreign Language film Oscar,[3] winner of the San Sebastián Golden Shell and five Goyas – to the recent offering, *Amador*, with viewing figures under 100,000 at the time of writing.

Zambrano's second film, *Havana Blues** (*Habana Blues* 2005), was a change of direction and location to music and Cuba. León de Aranoa, in contrast, has maintained his commitment to *cine social* across five features, making his work an obvious target for detractors of the tendency, like Àngel Quintana. Drawing on the arguments of Carlos Losilla and José Enrique Monterde, who observe that the *cine social* fails to be formally innovative, (summarized in Quintana 2008, 254) and is generically repetitive, favouring a 'half-way house between melodrama and sentimental comedy' (summarized in Quintana 2008, 254), Quintana defends a thesis of 'timid realism'. The problems with what he calls the 'recuperation of certain realist tendencies' (251) in Spanish cinema of the 2000s are both thematic and formal. First, the *cine social* fails to establish 'a strong political discourse' and denounce 'concrete problems', like those associated with the right-wing PP (252). Moreover it fails to be aesthetically explorative, self-reflective or questioning, and offers script- and star-led dramatizations, with a 'certain realist background' (252–3). Thus in *Mondays* a 'realist background' is provided by the documentary images of shipbuilders' demonstrations in Gijón during the opening credits, but there follows a script-led 'traditional work of drama' (254) starring Javier Bardem, whose performance becomes a 'spectacle' (253).[4]

What lies behind Monterde, Losilla and Quintana's response is a critical framework that cannot contain middlebrow cinema. The problem is the blurring, or fusion, of diverse elements. The *cine social* partially, but insufficiently, addresses the social problems and adopts the aesthetic forms of Italian Neorealism (Quintana 2008, 253), but unsettlingly fuses these with 'drama', or more specifically 'melodrama' and 'comedy', while betraying awe for the Spanish star system. This response is similar to that of Esteve Riambau to Mirovian cinema, analysed in Chapter 6, which he influentially condemned as a 'multipurpose' (1995, 424). Just as I revise Riambau's formula to suggest a methodology that analyses the overlap between, rather than lists the existence of, formal elements, so I propose a similar response to interpreting the 'popular' or 'timid' *cine social* as middlebrow.

Beginning with a documentary treatment of the specific (but not specific enough for Quintana) demonstrations of the sacked shipworkers of Gijón (Asturias), León de Aranoa scripts a fictional narrative of the lives of four such men in Vigo, in neighbouring Galicia. Inspired by British efforts *The Full Monty* (Cattaneo 1997) and *Billy Elliot* (Daldry 2000), *Mondays* dramatizes the

FIGURE 7.1 *Star Actor and Social Realism. Javier Bardem's Santa at the Vigo Docks.* Mondays in the Sun *(Los lunes al sol León de Aranoa 2002)*

consequences of unemployment on the lives of Santa (Bardem), José (Luis Tosar), Lino (José Ángel Egido) and Amador (Celso Bugallo), through questions of gender (Fouz-Hernández and Martínez-Expósito 2007, 68; Whittaker 2011, 125–45). The obvious trials of economic disadvantage are nuanced and humanized by examining them in connection with a masculinity that becomes reconfigured in physical, familial and spatial terms. Bardem as Santa famously developed a paunch and added a waddle to his gait to convey the effects of enforced inactivity on a former manual worker's body; his body becomes one of 'consumption rather than production', in Tom Whittaker's felicitious phrase (2011, 136). (By way of contrast, in the 'Naval' (Shipyard) bar where the four friends drink, photos of the half-naked muscled torsos of male boxers and other sportsmen can be seen, calling to mind Bardem's 1990s 'macho' star image, in films like *Ham Ham* [*Jamón jamón* Bigas Luna 1992].) Through the other characters, León de Aranoa explores the impact of unemployment on the family, with José's resentment of his wife's work, middle-aged Lino's displacement by the modern look and computer literacy of his son's generation, and alcoholic Amador's abandonment by his spouse. As Whittaker points out, in this film that links local unemployment with global currents of financial restructuring (the shipyards have been closed as the vessels can be made more cheaply in Korea), the transformations of domestic and public spaces are key (2011, 125–38). Domestic ones are unwittingly disrupted by the presence of unemployed men, public ones are also transformed, both consciously and unconsciously. The film takes its title and promotional poster from the accidental presence of inactive, working-age men sitting in the sun in public spaces on a Monday (on the Vigo ferry we see Santa and José; on the rocks overlooking the sea, Santa and Lino). The film ends with the men's purposeful disruption of the space in a small act of defiance. They 'borrow' the ferry that transports workers across the estuary for a trip to scatter Amador's ashes in the ocean. To the annoyance of the commuting workers, the men set the ferry adrift, an apt metaphor for the enforced directionlessness of their own lives. Depressingly enough, ten years on, *Mondays* today seems doubly prescient. The unemployment it takes as its focus looks grimly set to continue to define post-2000 Spain for the time being. The indignation yet sense of community among León de Aranoa's fictional characters also looks forward to the recent phenomenon of 'Los indignados', or 'The Outraged', groups of many young unemployed people peacefully protesting against their lack of opportunities.

The incontestably serious subject of unemployment is portrayed by León de Aranoa's partial adoption of the high-culture references to Italian Neorealism, in a similar manner to Zambrano's *Alone*. Formal techniques of cinematography, editing and mise en scène are all harnessed for a political critique that blames testing individual circumstances on repressive socio-economic contexts. As Whittaker notes, the documentary inspiration and credit sequence of the shipworkers' demonstrations not only takes inequality as its subject but adopts politically-coded formal techniques, such as framing characters in medium long shots: 'Often used in Italian neo-realist films [...], this visual strategy serves to represent the characters as metonymic agents within a greater class struggle' (2011, 128). A combination of medium shots, a single long shot, together with significant mise en scène, is mobilized in the treatment of Santa's visit to Amador's apartment. León de Aranoa devotes three and a half minutes to the sequence, which offers a montage of hand-held medium shots, some of which include Santa in the frame, all of which track, swivel and probe into the rooms to record the apartment's wretched state of abandonment, with piles of discarded rubbish and unwashed crockery in seemingly every gloomy corner. When Santa opens the bedroom window: 'a sharp pull focus emphasizes the derelict shipbuilding yard which lies below, as if to suggest the reason for Amador's decline' (Whittaker 2011, 134).

This description may read like text-book social realism, but three other elements are crucial to the pivotal scene at the apartment: actor, music and narrative structure. The cinematography includes a number of point-of-view shots, encouraging us to understand and interpret the squalor by identifying with Santa. This process of identification is underscored by casting star actor Bardem, whose Socialist background and views are well-known to domestic audiences. Further, when the subjective cinematography begins, León de Aranoa introduces the emotive tones of the piano and strings of Lucio

Godoy's original score (he was nominated for best original score for this film at the CEC awards, and won best score at the Spanish Music Awards). Subjective cinematography, casting and music all feed into narrative here. Via the image-track we connect Amador's decline to unemployment, but via the soundtrack our emotional response to the situation is encouraged. Finally, via Santa we are encouraged to condemn the situation through the character's bitter views on the labour dispute and mass redundancies, which are voiced throughout the film. On a second viewing, we may also appreciate the centrality of the apartment scene in connection with narrative structure, for the window and the long shot of the yard look forward to the climax: Amador will commit suicide by leaping from the window, an act which the film, through this image, blames on unemployment.

Carefully constructed narrative, identification of character, heavily narra-tivized mise en scène in a domestic space and an emotive musical score are techniques that are not associated with social realism, but with melodrama. *Mondays* thus blurs, or fuses, genres. For Quintana this is a process of weakening, whereby 'modern realism' (2008, 253) deteriorates to 'timid realism' (2008). For Whittaker, however, this blurring may be productive. 'Formal tension between social realism and melodrama results in spatial tension', he writes, arguing that domestic and working spaces are refigured in gender terms, with both subject to the alluring but nefarious forces of post-industrial globalization. Whittaker's is a refreshing response to poe-faced complaints about generic purity. Thus where Stephen Brown questions cinematographer Alfredo Mayo's favouring of a 'bright, warm, sunlit' palette to portray unemployment in the famously rainy Galicia (2005, 69), an effect achieved by the use of Agfa rather than Kodak stock, Whittaker notes that while 'the glowing colours [...] are strikingly at odds with the bleak socio-economic milieus of the characters' the tension created in fact usefully points to the characters' negotiation of 'utopia and reality' (2011, 141).

Mondays is therefore another example of a middlebrow film that runs the risks of blurring. It combines serious questions like unemployment with elements of the revered social-realist traditions of auteurist cinema, but riskily fuses these with the high production values of the accessible genre of melodrama. Thus we encounter the familiar (though rounded and bearded) face of Bardem in the lead role, alongside top-notch Tosar, Egido and Bugallo (as we will see, the ascendance of actor Tosar took place post-*Mondays*) and our involvement with and understanding of the narrative is achieved by our identification with them. Our emotions are also cued by way of award-winning non-diegetic music. The collision of melodrama and social realism is particularly striking in the opening sequence, for León de Aranoa adds Godoy's original score as the only sound to an image track of documentary images of workers' clashes with police. Mise en scène, meanwhile, is deployed in a manner that interestingly hovers between both genres, imbued with the political significance that characterizes social realism, and the narrative significance that characterizes melodrama. Rather than condemning it as 'timid', we may approach a middlebrow film like *Mondays* on its own terms: accepting the tensions that arise from fusion and exploring their wider significance.

Take My Eyes (*Te doy mis ojos* Bollaín 2003)

Like *Mondays*, Icíar Bollaín's third feature, *Take My Eyes* (*Te doy mis ojos*) met with commercial and critical acclaim on its release, with a respectable audience of a million and an impressive seven Goya wins. As Paul Begin has recently written, critical attention to the film has been thus far divided between a thematic interest in its study of domestic violence and a formal interest in its intertextual references to pictorial art, and, to a lesser extent, architecture (2010, 32). For the critics that have addressed the film according to genre it has been labelled both 'timid realism' (Quintana 2008, 251) and 'popular social realism' (Jordan and Allinson 2005, 163), while Alberto Mira avoids 'realism' altogether in describing the film as a 'melodrama and as a contribution to social debate' (2010, 290).

This fusion of serious subject matter and high-cultural reference with an accessible formal treatment that apparently draws on both social realism and melodrama, and is characterized by high production values (recognized by awards for acting, screenplay and sound as well as directing), offers another example of middlebrow cinema, newly solemn here given the film's harrowing theme. Bollaín's willingness to broach a controversial topic highlights the potential for accessible-yet-serious middlebrow cinema to play a social role. While *Mondays* explored unemployment, this was too wide a theme for the film to make a specific intervention in the debate (Quintana, we recall, is critical of the film's failure to engage with specific PP policies [2008, 252]). *Take My Eyes*, meanwhile, successfully fashions the single-issue film for the 2000s, which Begin helpfully terms 'social issue cinema' (2010, 31). Part of its success may be measured by imitation, for Alejandro Amenábar similarly took on a single issue in his Oscar-winning *The Sea Inside* (*Mar adentro* 2004; Best Foreign Language Oscar 2005), which explored euthanasia through the real life story of Ramón Sampedro. Thus for Brian Goss, *Take My Eyes* is an 'intervention' in the public debate on domestic violence (2008, 34), while Jacqueline Cruz notes the film's participation in current media debates of the problem prior to its legal recognition in 2004 (Martínez-Carazo 2007, 394n.

2) and approvingly notes the accuracy and detail of Bollaín and fellow script-writer Alicia Luna's carefully-researched script, which pays judicious attention both to the victim of abuse and, importantly, its perpetrator (Cruz 2005, 67, 69). For Begin, this successful intervention goes to show that 'film, more so than any other medium, is the most capable for dissecting and treating social issues' (2010, 42). In the context of this book I would stress that it is middlebrow film in particular that can 'dissect' and 'treat' issues in this way. In the wider context of screen studies, Paul Julian Smith has shown that television, with its vastly higher viewing figures and ability accessibly to connect with the rhythms of everyday life, is oftentimes even more 'capable' than film to 'work through' social issues with audiences.[5]

The intermedial connections between Bollaín's film and high art have been a frequent critical approach to this much-analysed film. Critics have carefully shown the highly intelligent – but easily intelligible – ways Bollaín takes five examples of Western pictorial art and sews them into the film narrative (e.g. González del Pozo 2008; Martínez-Carazo 2008). Intermedial relations between pictorial art and feature film may of course take multiple forms. In Spanish film we have Luis Buñuel's wicked, witty references to Leonardo Da Vinci's *Last Supper* and Millet's *Angelus* in *Viridiana* (1961). Buñuel's godless characters recreate the holy scenes of the paintings in space, then hold the poses in time, so that viewers may appreciate the blasphemous irony of the intertext. Another example from auteur film is Víctor Erice's minutely-observed documentary study of artist Antonio López's unfinished painting of the eponymous tree, *The Dream of Light* (*El sol del membrillo*, literally, *The Quince Tree Sun*, 1992). Bollaín's middlebrow approach, however, recalls Antonio Mercero's in *A Time for Defiance* (1998) (see Chapter 6). In Mercero's film, Goya symbolizes liberalism and anti-war protest, both of which are rather simplistically associated with the Civil-War experience of a fictional anarchist family. *Take My Eyes* is more complex, with Bollaín's five pictorial intertexts working on a number of levels, including gender, power relations and trans-nationality, all of which are convincingly interwoven into the narrative of one woman's suffering with, then escape from, domestic abuse.

Thus at the start of the film a nervous Pilar, who has fled her abusive marital home and taken refuge at her sister, Ana's house, goes to Toledo cathedral where her sister works as a restorer. A low-angle tracking shot from Pilar's point-of-view reveals her perspective on a series of portraits of venerable former cardinals (all male, of course). But her eyes come to rest on Luis de Morales's *Mater Dolorosa* (1570s). The virgin's expression of resignation and suffering exactly matches Pilar's own. For Cristina Martínez-Carazo, this moment of recognition shows, 'on the one hand, the starting point of [Pilar's] emotional trajectory and on the other, the power of painting to replicate her emotional state' (2007, 396). In a later scene, Pilar hears a museum guide's description of El Greco's *The Burial of the Count of Orgaz* (1586–8). The lower half of the canvas, which portrays a group of mourning Spanish noblemen, seems to 'replicate' the darkness of her own abusive, moribund marriage to a Spaniard. In contrast, the guide's description of the re-birth of Orgaz in heaven in the upper half of the painting matches the protagonist's 'emotional trajectory' as she imagines her own re-birth in a future separated from her husband.

From then on, Pilar immerses herself in the study of art, then trains to become a guide herself. Thus Bollaín's inclusion of three further works, *Orpheus and Eurydice* (Rubens 1636–8), *Danae* (Titian 1554) and *Composition VIII* (Kadinsky 1923) is justified diegetically. Pilar's explanation of the first to her son matches the development of her relationship with her husband Antonio. Pilar, like Eurydice, has been taken to hell by Antonio, represented by Orpheus. In the Greek myth, Orpheus may rescue his wife if he can resist looking at her in their journey through the underworld. Rubens depicts the moment Orpheus gives in to temptation, looks at his wife, and thus loses her forever. Antonio's violence similarly plunges his wife in hell, but his assurance he will change, attendance at therapy, and touching attempts at seduction convince Pilar to return home. With the tragic inevitability of the Greek myth, Antonio will return to his old, violent ways and lose Pilar forever: the film's upbeat message is that his loss occurs thanks to her affirmation of her own identity by leaving him, rather than the other perfectly possible dénouement that he kills her.[6] Bollaín's use of the further Greek myth of Danae is similarly suggestive in narrative terms. Trainee guide Pilar introduces this painting to a group museum visitors, which, unbeknownst to her, includes Antonio. Of especial relevance here are the material afterlives of the erotic painting. Pilar describes a series of male regal owners who sought jealously to hide it away for their personal pleasure, or even destroy it so that others could not enjoy it – behaviour that of course matches Antonio's. By cleverly positioning Pilar in front of the projection of the painting, her association with the female Goddess is absolute, with the pixels of the projection flickering on her own skin, hair and clothes. This visual blurring conveys the way Antonio is unable to distinguish between the two females before him: the erotic female body on display (Danae) and the authoritative museum guide (his wife). When Pilar returns home, Antonio punishes the guide for the Titian's erotic portrayal of Danae's exhibitionism by physically attacking her in a fit of rage.[7] Bollaín's final artistic intertext constitutes a veritable intermedial symphony, for the colours of Kadinsky's abstract *Composition VIII* correlate with both the expression of emotion in music and Pilar's reading of Antonio's diary, which is also colour-coded according to emotion. Jorge González del Pozo explains the overlaps as 'the physical text of Antonio's diary becomes the visual text of *Composition VIII* and from there becomes the oral text of Pilar's words as she combines these narratives to reach a conclusion about her own feelings' (2008, n.p.).

Antonio's punishment of Pilar through humiliation is a textbook example of a neurotic and criminal response to her perceived threat. This may be understood in gender terms as castration anxiety (see note 7), but there is also a class dimension to his anxiety. Pilar's new life buys her two types of capital that Antonio is anxious about lacking. First, economic capital, for Pilar's current and future salary and new upper-bourgeois female friends throw into relief Antonio's membership of the petite bourgeoisie (he is an assistant in an electrical shop), about which he complains when the family visit his wealthy friend's second home in the country. Second, Pilar's acquisition of cultural capital through education also throws into relief Antonio's exclusion from high-culture. Bollaín captures this exclusion in the way she films Antonio's visit to the museum in Toledo to find his wife. Long shots diminish his figure as he scurries past a series of vast tableaux and sculptures whose presence he ignores.

The deployment of artistic intertexts is thus central to the characterization and plot development in *Take My Eyes*. It is important to note too that the means of that deployment is middlebrow, for, as González del Pozo emphasizes, this accessible film puts high art in reach of all audiences, culturally initiated or otherwise (2008, n.p.). Thus while prior knowledge is necessary fully to appreciate *Viridiana*'s intertextuality, in *Take My Eyes*, as in Mercero's *A Time for Defiance*, it is not, for the filmmakers provide full instruction. This makes both *Take My Eyes* and *A Time for Defiance* particularly accessible examples of the middlebrow, for other examples analysed in this book offer only initiated audiences the pleasure of recognition of well-known examples (as in the deployment of Goya's *The Spell* in *Spaniards in Paris*, or Velázquez's *Las meninas* in *Half of Heaven*). Art cognoscenti or not, Bollaín or Mercero's audiences enjoy the middlebrow pleasure of confirming their high-cultural capital through an accessible form.

While Mercero is uninterested in Goya's artistic form, Bollaín does not shy away from details of technique, linking, for example, the flowing pastel forms of El Greco's depiction of heaven in *The Burial* to Pilar's glimpse of a life of freedom and colour. It is ironic, therefore, that much critical response to Bollaín's oeuvre regards it as formally invisible. Prior to *Take My Eyes*, Susan Martin-Márquez writes of the 'deceptively "simple" surface' (2002, 261) of Bollaín's first two films. Martin-Márquez also notes that the critical tendency to stress 'simplicity', like Carlos Heredero's references to Bollaín's 'aesthetic nakedness' or 'expressive nakedness', is often a case of critics damning with faint praise, a fate that she argues is frequently reserved for female filmmakers (2002, 270–1n. 6). Writing on *Take My Eyes* specifically, Begin points out that a discussion of the film's form constitutes a critical blind spot (2010, 31–2). Begin aims to throw light on this area by discussing the film's 'realism', an area he argues is often ignored for its apparent invisibility, in favour of 'works of art that demonstrate touches of experimentalism' (2010, 32). Begin partially meets his objective by showing, first, how sound, or more accurately, lack of sound, is suggestively deployed in the film to cue emotion, especially in connection with timid Pilar,[8] and second, how the combination of cinematography, editing and mise en scène in Bollaín's tightly-framed shots conveys meaning, especially in connection with Antonio. Begin's final example focuses on the troubling sex scene between the married couple, in which the characters' nudity, the medium shot, and the simultaneous presence in the frame of both a partially-obscured Antonio and fully-displayed Pilar disturbingly replicate the gendered power relations of the look explored in connection with Titian's *Danae*, forcing the viewer into an uncomfortable decision between 'empathy or voyeurism?' (2010, 41). The knowing pictorialism of Bollaín's film techniques in this scene offers an example, however, of precisely the 'experimentalism' that Begin claims she avoids. Like Begin, I suggest that film form of *Take My Eyes* has been under-analysed, in favour of its social-issue focus and artistic intertexts. Unlike Begin, I will suggest that *Take My Eyes* is not an example of social realism at all. I will devote the remainder of this section to arguing that *Take My Eyes* is such a successful example of middlebrow cinema because of the ready readability of its genre, which, as Alberto Mira points out, is melodrama.

Take My Eyes is a film about physical violence in which we never see physical violence, though its effects and its threat hang heavy throughout. This does not suggest the documentary origins of social realism, but rather the displacement strategies more commonly associate with melodrama. Thus when Ana visits Pilar and Antonio's apartment to pick up her sister's belongings after her sister's initial departure, we see, from Ana's perspective, the visual aftermath of one of her brother-in-law's fits of rage: broken panes of glass and tomato sauce spattered over the kitchen from a plate of food flung in anger. While a documentary approach might have portrayed an actual attack, the melodramatic one displaces the act into mise en scène, thus spilled blood is evoked through the red sauce splashed on the kitchen tiles. This approach is not to be dismissed for timidity for, as Mira writes, 'not seeing [the acts of violence] only increases our perception of the horror' (2010, 290). Perhaps the fact that the viewer becomes used to this displacement of violence, even if it makes it more horrific, makes Antonio's depressingly inevitable loss of control and humiliation of Pilar towards the end of the film all the more difficult to watch.

The displacement of emotion into mise en scène is thus one of Bollaín's melodramatic strategies. The family focus of the plot is also typical, as is the strong female lead (played by Laia Marull), who is the focus of our identification, though unlike previous examples of the genre discussed in this book like *Life Goes On** (Fernán Gómez 1964, see Chapter 3) and *The Flower of My Secret* (Almodóvar 1995, see Chapter 6), the male partner (Luis Tosar) is also treated with nuance. Considering the film through the generic conventions of melodrama rather than social realism also allows us more subtly to account for setting. Spain's former medieval capital Toledo is frequently evoked through architectural landmarks, like the iconic cityscape-vista of the historic centre (the 'casco'), the Alcázar (military fortress), the cathedral, the city's narrow streets, and the characteristic living quarters of its historic centre, seen through Ana's house. A social-realist approach that seeks to link individual behaviour to environment might lead to the interpretation of the ancient city as a cipher for centuries of patriarchal repression, as in Pascale Thibaudeau's description of the Toledo's role in the film as a 'paragon of patriarchy' (2008, 234; 237–41). The specific scene of Pilar and Antonio's sexual encounter in Ana's house seems to confirm this. It begins with a shot of the Alcázar from the bedroom window. After the sex, as Antonio becomes angry and demands Pilar return to the marital home, Bollaín's camera takes in a second view of the military fortress from the window. Abusive Antonio's demands on Pilar are thus linked to the militaristic and patriarchal values of the monument, which is a famous symbol of Nationalist resistance during the Civil War.

The significance of the city is more subtle than this. For a start, its historic centre is presented as a site of refuge for the desperate Pilar, who escapes to it with her son from the marital home on the city's modern outskirts (the 'polígano'). It is also the artistic collections held by the historic city that provide an independent Pilar with a job, and trigger her 'liberation through art', as González del Pozo describes it (2008), for painter El Greco and the city Toledo where he lived are inextricably associated. The historic centre, its streets and its restaurants are also coded as welcoming and liberating feminine spaces for Pilar, for in them she spends time with the group of new female friends she makes through work. There is a further, specific scene at Ana's house in the historic centre that counters the patriarchal associations of the Alcázar-bedroom scene. Pilar and Ana are talking and hanging out washing on the roof-top terrace, from which the Alcázar can be seen, and the sisters' mother arrives wielding Pilar's wedding dress, which she wants Ana also to wear in her forthcoming marriage. Ana refuses, and begins angrily to question Pilar about the abuse she has suffered at the hands of her husband. Emotions are displaced onto objects once again as the beaten wife grabs the white gown that once represented her hopes for marriage and flings it in fury from the balcony top. Bollaín, as we have seen, is not interested in making films that are intelligible to the initiated only, and this scene standing alone brilliantly encapsulates the failed attempt at sisterly support in the context of marital abuse. The fact that the roof of Toledo's cathedral can be seen in the background of this scene perhaps stands for the patriarchal power of the Church and expectation of female obedience embodied by the attitude and life of the sisters' mother. However, the combination of the laundry in the foreground and the architecture in the background also recalls feminist filmmaker Marta Balletbò-Coll's similar composition in *Costa Brava* (1995). Just as in Balletbò-Coll's film the laundry invites us to question the significance of the 'phallic' towers of Gaudí's Sagrada Familia cathedral in Barcelona (Martin-Márquez 1999, 288), so in *Take My Eyes*, the presence of the laundry 'dress' the Alcázar and the cathedral differently, offering a feminist questioning of its patriarchal power.

I have argued that a key characteristic of middlebrow cinema is a focus on a serious subject matter, but unlike earlier efforts *Take My Eyes* engages with a specific issue, domestic violence, at the very moment it was debated in the media and law courts. Another characteristic is the deployment of high-cultural intertexts, but *Take My Eyes* is particularly skilful in stitching these artistic references into the fabric of its own narrative. On the page, the combination of domestic violence and intertextuality may look odd. Bollaín's accessible combination of the two, via a multi-dimensional vision of the city of Toledo, is one her great achievements in this film.

FIGURE 7.2 *Ana 'Dresses' Toledo's Alcázar.* Take My Eyes *(Te doy mis ojos Bollaín 2003)*

Carol's Journey (El viaje de Carol Uribe 2002)

While the connection between *Take My Eyes* of 2003 and the PSOE's legislation on domestic violence in 2004 is close, the correlation between films about the Spanish Civil War and Francoism and the Socialists' legislation on 'Historical Memory' in 2007 is more diffuse. It is nonetheless rewarding to place Imanol Uribe's *Carol's Journey* (*El viaje de Carol* 2002) and David Trueba's *Soldiers of Salamina* (2003), the subjects of this section and the next, in the contexts of the civic and political activism that preceded the 2007 law. This activism included the establishment in 2000 of the Association for the Recuperation of Historical Memory, which co-ordinates the opening up of mass graves, and the supporting bill of 2002 that 'condemned Francoism and rendered homage to its victims (including an obligation for public administrations to facilitate access to common graves and aid in the identification of remains)' (Paloma Aguilar quoted in Ballesteros 2005, 6). In 2005 Isolina Ballesteros expressed the hope that films like *Salamina* would 'continue to act as memory vectors to generate a real change in government policy and in its attitude towards the victims of Francoism' (2005, 6). In the 2007 law we might say that this hope was partially met. These connections and correlations between certain films of the 2000s and some areas of legislation do not point to a thesis of culture as just an illustration of context. The overlaps suggest, rather, that middlebrow cinema, with its accessible treatment of serious themes, may provide a productive forum in which to explore pressing contemporary concerns.

Released within one year of each other, *Carol's Journey* and *Salamina* share the motif of the journey in their otherwise very different approaches to the Civil War. The character arcs of the protagonists of both films trace a journey of self-discovery, a process that is acknowledged in the title of Uribe's film. Extra-diegetically the experience of watching the films may be likened to another journey of discovery, as both films take it on themselves to address their audiences on the serious subject of the War. The films are at opposite ends of the scale here, however. While *Carol's Journey*'s treatment offers a simplistic Manichaeism, *Salamina* explores details of battles, military strategy and participants that might only be familiar to a specialist audience. Despite these differences, both films invite a reading that relates these diegetic and extra-diegetic journeys to Spain of the early 2000s, though *Carol's Journey* offers a closed fiction set in 1930s Galicia, and *Salamina* a reflection on the Civil War that connects fictional present of 2003 and factual past, in particular the retreat of Republican forces in 1939 in Catalonia. The journey motif is especially prominent in the closing images of both films. *Carol's Journey*, which opens with Carol's arrival in Spain by train, closes with the girl's departure for America by taxi. As she moves forward in the car she looks back to see her three Spanish friends, one of whom, slain in error by a Nationalist bullet, is just a ghostly apparition. Trueba also employs oxymoronic movement in portraying Lola's departure from Miralles in *Salamina*. She is in another taxi which moves forward as she stares back in tears. Both Carol and Lola seem to evoke a Janus-faced Spain, pulled between past and future. As Arthur Hughes writes of Trueba's film, 'The visual contradiction of the taxi's forward motion against Lola's backward look is a distillation of contemporary Spanish society' (2007, 371).

The differences between the films stem from the ages of the protagonists: a twelve-year old girl on the cusp of adolescence and a middle-aged woman in the throes of a mid-life crisis. The characterization and plot of *Carol's Journey* are indebted to Montxo Armendáriz's 1997 *Secrets of the Heart*, a film which Uribe co-produced. Childhood journeys of discovery are central to this similarly middlebrow treatment of a child growing up in 1960s dictatorship Spain. A key motif is protagonist Javi's crossing of the village river on stepping stones: fear prevents him from doing so at the opening of the film, but he makes the literal journey across the water and completes the figurative voyage of self-discovery by the end. River-crossings feature among Carol's 2002 journeys too, though Uribe uses them as an image of development from girlhood to womanhood by having Carol kiss Tomiche halfway across one. The accidental shooting of Tomiche also occurs halfway across the river, visually illustrating that the boy's life is, tragically, barely half-lived. Uribe reprises Armendáriz's use of linguistic discovery too. While Javi's young age justifies his questions ('¿Qué significa "chingar"?' [What does 'screw' mean?]), bilingual Carol's are explained by her lesser familiarity with Spanish ('¿Qué significa "deshuevado"'?' [What does 'done in' mean?]).

A gentle treatment of the newly urgent question for 2000s Spain of the Civil War, and a highly accessible melodrama that features journeys and questions that are clearly symbolic in a national context, my approach to this middlebrow film will rest on its use of the child protagonist. Such films are so important in Spanish cinema that they have a generic label of their own, 'cine con niño' (films with a child). Alberto Mira has identified two traditions here, and although longer studies might point out the disruptions, contradictions and overlaps between both tendencies, the division is nonetheless useful. The first tradition, writes Mira, 'uses the child, normally an orphan, as a spectacular object in comedy, melodrama or, most often, in musicals. It has its golden period in the 1950s and 1960s' (2010, 77–8) and its most prominent representatives are Pablito Calvo, who shot to fame in Ladislao Vajda's blockbuster *The Miracle of Marcelino* (*Marcelino, pan y vino* 1955), and Marisol, discussed in Chapter 3. Mira's second tradition begins with Víctor Erice's *The Spirit of the Beehive* (*El espíritu de la colmena* 1973) 'which uses the child as a witness and as an anchor for audience identification' (2010, 78) in films that are political critiques of the dictatorship; Armendáriz's *Secrets of the Heart* revived this approach in the 1990s (Mira 2010, 80). Antonio Mercero's treatment of Lolo García in middlebrow *Daddy's War* (1977) blurred the popular, escapist 'spectacular object' tradition and the auteurist, political 'child as witness' strand, as discussed in Chapter 4. My thesis in this analysis of *Carol's Journey* is that a middlebrow fusion of popular and auteurist strands similarly occurs.

Middlebrow cinema may, as we have seen, appeal to high-cultural inter-texts from art, literature or theatre, or may, as in the case of the connections between the *cine social* and Italian Neorealism, appeal to the auteurist traditions of cinema itself. In *Carol's Journey* the privileged intertext is Erice's *The Spirit of the Beehive*, the key reference point of Spanish cinema's auteurist tradition. Both films are sympathetic to the Republican losers of the Civil War. *The Spirit of the Beehive* features the assassination of a Republican *maquis* and chronicles the post-war solitude, silence and monotony to which Ana's family, in its rambling country house, is condemned. *Carol's Journey* turns the clock back to the conflict itself, narrating the capture of Carol's father, a North-American pilot for the Republic-defending International Brigades, and the sadness of the girl's bereaved grandfather in his rambling old house, who burns his leftist literature and suffers the violation of his home through external anti-American graffiti and an internal, unauthorized search by his Nationalist son-in-law.

More substantial than the loose political leanings of the plots is the child protagonist. Erice's is the original child-as-witness film, though it reprises the way Carlos Saura uses adolescent Enrique's inquisitive youthful perspective on the Civil War conflict in *The Hunt* (*La caza* 1966). Through subjective cinematography, elliptical narrative and clever interweaving of a viewing of James Whales's *Frankenstein* (1931), we share Ana's partial, confused point-of-view as she witnesses the aftermath of conflict, befriending the *maquis* and attempting to decipher her parents' enigmatic lives. Alongside the horror film intertext Erice profitably deploys references to the natural world, most notably the beehive, which delicately combines a child's fascination with the natural environment and the weighty symbolism with which the structure has been imbued by Spanish authors like Camilo José Cela's nihilistic condemnation of post-war Spain in 1951 *The Beehive* (*La colmena*) and Belgian poet Maurice Maeterlinck in his 1901 *The Life of the Bee* (Stone 2002, 89).

The horror film intertext is missing from Uribe's gentle treatment, but he retains our identification with the child through plot and cinematography, and similarly interweaves references to the natural world. Point-of-view shots are employed from the moment Carol wakes up on the train to observe the priest and altar boy's shock when they see her mother smoke, to the look backwards at her friends on her departure, discussed above. Her confrontation with the ongoing conflict involve understanding that her father is fighting on the losing side and witnessing the violence of the period, which takes the mildly amusing form of soldiers mistaking a balloon dropped from her father's aircraft for a bomb, and the more sinister forms of discovering the meaning of 'dar un paseo' (to be shot in the head) and witnessing the accidental shooting dead of her friend Tomiche. Carol shares Ana's fascination with the natural world, and the film explores her connection to the birds that Tomiche and his friends capture in the mountains, and a reference to insects in particular through her friend Maruja's silk worms and butterflies.

However, the difference between middlebrow *Carol's Journey* and auteurist *The Spirit of the Beehive* is vast, and hinges on the questions of intelligibility and interpretation. This is not to say that Erice's film is unintelligible and unintepretable, but, rather, that his audience has to travel further, for greater reward. Each of the encounters between six-year-old Ana and the adult world of conflict and silence, the film world of monstrosity and the natural world of wonder is governed by complexity, bewilderment and an ambiguous lack of resolution. Thus the aftermath of the Civil War that causes the slaying of the *maquis* remains a mystery to Ana, while the viewer may begin to comprehend it by bringing to bear their historical knowledge of post-war repraisals in the period. Likewise, her parents' world remains impenetrable, though viewers may partially comprehend it through references to the father's intellectual past, evoked through photographs, and present, evoked through the Maeterlinck study. Plural cultural references might be brought to bear to comprehend the beehive metaphor, which remains an elusive wonder to Ana. Importantly, though, no neat division between on-screen childhood incomprehension and off-screen adult comprehension is made. Ana, for example, intuits the significance of a number of monster-figures in her surroundings, including Frankenstein. The audience, meanwhile, is left with a number of enigmas, like the meaning of Ana's final nocturnal address to the monster 'soy Ana' (I am Ana), which may be endlessly interpreted and re-interpreted as an obsession with monstrosity and surrender to her repressive surroundings, or a rebellious act of self-identity and affirmation against those same surroundings.

While Erice's child perspective thus leads to bewilderment and the requirement for often unsettling audience involvement, Uribe's leads to comprehension and comforting simplification that ends up spiralling off into a sentimental treatment of childhood that has little to do with its Civil War context. Thus the war leads to Carol's inconvenient separation from her father, compensated for by the adventures she has with Tomiche in order to send him letters, and his airborne visit and parachuted present. The natural world provides further keys for comprehension as the birds are symbol of freedom and flight, like her father, and Maruja herself performs the act of interpretation for the audience when Carol explores the secret room of silk worms and butterflies: 'tu también estás dentro de un capullo, pero pronto se abrirá' (you're in a cocoon too, but it'll soon open), to which Carol replies with refreshing sarcasm 'y yo me convertiré en una mariposa de seda' (and I'll become a silk butterfly). While the rambling old house of *The Spirit of the Beehive* is full of fear and mystery, Carol's house in *Carol's Journey* is a space of affirmation and comprehension. Thus when Torrent's Ana hears heavy footsteps as she lies in bed, she never learns, as the viewer does, that they are her father's, not a monster's. In contrast, when Lago's Carol is awakened by unfamiliar sounds and creeps downstairs to investigate, she discovers the welcome sight of her father talking to her grandfather in the warmly-lit family kitchen, ready with a bear hug for his daughter. Consequently, while *The Spirit of the Beehive* ends with Ana's enigmatic confrontation of a monstrous post-war Spain, Carol takes an improbably jolly taxi-ride through a supposedly war-torn country to escape to a sunny future in America, to which, she is promised, her imprisoned father will return and her grandfather will soon visit.

Secrets of the Heart also ends with the affirmative completion of a journey and confirmation of filial love for the father. For Rob Stone, what saves the film from the 'golden-hued nostalgia for childhood' is 'the chronology which

FIGURE 7.3 *Maruja Over-explains the Significance of the Cocoons to Carol.* Carol's Journey *(El viaje de Carol Uribe 2002)*

identifies Javi, who would be 21 at the time of Franco's death, with the generation that came of age in the political transition' (2002, 106). With no such
chronology, I would suggest, *Carol's Journey* leaves us just with the 'golden-
hued nostalgia' that characterizes the first child-cinema tradition identified by
Mira. Rather than treat the child as a subject with whom audiences might
identify as a witness to key events, in this first tradition, we recall, the child is
treated as a 'spectacular object'. Such a treatment reduces character to stereotype, and *Carol's Journey* piles one such on top of the other. Like Pablito and
Marisol, Carol is for all intents and purposes an orphan, as her mother dies
early in the picture and her father is absent. Like Cinderella, she has, however,
a fairy godmother in the shape of wise, fun-loving, nurturing Maruja (Rosa
María Sardà), who does not have a magic wand but does have a magic room
of silk worms that transform the leaves they eat into silk cocoons. She also
has an ugly stepmother, the not-accidentally named embittered *beata* Dolores
(Lucina Gil), whose husband Adrián (played by a menacing Carmelo Gómez
whose talent goes mostly underused) has married her on the rebound and
an ugly sister, Dolores's daughter Blanca, complete with blonde plaits and
prim dresses. The Civil War context adds further characters to the tale, but no
nuance, thus Nationalist Adrián is in cohoots with the local Falangist Alfonso
(Alberto Jiménez), both of whom sport Hitleresque moustaches. Alongside
such stereotypes, Carol's outsider status as a dungarees-wearing Tomboy
with cropped hair scarcely undergoes any 'journey' at all, other than the
sentimental one of acquiring her first boyfriend. She begins as the outsider
daughter of an American air pilot and ends returning to that outside space of
America once again, having failed to fit in.

If stereotyped characterization discourages an appreciation of subjectivity
and transformation, cinematography and music also underscore the treatment
of Carol as an object to be contemplated. Her location against the verdant
mountain and rural landscapes of the film, shot in Galicia and Portugal, are
diegetically justified by Carol and her friend's adventures in the natural world,
but the beauty of this mise en scène leads to the static contemplation of
spectacle, rather than dynamic investigation of change. Bingen Mendizábal's
original score plays a key role in emphasizing the saccharine elements of the
visual track. If not making the military dimension of characters' behaviour
obvious by adding drum rolls – as when the children witness a truck-load of
prisoners being driven through the night to their execution, or when Adrián
pushes past his father-in-law to search the house for Carol's father – or adding
a jaunty accompaniment to the portrayal of childhood mischief – as when
Tomiche pinches Carol's hat – Mendizábal offers soaring strings, rippling
keyboard notes, and comfortingly repeated phrases that are linked to Carol.
These, predictably, underscore moments of emotional intensity, like the

moments when Carol receives letters from her father, or her first kiss with Tomiche, and thus serve throughout to exaggerate moments that are already highly sentimental.

We have seen over the course of this book that the middlebrow can be a tricky balancing act between serious thematic concerns and accessible formal treatment. *Carol's Journey* seems to be an example of a film where the balance tips so far in favour of the accessibility of popular child-cinema that it compromises the serious concerns that align it with auteurist child-as-witness cinema. For a director of the standing of Uribe, its audience figures were correspondingly modest at 374,000 viewers, though it won the Crystal Bear (Special Mention) at Berlin in 2003 along with 3 Goya nominations. *Carol's Journey* seems to constitute Spanish child-cinema at a point of creative exhaustion, a point confirmed by David Trueba's effective decision to challenge the inter-generational inheritance narrative in his exploration of the Civil War in *Salamina* of the following year. It is perhaps surprising to note, then, that in 2006 another renowned director would cast another twelve-year-old girl as the protagonist of another fictional feature about the Civil War: Mexican Guillermo del Toro in *Pan's Labyrinth* (*El laberinto del fauno*).[9] Del Toro's piece boasted superb actors like Ivana Baquero (Ofelia), Maribel Verdú (Mercedes), Sergi López (Vidal) and Ariadna Gil (Carmen) – but then so did Uribe's with 'revelation' actress Lago (Galán 2006), male adolescent favourite at the time José Juan Ballesta (Tomiche), plus Carmelo Gómez (Adrián), María Barranco (Aurora) and Rosa María Sardà (Maruja). Both reprise the nationally-symbolic female child's journey of discovery, but the success of multiple-award-winning *El laberinto* (it won Oscars for art direction, cinematography and make-up) might be best explained in its attentive reading of Erice's original treatment of 1973. Unlike Uribe, del Toro develops the investigation of fantasy begun by the *Frankenstein* intertext in Erice's *The Spirit of the Beehive* into a key component of the film, whereby the socio-realist narrative of the Civil War is mirrored by Ofelia's investigation of a subterranean world of fantasy and myth. Amparo Aliaga Sanchis's comparison of the two films sums up the difference succinctly 'both varnish the sadness of the period: [Uribe] through sentimentalism and [Del Toro] through fantasy' (2008, 2).

Soldiers of Salamina (*Los soldados de Salamina* Trueba 2003)

Isolina Ballesteros has likened the impact of Javier Cercas's immensely successful novel *Soldados de Salamina*[10] on public awareness of the Spanish

Civil War to the 'Spielberg effect' that *Schindler's List* (1993) had on awareness of the Holocaust (2005, 6). As is standard practice in commercial cinema, David Trueba's movie adaptation of the same name piggy-backs on the success of the novel, with a view to converting its readers into the film's audience, and it succeeded in attracting 433,000, which no doubt included many of them. It would be wrong, however, to dismiss the film for a lack of originality. In this section I will suggest that the creative challenge of adaptation leads Trueba to make two original contributions to historical cinema in Spain. First, by finding cinematic equivalents for the investigation of memory in the original novel[11] Trueba offers an new exploration that switches between a fictional present and a Civil-War past evoked through interwoven images from the documentary archive and fictional historical recreations. Second, Trueba's transformation of Cercas's male protagonist Javier into the female character Lola is a brilliant move. This change allows him to move away from the original novel and explore questions of inter-generational inheritance and childlessness that mark a new departure from the numerous Spanish Civil-War films, like *Secrets of the Heart* (Armendáriz 1997) and *Carol's Journey* (Uribe 2002) discussed in the previous section, that have now almost exhausted the child-protagonist and child-as-witness trends.[12]

David Trueba, brother of Fernando (whose *First Work* is analysed in Chapter 5), is one of the 'New Directors' discussed by Carlos Heredero in *20 New Spanish Film Directors* (1999) (*Salamina* is his third feature). Although Heredero traces Trueba's literarity through his 1990s work as a novelist, journalist and particularly successful scriptwriter before moving behind the camera (1999, 322–4), the 'middlebrow turn' I analyse in Pedro Almodóvar's 1995 *The Flower of my Secret* (Chapter 6) also seems influential. Literarity is central to *Salamina*, as it was to *Flower*, because both films feature writers as protagonists, both portray a crisis in creativity, and both explore the inter-connections between the writers' lives and art. Trueba also reprises Almodóvar's interest in a middle-aged female protagonist, though in *Flower* this focus leads to an intense melodrama of marital breakdown, whereas in *Salamina* it leads to a preoccupation with childlessness that is entirely absent from Almodóvar's world. Thus Trueba's post-credit sequence, in which the mobile camera sweeps over novels and notebooks eventually to rest on Lola at her desk repeats Almodóvar's post-credit sequence, in which we meet Leo in an identical scenario. As discussed in Chapter 6, Almodóvar's middlebrow turn in *Flower* may be related to studies that indicate a new appetite among 1990s audiences for serious yet accessible films with cultural capital secured by high-cultural references. The reasonable viewing figures for *Salamina* of 433,000 were less than half those of *Flower* (982,000), but nonetheless indicate the continued existence of an audience for middlebrow films.

The high-cultural references of *Salamina* turn on the film's literarity. The privileged intertext here is the source novel. For its readers, the film, like any literary adaptation, offers the pleasures of recognizing previously-encountered characters, scenes and plot twists, and the often perverse pleasures of annoyance at changes to the original – this annoyance enables readers to confirm the cultural capital represented by their knowledge of the original. In addition to the connection to Cercas, *Salamina* continually reminds the viewer of its literarity. It emphasizes its protagonist's occupation as a writer and academic, features writerly locations like libraries and the author's study, and includes on its image-track numerous medium shots of books, notebooks, newspapers, word documents on computer screens, letters, manuscripts and other archival texts – plus close-ups of specific pages – and on its sound-track many voiceover readings of those sources. Moreover, its plot covers a range of literary activities: research on two Spanish writers (after Lola's brief consideration of internationally renowned poet Antonio Machado in her original newspaper article, 'El secreto esencial' [The Essential Secret], she focuses on founder of the Falange and middle-ranking writer Rafael Sánchez Mazas), the frustration of writer's block, frenzied typing on a computer keyboard, petulant hurling of manuscripts into the bin and of books across the room, and even the encouragement of two unlikely literary fairy godmothers: Conchi, the Sancho Panza to Lola's Don Quijote,[13] and the even more improbable Aguirre, who motions to Lola to get on with writing her novel under the belting rain mid-way across another Girona bridge.

What rescues the film from being a library piece, and brings the accessibility and high production values that are typical of the middlebrow, is the casting of Ariadna Gil. Gil happens to be Trueba's partner, but her star persona is ideal for the fusion of a dusty library study with the emotional journey of a partnerless, childless middle-aged woman. Born (like Trueba) in 1969, fans of the actress might protest her youthfulness, but in *Salamina* she performs a middle age beyond her years. Intelligent adaptability characterizes her filmography pre-*Salamina*. A 'pretty face' taken more seriously as an artist after playing lesbian Violeta in David's brother's *Belle Epoque* (Fernando Trueba 1992), Alberto Mira describes her strengths as 'a strong sensuality and a husky voice, which can suggest depths of mystery, but she has always resisted typecasting, and even in her roles as object of desire, there is a sense of intelligent distance' (2010, 145). With the serious subject of the Civil War and a popular actress as protagonist, Trueba's *Salamina* offers an effective middlebrow version of historical cinema that focuses on memory, through Gil's mind (Mira's 'intelligent distance'), and childlessness, through Gil's body (Mira's 'sensuality ... desire').

Lola imagines the past in *Salamina* in two ways: first, through an academic investigation of historical events and second, through an imaginative recreation of them in her own writing. Lola may be a writer, and the physical act of writing is frequently shown, but most of this investigation and imagination is visually presented, as Trueba uses both authentic archive footage and fabricated historical recreations to portray Lola's thoughts, or mind's eye, as she becomes fascinated by the moment of comradeship between Sánchez Mazas and the militiaman/Miralles towards the end of the Civil War. For example, as Lola reads her article 'The Essential Secret' to her father, her voiceover is accompanied by archive images that represent the recreation, in her imagination, of the events she describes (these include both authentic sources and fictitious historical recreations with Ramón Fontserè as Sánchez Mazas). The introduction of Miralles is similar. Lola reads her student Gastón's essay – conveyed to the audience through a voiceover read by the actor who portrays him, Diego Luna – and we see, in her mind's eye, a series of images that are both real – photographs and newsreels – and fictitious – for instance, the actor Alberto Ferreiro in the role of the militiaman. Throughout the film, Trueba plunders the authentic archive of newsreel, photographs and newspapers from the period, mixes them with historical recreations featuring the actors Fontserè as Sánchez Mazas, Ferreiro as the militiaman, and others, and even alters the original archive to include super-imposed images of these contemporary actors (for instance, in the case of the ceremony where Sánchez Mazas [played by Fontserè] swears his allegiance to Franco [authentic footage]).[14]

Trueba's use of the audiovisual archive evokes a number of processes that Laura Mulvey has termed 'Delayed Cinema'. When Lola imagines the past, Trueba likens her to Mulvey's description of the film fan, who returns to old films and finds new meaning in them by discovering 'some detail has lain dormant, as it were, waiting to be noticed' (2006, 22). The historical detail that for Lola has 'lain dormant' is the moment when Sánchez Mazas and the militiaman exchange a look beneath the pouring rain in the undergrowth after the Falangist's escape from the Republican firing squad at the end of the war, a moment that the film repeats four times in slow motion. Trueba portrays Lola's shift of focus from Sánchez Mazas to the militiaman in a similar way. The moment when he sings 'Suspiros de España' (Sighing for Spain) in the rain becomes another detail that has 'lain dormant' awaiting her discovery, and it is repeated twice in slow motion from the perspective of her mind's eye.

Thus, while Trueba's plot is not original (an adaptation of a novel), he offers a version of 'Delayed Cinema' to highlight Lola's engagement with the past through her imagination. However, Lola is far more than a disembodied eye that sees events, or a mind that imagines events. Despite her characterization as the aloof, ascetic intellectual – repeatedly thrown into relief by María Botto's lusty portrayal of her earthy, sensual friend, Conchi – the use of Gil's body is key.[15] Lola's childlessness and middle age are particularly important here. We know Lola as an adult for whom no trauma about the Civil War has been transmitted via her family; her father's amnesia further reinforces this point. Through her childlessness Trueba also sweeps away the questions of lineage and inheritance that characterize films with parents as protagonists. Multiple examples of Spanish cinema condemn bad parents, both fathers and father-figures (reclusive Fernando Fernán Gómez's character in *The Spirit of the Beehive*; Héctor Alterio's war-obsessed fathers of *Raise Ravens* [*Cría cuervos* Saura 1976] and *Daddy's War*; Sergi López's terrifying Captain Vidal in *Pan's Labyrinth*) and mother and mother-figures (Aurora Bautista's overbearing aunt in *Aunt Tula* [*La tía Tula* Picazo 1964]; Lola Gaos's incestuous monster in *Poachers** [*Furtivos* Borau 1975]).[16] In a cultural context where the portrayal of cross-generational trauma has grown familiar, Lola's childlessness could have offered a liberation of sorts: since trauma cannot be passed down the generations, the future is no longer held prisoner of the past. However, in Trueba's hands, childlessness is a source of regret, never one of release. In what follows, I will bring to the fore the apparently incidental background details regarding Lola's childlessness and suggest that they gesture towards stasis and an inability to move forward. *Salamina* therefore forces the viewer to consider questions about the future that are potentially more terrifying than those posed by the cross-generational narrative: not how will it be affected, but, will it exist?

As I have indicated, the plot of *Salamina* relies heavily on archive footage. Given that Trueba is pitching his work as a middlebrow balance of seriousness and accessibility, this reliance may seem excessive. It is tolerated by the viewer thanks to the central role played by Lola as protagonist. As we have seen, her exploration of the past is at first an intellectual investigation, but it also shifts to a perceptual experience: at first, she re-lives past time in her imagination, but, as she becomes increasingly involved in the story, she re-lives it also through her own body. This process begins with the biography she writes on Sánchez Mazas. When she phones Conchi's TV show, she gives away her intellectual identification with the Falangist author by playfully giving her name as Lola Sánchez, rather than Lola Cercas. However, when she visits the woods where the shooting took place, she re-lives some of Sánchez Mazas's experiences – albeit very partially – in her own skin. Thus, as she explores the area where the Falangist was hunted down to be killed, she likewise fears for her own life as she realizes that hunters are firing shots but are unaware of her presence.[17] Just as Sánchez Mazas endures physical suffering 'durante nueve días con sus noches de invierno' (during nine days with their winter nights) (as Lola writes in her account), she suffers too, cutting her wrist as she falls in the undergrowth and, once back at home, holding her breath for several seconds under water in the bath. As she delves deeper into Sánchez Mazas's bodily suffering in her account, so her body suffers further too. She has a nervous fit at the computer and stops breathing – a moment of disturbance that Trueba portrays with a canting shot – and ends up lying on the floor. For Hughes, the cinematography in the sequence of the fit indicates a 'dis-identification' between Lola and Sánchez Mazas (2007, 384). However, if we read Gil's Lola as embodying time, the cinematography points here to a profound identification between writer and history through the body.

Thus Lola's embodiment of time via her identification with Sánchez Mazas points to a past that might be sympathetically recovered. However, Trueba also brings out the female body's special relation to time: a finite period of fertility. By emphasizing Lola's childlessness and stressing, through middle age, that her fertility is nearing its end, Trueba hints both at the future, and the possible lack of a future. Crucial to this is Trueba's change of Cercas's original Javier to the film's Lola, which allows him to introduce 'new perspectives', as he himself stated in interview (Harguindey 2002).[18] One such 'perspective', which draws on the 'sensuality' and 'desire' Alberto Mira identifies in Gil's star persona is female sexuality. In an original move, Trueba rejects the ever-familiar sexualized female body (glimpsed in Lola's truncated relationships with both male student Gastón and female friend Conchi) and deploys Gil's 'sensuality' and 'desire' to explore an anxiety rarely addressed on screen – childlessness.

While Conchi, the professional tarot-card-reading Cassandra, conjures up the future through cheerful chatter, for Lola, until the final scene of the film, it may only be glimpsed through wordless gazes not obviously connected to the narrative. The first such non-diegetic moment occurs in Madrid, where she has travelled to begin her research on Sánchez Mazas. The business of the narrative here concerns research; apparently irrelevant then is her chance encounter with her ex-boyfriend, Carlos, mid-way across one of the capital's busy parks. When Lola turns back to look at him walk away, we share a point-of-view shot that reveals he is carrying a bag from Prenatal, Spain's best-known baby shop. Again, when Lola borrows a car from a colleague to travel to the Collell sanctuary and surrounding woods, she finds a child's rattle in the empty passenger seat. The business of the narrative again concerns research on Sánchez Mazas, but as Lola wordlessly studies the rattle, Trueba hints that this research is somehow entangled with the search for a child of her own. Similarly, when Lola arrives at the ruined country house where Sánchez Mazas took refuge, she passes by a group of children playing war games. The bleak suggestion here that man is eternally condemned to repeat his mistakes and that each generation will engage in new wars, is not original – it can be found through similar images of children's war games in *From Pink ... to Yellow* (*Del rosa al amarillo* Summers 1963) and *Bicycles are for Summer* (*Las bicicletas son para el verano* Chávarri 1984), for example. The shift of focus to Lola's childlessness is original, however. Likewise, in a sequence at her office at Girona university, we find her silently remove a child's drawing from a wall and study it sadly.

Another example of a wordless reference occurs as Lola waits for Jaume Figueras in Girona's El Núria café in order to interview him about his father. At their first appointed meeting, Figueras doesn't show up, and it may at first seem surprising that Trueba bothers to portray his protagonist simply waiting. There are two sections to this portrayal of her wait. In the first, jump cuts convey Lola's annoyance that her interviewee hasn't arrived. In the second section, the camera moves outside the café window, and a long take replaces the jump cuts; there follow three point-of-view shots from Lola's perspective of children in a playground, and the section closes with a close-up of the character's face. In the long take shot through the window pane, we see both Lola's face as she stares out at the children, and, simultaneously, the reflection of those same children at play. Trueba's use of reflections of Lola's face is a visual motif repeated throughout the film to underscore narrative: when Lola reads her article to her father, Trueba captures both Gil and her mirror reflection in the same frame; when Lola leaves Daniel Angelats in Banyoles, then Miralles in Dijon, the camera captures both Gil's face and its reflection in the bus windows (the face and its reflection as Lola leaves Banyoles is used on the DVD cover). In the taxi in Dijon, Miralles's face is also

FIGURE 7.4 *Lola Gazes at the Children at Play.* Soldiers of Salamina *(Los soldados de Salamina Trueba 2003)*

superimposed on Lola's through the reflection of the window pane. These reflections seem to convey Lola as Janus-faced, caught between past and present. Further, in the example at the Núria café, the use of reflection also underscores the film's subtle study of childlessness. Finally, with Miralles, we see Lola watch a group of children pass by the gates of the old people's home in single file. Tellingly, just as Miralles articulates Lola's struggle to understand anonymous heroism, so the old man also raises the question of childlessness by acknowledging the children's presence, questioning whether Lola has children, then affirming their importance: 'Cuando los miras, te das cuenta de que lo único que importa es estar vivo. Con eso basta' (When you look at them you realize that the only thing that matters is to live. That's enough).[19]

Thus middlebrow *Salamina* makes an original contribution to Spanish historical cinema. While following enough of the original novel to attract readers, Trueba simultaneously offers an original treatment of the representation of the Civil War via Lola's mind, and a representation of a (threatened) future via Lola's body. The role played by Gil as the protagonist is thus central, and her interaction with particularly effective supporting actors like Botto and Luna temper the seriousness of the historical investigation with an accessible treatment of Lola's life and relationships.

Alatriste (Díaz Yanes 2006)

An especially loose, though nonetheless useful, generic marker, it is today possible to assess three decades of 'heritage cinema', noting the shifts in critical debates and the applicability or otherwise of the term to Spanish cinema. Though coined to refer to 1940s British period cinema (Barr 1986, 11), as we have seen in Chapter 6, the term describes films of the 1980s onwards that use historical settings in a particular way. In 1993 Andrew Higson stressed that 'the past is displayed as visually spectacular pastiche, inviting a nostalgic gaze that resists the ironies and social critiques so often suggested narratively' (2006, 91), though this hostile interpretation was quickly revised by critics sympathetic to the treatment of gender and sexuality (eg Monk 1995), and the democratization of history (Sargeant 2000), in films like *A Room with a View* (Ivory 1985). Proof of the looseness of the marker comes with the fact that, after barely a decade and a half, a new term, 'post-heritage' (coined by Claire Monk in 1995),[20] was needed to describe the way the genre had come to emphasize sex and violence (Monk 2011, 23). Films like *La reine Margot* (Chéreau 1994) and *Elizabeth* (Kapur 1998) thus sought cross-over appeal to younger audiences brought up on thrillers like *Pulp Fiction* (Tarantino

1994). Higson, again, revised in 2003 his earlier critique to argue for 'a tension between narrative and spectacle' in heritage and post-heritage cinema, 'while the first is often progressive, stressing the conflicts at the heart of inheritance, the second is generally reactionary, consoling threatened audiences for the loss of imperial power or class privilege' (summarized in Smith 2006, 112).

'Heritage film' can only be used of Spanish cinema of the 1980s with qualifications, for while Mirovian cinema displays some characteristics like high production values and a tendency towards literary adaptations (Chapter 5), the particular circumstances of a country emerging from dictatorship with a political desire to recuperate oppositional texts of the Franco period are a key difference. However, examples of films from the next decade, like *The Dumbfounded King* (1991) and *The Dog in the Manger* (1997) (discussed in Chapter 6) reveal a Spanish cinema in step with transnational heritage trends. This section and the next will argue that Agustín Díaz Yanes's *Alatriste* (2006) and Andrucha Waddington's *Lope* (2010) also bear comparison with post-heritage examples.[21] Crossover heritage-thriller *Elizabeth* offers a model for Díaz Yanes's fusion of heritage with the western in his adaptation of five novels of Arturo Pérez-Reverte's much-loved historical series about Captain Alatriste. Waddington's *Lope*, meanwhile, in returning to the formative years and amorous entanglements of the young playwright, takes *Shakespeare in Love* (Madden 1998) as an obvious model.

I include the 'heritage' and 'post-heritage' debates here in order to portray the alignment of these Spanish films with non-Spanish examples. These films were not aimed at foreign audiences, however. *The Dumbfounded King*, *The Dog in the Manger*, *Alatriste* and *Lope* all had limited distribution outside Spain:[22] Spanish heritage thus constitutes an 'indigenization' of foreign heritage trends intended for Spanish audiences.[23] Intersecting synchronically with non-Spanish trends exemplified by *Elizabeth* (which was a box office hit in Spain [Smith 2006, 106]), Spanish heritage connects diachronically with the domestic cinema's middlebrow tendency, which has been the focus of this book. Rather than admitting the failure of generic descriptors by adding prefixes like 'post-' (what will come next?) the 'middlebrow' approach may be adapted to new tendencies. The applicability of 'middlebrow' to both, say, *Spaniards in Paris* (Bodegas 1971) and, forty years on, *Lope*, does not flatten the field, but teases out its continuities of an emerging (1970s), then consolidated (2000s), middle-class audience enjoying varied middlebrow films that are nonetheless all identifiable through their fusion of serious subject matters, high-cultural references, high production values and an accessible treatment.

Díaz Yanes's third feature *Alatriste*, which began as a commission when the director was approached by the author Pérez-Reverte and the producer Antonio Cardenal ('Review of *Alatriste*' 2006), reprises these four traits but marks a new departure for Spanish cinema in its incredibly high production values (carefully reporting each stage of the project, the press repeated ad nauseum that these were bought at a price of 24 million euros, making the film the most expensive Spanish feature ever made).[24] A tale that spans 25 years in the life of veteran soldier and occasional mercenary Captain Alatriste (played by American Viggo Mortensen, of recent *The Lord of the Rings: The Return of the King* [Jackson 2003] fame, who is the only non-Spaniard in the cast), it takes in the key battles of Flanders in 1622 (the opening scene), the surrender of Breda in 1625 (which relies on Velázquez's renowned painting of that name) and Rocroi of 1643 (the final scene, in which we are led to understand the hero might die). The plot also takes in civilian life. It ranges from heritage cinema's familiar terrain of the aristocracy, with scenes involving the Count-Duke of Olivares (an unlikely Javier Cámara), the King Felipe IV's favourite, who is often located in El Escorial's sumptuous library, and Alatriste's protector, Count Guadalmedina (Eduardo Noriega), a figure also associated with richly decorated interiors. (Wisely, Díaz Yanes conveys the monarch Felipe through absence: supposedly all-powerful, he is only glimpsed in a handful of scenes, which suggests his status as a mere puppet manipulated by Olivares.) More typical of the post-heritage trend is the film's equal attention to Madrid's brutal street brawls, and violent disputes in unruly taverns. A student of history before turning to film, the didactic aim of Díaz Yanes' project to explore Spain's simultaneously glorious-yet-grim Golden Age on screen and link the period to contemporary concerns, like the overlap between the Spanish soldiers' experience in Flanders in 1622 and American soldiers' experience in Iraq in 2003 (Liz 2011, 147–8), was perhaps too obvious for some. However, viewing figures of over three million, which made the film the Spanish hit of the year and contributed substantially to the rare achievement of a 20 per cent domestic audience share for national films in 2006, suggest great public success (though doubt has been cast on whether these figures enabled producers to recoup the vast production costs [Mira 2010, 7]).

Central to the film's successful treatment of a serious subject matter, even if it was too didactic for some, was the fact it was based on Pérez-Reverte's literary original. This former war reporter is an immensely successful historical novelist: his books have been translated into 40 languages and a recent count estimates sales of four and a half million (García 2006). Key too is the didactic aim of Pérez-Reverte's Alatriste series (currently numbering seven novels). Spurred by the inadequacy of coverage of the seventeenth century in his daughter's school books, Pérez-Reverte co-authored the first volume of the series, *Capitán Alatriste* (first published in 1996), with the then twelve-year-old Carlota. Such were the books' success that they are now on the Spanish school curriculum (Walsh 2007, 68). In adapting five of the Alatriste novels to film, Díaz Yanes secured, first, the books' many fans as viewers; crucially Pérez-Reverte declared to the press that he approved of both the project (Mora 2003) and the finished film (Ruiz Mantilla 2006a; 2006b), a supportive role confirmed in interviews included in the DVD Extras (distributed by C20 Fox, 2007). Second, Díaz Yanes also borrowed the books' middlebrow mission to explore accessibly the serious matter of the history of Spain's Golden Age.

I begin with an apparently incidental, wordless and brief scene, a relatively rare moment in which the film appears to gather itself together in among all the rapidly edited and dynamically shot battle scenes and street sword fights. I will use this scene, first, to explore those characteristics of the film that make it a middlebrow success before considering, second, why it has been taken as a critical failure. On Alatriste's return from Flanders, he gets into trouble by pardoning the lives of the two English noblemen he has been hired by the Inquisition to assassinate. The scene begins with Alatriste's meeting with his protector, Guadalmedina, at which his ward Iñigo Balcoa (Nacho Pérez) is also present (the character is the narrator of the novels, a role never fully replicated in the film). Guadalmedina casually mentions the painting he has bought 'from a Sevillean painter who works for the king' (Velázquez was born in Seville and moved from his birth place to work in the Madrid court), which is propped up on the floor with two pieces of material casually draped over each corner. When the count leaves the room, Alatriste examines the image, *The Waterseller of Seville* (1620), which details a humble old man giving a glass of water to a young boy, while a man drinks from a glass in the background. In a gesture suggested by Mortensen and accepted by Díaz Yanes,[25] Alatriste then kneels down to the canvas to touch the drop of water Velázquez paints in glistening verisimilitude as it drips down the side of the earthenware jar. A shot-reverse shot ensures that the viewer identifies with Alatriste's contemplation of the work.

First, this scene displays the middlebrow tendency to evoke intertextually high culture. While the heritage genre may often choose canonical literature, high art references are common too, and Díaz Yanes, following novelist Pérez-Reverte, deploys them by explaining them and linking them to the narrative. Guadalmedina mentions Seville, not the name of the painter, and it is for the viewer to make the admittedly not complicated link between the pictorial treatment of the relationship between men on the canvas and the developing relationship between men on screen. Velázquez's older man offers life-giving water to a younger boy; the image of a man drinking in the background perhaps a future projection of the boy's manhood. Similarly, the

FIGURE 7.5 *Alatriste Examines Velázquez's* The Waterseller of Seville. Alatriste *(Díaz Yanes 2006)*

film details Alatriste's relationship with Iñigo. His protection of the boy is also life-giving, and the two characters will age over the twenty-five years of the narrative. The focus here is not negatively on masculine ageing, but positively on masculine maturity, for Díaz Yanes explores apprenticeship then veteran status through the male characters, but reserves physical weakness and illness for the female characters: for all the wounding on the battlefield, only María de Castro, Alatriste's love interest played by Ariadna Gil, ends up in a hospital. Uncomplicated too is the formal link between Velázquez's colour palette and Díaz Yanes's mise en scène, which is underscored by the coloured cloths draped over each top corner of the canvas. Fusing pictorial and filmic worlds, these pieces of material thus link the colours and textures of the painting to the colours and textures of the film. (We have seen this replication of Baroque painting in *The Dumbfounded King* [1991] and Díaz Yanes admits in interview [DVD Extras] that his and cinematographer Paco Femenia's inspiration in Velázquez is not original.) Besides lending its colours to the mise en scène of the film in a general way, another particular Velázquez intertext is central to the Breda sequence. Here Díaz Yanes follows Pérez-Reverte's original use of *The Surrender at Breda* (1635), a painting familiar to anyone schooled in Spain (Walsh 2007, 79) and which Anne Walsh describes as part of the author's intertextual strategy to use well-known high-cultural references as 'a platform from which the subjects in question take on life' (2007, 79). After the fast-moving battle scenes Díaz Yanes arrests the narrative flow with a comparatively long take (four seconds) of a group of observers of victors and vanquished that includes Iñigo, then another longer take (ten seconds) of the actors taking up positions to recreate Velázquez's painting; the take ends with a fade to a rather clichéd keyhole. Should any viewer have missed the reference, it is sewn into the subsequent narrative: Iñigo sees Velázquez's canvas as it is carried across the patio at court in El Escorial; he then describes the picture to his protector on his return to Spain. In a similar way Díaz Yanes stitches references to canonical literature into the fabric of the film. Quevedo and Lope de Vega make appearances, not as lofty references for the initiated, but as a man of the people played by cuddly actor Juan Echanove in the first case, and as a snippet of a play (*The Dog in the Manger* again) performed by actress María de Castro, in the second. The film exemplifies throughout, then, a middlebrow fusion of high art and accessible treatment.

Returning to the *Waterseller*, the scene also displays the centrality of Mortensen to the film, especially as in this instance the actor took the creative lead. Díaz Yanes's determination to secure an actor who was both a Castilian-speaker and an 'action hero' (DVD Extras) crystallizes the way this film is an indigenization of non-Spanish heritage. The insistence on language reveals that the project, despite its enormous budget, was always a domestic one, given the failure of Spanish heritage on international circuits noted above. The insistence on the 'action hero' reveals Díaz Yanes's determination to make the film as accessible as possible. Díaz Yanes insists Mortensen was the first choice and that without him the film would not have been made. Some critics are sniffy about his accented Castilian (a New York resident, his childhood was divided between Argentina and Norway), but its idiosyncracy compliments his life story as a loner and outsider, who is uncomfortable and scruffy at court (he insists on wearing tatty boots in his interview with Olivares). Of course the loner and the outsider, played by an acting star, is a staple of the Western, an archetypal example of which would be John Wayne's Ethan Edwards in *The Searchers* (Ford 1956). The director has stressed in interview (DVD Extras) his intention to incorporate the western genre, and his consideration of *Alatriste* as a kind of 'seventeenth-century Spanish Western', with the bullfighter rather than the cowboy the model for some of Mortensen's gestures, like the efficacious sweeping of the cape in the convent battle scene, or the positioning of the sword in the final image of the film, which offers a medium shot of the warrior poised for battle like a matador poised for the kill. Elaborate and deadly swordfights which gesture towards tauromachy thus replace gunfights, but the characterization of the hero survives intact the shift from the American West to Imperial Spain, for the film is nothing short of a hymn to heterosexual masculinity. Short on words, Mortensen's Alatriste is long on physical strength and skill, bravery, honour (or rather a modern conception on honour that sidesteps religion and stresses Socialism), fatherly responsibility and heterosexual love. The sword fights, choreographed by world expert Bob Anderson (as the DVD extras frequently insist), are especially impressive when they involve Mortensen, who had worked with Anderson on *Lord of the Rings*. Bravery characterizes each of Alatriste's interventions on the battle field (if he's not knifing Dutch protestants he's successfully bombing their headquarters or refusing to surrender to the French by explaining to opponents at Rocroi 'éste es un tercio español' [this is a Spanish regiment]), while honour rules his actions when in Madrid, as when he refrains from killing the Englishmen he has been hired to assassinate, or refuses to loot the booty of a Dutch galleon Guadalmedina has ordered him to ambush. His devotion to Iñigo, which ranges from training in matters of war, advice on matters of love, and paying off captors when he gets into trouble, knows no bounds. Intimate scenes with his love interest María de Castro complete the picture, where the fact of his apparent life-long fidelity to her does away with the inconvenient matter of her marriage to another man.

The *Waterseller* scene offers one last interpretative lead that ironically explains both the greatest success of the picture, and, for many critics, its greatest flaw. As a self-contained scene, the episode works brilliantly. As we have seen, it deploys the Velázquez intertext suggestively to underscore the narrative of filial relations, masculinity and ageing and effectively to enhance the film's mise en scène with the painter's rich Baroque tones. But this is not an example of the 'museum aesthetic' (Vincendeau 2001, xviii) of early heritage cinema that focussed on the bourgeoisie and aristocracy. Díaz Yanes chooses a Velázquez piece that portrays humble life, and the film likewise leaves the marvellous settings of El Escorial for violent street and tavern brawls and the hand-to-mouth existence of soldiers on the delayed, diminished, or sometimes non-existent pay of which Alatriste often complains. Other self-contained episodes in the film work similarly well. Critics may continue to moan that a Spanish director cannot stage impressive battle scenes like Hollywood (Pérez Gómez 2010), but Díaz Yanes affirmatively and resoundingly answers the question of whether Spanish cinema has the 'technical maturity' (Mira 2010, 7) to handle big-budget films and offer high production values. For example, the opening scene immediately impresses the viewer by effectively portraying the watery 'birth' of Alatriste in the misty, blue-tinged Flemish moat as the action begins *en media res* with a night-time ambush of a Dutch outpost (the film had José Manuel Guerrero as military consultant). Convincing too are the sequences at Breda, especially the depiction of the misery of the rain-drenched trenches, and the terrifying claustrophobia of tunnels in the bombing mission. The film then stages another watery 're-birth' when Alatriste and his men desperately drink from the muddy puddles of the trenches after the mission, especially when Alatriste clears his comrade's mouth of sulphur like a midwife encouraging a newborn child to breathe. The especially expensive final battle of Rocroi, complete with multiple extras and horses, also mobilizes tracking shots, rapid editing and low camera angles beneath lances and legs, both human and equestrian, to great effect.

An argument could be made that water imagery links this long film together. The *Waterseller* scene stresses that the liquid bestows life, a quality confirmed by these scenes of Alatrtiste's 'birth' and 're-birth', and reinforced by his beach landing after the Flanders campaign, and Iñigo's beach landing after a year in the galleys. The links, however, are not sufficiently stressed and it is probably fair to note that each one works best in isolation. The problem with the film, most critics agree, is then that Díaz Yanes fails to make it more than a sum of these impressive parts. The reviewer for *Cine para leer* attributes this to the director's simple inability to write a coherent script (Pérez Gómez 2010) (though he has either won, or been nominated, for Goyas for best screenplay for all four of his features to date, including a nomination for *Alatriste*). The failure might alternatively be attributed to Díaz Yanes's excessive concern to keep Pérez-Reverte's readers happy by including all of their favourite scenes, meaning viewers not acquainted with the originals supposedly became confused (Mira 2010, 7). It may be true that a different medium might have served the novels better here, with the longer reach of a television series better able to replicate narrative development (the director's pushing to the longer end of a feature-length running time at 140 minutes also hints at the limitations of the feature-length medium). An alternative reason for the critical intolerance of the somewhat disjointed narrative (which, it should be noted, three million viewers didn't seem to mind) lies in the depressingly persistent knee-jerk dismissal in Spain of the portrayal of history on screen by Spanish directors. Even thirty years after the dictator's death, must such efforts always be linked to the derided CIFESA super-productions of the 1940s and 1950s (Pérez Gómez 2010), which, in any case only amounted 4 features (Labanyi 2007, 25) (see Chapter 2)? Bernard Bentley is surely right to connect *Alatriste* with these only to underline differences, for Díaz Yanes's sceptical view of Spanish imperialism 'implicitly gives the lie to the glory of Francoist historical films [...] and points to the vanity of military interventions in foreign lands' (2008, 330).

I would suggest, conversely, that the critical intolerance of some narrative incoherence is a consequence of Díaz Yanes's middlebrow fusion of the genres of heritage cinema and western. Heritage cinema not only emphasizes, but celebrates spectacle. If the genre began in the 1980s with the much-criticized focus on British country estates in the Edwardian period, this post-heritage, Spanish example shows that mise en scène can be deployed to fuse sumptuous interiors (with the exception of one shot of the King hunting at the Retiro, Díaz Yanes is not interested in picturesque exteriors) with the humble circumstances of penniless soldiers and poets. The close-up tracking shot of Alatriste's tatty boots in Olivares's magnificent El Escorial study (included in the film's trailer) sums up this productive collision of the plush focus of some early British examples with the grittiness of post-heritage versions. The western, meanwhile, is all about action, character arc, and a dynamic and inexorable move forwards to a climatic resolution – as in Ethan's relentless 'search' for his niece in *The Searchers* which results in her discovery, recovery and a return to order. In *Alatriste* the balance tips towards a post-heritage interest in spectacle, and away from the narrative tenacity that audiences associate with the Western. This fusion of genres brings out about what I would defend as the film's great success as middlebrow cinema: a serious study of three turbulent decades in Spain's historically and culturally pivotal seventeenth century, whose didacticism does not detract from its interest; an effective interweaving, at the levels of both narrative and form, of contemporary high-cultural references like Velázquez; an exceptionally high budget deployed on the kind of high production values that were a first in Spanish cinema; and highly accessible form of the star-led western. As I have argued throughout this book, however, middlebrow fusion is a difficult balancing act, and in this instance the crossover between niche heritage and mainstream Western was too unsettling for some. Spanish critics, who were possibly still mindful of the Francoist cinema, or perhaps aware of the failure of previous Spanish big-budget efforts like Carlos Saura's *El dorado* (1987), seized on the failure to replicate the action-led scripts of the last of these four aspects, which unfairly detracts from what is an otherwise impressive achievement.

Lope (Waddington 2010)

The stage appeared to be set for Andrucha Waddington's *Lope* to repeat *Alatriste*'s success.[26] Enthusiasm among Spanish audiences for foreign heritage cinema[27] had been domestically harnessed by directors like Imanol Uribe (*The Dumbfounded King* 1991) and Pilar Miró (*The Dog in the Manger* 1996) in the 1990s, then Vicente Aranda (*Madness of Joan* [*Juana la loca* 2001]) and Agustín Díaz Yanes (via Arturo Pérez-Reverte) in the 2000s, and a modest Spanish heritage cinema appeared to be flourishing. *Alatriste* seemed to prove that Spain could at last take advantage – in domestic markets at least

– of the kind of historical and cultural heritage that had helped make British cinema such a success from the 1990s on. In this context, Paul Julian Smith notes that Spain and Britain are 'Post-imperial powers coping with prolonged national decline' (2006, 101), signalling the attraction, for heritage audiences, of a simultaneous celebration of national prominence and consolation for its disappearance – the disappearance being much longer in the Spanish case. *Alatriste* also seemed to prove that Spanish cinema was fertile terrain for the newly gritty post-heritage trend. A nation that associates its Renaissance as much with the picaresque pranks of a destitute beggar boy in *Lazarillo de Tormes* (published by an anonymous author in 1554) as with the aristocratic leisure pursuits at the Buen Retiro palace (completed under Felipe IV in 1640, the park attached to the now disappeared building still constitutes central Madrid's principal open space), directors like Díaz Yanes and Waddington (and Pérez-Reverte before them) did not have to look hard for grittiness. Like Lazarillo, the fictional Lope created on paper by scriptwriters Jordi Gasull and Ignacio del Moral and on screen by director Andrucha Waddington and actor Alberto Ammann, is also initially destitute, also has a blind protector (the equivalent of Lazarillo's guardian is Lope's mother), is also keenly aware of a society based on appearances (while Lazarillo uncovers the sham pretensions of a penniless nobleman, Lope borrows clothes to impress), and is also bent on upward social mobility (Lazarillo rises from urchin to the morally dubious but personally comfortable position of cuckold to an archbishop, while Lope ascends from broke soldier to rising literary star). A cross-over between heritage and romantic comedy, *Lope* looked set fair to add its name to Spanish cinema's successful middlebrow trend. It takes the uncontroversial theme of the creative forging of the playwright in the late sixteenth century as it subject matter, fuses this with accessible romantic comedy, spends a mid-budget of 13 million euros (Montilla 2009) on high, if not *Alatriste*-level, production values, and treats the viewer to the high-cultural references of snippets of Lope's plays and poems and the odd pictorial intertext. A box office success with 604,789 viewers, I will devote the rest of my analysis to examining these four middlebrow characteristics (serious subject matter, accessible treatment, high production values and high-cultural references) to ask why the film nonetheless fails on middlebrow terms.

In its moderately serious aim to bring canonical literary figure Lope de Vega to a wide public, *Lope* exemplifies the pedagogical tendency of much middlebrow work. Pedagogy is not a dirty word in Spanish screen studies. Manuel Palacio, for example, uses it to describe the drive to promote democratic values through literary classics in television adaptations of the transition period, like *Fortunata y Jacinta* (Camus 1980), or great-life biopics such as *Cervantes* (Ungría 1980) (2001, 153); the description likewise fits the promotion of a left-wing cultural tradition in the PSOE government's Mirovian films (see Chapter 5). But when does the worthy desire to respond to a socially- and culturally-aspirant audience become a paternalistic desire to educate school children? The versions of Alatriste offered by both Pérez-Reverte and Díaz Yanes perhaps manage to be both suitable for school children (like the author's twelve-year-old daughter Carlota) and rewarding for adults. However, *Cine y Letras* critic Vicente Díaz argues that with *Lope* the balance tips towards the school children (2010). The inclusion of a number of the love poems works well enough, in the manner of the film's obvious model *Shakespeare in Love* (Madden 1998), and the moment when Elena (Pilar López de Ayala) draws her finger over Lope's signature at the end of ballad he has just written for her is particularly successful (ballad V, 'Contemplando estaba Filis, /a la media noche sola/ una vela...' [At mid-night, alone, Filis contemplated a candle...]).[28] Smudging the ink combines the literary and physical nature of her attraction. The treatment of the plays is less rewarding. There is much focus on the material conditions of their composition, with Madden-inspired close-ups of ink-stained fingers grasping extravagant quills poised over rough parchment (both items fashioned especially for the film); and the narrative of Lope's loyalty to, then rebellion against, theatre manager Jerónimo Velázquez (Juan Diego) also pays attention to the practical conditions of their performance. As for the plays themselves, we only see the opening of what could be *El nuevo mundo, descubierto por Cristobal Colón* (*The New World, Discovered by Christopher Columbus*) (1596–1603), which includes an introduction by the narrator and a scatalogical joke, but offers disappointingly little evidence of the creative brilliance that is much described throughout. This, perhaps, is the problem: Gasull and Del Moral's script spends too long on exegesis, explaining too often how the playwright is revolutionizing the theatre by breaking rules, mixing previously separate genres and stressing realism, and showing it too little through performance of the plays. In response to this approach 'which recalls someone marking their notes with a highlighter pen', Díaz suggests matinee screenings for school audiences (2010). By the time the DVD version was released, it in fact included a 'Special Teaching Version'. No less revealing than the decision to include this as an extra is the version's content: it is identical to the original version, with only two brief clothed but suggestive sex scenes between Lope and Elena cut.

If over-exegesis is understandable for scriptwriters and director working with early-modern material for the first time, less understandable is the unadventurous use of one of the best-known genres of all time: romantic comedy. As we saw with Pilar Miró's 1996 film version of Lope's *The Dog in the Manger*, adopting the conventions of this highly familiar genre is key to crossover, as they make the high-culture references accessible. Thus the performances of

Miró's actors, and her other decisions in mise en scène, cinematography and editing, make the repetition of achingly familiar scenarios like lovers' tiffs, love triangles and the locus amoenus satisfyingly knowing and playful. *Lope* lacks this postmodern edge, so there is little ironic distance from the over-familiar: it becomes instead clichéd and derivative. New golden boy of Hispanic cinema (Marañón 2010), Ammann offers a decent turn as the playwright, though he has to repeat much of the ground covered by Joseph Fiennes in *Shakespeare in Love* and Gérard Depardieu in *Cyrano de Bergerac* (Rappeneau 1990). His relationship with Elena is the best aspect of the film. The self-awareness of the actress who starred as Juana la loca in Aranda's eponymous 2001 film brings a productive world-weariness to her role as femme fatale Elena: this experienced heritage actress brings out the best in Ammann's performance. However, despite her usually assured touch, Leonor Watling is unable to lift her admittedly trickier role as the nervous virgin Isabel de Urbina above cliché. While Elena's relationship with Lope unfolds in the productively used and suggestively unorthodox liminal spaces of the back-stage dressing room, cramped stairwells, and the rooftops above the city, Watling struggles with an Isabel bound to the incredibly clichéd settings of a hay loft locus amoneus, an absurdly contrived horseback elopement to Lisbon, then nothing less than riding into the sunset with her man at the end of the film.

If the film's handling of both the literary intertext and the filmic genre is problematic in places, uneven too is the question of anachronism. Striving for period authenticity is just one approach to screening the past on film, and, following films like *William Shakespeare's Romeo and Juliet* (Luhrmann 1997), post-heritage audiences are used to creative anachronism. Thus the fact that the wardrobe department was not interested in precise period authenticity (DVD Extras) (neither was *El perro*'s) does not detract from its contribution to mise en scène (Tatiana Hernández won one of the film's two Goyas for Best Costume Design). Costume design and set design are also complemented by the slightly anaemic tones of the colour palette overall, which sets the film apart from those inspired by the rich tones of Velázquez, seen in *Alatriste*. An alternative pictorial source might be Egidio Menéndez here, for the muted colour palette of a still life like *Still Life with Oranges and Walnuts* (1772) seems especially relevant to the scene where Lope and Elena drink orange juice at a kitchen table complete with fruit, basket and ceramic jug. That eighteenth-century artist Egidio is an anachronistic intertext to a film set in the late sixteenth century (as the opening intertitle announces) seems an academic point given the overall success of the film's drained visuals. Forgivable too is the script's adoption of contemporary Castilian rather than the strictly authentic early-modern forms (the most noteworthy difference concerns the frequently-used second person: *Alatriste* retains the authentic 'vos' with its particular conjugation of the verb; *Lope* uses today's 'tú', which conjugates differently).[29] Even the obvious contemporary references in the script like Fray Bernardo's assurance that 'el dinero está en la construcción' (the real money is in construction) is 'a deft comment on Spain's current economic woes' (Holland 2010). Where Waddington's creative anachronism fails is with the character of Isabel, and the more extravagant adventure scenes associated with her. Watling states in interview that Waddington sought a 'very contemporary and very naturalistic' treatment of her character (J. B. 2010) but even an actress of her standing cannot pull this off. The elopement of the high-born noble-woman from Madrid to Lisbon with little food, no shelter, and a cheerful 'seré tu puta' (I'll be your whore) comes across as ridiculous. Absurd too is the sequence where she merrily follows her 'husband', now an enchained felon, back to the capital: she may have covered over three hundred miles on horseback unprotected, but she still has time to pin and braid her hair before re-entering the city.

Still commanding a substantial audience, the film therefore suffers from some unevenness of tone and some mishandling of the various balancing acts involved with the middlebrow. In its treatment of serious subject matter and high-cultural references the balance tips away from the rewardingly didactic towards the excessively educational and its handling of accessible form veers towards naive derivation rather than knowing reference. Two critics sum up these problems with what is often the most insulting adjective a film critic can muster: 'televisual' (Pérez Gómez 2010; Díaz 2010). It is undeniable that aspects of *Lope* are flawed. I started this section with a summary of the similarities between the 2010 film and *Alatriste*, but end it with the key differences. First, *Lope* lacks the mediating role of exceptionally successful middlebrow historical author Pérez-Reverte. Second, while I argue

FIGURE 7.6 *Elena and Lope Via the Menéndez Intertext.* Lope *(Waddington 2010)*

that heritage-western cross-over *Alatriste* might be comparable to a foreign predecessor like heritage-thriller cross-over *Elizabeth* (Kapur 1998), Díaz Yanes's film stands alone for its originality. All the largely hostile responses to *Lope* in the Spanish press (and even the positive review of the film in the trade press *Variety*) point out that Waddington's movie compromises its originality by its excessive proximity, with regards both narrative conception and even the repetition of entire scenes, to *Cyrano de Bergerac* and *Shakespeare in Love* (Javier Ocaña, for example, points out that the scene where the rich but tongue-tied Portuguese nobleman passes off poems written by Lope as his own is lifted from Rappeneau's film [2010]).

Critics Ángel Pérez Gómez (2010) and Vicente Díaz's (2010) comparisons of the film to television are intended as a criticism but I would suggest that, ironically, they underline *Lope*'s partial middlebrow success. The use of 'televisual' as an adjective to criticize 'film' is a reminder of how tenacious remains the artistic hierarchy between large and small screens in film criticism (Smith 2006, 1–2). However, scholars have begun to question it: in 2004 I included two major TV serials in a monograph on literary adaptations (*Fortunata y Jacinta* [Camus 1980] and *La Regenta* [Méndez Leite 1995] [Faulkner 2004, 79–125]); in 2009 Paul Julian Smith offered a wide-ranging book on precisely 'the inextricability of cinema and television as twin vehicles for screen fiction in Spain' (2009, 11). While *A History of Spanish Film* has sought to revise previous critical approaches by placing both the ignored category of the 'middlebrow', and the often overlooked 'middlebrow films', in the foreground, Spanish television studies pay attention to the middlebrow from the outset (Faulkner 2004, 13; Smith 2006, 27–57). Examples like rural dramas of the 1970s (*Chronicles of a Village* [*Crónicas de un pueblo*, multiple authors including creator Antonio Mercero, 1971–4]), literary adaptations of the 1980s (*The House of Ulloa* [*Los Pazos de Ulloa* Suárez 1985]), and historical dramas from the 1990s onwards (*Tell Me How It Happened* [*Cuéntame cómo pasó* multiple authors, creator Miguel Angel Bernardeau, 2001–]) all variously display the key characteristics of serious subject matter, accessible treatment, high-cultural references and high production values. In the new millennium history on screen in particular has received much successful middlebrow treatment on television with *14 April: The Republic** (*14 de abril. La República* multiple authors, 2011), for example, set in the 1930s and *Aguila roja* (multiple authors, 2009–), set in *Alatriste*'s 1600s. The fact that the latter TV series is now also a commercially successful feature film *Aguila roja, the Film** (*Aguila roja, la película* Ayerra 2011)[30] is an example of a multimedia synergy that confirms the convergence in the Spanish audiovisual environment highlighted by scholars (Riambau and Torreiro 2008; Smith 2009; 2012). Even though the feature film *Lope* partially fails, to label it televisual in fact positively places it in the company of these considerable middlebrow successes of the small screen.

This book has focussed on cinema, it has recorded the traces of social mobility from the beginning of the twentieth century on screen, and has argued that the Spanish middlebrow film, dating from 1970s on, responds to social mobility off screen through the advent of a socially- and culturally-aspirant middle-class audience. Television has been back stage in many of my readings of middlebrow films, with their financing often including TV companies, their personnel often trained on the small screen, and their serious-yet-accessible treatment often converging with the approach of the newer medium. The next study of the middlebrow in Spanish screen culture might place television centre stage.

Notes

1 This is just one interpretation. Homogenization of cinematic output proved disasterous in the 1980s, when the Miró legislation stifled alternative trends. Rob Stone is concerned about such stifling in the contemporary period, but optimistically suggests that today, with recognition in the Spanish Cinema Law of 2007, free-to-view short films on the internet are 'upholding a magnificent, often subversive tradition in Spanish cinema' (2011, 56).

2 This is the focus, for example, of special issues of the *Hispanic Research Journal* (8, 1, 2007) and *Studies in Hispanic Cinemas* (7, 1, 2010).

3 Controversially chosen in preference to Almodóvar's *Talk to Her* (*Hable con ella* 2002), which went on to win Best Original Script at the ceremony.

4 The contemporary boom in Spanish documentaries may be implicit in Quintana's critique. The radically socialist, multi-authored *There's Good Cause!** (*¡Hay motivo!* 2004), for example, provides the direct thematic address to the PP's policies, and the experimental, self-reflexive formal treatment that Quintana prizes.

5 See his comparison of the issue of euthanasia in feature film *The Sea Inside* and television series *Journalists* (*Periodistas* 1998–2202, episode 8) (2009, 105–21). Roberto Bodegas, director of an early Third-Way middlebrow film examined in this book, *Spaniards in Paris* (1971) (Chapter 4), also directed a TV dramatization of the question (*Condemned to Live* [*Condenado a vivir* 2001]). There is much overlap between middlebrow film and middlebrow television, full examination of which lies outside the scope of this book.

6 For further details of the overlap see González del Pozo 2008, 8–9.

7 Begin reads the blurring differently, as Antonio's failure to distinguish between 'art as contemplation and art as arousal' (2010, 39). For González del Pozo, Antonio's investigation of his wife's new life by visiting the museum, then humiliation of her for it through violent attack, may be

interpreted through Laura Mulvey's use of psychoanalysis. Antonio's behaviour relates to two responses to castration anxiety: 'the male unconscious has two avenues of escape [...]: preoccupation with the re-enactment of the original trauma (investigating the woman demystifying her mystery), counterbalanced by the devaluation, punishment or saving of the guilty object' (González del Pozo 2010, 9–10).

8 Antonio's association of Pilar with the rustling sounds of her quiet presence within the home conveys his fundamental misunderstanding of her character. Sight, not sound, is key to her identity, hence her refusal, ultimately to 'give Antonio her eyes' ('I give you my eyes' is a literal translation of the title) and realization that she must visualize herself anew once she has left him: 'necesito verme' (I need to see myself).

9 This followed his 2001 *The Devil's Backbone* (*El espinazo del diablo*) which, with its orphanage setting, was also child-focussed.

10 *Soldiers of Salamina*. Its runaway success became known as the 'Salamina phenomenon' (Alegre 2003, 7). Its success was not without controversy. By avoiding the ideological divisions entrenched over a 36-year dictatorship (these divisions are also avoided in Trueba's film), the book was condemned by many as a shameful acceptance of consensus politics. Alison Ribeiro de Menezes summarizes the ways in which critical response to the novel has shown that Cercas's 'treatment of the political element of his narrative remains ethically questionable' (2010, 3).

11 The publication of *Diálogos de Salamina* is testament to the apparently helpful role of Cercas in the adaptation and to the productive relationship between novelist and director. For a full study of the film as an adaptation, see Ballesteros 2005.

12 My thanks to Alison Ribeiro de Menezes, who encouraged me to develop my ideas about this subject in response to a paper I delivered at 'Contested Memories: War and Dictatorship in Contemporary Spanish and Portuguese Culture', Instituto Cervantes, Dublin, 2007, and to Chloe Paver for her valuable comments on an earlier version of this section.

13 Lola is even described as wearing 'armour' by Conchi, in the scene that follows the completion of her book.

14 This implied equivalence between the fictitious and the real is problematic, but Pascale Thibaudeau shows how the use of archive material, its falsification, and its combination with fictitious material, is in fact employed to cast doubt on the '"truth" of the image' (2006, 129).

15 In Vicente Aranda's flawed *Freedomfighters* (*Libertarias* 1996), Gil's body is similarly crucial to meaning as a conduit for viewers' emotional responses, registering fear, despair, violation and – especially in the film's graphic and bloody dénouement – horror at physical violence.

16 This tendency is tempered by a complimentary, compensatory drive to locate positive parenting away from Spain as in Carol's beloved North-American father in *Carol's Journey*. Even non-history films repeat this motif, as in the contrast drawn between loving Scottish Uncle John (David

Mooney) in *Take My Eyes* and perpetrator of domestic violence Spanish father Antonio (Luis Tosar). In this context Rob Stone notes the important change of direction marked by the 'uncle' (Carmelo Gómez) in *Secrets of the Heart*, which 'recuperates the figure of the father from a cinematic tradition that suffered and reflected the patriarchal state of the dictatorship' (2002, 107), though the recuperation is somewhat spoiled by the fact that the uncle turns out to be Javi's biological father, an act of infidelity that led to his original father's suicide.

17   Hughes notes that this 'modern day rendition of Sánchez Mazas coming under fire' differs significantly from the novel (2007, 383).

18   This change enables Trueba to avoid the sexist elements of the novel criticized by Eva Antón (2003).

19   This exchange is casual in the novel (Cercas 2003, 188). Lola's confession that she was about to have children is added, as is Miralles's philosophical comment about life.

20   Harri Kalpi's suggests 'alternative or dark heritage' as other qualifiers (2004, n.p).

21   Paul Julian Smith has placed *Madness of Joan* (*Juana la loca* Aranda 2001) and *Theresa: The Body of Christ* (*Teresa, el cuerpo de cristo* Loriga 2007) in heritage and post-heritage contexts (2006 and 2011 respectively).

22   If we take release in the US as a test case, *The Dumbfounded King* had no release, *The Dog in the Manger* was released only at the Chicago film festival, *Alatriste* only at the Miami film festival and *Lope* only at the Palm Springs film festival. Vicente Aranda's *Madness of Joan* (2001) did achieve limited US distribution, but flopped among audiences who had no cultural context in which to place it (Smith 2006, 110).

23   I borrow the term from television studies: Buonanno 2008. See Smith 2012, 512, for its use in the Spanish televisual context.

24   Writing in 2011, Mariana Liz has revised this down to the second most expensive feature (147).

25   Recounted by the director in the interview on the DVD Extras

26   Its many financial backers included Jordi Gasull, producer and co-scriptwriter, who instigated the project (J. B. 2010). Production companies eventually included Ikiru Films, Antena 3 Films, El Toro Pictures and Conspiraçao, with TVE and Canal Plus; alongside Gasull, its producers included Mercedes Gamero, Edmon Roch and Waddington (Holland 2010).

27   For example *Cyrano de Bergerac* attracted 1,565,104 in 1991; *Elizabeth*, 254,042 in 1998; *Shakespeare in Love*, 2,863,088 in 1999.

28   Text transcribed from the film. The ballad was included in Lope's *Romancero General* in 1600.

29   In the book based on the film, Verónica Fernández's *Lope* (2010), the archaic 'vos' form is partially used, suggesting readers were deemed more tolerant than filmgoers of perceived linguistic difficulty.

30   My thanks to Will Higbee for pointing out this example to me.

Abbreviations and glossary

For acronyms, I have given the abbreviation included in the main body of the text first, then the full name or term in Spanish, then an English translation and explanation where necessary.

AACC Academia de las Artes y las Ciencias Cinematográficas de España. Spanish Film Academy.

ACE Asociación de Cronistas de Espectáculos. Association of Latin Entertainment Critics.

Autarky Economic isolationism.

Barcelona School Catalan Avant-garde film movement of the late 1960s.

Caudillo Leader. The title used by Franco.

CEC Círculo de Escritores Cinematográficos. Screenwriters' Circle.

Desencanto Disenchantment. The word is associated especially with the disillusionment that came with the re-establishment of democracy in Spain in the late 1970s and early 1980s.

Desastre The 'Disaster' refers to Spain's loss of its final colonies, Cuba and the Philipines, to the US in 1898.

EEC European Economic Community.

Españolada A colloquial, pejorative term for the Spanish folkloric film that stresses its promotion to domestic audiences of the stereotypes commonly held by foreigners about Spain.

Esperpento A deformed, exaggerated aesthetic developed by Ramón del Valle-Inclán in his 1920 play *Bohemian Lights* (*Luces de Bohemia*).

Falange Falangism. Spanish Fascist Party founded in 1933 by José Antonio Primo de Rivera (son of the ex-dictator, Miguel). In 1937 it merged with other parties to form the official Francoist party FET y de las JONS.

FET y de las JONS Falange Española Tradicionalista y de las Juntas de Ofensiva Nacional-Sindicalista. Franco's ruling party, created in 1937, by an enforced amalgam of Falangists and Traditionalists (the Carlist Communion).

FILESA scandal A company set up by prominent figures in Felipe González's PSOE to launder illicit income.

GAL Grupos Antiterroristas de Liberación. Anti-Terrorist Liberation Squads.

Generation of 1898 A period of introspective cultural reflection on Spanish identities and problems following the 'Disaster' (Spain's loss of its final colonies, Cuba and the Philipines, to the United States in 1898).

Goya prizes The equivalent of the 'Oscars' in Spain. The prizes are awarded by the AACC.

Interés especial Special Interest. An award made by the Francoist authorities (from 1964) which gave a subsidy of 15–50 per cent of production costs to a film.

Interés nacional National Interest. An award made by the Francoist authorities (from 1944–63) which gave a subsidy of up to 50 per cent of production costs to a film. In addition, a film with such an award could attract up to 15 import licences for its producer.

Maquis Republican guerrilla fighter, associated with rough living conditions in rural environments, 1939–51.

Misiones pedagógicas Pedagogical Missions. Travelling teams who took education and culture to the rural populace. Their intellectual influences date back to nineteenth-century Krausism, some 'Missions' took place in the 1920s, but they were officially established by the Second Republic (1931–6).

Movida The explosion of culture associated with the end of the Franco dictatorship and the city of Madrid.

Movimiento Nacional National Movement. The 'movimiento' (movement) was Franco's political party when in power.

NCE Nuevo Cine Español. New Spanish Cinema. Franco's Director General of Cinema, José María García Escudero (1962–7) put

in place a series of measures including subsidies to promote the politically left-wing and aesthetically-innovative art films of the graduates of the State Film School, with a view to their distribution beyond Spain at foreign film festivals.

NO-DOs Noticiarios y documentales. State-authored newsreels screened obligatorily before films throughout the Franco period (1943–81, though they ceased to be obligatory from 1975).

PP Partido Popular. Popular Party. Right-wing, conservative political party

Progre Radical, leftie.

PSOE Partido Socialist Obrero Español. Spanish Socialist Workers' Party.

Sainete One-act low-life farce.

SNE Sindicato Nacional de Espectáculo. National Performers Guild.

TVE Televisión Española. Spanish state television broadcaster.

UCD Unión de Centro Democrático. Union of the Democratic Centre. A centre/centre-right coalition headed by Alfonso Suárez and in power in the key years of the Spanish Transition from 1977–82.

VCE Viejo Cine Español. Old Spanish Cinema. The commercially-orientated and often crude popular cinema that existed in the same period as the NCE, and was thus assigned the opposite label.

Ye-yé Trendy and associated with youth culture. Relates especially to the 1960s.

Zarzuela Popular operetta.

Bibliography

Acevedo-Muñoz, Ernesto. 2007. *Pedro Almodóvar*. London: British Film Institute.

'Alatriste, la película'. 2006. *Cine y letras*, March 4. Available at http://www.thecult.es/Critica/alatriste-la-pelicula.html (Accessed 30 August 2012).

Alberich, Ferran. 2002. *Antonio Drove: la razón del sueño*, Madrid: 32 Festival de Cine de Alcalá de Henares; Comunidad de Madrid; Ayuntamiento de Alcalá de Henares; Fundación Colegio del Rey.

Alegre, Luis. 2003. *Diálogos de Salamina: un paseo por el cine y la literatura*. Barcelona: Tusquets; Madrid: PLOT.

Aliaga Sanchis, Amparo. 2008. 'La memoria de la guerra civil en *El viaje de Carol* (Imanol Uribe) y *El laberinto del fauno* (Guillermo del Toro)'. Paper presented at the 17th Congreso Nacional de Historia del Arte, Art i Memòria, Barcelona, 22–6 September. Available at http://www.ub.edu/ceha-2008/pdfs/09–m01–s01–com_07–aas.pdf (Accessed 4 September 2012).

Allen, Robert. 1995. 'William Fox presents *Sunrise*'. In *The Studio System*, edited by Janet Staiger, 127–39. New Brunswick: Rutgers University Press.

Allinson, Mark. 1999. 'Pilar Miró's Last Two Films: History, Adaptation and Genre'. In *Spanish Cinema: Calling the Shots*, edited by Rob Rix and Roberto Rodríguez-Saona, 33–45. Leeds: Trinity and All Saints.

—2001. *A Spanish Labyrinth: The Films of Pedro Almodóvar*. London: I. B. Tauris.

—2005. '*Calle Mayor/Main Street*'. In *The Cinema of Spain and Portugal*, edited by Alberto Mira, 78–87. London: Wallflower

Almodóvar, Pedro. 1996. *The Flower of My Secret*. Translated by Peter Bush. London: Faber and Faber.

Álvarez Junco, José. 1995. 'Rural and Urban Popular Cultures'. In *Spanish Cultural Studies: An Introduction*, edited by Helen Graham and Jo Labanyi, 82–90. Oxford: Oxford University Press.

Amann, Eizabeth. 2010. 'Mortgaged Dreams: The Economics of Seduction in J. A. Bardem's *Calle Mayor*' *Journal of Spanish Cultural Studies* 11, 1: 17–32.

Antón, Eva, n.d. (2003?), '*Soldados de Salamina*: guerra y sexismo: otro ejemplo narrativo de la reacción patriarcal' *Mujeres en red: El periódico feminista*. Available at: http://www.nodo50.org/mujeresred/cultura/soldados_de_salamina.html (Accessed 31 August 2012).

Aranda, Francisco. 1971. 'Introduction'. In *'Tristana': A Film by Luis Buñuel*, edited by Francisco Aranda, trans. by Nicholas Fry, 5–11. London: Lorrimer Publishing.

Arroita Jauregui, Marcelo. 1974. 'Galdós como coartada'. *Arriba*, September 4.

Ballesteros, Isolina. 2005. 'La exhumación de la memoria histórica: nostalgia y utopía en "Soldados de Salamina" (Javier Cercas, 2001; David Trueba, 2002)' *Film-Historia Online*, 16, 1: 1–7.

Balló, Jordi, Ramón Espelt and Joan Lorente. 1990. *Cinema català 1975–1986*. Barcelona: Columna.

Barr, Charles. 1986. 'Introduction: Amnesia and Schizophrenia'. In *All Our Yesterdays: Ninety Years of British Cinema*, edited by Charles Barr, 1–30. London: British Film Institute.

Barton, Simon. 2004. *A History of Spain*. Hampshire: Palgrave Macmillan.

Beck, Jay and Vicente Rodríguez Ortega. 2008. 'Introduction'. In *Contemporary Spanish Cinema and Genre*, edited by Jay Beck and Vicente Rodríguez Ortega, 1–23. Manchester: Manchester University Press.

Begin, Paul. 2010. 'Regarding the Pain of Others: The Art of Realism in Icíar Bollaín's *Te doy mis ojos*' *Studies in Hispanic Cinema* 6, 1: 31–44.

Benet, Vicente, Juan M. Company, Jesús González Requena, José Luis Guarner, Carlos Heredero, Juan López Gandía, Carlos Losilla, José Monterde, Pilar Pedraza, Vicente Sánchez Biosca, Rafael Tranche, Paulino Viota and Santos Zunzunegui. 1989. *Escritos sobre el cine español: 1973–1987*. Valencia: Filmoteca Generalitat Valencia.

Bentley, Bernard. 1995. 'The Credit Sequence of *La mitad del cielo* (1986)' *Forum for Modern Language Studies* 31, 1: 259–73.

—2008. *A Companion to Spanish Cinema*. Woodbridge: Tamesis.

Bonaddio, Federico. 2004. 'Dressing as Foreigners: Historical and Musical Dramas of the Early Franco Period'. In *Spanish Popular Cinema*, edited by Antonio Lázaro Reboll and Andrew Willis, 24–39. Manchester: Manchester University Press.

Bourdieu, Pierre. 1999. *Distinction: A Social Critique of the Judgement of Taste*. Translated by Richard Nice. London: Routledge.

Blasco Ibáñez, Vicente. 1967. *Obras completas. Tomo II*. Madrid: Aguilar.

Brown, Stephen. 2005. 'Mondays in the Sun' *Sight and Sound* 15: 68–9.

Buñuel, Luis. 1994. *My Last Breath*. Translated by Abigail Israel. London: Verso.

Buonanno, Milly. 2008. *The Age of Television: Experiences and Theories*. Bristol: Intellect.

Busquet, Jordi. 2008. *Lo sublime y lo vulgar: la cultura de masas o la pervivencia de un mito*. Barcelona: UOC.

C.P.A. 1999. 'Ya no están solas'. *La Nueva España*, 17 April.

Cagle, Chris. 2007. 'Two Modes of Prestige Film' *Screen* 48, 3: 291–311

Canning, Elaine. 2005. '"Not I, my Shadow": Pilar Miró's Adaptation of Lope de Vega's *The Dog in the Manger* (1996)' *Studies in European Cinema* 2, 2: 81–92.

Cañique, Carlos and Maite Grau. 1992. *¡Bienvenido Mrr. Berlanga!*. Barcelona: Destino.

Caparrós Lera, José María. 1983. *El cine español bajo el régimen de Franco*. Barcelona: Edicions de la Universitat de Barcelona.

Casals, Montserrat. 1984. 'El éxito final de un proyecto incierto'. *El País*, 7 January.

Castro de Paz, José Luis. 2002. *Un cinema herido. Los turbios años cuarenta en el cine español (1939–1950)*. Barcelona: Paidós.

Castro de Paz, José Luis and Josetxo Cerdán. 2011. *Del sainete al esperpento. Relecturas del cine español de los años 50*. Madrid: Cátedra.

Cela, Camilo José. 1998. *La colmena*. Madrid: Cátedra.

Cercas, Javier. 2003. *Soldados de Salamina*. Barcelona: Tusquets.

—2009. *Anatomía de un instante*. Barcelona: Mondadori.

Charchalis, Wojciech. 2005. *El realismo mágico en le perspectiva european. El caso to Gonzalo Torrente Ballester*. New York: Peter Lang.

Cobb, Christopher. 1995. 'The Republican State and Mass Educational-Cultural Initiatives 1931–1936'. In *Spanish Cultural Studies: An Introduction*, edited by Helen Graham and Jo Labanyi, 133–8. Oxford: Oxford University Press.

Company, Juan Miguel. 1997a. '*Dos cuentos para dos 1947*'. In *Antología crítica del cine español 1906–1995*, edited by Julio Pérez Perucha, 217–19. Madrid: Cátedra; Madrid: Filmoteca Española.

—1997b. '*El clavo 1944*'. In *Antología crítica del cine español 1906–1995*, edited by Julio Pérez Perucha, 178–80. Madrid: Cátedra; Madrid: Filmoteca Española.

—1997c. '*Tristana 1969 [1970]*'. In *Antología crítica del cine español 1906–1995*, edited by Julio Pérez Perucha, 674–6. Madrid: Cátedra; Madrid: Filmoteca Española.

Company Ramón, Juan Miguel. 1989. 'La conquista del tiempo: las adaptaciones literarias en el cine español'. In *Escritos sobre el cine español: 1973–1987*, by Vicente Benet et al., 79–88. Valencia: Filmoteca Generalitat Valencia.

Cruz, Jacqueline. 2005. 'Amores que matan: Dulce Chacón, Icíar Bollaín y la violencia de género'. *Letras Hispanas: Revista de Literatura y Cultura* 2, 1: 67–81.

D'Lugo, Marvin. 1991. *The Films of Carlos Saura: The Practice of Seeing*. Princeton: Princeton University Press.

—1997. *Guide to the Cinema of Spain*. Westford, Conneticut: Greenwood Press.

Davies, Ann. 2011. 'Introduction: The Study of Contemporary Spanish Cinema'. In *Spain on Screen: Developments in Contemporary Spanish Cinema*, edited by Ann Davies, 1–18. Hampshire: Palgrave Macmillan.

De Riquer i Permanyer, Borja. 1995. 'Social and Economic Change in a Climate of Political Immobilism'. In *Spanish Cultural Studies: An Introduction*, edited by Helen Graham and Jo Labanyi, 259–71. Oxford: Oxford University Press.

Del Rey Reguillo, Antonia. 1998. *Modos de representación en el cine español de los años veinte: cuatro ejemplos significativos*. Valencia: University of Valencia.

Delgado, María. 1999. 'Saura's *Los golfos* (1959; Released 1962): Heralding a New Cinema for the 1960s'. In *Spanish Cinema: The Auteurist Tradition*, edited by Peter Evans, 38–54. Oxford, Oxford University Press.

Delibes, Miguel. 1974. *El príncipe destronado*. Barcelona: Destino.

Deveny, Thomas. 1990. 'Living Underground: The Mole in Contemporary Spanish Cinema' *RLA: Romance Languages Annual* 2: 391–4.

—1993. *Cain on Screen: Contemporary Spanish Cinema*. London: Scarecrow.

—1999. *Contemporary Spanish Film from Fiction*. Lanham: Scarecrow.

Díaz, Vicente. 2010. '"Lope" (2010), la película de Andrucha Waddington'. *Cine y Letras*, 27 August. Available at http://www.thecult.es/Critica/lope-2010-la-pelicula-de-andrucha-waddington.html (Accessed 31 August 2012).

Dyer, Richard and Ginette Vincendeau. 1992a. 'Introduction'. In *Popular European Cinema*, edited by Richard Dyer and Ginette Vincendeau, 1–14. London: Routledge.

Dyer, Richard and Ginette Vincendeau (eds). 1992b. *Popular European Cinema*. London: Routledge.

Edwards, Gwynne. 1982. *The Discreet Art of Luis Buñuel: A Reading of his Films*. London: Boyars.

Eidsvick, Charles. 1981. 'Dark Laughter: Buñuel's *Tristana* (1970) from the Novel by Benito Pérez Galdós'. In *Modern European Filmmakers and the Art of Adaptation*, edited by Andrew Horton and Joan Magretta, 173–87. New York: Ungar.

Ellis, John. 2002. *Seeing Things: Television in the Age of the Uncertainty*. London: I. B. Tauris.

Elsaesser, Thomas. 1990. 'Introduction'. In *Early Cinema: Space, Frame, Narrative*, edited by Thomas Elsaesser, 153–73. London: British Film Institute.

Epps, Brad and Despina Kakoudaki. 2009. 'Approaching Almodóvar: Thirty Years of Reinvention'. In *All About Almodóvar: A Passion for Cinema*, edited by Brad Epps and Despina Kakoudaki, 1–34. Minneapolis: University of Minnesota Press.

Evans, Peter. 1991. 'Buñuel and *Tristana*: Who is doing What to Whom?'. In *Carnal Knowledge: Essays on the Flesh, Sex and Sexuality in Hispanic Letters and Film*, edited by Pamela Bacarisse, 91–8. Pittsburgh: Ediciones Tres Ríos.

—1995. 'Cifesa: Cinema and Authoritarian Aesthetics'. In *Spanish Cultural Studies: An Introduction*, edited by Helen Graham and Jo Labanyi, 215–22. Oxford: Oxford University Press.

—1997. 'From Golden Age to Silver Screen: The *comedia* on Film' *Papers in Spanish Theatre* 5: 1–13.

—1999. 'Introduction'. In *Spanish Cinema: The Auteurist Tradition*, edited by Peter Evans, 1–7. Oxford, Oxford University Press.

—2000. 'Satirizing the Spanish Christmas: *Plácido* (Luis García Berlanga 1961)'. In *Christmas at the Movies: Images of Christmas in American, British and European Cinema*, edited by Mark Connelly, 211–21. London: I. B. Tauris.

—2004. 'Marisol: The Spanish Cinderella'. In *Spanish Popular Cinema*, edited by Antonio Lázaro Reboll and Andrew Willis, 129–51. Manchester: Manchester University Press.

Evans, Peter, Chris Perriam and Isabel Santaolalla (eds), 2007. Special issue of *Hispanic Research Journal* 8, 1: 3–90.

Fanés, Felix. 1989. *El cas Cifesa: vint anys de cine español (1932–1951)*. Valencia: Filmoteca de la Generalitat Valenciana.

Faulkner, Sally. 2004. *Literary Adaptations in Spanish Cinema*. Woodbridge: Tamesis.

—2006a. *A Cinema of Contradiction: Spanish Film in the 1960s*. Edinburgh: Edinburgh University Press.

—2006b. 'The Contradictions of Nostalgia: Ruralist Cinema and Mario Camus's *Los santos inocentes* (1984)'. In *Representing the Rural in the Cinema*, edited by Catherine Fowler and Gillian Helfield, 35–47. Detroit: Wayne State University Press.

—2007. '*Solas* (Zambrano, 1999): Andalousian, European, Spanish?'. In *Spanishness in the Spanish Novel and Cinema of the 20th–21st Century*, edited by Cristina Sánchez-Conejero, 237–46. Newcastle: Cambridge Scholars Publishing.

—2012. 'Literary Adaptations'. In *A Companion to Spanish Cinema*, edited by Jo Labanyi and Tatjana Pavlovic, 493–504. Oxford: Wiley–Blackwell.

—2013. 'The Galdós Intertext in Buñuel's Viridiana'. In A Companion to Luis Buñuel, edited by Julián Daniel Gutiérrez Albilla and Rob Stone, 381–98. Oxford: Wiley-Blackwell.

Fernández, Verónica. 2010. *Lope. La novela basada en la película*. Madrid: Planeta.

Fernández Colorado, Luis. 1997. '*El misterio de la Puerta del Sol* 1929'. In *Antología crítica del cine español 1906–1995*, edited by Julio Pérez Perucha, 80–2. Madrid: Cátedra; Madrid: Filmoteca Española.

Fernández Soto, Concepción and Francisco Checa y Olmos. 2010. 'El cine de Pilar Miró. Homenaje y puente hacia la literatura' *Arbor* 186, 741: 79–88.

Fernández-Santos, Ángel. 1998. 'Un Rey Lear contemporáneo'. *El País*, 1 November.

Fernández-Santos, Elsa. 1999. 'Benito Zambrano recupera en su película *Solas* la dignidad de la mujer rural'. *El País*, February 27. Available at http://elpais.com/diario/1999/02/27/cultura/920070001_850215.html (Accessed 4 September 2012).

Fiddian, Robin. 1999. '*La vida alegre* (Colomo, 1986)'. In *Spanish Cinema: The Auteurist Tradition*, edited by Peter Evans, 242–53. Oxford, Oxford University Press.

Fiddian, Robin and Peter Evans. 1988. *Challenges to Authority: Fiction and Film in Contemporary Spain*. Woodbridge: Tamesis.

Font, Domènec. 2003. 'D'un temps, d'un país y de un cine anfibio: sobre la Escuela de Barcelona'. In *Los nuevos cines en España: ilusiones y desencantos de los años sesenta*, edited by Carlos Heredero and José Enrique Monterde, 175–94. Valencia: Festival Internacional de Cine de Gijón; Institut Valencià de Cinematografía Ricardo Muñoz Suay; Centro Galego de Artes da Imaxe; Junta de Andalucía, Consejería de Cultura; Filmoteca de Andalucía; Filmoteca Española.

Fouz-Hernández, Santiago and Alfredo Martínez-Expósito. 2007. *Live Flesh: The Male Body in Contemporary Spanish Cinema*. London: I. B. Tauris.

Fowler, Bridget. 1995. 'Literature Beyond Modernism: Middlebrow and Popular Romance'. In *Romance Revisited*, edited by Lynne Pearce and Jackie Stacey, 89–99. London: Lawrence and Wishart.

Fuentes, Víctor. 2000. *Los mundos de Buñuel*. Madrid: Ediciones Akal.

Galán, Diego. 2000. 'El cine español de los años cuarenta'. In *Un siglo de cine español*, edited by Román Gubern, 119–34. Madrid: AACC.

—2003. 'Almodóvar elige a Fernán-Gómez'. *El País*, November 21.

Galt, Rosalind. 2011. *Pretty: Film and the Decorative Image*. New York: Columbia University Press.

García, Rocío. 2006. 'La corte de Alatriste'. *El País*, August 6. Available at http://elpais.com/diario/2006/08/06/eps/1154845611_850215.html (Accessed 4 September 2012).

García Jambrina, Luis, 'Review of *El abuelo*'. *ABC*, December 19.

García Ochoa, Santiago. 2012. 'Automóvil y cine en la España desarrollista: *Peppermint frappé* (Carlos Saura, 1967)' *Hispanic Research Journal* 13, 2: 111–30.

García-Posada, Miguel. 1997. 'Un perro muy particular'. *El País*, June 2.
Available at http://www.elpais.com/articulo/cultura/perro/particular/
elpepicul/19970206elpepicul_6/Tes (Accessed 22 May 2010).
George, David. 2007. 'Cinematising the Crowd: V. Blasco Ibáñez's Silent *Sangre y
arena* (1916)'. *Studies in Hispanic Cinema* 4, 2: 91–106.
George, David, Susan Larson and Leigh Mercer. 2007. 'Disintegrating Pictures:
Studies in Early Spanish Film'. *Studies in Hispanic Cinema* 4, 2: 73–8.
Ginger, Andrew, 2000. 'Dashing on the Silver Screen: *Don Juan Tenorio* (1922)
Dir. Ricardo de Baños (based on the play of the same title by José Zorrilla
(1844)'. In *Selected Interdisciplinary Essays on the Representation of the Don
Juan Archetype in Myth and Culture*, edited by Andrew Ginger, Huw Lewis
and John Hobbs, 187–213. Lewiston: Edwin Mellen Press.
—2007. 'Space, Time, Desire, and the Atlantic in Three Spanish Films of the
1920s' *Hispanic Research Journal* 8, 1: 69–78.
Gómez, Asunción. 2002. 'La representación de la mujer en el cine español de
los años 40 y 50: del cine bélico al neorrealismo' *Bulletin of Spanish Studies*
79: 575–89.
Gómez B. de Castro, Ramiro. 1989. *La producción cinematográfica española: de
la transición a la democracia 1976–1986*. Bilbao: Mensajero.
González del Pozo, Jorge. 2008. 'La liberación a través del arte en *Te doy mis
ojos* de Icíar Bollaín' *Ciberletras* 19: n.p.
González López, Palmira. 1997. '*Don Juan Tenorio* 1910'. In *Antología crítica
del cine español 1906–1995*, edited by Julio Pérez Perucha, 28–30. Madrid:
Cátedra; Madrid: Filmoteca Española.
Goss, Brian. 2008. '*Te doy mis ojos* (2003) and *Hable con ella* (2002): Gender in
Context in Two Recent Spanish Films' *Studies in European Cinema* 5, 1: 31–44.
Graham, Helen. 1995. 'Popular Culture in the "Years of Hunger"'. In *Spanish
Cultural Studies: An Introduction. The Struggle for Modernity*, edited by Helen
Graham and Jo Labanyi, 237–45. Oxford: Oxford University Press.
Graham, Helen and Jo Labanyi. 1995. 'Culture and Modernity: The Case
of Spain'. In *Spanish Cultural Studies: An Introduction. The Struggle for
Modernity*, edited by Helen Graham and Jo Labanyi, 1–19. Oxford: Oxford
University Press.
Gubern, Román. 1977. *El cine sonoro de la II República (1929–1936)*. Barcelona:
Lumen.
—1981. *La censura: función política y ordenamiento jurídico bajo el franquismo
(1936–1975)*. Barcelona: Ediciones península.
—1986. *1936–1939: la guerra de España en la pantalla: de la propaganda a la
historia*. Madrid: Filmoteca Española.
—1994. *Benito Perojo: Pionerismo y supervivencia*. Madrid: Filmoteca Española;
ICAA; Ministerio de Cultura.
—1995. 'Precariedad y originalidad del modelo cinematográfico español'. In
Historia del cine español, by Román Gubern et al., 9–17. Madrid: Cátedra.
—1996. 'Los difíciles inicios'. In *Primeros tiempos del cinematógrafo en España*,
edited by Juan Carlos de la Madrid, 11–24. Gijón: Trea.
—1997. '*Esa pareja feliz* 1951'. In *Antología crítica del cine español 1906–1995*,
edited by Julio Pérez Perucha, 303–5. Madrid: Cátedra; Madrid: Filmoteca
Española.

—1998. 'Benito Perojo's *La verbena de la paloma'*. In *Modes of Representation in Spanish Cinema*, edited by Jenaro Talens and Santos Zunzunegui, 47–57. Minneapolis: Minneapolis University Press.

Gubern, Román, José Enrique Monterde, Julio Pérez Perucha, Esteve Riambau and Casimiro Torreiro. 1995. *Historia del cine español*. Madrid: Cátedra.

Hallam, Julia, with Margaret Marshment. 2000. *Realism and Popular Cinema*. Manchester: Manchester University Press.

Harguindey, Ángel, 2002, 'Muerte y resurrección de Sánchez Mazas'. *El País*, May 3. Available at http://elpais.com/diario/2002/05/03/cine/1020376801_850215.html (Accessed 31 August 2012).

Havard, Robert. 1982. 'The Seventh Art of Luis Buñuel: *Tristana* and the Rites of Freedom' *Quinquereme* 6, 1: 56–74.

Heredero, Carlos. 1989. 'El reflejo de la evolución social y política en el cine español de la transición: historia de un desencuentro'. In *Escritos sobre el cine español: 1973–1987*, by Vicente Benet et al., 17–32. Valencia: Filmoteca Generalitat Valencia.

—1993. *Las huellas del tiempo: cine español 1951–1961*. Valencia: Filmoteca de la Generalitat Valenciana.

—1999. *20 nuevos directores del cine español*. Madrid: Alianza Editorial.

—2000. '1951–1961: Conformismo y disidencia'. In *Un siglo de cine español*, edited by Román Gubern, 135–50. Madrid: AACC.

Herrera, Javier. 2005. *El cine en su historia. Manual de recursos bibliográficos e internet*. Madrid: Arcos.

Hess, Jonathan. 2009. 'Beyond Subversion: German Jewry and the Poetics of Middlebrow Culture'. *German Quarterly* 82, 3: 316–35.

Higson, Andrew. 1993. 'Re-presenting the National Past: Nostalgia and Pastiche in the Heritage Film'. In *British Cinema and Thatcherism: Fires Were Started*, edited by Lester Friedman, 109–29. London: UCL Press.

—2003. *English Heritage, English Cinema: Costume Drama since 1980*. Oxford: Oxford University Press.

—2006. 'Re-presenting the National Past: Nostalgia and Pastiche in the Heritage Film'. In *British Cinema and Thatcherism: Fires Were Started*, 2nd edn, edited by Lester Friedman, 91–109. London: Wallflower.

Hinds, Hilary, 2009. 'Ordinary Disappointments: Femininity, Domesticity, and Nation in British Middlebrow Fiction, 1920–1944'. *Modern Fiction Studies* 55, 2: 293–320.

Holland, James. 2010. '*Lope'*. *Variety*, September 10. Available at http://www.variety.com/review/VE1117943501/ (Accessed 30 August 2012).

Hontanilla, Ana. 2006. 'Hermafroditismo y anomalía cultural en *Mi querida señorita' Letras Hispanas* 3, 1: 113–22.

Hopewell, John, 1986. *Out of the Past: Spanish Cinema after Franco*. London: British Film Institute.

—1999. '*El corazón del bosque* (Gutiérrez Aragón, 1979)'. In *Spanish Cinema: The Auteurist Tradition*, edited by Peter Evans, 164–75. Oxford: Oxford University Press.

Hueso, Ángel Luis. 1997. '*Mi querida señorita 1971'*. In *Antología crítica del cine español 1906–1995*, edited by Julio Pérez Perucha, 689–91. Madrid: Cátedra; Madrid: Filmoteca Española.

Hughes, Arthur. 2007. 'Between History and Memory: Creating a New
    Subjectivity in David Trueba's Film *Soldados de Salamina*' *Bulletin of Spanish
    Studies* 84, 3: 369–86.
J. B. 2010. 'No es un documental, es un filme inspirado en una vida'. *ABC*,
    September 1. Available at http://www.abcdesevilla.es/20100901/cultura/
    documental-filme-inspirado-vida-20100901.html (Accessed 31 August 2012).
Jagoe, Catherine. 1994. *Ambiguous Angels: Gender in the Novels of Galdós*.
    Berkeley: University of California Press.
Jordan, Barry. 1999. 'Promiscuity, Pleasure and Girl Power: Fernando Trueba's
    Belle Époque'. In *Spanish Cinema: The Auteurist Tradition*, edited by Peter
    Evans, 286–309. Oxford, Oxford University Press.
—2000a. 'How Spanish is it? Spanish Cinema and National Identity'. In
    Contemporary Spanish Cultural Studies, edited by Barry Jordan and Rikki
    Morgan-Tamosunas, 68–78. London: Arnold.
—2000b. 'The Spanish Film Industry in the 1980s and 1990s'. In *Contemporary
    Spanish Cultural Studies*, edited by Barry Jordan and Rikki Morgan-
    Tamosunas, 179–92. London: Arnold.
—2003. 'Revisiting the *comedia sexy ibérica*: *No desearás al vecino del quinto*
    (Ramón Fernández, 1971)' *International Journal of Iberian Studies* 15, 3: 167–86.
—2005. 'Late-Francoist Popular Comedy and the "Reactionary" Film Text'
    Studies in Hispanic Cinemas 2, 2: 83–104.
—2011. 'Audiences, Film Culture, Public Subsidies: The End of Spanish Cinema?'.
    In *Spain on Screen: Developments in Contemporary Spanish Cinema*, edited
    by Ann Davies, 19–40. Hampshire: Palgrave Macmillan.
Jordan, Barry and Mark Allinson. 2005. *Spanish Cinema: A Student's Guide*.
    London, Hodder Arnold.
Jordan, Barry and Rikki Morgan-Tamosunas. 1998. *Contemporary Spanish
    Cinema*. Manchester: Manchester University Press.
Kalpi, Harri. 2004. 'The Wretched of the Earth: Thomas Hardy, "Heritage"
    Cinema and British Society 1967–2000' *Wider Screen* 1, n.p. Available at
    http://www.widerscreen.fi/2004/1/wretched_of_the_earth.htm (Accessed 4
    September 2012).
Kawin, Bruce. 1978. *Mindscreen: Bergman, Godard, and First-Person Film*.
    Princeton: Princeton University Press.
Kember, Joe and Simon Popple. 2004. *Early Cinema: From Factory Gate to
    Dream Factory*. London: Wallflower.
Kinder, Marsha. 1993. *Blood Cinema: The Reconstruction of National Identity in
    Spain*. Berkeley: University of California Press.
—1997. 'Refiguring Socialist Spain: An Introduction'. In *Refiguring Spain: Cinema/
    Media/Representation*, edited by Marsha Kinder, 1–32. Durham, NC: Duke
    University Press.
Kowalsky, Daniel. 2004. 'Rated S: Softcore Pornography and the Spanish
    Transition to Democracy, 1977–82'. In *Spanish Popular Cinema*, edited
    by Lázaro Reboll, Antonio, and Andrew Willis, 188–208. Manchester:
    Manchester University Press.
Labanyi, Jo. 1995. 'Masculinity and the Family in Crisis: Reading Unamuno
    through *Film Noir* (Serrano de Osma's 1946 Adaptation of *Abel Sánchez*)'
    Romance Studies 26: 7–21.

—1997. 'Race, Gender and Disavowal in Spanish Cinema of the Early Franco Period: The Missionary Film and the Folkloric Musical' *Screen* 38: 215–31.

—1999. 'Fetishism and the Problem of Sexual Difference in Buñuel's *Tristana*'. In *Spanish Cinema: The Auteurist Tradition*, edited by Peter Evans, 76–92. Oxford, Oxford University Press.

—2000. 'Feminizing the Nation: Women, Subordination and Subversion in Post-Civil War Spanish Cinema'. In *Heroines without Heroes: Reconstructing Female and National Identities in European Cinema 1945–51*, edited by Ulrike Sieglohr, 163–84. London: Cassell.

—2001. 'Música, populismo y hegemonía en el cine folklórico del primer franquismo'. In *La herida de las sombras*, edited by Luis Fernández Colorado and Pilar Couto Cantero, 83–98. Madrid: AACC.

—2002a. 'Musical Battles: Populism and Hegemony in the Early Francoist Folkloric Film Musical'. In *Constructing Identity in Contemporary Spain: Theoretical Debates and Cultural Practice*, edited by Jo Labanyi, 206–21. Oxford: Oxford University Press.

—2002b. 'Introduction: Engaging with Ghosts; or, Theorizing Culture in Modern Spain'. In *Constructing Identity in Contemporary Spain: Theoretical Debates and Cultural Practice*, edited by Jo Labanyi, 1–14. Oxford: Oxford University Press.

—2004. 'Costume, Identity and Spectator Pleasure in Historical Films of the Early Franco Period'. In *Gender and Spanish Cinema*, edited by Steven Marsh and Parvati Nair, 33–52. Oxford: Berg.

—2007a. 'Cinema and the Mediation of Everyday Life in 1940s and 1950s Spain' *New Readings* 8: 1–24.

—2007b. 'Negociando la modernidad a través del pasado: el cine de época del primer franquismo'. In *Hispanismo y cine*, edited by Javier Herrera and Cristina Martínez-Carazo, 21–44. Madrid: Iberoamericana; Frankfurt: Amsterdam.

—2010. *Spanish Literature: A Very Short Introduction*. Oxford: Oxford University Press.

Larson, Susan, 2005. 'Stages of Modernity: The Uneasy Symbiosis of the *género chico* and Early Cinema in Madrid'. In *Visualizing Spanish Modernity*, edited by Susan Larson and Eva Woods, 263–82. Oxford: Berg.

—2007. 'Nemesio M. Sobrevila, Walter Benjamin, and the Provocation of Film'. *Studies in Hispanic Cinema* 4, 2: 107–19.

Lázaro Reboll, Antonio and Andrew Willis. 2004a. 'Introduction: Film Studies, Spanish Cinema and Questions of the Popular'. In *Spanish Popular Cinema*, edited by Lázaro Reboll, Antonio, and Andrew Willis, 1–23. Manchester: Manchester University Press.

Lázaro Reboll, Antonio, and Andrew Willis, (eds) 2004b. *Spanish Popular Cinema*. Manchester: Manchester University Press.

Leahy, Sarah. 2007. 'A (Middle) Class Act: Taste and Otherness in *Le Goût des autres*'. In *France at the Flicks: Trends in Contemporary French Popular Cinema*, edited by Darren Waldron and Isabelle Vanderschelden, 116–29. Cambridge: Cambridge Scholars Publishing.

Leonard, Candyce. 2004. '*Solas* and the Unbearable Condition of Loneliness in the Late 1990s'. In *Spanish Popular Cinema*, edited by Antonio Lázaro Reboll and Andrew Willis, 222–36. Manchester: Manchester University Press.

Liz, Mariana. 2011. '*Alatriste*'. In *Directory of World Cinema: Spain*, edited by
   Lorenzo J. Torres Hortelano, 147–8. Bristol: Intellect.
Llinás, Francisco, ed.. 1989. *Directores de Fotografía del cine español*, Madrid:
   Filmoteca Española.
—1998. 'Redundancy and Passion: Juan de Orduña and CIFESA'. In *Modes
   of Representation in Spanish Cinema*, edited by Jenaro Talens and Santos
   Zunzunegui, 104–12. Minneapolis: Minneapolis University Press.
Longhurst, Alex. 1995. 'Calculating the Incalculable: Reflections on the Changing
   Class Structure of Contemporary Spain'. *Association for Contemporary Iberian
   Studies* 8, 2: 2–18
—1999. 'Class'. In *Encyclopedia of Contemporary Spanish Culture*, edited
   Eamonn Rodgers, 113–14. London: Routledge.
Losilla, Carlos. 1989. 'Legislación, industria y escritura'. In *Escritos sobre el
   cine español: 1973–1987*, by Vicente Benet et al., 33–44. Valencia: Filmoteca
   Generalitat Valencia.
López, Ana. 2011. Special issue of *Studies in Hispanic Cinema* 7, 1: 3–72.
López Sánchez, Lorenzo. 1974. '*Tormento*, buen espejo galdosiano de
   situaciones pasadas para realidades de hoy'. *ABC*, 8 September.
Marañón, Carlos, 2010, 'Lope' *Cinemanía*, 3 September. Available at http://
   cinemania.es/criticas/detalle/3724/lope_1 (Accessed 31 August 2012).
Marsh, Steven. 1999. 'Enemies of the *Patria*: Fools, Cranks and Tricksters in the
   Film Comedies of Jerónimo Mihura' *Journal of Iberian and Latin American
   Studies* 5, 11: 65–75.
—2002. *Popular Spanish Film under Franco: Comedy and the Weakening of the
   State*. Hampshire: Palgrave Macmillan.
Martín, Celia. 2003. 'Defying Common Sense: Casting Pepa Flores/Marisol as
   Mariana Pineda' *Journal of Iberian and Latin American Studies* 9, 2: 149–61.
Martin-Márquez, Susan. 1999. *Feminist Discourse in Spanish Cinema: Sight
   Unseen*, Oxford: Oxford University Press.
—2002. 'A World of Difference in Home-Making: The Films of Icíar Bollaín'. In
   Women's Narrative and Film in 20th Century Spain, edited by Ofelia Ferrán and
   Kathleen Glenn, 256–72. New York: Routledge.
Mercer, Laura. 2007. 'Fear at the hands of technology: The proto-Surrealism of
   the films of Segundo de Chomón' *Studies in Hispanic Cinemas* 4, 2: 79–90.
Metz, 2007. 'From *Film Language*'. In *Film Theory and Criticism: Introductory
   Readings*, edited by Leo Braudy and Marshall Cohen, 68–79. Oxford: Oxford
   University Press.
Mira, Alberto. 2005. 'Introduction'. In *The Cinema of Spain and Portugal*, edited
   by Alberto Mira, 1–11. London: Wallflower Press.
—2010. *The A-Z of Spanish Cinema*. Lanham: Scarecrow.
Mitchell, Philip. 2004. 'Re-appraising Antonio Mercero: Film Authorship and
   intuición popular'. In *Spanish Popular Cinema*, edited by Antonio Lázaro Reboll
   and Andrew Willis, 169–87. Manchester: Manchester University Press.
Molinero, Carme. 2008. 'La transición y la "renuncia" a la recuperación de la
   "memoria histórica"' *Journal of Spanish Cultural Studies* 11,1: 33–52.
Monk, Claire. 1995. 'Sexuality and the Heritage' *Sight and Sound* 5, 10: 32–4.
—2011. *Heritage Film Audiences: Period Films and Contemporary Audiences in
   the UK*. Edinburgh: Edinburgh University Press.

Monterde, José Enrique. 1989. 'El cine histórico durante la transición política'. In *Escritos sobre el cine español: 1973–1987*, by Vicente Benet et al., 45–64. Valencia: Filmoteca Generalitat Valencia.

—2003. 'La recepción del "nuevo cine". El contexto crítico del NCE'. In *Los nuevos cines en España: ilusiones y desencantos de los años sesenta*, edited by Carlos Heredero and José Enrique Monterde, 103–19. Valencia: Festival Internacional de Cine de Gijón; Institut Valencià de Cinematografía Ricardo Muñoz Suay; Centro Galego de Artes da Imaxe; Junta de Andalucía, Consejería de Cultura; Filmoteca de Andalucía; Filmoteca Española.

Montiel Mues, Alejandro. 2002. '¿Dulce o agria transición? Benito Perojo (1938–1942)'. In *La herida de las sombras*, edited by Luis Fernández Colorado and Pilar Couto Cantero, 237–56. Madrid: AACC.

Montilla, Cristóbal, 2009, 'Leonor Watling y Pilar López de Ayala, las amantes de *Lope*'. *El mundo*, 20 April. Avaialable at http://www.elmundo.es/elmundo/2009/04/20/andalucia_malaga/1240255086.html (Accessed 31 August 2012).

Mora, Miguel. 2003. 'Alatriste, nos vemos en el cine'. *El País*, 26 October . Available at http://elpais.com/diario/2003/10/26/cultura/1067119201_850215.html (Accessed 4 September 2012).

Moreno Hernández, Carlos. 1995. *Literatura y 'Cursilería'*. Valladolid: Universidad de Valladolid.

Morris, C. B.. 1980. *This Loving Darkness: The Cinema and Spanish Writers 1920–1936*. Oxford: Oxford University Press.

Mulvey, Laura. 2006. *Death 24x a Second: Stillness and the Moving Image*. London: Reaktion.

Munsó Cabús, J. 1971. '*Tristana*, la mejor película del año'. *Solidaridad Nacional*, 3 February.

Murphy, Katharine. 2010. 'Images of Pleasure: Goya, Ekphrasis and the Female Nude in Blasco Ibáñez's *La maja desnuda' Bulletin of Spanish Studies* 87, 7: 939–57.

Nair, Parvati. 2004. 'Borderline Men: Gender, Place and Power in Representations of Moroccans in Recent Spanish Cinema'. In *Gender and Spanish Cinema*, edited by Steven Marsh and Parvati Nair, 103–18. Oxford: Berg.

Napper, Lawrence. 2009. *British Cinema and Middlebrow Culture in the Interwar Years*. Exeter: Exeter University Press.

Navarrete, Ramón. 2003. *Galdós en el cine español*. Madrid: T. & B.

Navarrete, Luis. 2009. *La historia contemporánea de España a través del cine español*. Madrid: Síntesis.

'*Noche de verano*, de Jorge Grau, estrenada con éxito en Italia'. 1963. *Ya*, 13 September.

Ocaña, Javier, 2010, 'El fénix de la corrección'. *El País*, 3 September. Available at http://elpais.com/diario/2010/09/03/cine/1283464807_850215.html (Accessed 31August 2012).

Palacio, Manuel. 2001. *Historia de la televisión en España*. Barcelona: Gedisa.

Parsons, Deborah. 2003. *A Cultural History of Madrid*. Oxford: Berg.

Pavlović, Tatjana. 2004. 'Gender and Spanish Horror Film'. In *Gender and Spanish Cinema*, edited by Steven Marsh and Parvati Nair, 135–50. Oxford: Berg.

—2008. '*Los paraísos perdidos*: Cinema of Return and Repetition (Basilio Martín Patino, 1985)'. In *Burning Darkness: A Half Century of Spanish Cinema*, edited by Joan Ramon Resina, 105–24. New York: SUNY Press.

—2011. *The Mobile Nation: España cambia de piel (1954–1964)*. Bristol: Intellect.

Pavlović, Tatjana, Inmaculada Álvarez, Rosana Blanco-Cano, Anitra Grisales, Alejandra Osorio, and Alejandra Sánchez. 2009. *100 Years of Spanish Cinema*. Malden: Wiley-Blackwell.

Payne, Stanley. 1987. *The Franco Regime 1936–1975*. Madison, WI: University of Wisconsin Press.

Pearson, Roberta and William Uricchio. 2004. 'How Many Times Shall Caesar Bleed in Sport: Shakespeare and the Cultural Debate about Moving Pictures'. In *The Silent Cinema Reader*, edited by Lee Grievson and Peter Krämer, 155–68. London: Routledge.

Peláez Paz, Andrés. 1997. '*Asignatura pendiente* 1977'. In *Antología crítica del cine español 1906–1995*, edited by Julio Pérez Perucha, 764–6. Madrid: Cátedra; Madrid: Filmoteca Española.

Pereira, Óscar. 1998. 'Pastiche and Deformation in José-Luis Garci's *Asignatura pendiente*'. In *Modes of Representation in Spanish Cinema*, edited by Jenaro Talens and Santos Zunzunegui, 155–70. Minneapolis: Minneapolis University Press.

Pérez Galdós, Benito. 1977. *Tormento*. Oxford: Pergamon.

—1982. *Tristana*. Madrid: Alianza Editorial.

—1999. *El abuelo*. Madrid: Alianza Editorial.

Pérez Gómez, Ángel. 2010. (n.d., 2010?). '*Alatriste*' *Cine para leer*. Available at http://www.cineparaleer.com/archivo/item/190 (Accessed 30 August 2012).

Pérez Perucha, Julio. 1992. *Cine español. Algunos jalones significativos (1896–1936)*. Madrid: Films 210.

—1995. 'Narración de un aciago destino (1896–1930)'. In *Historia del cine español*, by Román Gubern et al., 19–121. Madrid: Cátedra.

Perriam, Chris, Michael Thompson, Susan Frenk and Vanessa Knights. 2000. *A New History of Spanish Writing: 1939 to the 1990s*. Oxford: Oxford University Press.

—2003. *Stars and Masculinities in Spanish Cinema*. Oxford: Oxford University Press.

Preston, Paul. 1993. *Franco: A Biography*. London: Fontana–HarperCollins.

—2012. *The Spanish Holocaust: Inquisition and Extermination in Twentieth-Century Spain*. London: Harper Collins.

Quintana, Àngel, 2008. 'Fernando León de Aranoa; *Princesas* (2005) y el realismo tímido en el cine español'. In *Miradas sobre pasado y presente en el cine español (1990–2005)*, special issue of *Foro Hispánico*, edited by Pietsie Feenstra and Hub Hermans, 251–64. Amsterdam: Rodopi.

Radway, Janice. 1993. *A Feeling for Books: The Book-of-the-Month Club, Literary Taste, and Middle-Class Desire*. Chapel Hill: University of North Carolina Press.

Ramos, Pablo. 1974, '*Tormento*, de Pedro Olea'. *El Alcázar*, 6 September.

'Review of *El abuelo*'. 1998. *La nueva España*, 31 October .

Riambau, Esteve. 1995. 'La década "socialista" (1982–1992)'. In *Historia del cine español*, by Román Gubern et al., 399–448. Madrid: Cátedra.

—1997. '*Mañana será otro día* 1966 [1967]'. In *Antología crítica del cine español 1906–1995*, edited by Julio Pérez Perucha, 635–7. Madrid: Cátedra; Madrid: Filmoteca Española.

—2000. 'El cine español de la transición (1973–1978): Una asignatura pendiente'. In *Un siglo de cine español*, edited by Román Gubern, 179–90. Madrid: AACC.

Riambau, Esteve, and Casimiro Torreiro, 2008, *Productores en el cine español: Estado, dependencias, y mercado*. Madrid: Cátedra.

Ribeiro de Menezes, Alison. 2010. 'From Recuperating Spanish Historical Memory to a Semantic Dissection of Cultural Memory: *La malamemoria* by Isaac Rosa' *Journal of Iberian and Latin American Research* 16, 1: 1–12.

Richards, Michael. 1998. *A Time of Silence: Civil War and the Culture of Repression in Franco's Spain*. Cambridge: Cambridge University Press.

Richardson, Nathan. 2002. *Postmodern 'Paletos': Immigration, Democracy, and Globalization in Spanish Narrative and Film, 1950–2000*, Lewisburg: Bucknell University Press.

Roberts, Stephen. 1999. 'In Search of a New Spanish Realism: Bardem's *Calle Mayor* (1956)'. In *Spanish Cinema: The Auteurist Tradition*, edited by Peter Evans, 19–37. Oxford, Oxford University Press.

Rodoreda, Mercè. *La plaça del diamant*. Barcelona: Club Editor.

Ross, Christopher. 2000. *Spain 1812–1996. Modern History for Modern Languages*. London: Hodder Arnold.

Rubin, Joan. 2002. *The Making of Middlebrow Culture*. Chapel Hill: University of North Carolina Press.

Ruiz, Luis Enrique. 2004. *El cine mudo español en sus películas*. Bilbao: Mensajero.

Ruiz Mantilla, Jesús. 2006a. 'Alatriste surca los desconocidos Egea y Mediterráneo del XVII'. *El País*, December 13. Available at http://elpais.com/diario/2006/12/13/cultura/1165964406_850215.html (Accessed 4 September 2012).

—2006b. 'La sombre de Alatriste'. *El País*, 27 August. Available at http://elpais.com/diario/2006/08/27/madrid/1156677856_850215.html (Accessed 4 September 2012).

Saíz, José Luis, 1999, 'Review of *Solas*'. *El Diario Palentino*, April 9.

Sánchez Noriega, José Luis. 1998. *Mario Camus*. Madrid: Cátedra.

Sánchez Salas, David. 2007. *Historias de luz y papel: el cine español de los años veinte, a través de su adaptación de la narrativa española*. Murcia: Murcia Cultural.

Sánchez Vidal, Agustín. 1991. *El cine de Florián Rey*. Zaragoza: Caja de ahorros de la Inmaculada Aragón.

—1997. '*La aldea maldita* 1930'. In *Antología crítica del cine español 1906–1995*, edited by Julio Pérez Perucha, 83–5. Madrid: Cátedra; Madrid: Filmoteca Española.

—2005 '*La aldea maldita/The Cursed Village*'. In *The Cinema of Spain and Portugal*, edited by Alberto Mira, 12–21. London: Wallflower Press.

Sánchez-Conejero, Cristina. 2006. *¿Identidades españolas? Literatura y cine de la globalización (1980–2000)*. Madrid: Editorial Pliegos.

Santaolalla, Isabel. 1999. 'Julio Medem's *Vacas* (1991): Historicizing the Forest'.

In *Spanish Cinema: The Auteurist Tradition*, edited by Peter Evans, 310–24. Oxford: Oxford University Press.

—2005a. *Los 'otros'. Etnicidad y 'raza' en el cine español contemporáneo*. Zaragoza: Prensas Universitarias de Zaragoza; Madrid: Ocho y medio.

—2005b. '*Los últimos de los Filipinas/Last Stand in the Philippines*'. In *The Cinema of Spain and Portugal*, edited by Alberto Mira, 50–9. London: Wallflower Press.

Santos Fontenla, César. 1966. *Cine español en la encrucijada*. Madrid: Editorial Ciencia Nueva.

Sargeant, Amy. 2000. 'Making and Selling Heritage Culture: Style and Authencity in Historical Fictions on Film and Television'. In *British Cinema, Past and Present*, edited by Justine Ashby and Andrew Higson, 301–15. London: Routledge.

Schnoover, Karl. 2009. 'Neo-Realism at a distance'. In *European Film Theory*, edited by Temenuga Trifonova, 301–18. London: Routledge.

Smith, Paul Julian. 1994. *Desire Unlimited: The Cinema of Pedro of Almodóvar*. London: Verso.

—1996. *Vision Machines: Cinema, Literature and Sexuality*. London: Verso.

—2000. *Desire Unlimited: The Cinema of Pedro of Almodóvar*. Second edition. London: Verso.

—2001. '*Solas*' *Sight and Sound* 11, 7: 56.

—2003. *Contemporary Spanish Culture: TV, Fashion, Art and Film*. Cambridge: Polity.

—2006. *Television in Spain: From Franco to Almodóvar*. Woodbridge: Tamesis.

—2009. *Spanish Screen Fiction: Between Cinema and Television*. Liverpool: Liverpool University Press.

—2011. 'Re-visions of Teresa: Historical Fictions in Television and Film'. In *Spain on Screen: Developments in Contemporary Spanish Cinema*, edited by Ann Davies, 60–78. Hampshire: Palgrave Macmillan.

—2012. 'Film and Television' In *A Companion to Spanish Cinema*, edited by Jo Labanyi and Tatjana Pavlovic, 504–17. Oxford: Wiley-Blackwell.

Stone, Rob. 2002. *Spanish Cinema*. Harlow: Longman.

—2004. '¡Victoria? A Modern Magdalene'. In *Gender and Spanish Cinema*, edited by Steven Marsh and Parvati Nair, 165–82. Oxford: Berg.

—2011. '*Al mal tiempo, buena cara*: Spanish Slackers, Time-images, New Media and the New Cinema Law'. In *Spain on Screen: Developments in Contemporary Spanish Cinema*, edited by Ann Davies, 41–59. Hampshire: Palgrave Macmillan.

Tellez, José Luis. 1997. '*El extraño viaje* 1964 [1966]'. In *Antología crítica del cine español 1906–1995*, edited by Julio Pérez Perucha, 585–7. Madrid: Cátedra; Madrid: Filmoteca Española.

Thibaudeau, Pascale. 2006. 'Réécriture filmique et écriture de l'histoire: de la survie à la dette dans *Soldados de Salamina*'. In *Traduction, adaptation, réécriture dans le monde hispanique contemporain*, edited by Solange Hibbs and Monique Martínez, 121–36. Toulouse: Presses universitaires du mirail.

—2008. 'El cine de denuncia social en España: El caso de *Te doy mis ojos* de Icíar Bollaín'. In *Miradas sobre pasado y presente en el cine español (1990–2005)*, a special issue of *Foro Hispánico*, edited by Pietsie Feenstra and Hub Hermans, 231–49. Amsterdam: Rodopi.

Torreiro, Casimiro. 1995a. 'Del tardofranquismo a la democracia (1969–1982)'. In *Historia del cine español*, by Román Gubern et al., 341–98. Madrid: Cátedra.

—1995b. '¿Una dictadura liberal? (1962–1969)'. In *Historia del cine español*, by Román Gubern et al., 295–340. Madrid: Cátedra.

Torres, Augusto M. 1992. *Conversaciones con Manuel Gutiérrez Aragón*. Madrid: Fundamentos.

Torres, Rosana. 1997. 'Pilar Miró: "Lope se adelanta a su tiempo en los personajes femeninos".' *El País*, March 5. Available at http://www.elpais.com/articulo/cultura/Pilar/Miro/Lope/adelanta/tiempo/personajes/femeninos/elpepicul/19970503elpepicul_7/Tes (Accessed 22 May 2010).

Tortella, Gabriel, 2000, *The Economic Development of Modern Spain*. Cambridge, Mass: Harvard University Press.

Tranche, Rafael. 1997. '*El mundo sigue* 1963'. In *Antología crítica del cine español 1906–1995*, edited by Julio Pérez Perucha, 531–3. Madrid: Cátedra; Madrid: Filmoteca Española.

Tranche, Rafael and Vicente Sánchez Biosca. 2002. *NO-DO: el tiempo y la memoria*. Madrid: Cátedra; Filmoteca Española.

Trenzado Romero, Manuel. 1999. *Cultura de masas y cambio político: El cine español de la transición*. Madrid: Centro de Investigaciones Sociológicas y Siglo XXI de España.

Triana-Toribio, Núria. 1999. '*¿Qué he hecho yo para merecer esto?* (Almodóvar, 1984)'. In *Spanish Cinema: The Auteurist Tradition*, edited by Peter Evans, 226–41. Oxford: Oxford University Press.

—2000a. 'A Punk called Pedro: *la movida* in the Films of Pedro Almodóvar'. In *Contemporary Spanish Cultural Studies*, edited by Barry Jordan and Rikki Morgan-Tamosunas, 274–82. London: Arnold.

—2000b. 'Ana Mariscal: Franco's Disavowed Star'. In *Heroines without Heroes: Reconstructing Female and National Identities in European Cinema 1945–51*, edited by Ulrike Sieglohr, 185–95. London: Cassell.

—2003. *Spanish National Cinema*. London: Routledge.

—2008. 'Auteurism and Commerce in Contemporary Spanish Cinema: *directores mediáticos*' *Screen* 49, 3: 259–76.

'*Tristana*, de Luis Buñuel'. 1970. *El Alcázar*, 30 March.

Valis, Noël. 2002. *The Culture of Cursilería: Bad Taste, Kitsch and Class in Modern Spain*. Durham: Duke University Press.

Van Liew, Maria. 2008. 'Immigration Films: Communicating Conventions of (In)visibility in Contemporary Spain'. In *Contemporary Spanish Cinema and Genre*, edited by Jay Beck and Vicente Rodríguez Ortega, 259–78. Manchester: Manchester University Press.

Vega, Félix Lope de. 1991. *El perro del hortelano*. Madrid: Espasa Calpe.

Vernon, Katy. 1997. 'Reading Hollywood in / and Spanish Cinema: From Trade Wars to Transculturation'. In *Refiguring Spain: Cinema/Media/Representation*, edited by Marsha Kinder, 35–64. Durham, NC: Duke University Press.

—1999. 'Culture and Cinema to 1975'. In *The Cambridge Companion to Modern Spanish Culture*, edited by David Gies, 248–66. Cambridge: Cambridge University Press.

Vidal, Belén. 2008. 'Love, Loneliness and Laundromats: Affect and Artifice in the

Melodramas of Isabel Coixet'. In *Contemporary Spanish Cinema and Genre*, edited by Jay Beck and Vicente Rodríguez Ortega, 219–38. Manchester: Manchester University Press.

Vilarós, Teresa. 1998a. *El mono del desencanto: una crítica cultural de la transición española (1973–1993)*. Madrid: Siglo veintiuno.

—1998b. 'Mother Country, Fatherland: The Uncanny Spain of Manuel Gutiérrez-Aragón'. In *Modes of Representation in Spanish Cinema*, edited by Jenaro Talens and Santos Zunzunegui, 188–202. Minneapolis: Minneapolis University Press.

Vincendeau, Ginette. 2001. 'Introduction'. In *Film/Literature/Heritage: A Sight and Sound Reader*, edited by Ginette Vincendeau, xi–xxxi. London: British Film Institute.

Waldron, Darren and Isabelle Vanderschelden. 2007. 'Introduction'. In *France at the Flicks: Trends in Contemporary French Popular Cinema*, edited by Darren Waldron and Isabelle Vanderschelden, 1–15. Cambridge: Cambridge Scholars Publishing.

Walsh, Anne. 2007. *Arturo Pérez-Reverte: Narrative Tricks and Narrative Strategies*. Woodbridge: Tamesis.

Whittaker, Tom. 2011. *The Films of Elías Querejeta: A Producer of Landscapes*. Cardiff: University of Wales Press.

Woods, Eva. 2004. 'Radio Free *Folklóricas*: Cultural, Gender and Spatial Hierarchies in *Torbellino* (1941)'. In *Gender and Spanish Cinema*, edited by Steven Marsh and Parvati Nair, 201–18. Oxford: Berg.

—2005a. 'Cinematic Legacy: Did the Propaganda Documentaries of the Civil War Establish Cinema as a Central Mode of Cultural Expression in Spain?; Viewpoint: No. Spain Had a Vibrant, Fully Developed Cinematic Tradition before the War'. In *History in Dispute. The Spanish Civil War. Vol. 18*, edited by Ken Estes and Daniel Kowalsky, 46–9. Columbia: SC; Manly/Detroit: St. James Press.

—2005b. 'Visualizing the Time-space of Otherness: Digression and Distraction in Republican Spain'. In *Visualizing Spanish Modernity*, edited by Susan Larson and Eva Woods, 283–300. Oxford: Berg.

—2008. 'Rehearsing for Modernity in *¡Bienvenido, Míster Marshall!* (Luis García Berlanga, 1952)'. In *Burning Darkness: A Half Century of Spanish Cinema*, edited by Joan Ramon Resina, 9–26. New York: SUNY Press.

—2012. *White Gypsies: Race and Stardom in Spanish Musicals*. Minneapolis: University of Minnesota Press.

Wright, Sarah. 2007. *Tales of Seduction: The Figure of Don Juan in Spanish Culture*. London: I. B. Tauris.

Zumalde Arregi, Imanol. 1997a. '*Plácido* 1961'. In *Antología crítica del cine español 1906–1995*, edited by Julio Pérez Perucha, 501–3. Madrid: Cátedra; Madrid: Filmoteca Española.

—1997b. '*Surcos* 1951'. In *Antología crítica del cine español 1906–1995*, edited by Julio Pérez Perucha, 294–6. Madrid: Cátedra; Madrid: Filmoteca Española.

Zunzunegui, Juan Antonio de. 1960. *El mundo sigue*. Barcelona: Noguer.

Zunzunegui, Santos. 1999. *El extraño viaje: el celuloide atrapado por la cola, o la crítica norteamericana ante el cine español*. Valencia: Episteme.

Zurián, Francisco. 2009. 'Pepi, Patty, and Beyond: Cinema and Literature in Almodóvar'. In *All About Almodóvar: A Passion for Cinema*, edited by Brad Epps and Despina Kakoudaki, 408–28. Minneapolis: University of Minnesota Press.

Index

This index covers the Introduction, chapters, figures (indicated by 'f.' after page number) and endnotes (indicated by 'n.' after page number). Asterisks indicate English film titles not listed in IMDb. Commonly abbreviated terms are not indexed in full.

'A combination of painstaking research, theoretical awareness, critical [...] [...]'

PETER EVANS, Emeritus Professor [...] University of London

'There has been nothing quite like Sally Faulkner's *A History of Spanish Film*. This [...] and ambitious volume combines a compelling general account of a vital national cinema with brilliant close analyses of individual titles. Moreover it skillfully places artistic and cultural questions within social and historical contexts. This book is required reading for both those who already know Spanish cinema and those who would like to discover it.'

PAUL JULIAN SMITH, Distinguished Professor, Hispanic and Luso-Brazilian Literatures and Languages, The Graduate Center, City University of New York, US

'This beautifully nuanced study gives the reader a series of intriguing new perspectives on the social crossovers produced by a cinema marked by class mobility and by realignments in taste in Spain. It concentrates on the active engagement of middle class culture—bizarrely under-estimated in most books on Spanish film—with fictions, markets and institutions. Sally Faulkner's indispensable history reveals a different continuity and disparate set of Spanish images to the ones we might have thought we knew.'

CHRIS PERRIAM, Professor of Hispanic Studies, School of Arts, Languages and Cultures, University of Manchester, UK

'Faulkner's close textual analysis of a diverse array of films complements the book's original and stimulating theoretical framework. *A History of Spanish Film* is a new and exciting contribution to intellectual discourses about class, modernity, and the production and reception of Spanish cinema. Students and scholars alike will find this work indispensable in their teaching and research.'

TATJANA PAVLOVIC, Associate Professor, 20th-Century Spanish Film and Literature, Tulane University, US

'Sally Faulkner's *A History of Spanish Cinema* is a moveable feast. Departing from the tendency to understand history as a rehearsal of grand ideologies and to view—and valorize—Spanish cinema in terms of denunciation and protest, subversion and experimentation, it charts the rise of the middle class and a corresponding 'middlebrow cinema'. Through an interlocking series of close, chronologically ordered readings of representative films in Spanish from before and after the Civil War, Faulkner's study grapples with complex questions of modernization, popular culture, education, entertainment, consumerism, class realignment, and social *mobility*—'upward, downward and stalled'—in *motion* pictures.'

BRAD EPPS, Professor of Spanish, University of Cambridge, UK

Sally Faulkner is Associate Professor of Hispanic Studies and Film at the University of Exeter, UK. She is the author of *Literary Adaptations in Spanish Cinema* (2004) and *A Cinema of Contradiction: Spanish Film of the 1960s* (2006) and was awarded a Fellowship from the British Arts and Humanities Research Council for 2011.

FILM

www.bloomsbury.com

Cover photo: *The Flower Of My Secret*, 1995, Dir. Almodovar ©CIBY 2000/ THE KOBAL COLLECTION

ISBN 978-0-8264-1667-4

90100

Also available from Bloomsbury

PETER BONDANELLA